Plants of Northern British Columbia

Plants of Northern British Columbia

Edited by Andy MacKinnon, Jim Pojar, Ray Coupé

Written by

George Argus
Ray Coupé
George Douglas
Andy MacKinnon
Rosamund Pojar

Frank Boas
Craig DeLong
Trevor Goward
Jim Pojar
Anna Roberts

Canada

CANADA-BRITISH COLUMBIA
PARTNERSHIP AGREEMENT ON
FOREST RESOURCE DEVELOPMENT:
FRDA II

The Publisher

Lone Pine Publishing
202A – 110 Seymour Street
Vancouver, British Columbia, Canada V6B 3N3

Lone Pine Publishing
206, 10426 – 81 Ave.
Edmonton, Alberta Canada T6E 1X5

Canadian Cataloguing in Publication Data

Plants of northern British Columbia
Includes bibliographical references and index.
ISBN 1-55105-015-3
1. Botany-British Columbia.   2. Plants-Identification.
I. MacKinnon, A. (Andrew), 1956–   II. Pojar, Jim, 1948–   III. Coupé. 1952–
QK203.B7P43 1992   581.9711'8   C92-091192-7

Front Cover Photo: Fred Chapman
Back Cover Inset Photos: B.C. Ministry of Forests, Ray Coupé, Anna Roberts
Editorial: Elaine Butler
Cover and Layout Design: Beata Kurpinski
Layout: Rusty Brown
Printing: Quality Colour Press, Edmonton, Alberta, Canada

Illustrations (see page 11) from *Moss Flora of the Maritime Provinces* by Robert T. Ireland,
1982, are reproduced with permission of the Canadian Museum of Nature, Ottawa, Canada;
from *Vascular Plants of the Pacific Northwest*, Volumes 1–5 by Hitchcock *et al.* 1955–69, are
reproduced with the permission of the University of Washington Press; and from *Flora of
Alaska and Neighboring Territories: A Manual of the Vascular Plants* by Eric Hultén are
reprinted with the permission of the publishers, Stanford University Press. © 1968 by the
Board of Trustees of the Leland Stanford Junior University.

Funding for this publication was provided by the British Columbia Ministry of Forests and the
Canada – British Columbia Partnership Agreement on Forest Resource Development:
FRDA II – a four-year (1991–1995) $200 million program cost-shared equally by the federal
and provincial governments.

The publisher gratefully acknowledges the assistance of Heritage Canada,
Alberta Community Development, and the financial support provided by the Alberta
Foundation for the Arts in the production of this book.

Table Of Contents

List of Keys

List of Conspectuses

Acknowledgements

We would like to first thank the authors who originally wrote or co-wrote the various sections of this book: Goerge Argus (willows), Frank Boas (mosses), Ray Coupé (shrubs and dwarf shrubs), Craig DeLong (grasses), George Douglas (composites, ferns and allies), Trevor Goward (lichens), Andy MacKinnon (lilies, orchids), Jim Pojar (trees, dwarf shrubs, other flowers), Rosamund Pojar (notes), and Anna Roberts (illustrated willow key, grasses, sedges and rushes). Their work has been edited (in some cases extensively) so responsibility for technical accuracy must rest with the editors. We would also like to thank all of the native groups from northern British Columbia who shared with us the information used throughout this guide.

Many individuals contributed their photographs to this guide: Frank Boas, Robin Bovey, Adolf Ceska, Ray Coupé, Blake Dickens, Katherine Enns, Ron Long, Robin Love, L. O'Hara, Robert Norton, George Otto, Jim Pojar, P.T. Rhead, Rick Riewe, Anna Roberts, Joan Rosenberg, Martin Ross, Hans Roemer, Rob Scagel, Nancy and Robert Turner, E.J. Underhill, W. van Dieren, Cliff Wallis, and Cleve Wershler. Photo credits are listed at the end of the book. Original line drawings have been prepared by Shirley Salkeld, Peggy Frank, Peggy Sowden, and Trevor Goward. Line drawings have been used with kind permission from Hitchcock et al. (1977), Hultén (1968), Ireland (1987) and a number of handbooks and guides from the Royal B.C. Museum: Brayshaw (1976, 1989), Douglas (1982), Schofield (1968), Szczawinski (1962), and Taylor (1966, 1973a, 1973b, 1974a, 1974b).

Assistance in organizing text and photos was provided by Louise Gronmyr, Beth Collins, Irene Ronalds, Neil West, There Britton, and Rusty Brown.

Many thanks are due to Lone Pine Publishing for their assistance in putting this guide together. Special thanks go to Rusty Brown (layout), Beata Kurpinski (design), Elaine Butler (editor), Tanya Stewart, Heather Peterson, Violet Poon, Gary Whyte, Shane Kennedy, and Lisa Koford.

Financial assistance in production of this guide has been provided by the B.C. Ministry of Forests, Research and Silviculture programs and by the B.C. Ministry of Forests and Forestry Canada under the Forest Renewal Development Agreement.

Andy MacKinnon, Jim Pojar, Ray Coupé

Introduction

From the first glorious fairyslipper orchids in the springtime to the last scarlet clusters of highbush-cranberries in the autumn woodlands, the plants of northern interior British Columbia are a fascinating, ever-changing subject to reward the careful observer. Most of us learn about our native flora for sheer enjoyment. Others (e.g., foresters) realize that the presence or abundance of certain key "indicator" species can tell them a lot about a site, and so give clues as to how it should be managed. Regardless of why you are interested in learning about the native plants in the northern interior, one thing is certain – the closer you look, the more you'll see. The large plants readily catch our attention, but mosses and lichens, which are abundant in the north woods, are small and frequently overlooked by most people. Those few individuals that do get down on their hands and knees to view them are well rewarded for their effort by the beauty and intricacies of these plants.

About the Guide

This guide is designed for anyone interested in learning about the flora of northern interior B.C. (page 12). It doesn't include all of the plants from the area, but does include all of the more common species. A number of authors have been recruited to write specific sections according to their areas of specialization. Illustrations usually include a colour photograph of a leaf with flower or fruit, accompanied by line drawings to illustrate habit (what the whole plant looks like) or details (where required). Keys are included to assist in separating some of the larger or more difficult groups, and there **are** some difficult groups.

This guide describes, for example, more than 40 species and subspecies of willows. Willows represent a very important part of the plant life of northern interior B.C., ranging from crawling dwarf shrubs to trees. Unfortunately, they are difficult to separate in some cases, and the willows described in this guide do not represent all of the species occurring in this region. A person wishing to become familiar with the flora of northern interior B.C. will never run out of challenges.

There are no other guides specifically covering the flora of northern interior B.C. Working with the plants of this area usually requires consulting several technical manuals for surrounding areas – Hultén (1968) or Welsh (1974) for Alaska; Porsild and Cody (1980) for the Northwest Territories; Moss (1983) for Alberta; Hitchcock and Cronquist (1973) for the U.S. Pacific Northwest; Scoggan (1978-1979) for Canada. Some (non-technical) field guides exist for various parts of our province – examples include Lyons (1974) for all of B.C. and Coupé et al. (1982) for the Skeena area. One guide has been published for part of the central and northern interior (Pojar et al. 1982), covering the Sub-Boreal Spruce (SBS) biogeoclimatic zone (see p.14). Most of these field guides are now out of print and unavailable. In addition, many excellent works exist for specific groups, and references are made to them throughout this guide. In particular, we recommend the handbooks produced by the Royal B.C. Museum in Victoria, covering various plant families in B.C.

This guide covers plant groups from trees and shrubs to mosses, liverworts and lichens (though purists will point out, of course, that lichens aren't really plants at all!). Algae have been deliberately excluded (except as they occur in lichens) because the group is poorly known in this area. They can be seen in ponds, in streams attached to rocks (usually as a brownish "scum"), on tree trunks as a greenish colouration, or as partners (with fungi) in lichens. Prescott (1964) is a good reference for identifying these organisms; you'll need a microscope and patience. A glossary and an index to common and scientific names are also included.

INTRODUCTION

Plant Names

Plants in this guide are listed with both common and scientific names. Scientific names are generally more widely accepted and stable than common names. For example, the scientific name *Vaccinium membranaceum* always refers to the same plant, even though different people in different places might call it a blueberry, a huckleberry, or a bilberry and "big," "big-leaved," or "black". There are, however, exceptions. The rein-orchids, for example, are placed in the genus *Platanthera* in this book, while other works may refer to the genus as *Habenaria*. In preparing this book the following works were used for the names: common names follow Meidinger (1987); scientific names follow Douglas *et al.* (1989, 1990, 1991) for vascular plants, Ireland *et al.* (1987) for mosses, Stotler and Crandall-Stotler (1977) for liverworts, and Noble *et al.* (1987) for lichens. Scientific and common names are listed alphabetically in the index at the end of this guide. Where alternative scientific or common names are in use in northern B.C., we've tried to include them.

Plant Descriptions

The characteristics most important for the species identification are in ***bold italics*** for easy reference. Plant descriptions are broken down into six sections, beginning with the **General** characteristics of the plant — how big it is, how long it lives, what you notice about the plant as you walk up to it.

This is followed by sections describing the **Leaves**, **Flowers** and **Fruits** of the plant (except, of course, for those groups that don't have leaves, flowers or fruit!). While some material has been taken from other works, every effort has been made to examine and re-describe species collected in northern B.C. (utilizing specimens from the herbaria, or dried plant collections, at Ministry of Forests offices in Prince George, Smithers, and Williams Lake). As with the **General** section, we have attempted to standardize the format of these sections to make it easier to compare one plant with another.

Next is the section called **Ecology**, which describes where the species is likely to be found. Several types of information are presented here — the species' habitat (e.g., streamsides), its commonness and abundance (e.g., uncommon but locally abundant), and its geographic range (e.g., at low to medium elevations in the northern part of the region). Physiographic regions (e.g., Coast Mountains, Quesnel Highland, Rocky Mountain Trench, Nechako Plateau, Liard Plain) are frequently used to specify geographic ranges. See Holland (1976) for a map and descriptions of these units. We also sometimes refer to the Haines Triangle, the Chilcotin, and the Peace River district — colloquial names for the far northwestern, southwestern, and northeastern (centred on the Peace River) parts of the region. (All references to "the region" or "this region" refer to the area outlined in the map on page 12).

Finally comes *Notes*, which presents additional information about the species, including notes about similar species, use of the plant by native groups, and/or derivation of the scientific or common names.

Plants are arranged within each section of the guide to group similar species; we think that this is the most useful arrangement for comparing these species and reducing the possibility of misidentification.

Illustrations

Each plant species is illustrated with one or two colour photographs showing leaves and (for most groups) flowers or fruits. Individuals whose photographs were used in the guide are listed in the Photo Credits on pg. 344. In addition, line drawings are used to illustrate details or general plant habit. These drawings include original illustrations and others used with permission from several reference works (see below).

Illustrations from *Vascular Plants of the Pacific Northwest*:
40 B*; 45 T, B; 50 T, B; 51 B; 52 B; 82 B; 88 B; 98 T; 99 T, B; 100 T, B; 101 T; 103 T, B; 104 T; 105 T, B; 117 T, B; 125 T, B; 126 T, B; 135 B; 139 B; 140 T, B; 142 T, 143 B; 144 T; 147 B; 148 B; 150 B; 151 B; 152 B; 153 T; 186 B; 187 T, B; 197 T; 198 B; 199 T, B; 200 T; 201 B; 202 T; 205 B; 206 T; 207 T, B; 209 B; 211 T; 215 T, B; 216 T, B; 220 T; 221 T; 222 T, B; 254 B; 255

Moss Flora of the Maritime Provinces:
298 B; 301 T; 303 T; 305 T; 307 T, B; 309 B; 312 T; 313 B; 314

Flora of Alaska and Neighboring Territories:
98 B; 104 B; 149 T; 153 B; 155 T, B; 182 B; 200 B; 204 B; 206 B; 210 T; 211 T; 217 T; 218 B; 239 B

*T=top; B=bottom

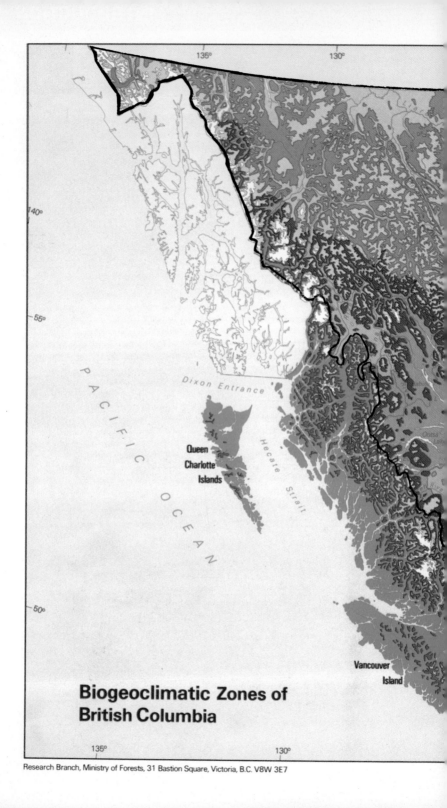

**Biogeoclimatic Zones of
British Columbia**

Research Branch, Ministry of Forests, 31 Bastion Square, Victoria, B.C. V8W 3E7

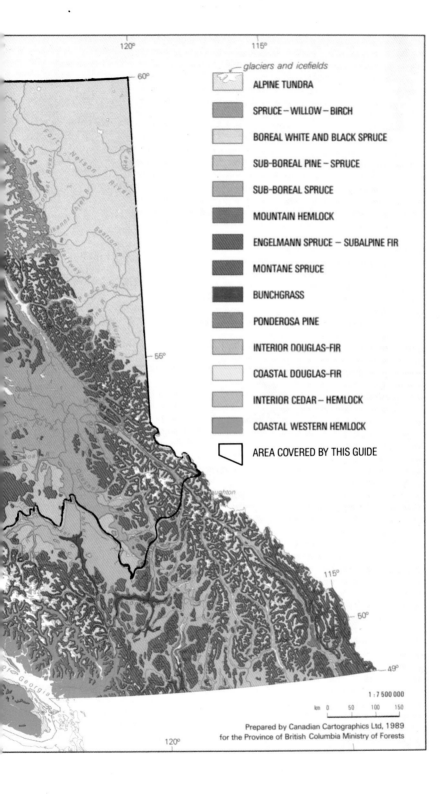

glaciers and icefields

ALPINE TUNDRA

SPRUCE – WILLOW – BIRCH

BOREAL WHITE AND BLACK SPRUCE

SUB-BOREAL PINE – SPRUCE

SUB-BOREAL SPRUCE

MOUNTAIN HEMLOCK

ENGELMANN SPRUCE – SUBALPINE FIR

MONTANE SPRUCE

BUNCHGRASS

PONDEROSA PINE

INTERIOR DOUGLAS-FIR

COASTAL DOUGLAS-FIR

INTERIOR CEDAR – HEMLOCK

COASTAL WESTERN HEMLOCK

AREA COVERED BY THIS GUIDE

1 : 7 500 000

km 0   50   100   150

Prepared by Canadian Cartographics Ltd, 1989
for the Province of British Columbia Ministry of Forests

Biogeoclimatic Zones Of Northern British Columbia

Biogeoclimatic zones are areas of broadly homogeneous climate. These climates are reflected in the patterns of vegetation across the landscape. For more information on the biogeoclimatic classification system, see Meidinger and Pojar (1991).

Eight of B.C.'s 14 biogeoclimatic zones are represented in the area covered in this guide, and they are described here to assist the user in understanding the broader-scale influences of topography on climate, and climate on vegetation, throughout northern B.C.

Sub-Boreal Spruce

This zone occurs in B.C.'s central interior, primarily on gently rolling plateaus. (Highway 16 from the Bowron River to Smithers runs through the Sub-Boreal Spruce zone.) The zone is intermediate (ecologically) between the interior Douglas-fir forests to the south and the boreal forests to the north. Forest productivity is moderately good, and although the climate is severe, the winters are shorter and the growing season longer than in boreal areas. Hybrid white spruce and subalpine fir are the dominant trees; extensive stands of lodgepole pine occur in the drier portions of the zone due to numerous past fires. Wetlands are abundant, dotting the landscape in poorly drained areas. Moose are common throughout this zone.

Sub-Boreal Pine — Spruce

This zone occurs on the high plateau of the west central interior in the rainshadow of the Coast Mountains. (Anahim Lake is in this zone.) Due to the cold, dry climate, the forests are generally of low productivity. The landscape is rolling and dotted with numerous wetlands, which are important for wildlife and hay production. The zone is also characterized by many even-aged lodgepole pine stands, the result of an extensive fire history. A minor amount of white spruce regeneration occurs. Lichens and/or feathermosses usually dominate the understory. Pinegrass and kinnikinnick are also common. The profuse ground lichens in the drier parts of the zone provide valuable winter range for caribou.

Interior Cedar — Hemlock

This zone occurs at lower to middle elevations in the interior wet belt and Skeena-Nass transition area of the province. (Purden Lake and Hazelton are in this zone.) Winters are cool and wet, and summers are generally warm and dry. This zone is the most productive in the interior and has the widest variety of coniferous tree species of any zone in B.C. Western hemlock and western redcedar are characteristic species, but hybrid white spruce and subalpine fir are common. Douglas-fir and lodgepole pine are generally found on drier sites. Wet sites are often easily recognized by a dense understory of devil's club and/or skunk cabbage.

Boreal White and Black Spruce

This zone is part of the extensive belt of boreal coniferous forest occurring across Canada. It occupies the northern valleys west of the Rocky Mountains and the gently rolling topography east of them. (Dawson Creek, Fort Nelson, Lower Post, Telegraph Creek, and Atlin are all in this zone.) Winters are long and cold, and the growing season short. The ground remains frozen for much of the year. The severe climate results in forests of low productivity. Numerous past fires have created extensive successional forests of trembling aspen and lodgepole pine. Where flat, the landscape is typically a mosaic of black spruce bogs and white spruce and trembling aspen stands. Valuable agricultural land is prevalent in the Peace River area. Moose and mosquitoes are very abundant.

Montane Spruce

This zone occurs in the south-central interior of B.C. and is included here because it occurs in the Chilcotin (on the Itcha, Ilgachuz, and Rainbow Ranges) in the southeastern portion of the area covered by this guide. The Montane Spruce zone occurs at middle elevations, and is most extensive in the southern interior in plateau areas. The winters are cold, and summers moderately short and warm. Engelmann spruce, hybrid white spruce and varying amounts of subalpine fir are the characteristic tree species. Due to past wildfires, successional forests of lodgepole pine are common and widespread. In this region, the Montane Spruce Zone provides important winter range for caribou.

Engelmann Spruce – Subalpine Fir

This is a subalpine zone occurring at high elevations throughout most of the interior. The climate is severe, with short, cool growing seasons and long, cold winters. Only those trees capable of tolerating extended periods of frozen ground occur. The landscape at the upper elevations is open parkland, with trees clumped and interspersed with meadow, heath, and grassland. Engelmann spruce and subalpine fir are the dominant trees; under drier conditions, lodgepole pine and whitebark pine can occur. White-flowered rhododendron and false azalea are common understory shrubs.

Spruce – Willow – Birch

This is a subalpine zone occurring in the severe climate of northern B.C., at elevations above the boreal forest and below the alpine tundra. At lower elevations, the zone is characterized by open forests of primarily white spruce and subalpine fir; upper elevations are dominated by deciduous shrubs including scrub birch and willows. In some high, wide valleys, cold air collects, resulting in a mosaic of scrub, grassland, and wetlands on valley floors below a band of forest on the valley sides. Above, the forest again gives way to shrubs, creating, in effect, a double treeline. This zone provides extensive moose, caribou, and, in the east, elk habitat.

Alpine Tundra

The alpine tundra, essentially a treeless zone characterized by a cold, harsh climate, is found on high mountains throughout the province. The long, cold winters and short, cool growing seasons create conditions too severe for the growth of most woody plants – except in dwarf form. Hence this zone is dominated by dwarf shrubs, herbs, mosses, and lichens. The zone has high recreational appeal. It also provides important range for caribou, mountain goat, and mountain sheep. Due to the severe climate, it is extremely sensitive to use. Disturbed landscapes require decades, or even centuries, to recover to their natural states.

Trees

Trees are single-stemmed, woody plants greater than 10 m in height when mature. Several of our willow species (notably Sitka, Scouler's, Pacific, and Bebb's willows) can grow to greater than 10 m in height; they're included in the Willows section (p. 54). Some small trees (e.g., alders, Rocky Mountain juniper, western yew) rarely reach 10 m in height, and are included in the Shrubs section.

Trees are the most obvious plants in most of northern interior B.C., creating the habitat in which most other plants live. Only areas where the climate becomes very severe — for example, in the alpine, or in the subalpine in the far North — lack trees. Some forest types, such as those dominated by hybrid white spruce, are fairly well restricted to central interior B.C.; others, such as the boreal forests further north, stretch (with minor variations) around the globe.

The severe climates of northern B.C. favour survival and growth of conifers — that is, the "cone-bearing" trees such as spruces. Coniferous trees are more suited ecologically to the long, cold winters and the relatively short growing seasons than are the broad-leaved trees such as maples, birches and the like. In the area covered by this guide all of the broad-leaved trees are deciduous (that is, they drop their leaves in the autumn); all of the conifers (except tamarack) are evergreen.

Trees were as important to the original inhabitants of northern B.C. as they are to the economy of the region today. Native peoples used trees for food, clothing, shelter, transport, cooking and storing, and medicine. The forest industry is the prime employer in northern B.C., processing trees into pulp, dimensional lumber, and specialty products. Trees provide food, shelter, and cover to most wildlife species in our area.

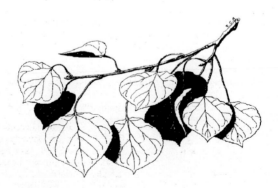

Key to Trees

1. Leaves needle-like or scale-like, mostly evergreen; seeds in cones, not enclosed in a fruit (conifers)
  2. Leaves mostly scale-like and appressed to twig, less than 1 cm long; bark often shredding and forming narrow, flat ridges on old trunks .... *Thuja plicata*
  2. Leaves needle-like and spreading from twigs, usually more than 1 cm long
    3. Leaves (needles) in clusters of two or more
      4. Needles deciduous, in clusters of 12-20, on woody projections .... *Larix laricina*
      4. Needles in clusters of 2 or 5 .... Pines (see *Pinus contorta*)
    3. Leaves (needles) not in clusters, borne singly on twig
      5. Needles angled (4-sided in cross-section), mostly 1-2 cm long; mature bark thin and scaly
        6. Cones about 2.5 cm long and egg shaped; branches often drooping with upturned ends; tree top knobby or club shaped; young twigs densely hairy; inner bark deep olive-green .... *Picea mariana*
        6. Cones 2.5-7.5 cm long and cylindrical to narrowly oval; lower branches often drooping but not with upturned ends; tree top rarely club-shaped; young twigs hairless or hairy; inner bark silvery white
          7. Cone scales flexible (not easily crushed), finely toothed (frayed) on margin and tapered at both ends; young twigs usually hairy; needles curved, often upwards; usually at subalpine elevations (over 1200 m) .... *Picea engelmannii* *
          7. Cone scales stiff with smooth, roundish margins; young twigs usually hairless; needles straight; usually found subalpine elevations .... *Picea glauca* *
      5. Needles flattened or semi-circular in cross-section, mostly 2-4.5 cm long; mature bark various
        8. Needles stalkless, curved upwards; bark of young trees smooth, gray and covered with resin blisters; buds 0.5 cm long with blunt tip; crown spirelike .... *Abies lasiocarpa*
        8. Needles stalked, not curved upwards; bark of young trees may be covered with resin blisters; buds 0.1-0.3 cm long or, if longer, then conical and sharp-pointed; crown various
          9. Cone bracts 3 pronged and prominent (usually longer than scales); buds conical and sharp pointed; needles usually of equal length and flat; leaf tips usually sharp-pointed; needle and stalk fall together leaving oval scars that are smooth to the touch; crown does not have drooping leader *Pseudotsuga menziesii* var. *glauca*
          9. Cone bracts minute and not 3 pronged; buds with blunt tips; needles often of unequal length and rounded on top, tips rounded or indented; needles fall from raised woody bases with scars pointing forward on twig; crown usually with drooping leader
            10. Needles flat and without taper, appearing two ranked and of variable length on twig; cones about 2 cm long; common at low to medium elevations (less than 1200 m) in wetter climates .... *Tsuga heterophylla*
            10. Needles rounded on top and narrowed abruptly to slender stalk, not appearing two-ranked, nearly equal in length; cones 3-6 cm long; at high elevations (greater than 1200 m), in our region only in the Nass Basin and surrounding mountains .... *Tsuga mertensiana*
1. Leaves broad and annually deciduous; seed enclosed in a fruit
            11. Bark with numerous conspicuous horizontal markings (lenticels) and peeling in large sheets; twigs dark reddish brown; leaves arranged singularly (alternate) on outer twigs but appearing to be in pairs on inner branches ... . *Betula papyrifera*
            11. Bark without conspicuous horizontal marking and not peeling in sheets; twigs brownish gray or orangey gray; leaves arranged singularly on all twigs
              12. Leaf stalk flattened; mature bark smooth and waxy but often becoming furrowed with age near base of trunk; terminal bud about 0.6 cm long and not resinous; leaves nearly circular in outline .... *Populus tremuloides*
              12. Leaf stalk round in cross-section; mature bark deeply furrowed; terminal bud about 2 cm long and very resinous (gummy); leaves broadly egg shaped
                13. Female flowers with 2 stigmas; capsules 2 valved; across the northern parts of our region, and east of the Rocky Mountains .... *Populus balsamifera* ssp. *balsamifera*
                13. Female flowers with 3 stigmas; capsules 3 valved; across central and southern parts of our region ...... *Populus balsamifera* ssp. *trichocarpa*

* Hybrids between Engelmann and white spruce are very common and have intermediate characteristics; see hybrid white spruce (page 19) for descriptions.

ENGELMANN SPRUCE — *Picea engelmannii*

General Straight, spire-like, up to 50 m tall; **young twigs usually hairy**, occasionally glabrous; bark with loose gray scales.

Leaves Needles 4-sided, sharp, but **not particularly stiff**, tending to twist toward upper side of branch; two whitish lines of stomata on upper and lower surfaces; with strong odour.

Cones Pollen (male) cones yellowish; seed (female) cones pendent, 4-5 cm long; scales green at flowering, becoming yellowish brown and papery thin **with jagged tip** at maturity.

Seedling Seedling with bottlebrush arrangement of usually 6 primary needle-like leaves, toothed.

Ecology Grows best on deep, rich, moist, loamy soils; **characteristically a subalpine species**, occurring between 1000 and 2000 m. As a pure species, occurs only in the southeast part of our region.

Notes: Commonly hybridizes with white spruce (*P. glauca*). Interior natives had a variety of uses for the wood and bark of spruces (see Turner 1979). The split roots were sewn into the seams of birch bark baskets and tightly woven into baskets. Both the pitch and bark were used for wound dressings and eye injuries. The Carrier chewed the emerging needles for coughs. • *Picea* is from ancient Latin *picea* meaning pitch-pine from *pix* or *picis* meaning pitch. Named after George Engelmann (1809-84), a botanist and authority on conifers.

WHITE SPRUCE — *Picea glauca*

General Stunted to erect, up to 40 m tall; **young twigs smooth and shiny**, not hairy; bark with loose gray scales.

Leaves Needles 4-sided, somewhat sharply pointed, **stiff**, tending to project from all sides of the branches (bottlebrush), aromatic when crushed.

Cones Pollen cones pale red; seed cones light brown to purplish, pendent, 2.5-3.5 cm long at maturity; scales papery, **stiffer and blunter than those of Engelmann spruce**.

Seedling 5-7 thick seed-leaves; juvenile leaves toothed.

Ecology Grows well on well-drained, moist soils. **Typically low to middle elevation forests**, but also at high elevations, especially in the North. As a pure species, occurs in the North, and also in the west Chilcotin.

Notes: Commonly hybridizes with Engelmann spruce; hybrids between white and Sitka spruce (sometimes called *P. lutzii*) are characteristic of much of the Skeena-Nass, coast-interior transitional area. Most parts of the tree were made into a wide variety of articles by interior native groups (see Turner, 1979), especially roots for tightly woven, coiled baskets. Spruce roots were also widely used for sewing the seams on objects made out of birch bark.

HYBRID WHITE SPRUCE — *Picea glauca x engelmannii*

General In most features, intermediate between white spruce and Engelmann spruce; young twigs usually variously hairy, but may be glabrous.

Cones Seed cones 3-4 cm long at maturity; scales with irregular, wavy tips.

Ecology Lowlands to timberline, but most abundant at low to middle elevations where it grows on upland slopes, as well as along streams and in swamps. Widespread throughout the southern half of our region, i.e., the upper Fraser, Skeena, and Peace drainages.

Notes: Hybrid white spruce is the common, widespread spruce of central British Columbia. In this area, from the Rockies to the Coast Mountains, and between roughly 52° and 57° N latitude, most spruce stands show evidence of hybridization. Individual trees resembling either parent (Engelmann or white spruce) can often be found, but most trees are intermediate in appearance, in general form, as well as in characters of the twigs, needles, and cones. Hence, it is easiest and probably most realistic to refer to the spruce trees of central interior B.C. simply as interior spruce or hybrid white spruce. In the middle Skeena-Nass transitional area, however, most spruce appear to be a hybrid between white and Sitka (often called *P. lutzii* or Roche spruce), or perhaps even involving Engelmann spruce.

BLACK SPRUCE — *Picea mariana*

General Small, often shrubby tree up to 20 m tall; branches short, sparse; in older trees, lower branches drooping, often rooting ("layering"), **uppermost branches clustered** to form a "crow's nest"; bark dark gray, scaly; **young twigs black-rusty hairy and glandular**.

Leaves **Needles short**, 4-sided, standing out on all sides or mostly pointed upwards; stomata present on all sides.

Cones Pollen cones dark red; seed **cones small** (less than 3 cm long), **purplish**, and persistent (hanging on) for several years.

Seedling 3-5 seed-leaves; juvenile leaves slender, lacking teeth.

Ecology Characteristic tree of cold, poorly drained, nutrient-poor sites; in bogs and swamps and upland sites near wetlands; also frequently with lodgepole pine and white spruce in boreal forests. Throughout all but the southernmost parts of the region, at low to medium elevations.

Notes: The long fibres make pulp of this tree favoured for manufacture of facial tissues and other paper products. The Carrier may have used the roots for making the encircling part of fish traps. The Carrier, Slave, and other Athabaskan groups chewed the pitch for pleasure. • *Mariana* is derived from Maryland, indicating the wide geographical range of this species.

SUBALPINE FIR — *Abies lasiocarpa*

General Tree up to 50 m tall (but usually 20-35 m tall), with narrow, spire-shaped crown, often stunted in exposed subalpine sites; branches short, thick, not spray-like; **buds blunt**; bark thin, grey, smooth, **with resin blisters**.

Leaves Needles 2-sided (as opposed to the 4-sided needles of spruce), **mostly blunt**, sometimes notched (may be pointed on very young growth at top of tree), all tending to turn upwards, crowded, bluish green, with white strip of stomata on both surfaces.

Cones Pollen cones small, bluish; seed cones large, cylindrical, usually deep purple, becoming lighter coloured with age, **erect**, near top of tree, disintegrating on the tree leaving only central core.

Seedling Four seed-leaves, 1-3 cm long, blunt-tipped without teeth.

Ecology Common and abundant at subalpine elevations throughout and also at low elevations in the moister parts of our region.

Notes: Wood, bark, and boughs were used by interior native people for roof shingles, bark baskets and bedding. Seeds were eaten by some groups. Pitch was used for coating canoe seams and rubbing on bowstrings. Rotten wood was used as a smudge for tanning hides. Pitch and bark preparations were used by Carrier and Gitksan for wounds, eye injuries or internally for respiratory ailments. • Often erroneously called balsam (fir); the true balsam fir (*Abies balsamea*) is an eastern species. Also called alpine fir, which is also something of a misnomer because alpine implies above tree-line or no trees present. The name *Abies* is derived from Latin *abeo* meaning to rise or arising and refers to the great height that some species attain. Fir is derived from the Old English *furh* or *fyrh* or Danish *fyrr* meaning fire (used as firewood).

INTERIOR DOUGLAS-FIR — *Pseudotsuga menziesii* var. *glauca*

General Large tree, up to 50 m tall in this region; crown of young trees pyramidal and with a stiffly erect leader; branches spreading to drooping; **buds sharply pointed**; bark ultimately very thick, fluted, ridged, rough, and dark brown.

Leaves Needles flat, **with pointed tip**, one groove on upper surface, and 2 white stomatal bands on lower surface; spirally arranged, and leaving small, flat scar on twig upon falling.

Cones Pollen cones small, reddish brown; young seed cones **pendent**, green at flowering, turning reddish-brown to grey; scales papery; **bracts prominently 3-forked**, extending beyond scales.

Seedling 5-9 seed-leaves, 1-3 cm long, not toothed.

Ecology Moist to very dry areas, generally at low elevations in the southern part of the region; tends to occur on dry, warm, rocky or gravelly habitats at the northern limits of its range, especially on calcareous soils, and often along large lakes (e.g., Babine, Stuart, McLeod).

Notes: The most important forest tree in western North America and one of the largest, though the interior variety never attains the same size as the coastal variety (var. *menziesii*). • All parts of the tree were used by southern interior natives (see Turner, 1979). The Carrier may have used the wood for making snowshoes and fish-traps. Under certain climatic conditions the twigs and leaves exude a white crystalline substance, called Douglas-fir sugar or wild sugar, which was highly prized by some interior groups whenever it was available. It contains a rare sugar — melezitose. The seeds, though small and pitchy, were eaten occasionally by the Shuswap. • This species was first described by naturalist-surgeon Dr. Archibald Menzies and is named after Northwest explorer-botanist David Douglas. The Latin name comes from *pseudo* (false) and *tsuga* (hemlock).

LODGEPOLE PINE — *Pinus contorta* var. *latifolia*

General A medium-sized straight tree up to 40 m tall with a pyramidal crown; bark scaly, light brown, dark gray to black; twigs yellowish when young becoming gray-brown and rough.

Leaves **Needles in twos**, often curved and twisted, deep green to yellowish green.

Pollen cones small, reddish green in clusters on tips of branches in spring; seed cones egg shaped, usually slightly curved; scales stiff and brown with sharp prickle on tip.

Seedling 3-6 seed-leaves, 1-3 cm long; juvenile leaves toothed on edges.

Ecology A highly adaptable species, tolerant of low-nutrient conditions; found from dunes and bogs to rocky hilltops and upland plains. In this region, primarily in lowland to montane forest, less commonly in the subalpine zone. Found throughout the region except in the upper Skeena and Nass drainages and in the Haines Triangle.

Notes: Pure stands of this species originated with fire. Whitebark pine (*Pinus albicaulis*) has needles in clumps of 5's, and is scattered at high elevations in the Coast, Cariboo, and Rocky Mountains south of 56°. • Jack pine (*Pinus banksiana*) occurs in northeastern B.C. just south of the Northwest Territories, and is similar to lodgepole pine in most respects, but can be distinguished by its shorter needles (1-4 cm long) and its non-prickly cone. Note that, in many parts of our region, lodgepole pine is commonly but incorrectly referred to as "jack pine." • Several interior native groups used the straight trunks in the construction of dwellings. Wood was also fashioned into drills and arrow shafts. The sweet, succulent cambium layer was almost a universal food among the interior groups. It was scraped off in the spring in long, fleshy ribbons ("noodles"), and eaten fresh, or sometimes stored. Pine cambium is a valuable emergency food, but removing the bark can damage or kill the tree. • The pitch was widely used as the base for various medicines. Mixed with grease or bear fat, it was applied to relieve pain or as a purification ritual. Young needles were eaten by Gitksan as a purgative and diuretic.

TAMARACK — *Larix laricina*

General A small tree rarely more than 15 m high in this region, with delicate foliage; bark thin, scaly; branches long, slender, pliable.

Leaves Needles borne on woody projections, in small lateral **clusters of 12 to 20**, more or less flat, blue-green, turning bright yellow in autumn and dropping off (**deciduous**).

Cones Pollen cones small, egg shaped; seed cones egg shaped, erect; scales dark red at flowering time, becoming leathery and brown with age; bracts do not project beyond scales; seeds winged.

Seedling With 4-6 slender seed-leaves.

Ecology Bogs, swamps, fens, and lower mountain slopes, especially where calcareous. Primarily in northeastern B.C., but with a few patches in the Central Interior in the Nechako Valley and south of Vanderhoof. Circumboreal distribution.

Notes: Larches (*Larix* spp.) are B.C.'s only native coniferous trees to shed their needles in the fall. As deciduous conifers, larches are somewhat of an ecological puzzle because they successfully live in what is normally considered an evergreen world. The evidence is that larches can construct, at relatively low carbon costs, a well-illuminated nitrogen-efficient canopy that provides a carbon gain comparable to evergreen conifers. • In our region, tamarack trees rarely grow large enough to be of commercial value. • The pitch of some species of *Larix* was mixed with grease and used by some interior natives as cosmetics for the skin or hair. In the days of wooden ships the roots were used by ship-builders to join ribs to deck timbers. • The name *Larix* may be derived from *lar* meaning fat because the tree produces resin.

TREES

WESTERN HEMLOCK — *Tsuga heterophylla*

General Tree 30-50 m tall with a narrow crown, a ***conspicuously drooping leader*** (growing tip), gracefully down-sweeping branches, and delicate, feathery foliage; bark rough, reddish brown, scaly.

Leaves Needles short, flat, widely and irregularly spaced, *of unequal length*, producing feathery flat sprays; yellowish green on top, whitish with stomata below.

Cones Pollen cones numerous, small; seed cones numerous, small (***1.5-2.5 cm long***), oblong, purplish-green when young, to light brown when mature.

Seedling Seed-leaves 3-6; juvenile leaves needle-like, arranged all around stem (bottlebrush).

Ecology Well adapted to grow on raw humus and on decaying wood; shade tolerant. Often the dominant tree in *low to moderate elevation forests* of the wetter parts of the southern half of our region.

Notes: The wood and bark were widely used by coastal natives for dishes, pots, and fishing gear. In the Interior, the Niska and Gitksan scraped off the cambium in the spring, baked it in earth ovens, and made it into cakes that were eaten fresh or dried. A favourite way to prepare the dried cambium in the winter was to whip it with snow and eulachon grease. Today it is frozen in plastic bags. The leaves may be used to make a tea. • The early settlers reportedly named this tree hemlock because the crushed needles emit an odour similar to that of the European weed of the same name. An alternative explanation is that it is derived from the New York aboriginal name for Canada, *Oh-ney-tah* (pronounced *hoe-o-na-dia*) meaning land of the hemlock. *Heterophylla* is Greek for other (or different) leaves; note the different lengths of needles on a branch of western hemlock.

MOUNTAIN HEMLOCK — *Tsuga mertensiana*

General Subalpine trees, erect, rarely up to 30-40 m tall, often stunted at higher elevations; leader only slightly drooping; branches drooping or spreading, but tending to have an upward sweep at the tips.

Leaves Similar to those of western hemlock, but *needles equal in length*, densely covering branches on all sides so sprays not flattened, and covered equally by stomata on upper and lower surfaces.

Cones Pollen cones bluish; seed cones light to deep purple, or brownish purple (sometimes green) at flowering, becoming brown at maturity; *longer (3-6 cm) than those of western hemlock* (the photo shows cones of western and mountain hemlock, side-by-side).

Seedling 3-6 seed-leaves; juvenile leaves needle-like, arranged all around stem, toothed.

Ecology *Subalpine to timberline*, forest and parkland; adapted to short growing seasons of snowy subalpine climates. Essentially a coastal species, but enters our region on the leeward side of the Coast Mountains and in the Nass Basin.

Notes: Western hemlock and mountain hemlock reportedly occasionally form hybrids where ranges overlap. Unlike most conifers, mountain hemlock does not provide good shelter from the rain because some of its branches slope upwards! • *Tsuga* is from the Japanese *Tsu-ga*, the elements for tree and mother, meaning treemother; *mertensiana* is named for Franz Karl Mertens, a German botanist.

22

WESTERN REDCEDAR *Thuja plicata*

General Large tree up to 50 m tall, with drooping leader; mature trees often fluted and buttressed at base; branches tending to spread or droop slightly and then upturn; branchlets spraylike, strongly flattened horizontally; **bark gray to reddish brown, tearing off in long fibrous strips**; wood aromatic.

Leaves *Scale-like*, in opposite pairs, closely pressed to stem in overlapping shingled arrangement; glossy yellowish green, turning brown and shedding in 3-4 year old branches.

Cones Pollen cones minute, numerous, reddish; seed cones with few scales, egg shaped, in loose clusters, green when immature, becoming brown; seeds winged.

Seedling Seed-leaves 2; young seedlings with many short, needle-like primary leaves in whorls of 3; lateral branches develop scale leaves during first year.

Ecology Mostly in moist to wet soils, usually in shaded forests at low elevations; grows best on seepage and alluvial sites, but also occurs in drier habitats, especially on richer soils. Abundant in the wettest, southern parts of the region, as in the wet belt southeast of Prince George, and the middle Skeena drainage around Hazelton.

Notes: Our provincial tree. • The most widely used and versatile of all plants used by the native peoples (see Turner, 1979). Everything from homes, canoes, and totem poles to cooking utensils and clothing were made from this tree. Some groups ate the cambial layer. • The name cedar is a misnomer as this species is not a true cedar, but rather a cypress. Sometimes called giant arborvitae — from *arbor* (tree) and *vitae* (life) — i.e., the tree of life because it seemingly never rotted, and because of its evergreen, pungently scented foliage. Jacques Cartier called *Thuja occidentalis* the *Arbre de vie* because a native chief showed him how to make a tea from the bark and foliage; after he gave the tea to his men who were dying of scurvy, they recovered. • The name *Thuja* is derived from *thuia*, an ancient Greek word for an aromatic evergreen tree (possibly a juniper) whose durable wood was highly prized for furniture making. *Plicata* means plicate or folded into plaits and refers to the arrangement of the scale-like leaves.

PAPER BIRCH · *Betula papyrifera*

General Small to medium-sized, deciduous tree up to 30 m tall; **bark peeling in papery strips**, white to copper-brown, smooth and marked with brown horizontal lines of lenticels.

Leaves Oval to round, sharp-pointed, sometimes very shallowly lobed; **margins doubly toothed**, usually 15-20 teeth per side; upper surface smooth to hairy, greener than lower surface; lower surface usually with hairy tufts in the angles of larger lateral veins toward base of leaf.

Flowers In 2-4 cm long catkins; flowering with or before leaves; catkins breaking up at maturity.

Fruits Nutlets with wings broader than body.

Ecology Open to dense, usually moist woods from the lowlands to lower mountain slopes; grows best on well-drained moist sites; thrives on burned-over and cutover areas where it often forms pure stands, later restricted to openings as the forest matures; readily sprouting from cut stumps. In this region, most abundant in the North and in the moister southern areas such as along the middle Fraser and Skeena rivers.

Notes: Alaska paper birch (*Betula neoalaskana*) occurs in northeastern B.C.; its twigs are densely covered with resin-glands. • Because of its watertight properties, the strong inner bark was widely used by central and northern interior natives to make canoes, baskets, dishes, snow goggles, and moose calls. The Shuswap were noted for their beautiful birch bark baskets. The Gitksan used bark to wrap food for storage or to envelop corpses. The Carrier say it makes excellent toboggans because it is slippery. Northern groups made digging or gambling sticks, snowshoe frames, and many other utensils from the wood (see Turner, 1979). The Shuswap made soap and shampoo from the leaves. • *Papyrifera* means paper-bearing, in reference to the bark.

TREMBLING ASPEN · *Populus tremuloides*

General Small to medium-sized, deciduous tree, up to 25 m tall, usually **colonial by suckers** from extensive shallow root system; **buds not resinous or fragrant**; bark greenish white turning blackish (**not peeling**) and somewhat roughened at base of tree with age.

Leaves Oval to nearly circular, with rounded to square-cut base, and sharp-pointed tip; **margins round-toothed**; leaf stalks flattened, allowing the leaves to tremble in the slightest breeze; no glands at base of blade.

Flowers In drooping catkins that appear before the leaves; male and female catkins on separate trees; male flowers with 6-12 stamens.

Fruits Capsules, with tufted-hairy seeds.

Ecology Dry ridges, upland slopes, moist depressions, or rich alluvial sites; tolerates a wide range of conditions, but grows best in well-drained, moist, loamy soils; will not grow in permanently saturated soils. Throughout the region, from low to medium elevations, rarely subalpine.

Notes: Clones of trembling aspen can cover several hectares; these are best differentiated in the spring or autumn, as entire clones leaf out or drop leaves simultaneously. • The cambium was sometimes eaten by interior natives. The Carrier lined baby cradles with rotten wood; it was soft and absorbent and made good diaper material. Bark and roots were chewed and applied to wounds to stop bleeding by the Carrier. The wood may have been used for fuel, poles, and sometimes canoes. In several aboriginal languages, the local name translates as woman's tongue or noisy leaf. The Okanagan believed that, "if the leaves began to shimmer when there was no perceptible wind, it would soon be stormy". (Turner, 1979). There are records of early settlers extracting a quinine-like substance from the bitter inner bark. • The wood of trembling aspen has been ignored by B.C. foresters in the past, but has recently been used to make pulp and chopsticks.

BLACK COTTONWOOD *Populus balsamifera* ssp. *trichocarpa*

General Large, tall, deciduous tree up to 40 m tall; buds very sticky (full of resin) and fragrant; old bark deeply furrowed, dark grey; *young shoots often angled in cross-section*.

Leaves Thick, oval, with rounded to heart-shaped base and sharp-pointed tip; margin finely round-toothed; surface pale and often stained with patches of brown resin beneath; leaf stalks round, often with a pair of glands at the junction with the blade.

Flowers Male and female flowers in separate catkins, and on different plants; male flowers with 40-60 stamens; *female flowers with 3 stigmas*; flowering before leaves open up.

Fruits *3-valved* green, hairy capsules; seeds with white, fluffy hairs attached.

Ecology On low to medium elevation, moist to wet sites; forms extensive stands on islands and floodplains along major rivers. Through-out the *southern half of our region*.

Notes: The cambium layer, of this subspecies especially, was widely harvested and eaten fresh by several northern interior groups. Shuswap natives applied the resin (gum) as an adhesive. All parts of the plant were used for a variety of purposes. Large cottonwoods were used by the Shuswap, Carrier, Tahltan, and Niska to make dug-out canoes and as a fuel source. Niska people sometimes made masks from the wood, temporary cabins from the bark, and rope from split roots. • Called cottonwood because of the cottony hairs on the mature seeds which float through the air like giant summer snowflakes!

BALSAM POPLAR *Populus balsamifera* ssp. *balsamifera*

General Tall tree but smaller than black cottonwood; bark becoming furrowed; *young shoots round in cross-section*.

Leaves Almost indistinguishable from those of black cottonwood.

Flowers In catkins; male flowers with 20-30 stamens; *female flowers with 2 stigmas*.

Fruits *2-valved*, smooth capsules; seeds with cottony hairs.

Ecology In moist soils along streams, rivers, floodplains; sometimes on rocky, colluvial slopes. Across *northern B.C. from the upper Stikine River and Atlin to east of Rockies*.

Notes: Balsam poplar is very difficult to distinguish from black cotton-wood. In our region, the ranges of the two overlap, and intermediate forms are common. However, black cottonwood is a larger tree with deeply furrowed older bark and thicker, larger leaves. It also has female flowers with 3 stigmas, and male flowers with 40-60 stamens. • Called balsam poplar because the sticky buds are full of a gummy resin that has a lovely fresh sweet, balsam odour. As buds open the springtime air is filled with this heady scent. • The Carrier used boiled fresh poplar bark as a poultice for wounds and gave it to children as worm medicine. The cambium layer was peeled off in the spring and eaten fresh. • Snowshoe hares are somewhat deterred from feeding on balsam poplar twigs during the winter by anti-feedant chemicals produced by the plants, especially in their juvenile phase. The hares much prefer to eat twigs of trembling aspen. Aspen produce a different chemical that somewhat deters ruffed grouse, which feed on the flower buds and catkins. There is evidence that willows, birches, and alders also produce their own brand of chemical defense against winter browsing.

Shrubs and Small Trees

Shrubs are woody plants less than 10 m tall when mature and usually multi-stemmed. Many of the shrubs in northern B.C. are willows, and they are included in a separate section (p. 54). Willows are distinguished from most other shrub species by their inflorescence − a catkin. Willows are also the only shrubs in our area to have a single bud scale. Shrubs 30 cm or less in height when mature have also been placed in a separate section: Dwarf Shrubs (p. 78).

The shrubs of northern B.C. represent a wide variety of plant families and genera; we've tried to group similar species together here. Many shrubs are accompanied by an illustration of a moose or squirrel standing next to them, for scale. The often delicious and nutritious fruits of our shrubs are a staple food of many northern animals, including our species. Records of the earliest European explorers document native use, as in this entry from the journal of Alexander Mackenzie (Friday, August 14, 1789):

> "...passed several of the native Campments. A River on the North side which appeared to be navigable, we camp'd at 1/2 past 6 oClk P.M. plenty of Berries which the men call *poires* (saskatoon, *Amelanchier alnifolia*), they are bigger than a pea, very well Tasted, some goose Berries (*Ribes* spp.) and a few Strawberries (*Fragaria* spp.)".

PRICKLY ROSE — *Rosa acicularis*

General Shrub, up to 1.5 m tall; ***stems usually densely covered with numerous straight, bristly prickles***.

Leaves Divided into ***5-7 oblong leaflets***, each doubly toothed, usually somewhat hairy on the underside.

Flowers ***Pink***, large, showy, ***solitary***, on short side branches.

Fruits Scarlet, globose to pear-shaped, fleshy "***hips***."

Ecology Open forest, thickets, rocky slopes, and clearings. Widespread at low to medium elevations throughout the region.

Notes: Rosa woodsii (wood rose), a species with glabrous leaves, nodal spines which differ from the internodal prickles (when present) and ***fruits and flowers in clusters***, is scattered on dry slopes in the drier parts of the region, particularly the Bulkley-Nechako and Peace River districts. For much of the material from the southern parts of our region, it is difficult to distinguish between *R. acicularis* and *R. woodsii. Rosa nutkana* (Nootka rose) has glabrous to pubescent leaves, pairs of large thorns at nodes with internodal prickles generally absent, solitary flowers and fruits, and occurs in moist thickets and woods. In northern B.C., it is typically a coastal species, but does occur in the central interior along the Skeena and Fraser rivers. • High in vitamin C content, rose hips were eaten on a casual basis or in times of scarcity by native people. The seeds were discarded and only the outside rind was eaten. The Gitksan warn that eating too many gives you an "itchy bottom." Today native people make them into jams and jellies. The Slave made tea from the petals. The Carrier scraped the cambium from the roots, soaked then boiled it, and applied the ointment to sore eyes. The Shuswap made arrows from rose wood (probably this species). • *Rosa* is the classical Latin name for the genus; *acicularis* means prickly.

RED RASPBERRY — *Rubus idaeus*

General An erect perennial shrub, up to 1.5 m tall; stems (canes) upright, almost unarmed to prickly bristly; shredding bark yellow to cinnamon brown; similar to cultivated raspberry.

Leaves ***3-5 leaflets*** on first-year canes, saw toothed and sharply pointed; mostly 3 leaflets on flowering canes, the terminal one being the largest.

Flowers ***White***, drooping, single or in small grapelike clusters.

Fruits A cluster of red drupelets (***a raspberry***); falling intact from plant; smaller but tastier than domestic raspberry.

Ecology Thickets, clearings, open woods. Throughout the region at low to moderate elevations, typically in disturbed habitats; rarely in mature forests.

Notes: Wild raspberries were eaten by all central and northern interior native groups − fresh or mashed and dried as cakes, although the Gitksan say they are too juicy to dry. They make jam and jelly from the fruit today. Teas were made from the leaves by the Carrier and used either as a beverage or for amenorrhea. An infusion of boiled stem was given to women for "sickness in their womb" (Carrier Linguistic Committee, 1973). • Originally called *rasps, raspis* or *raspises* (16th century). Possibly derived from a fruit from which a drink could be made like a *raspis* or a sweet red French wine; *vinum raspatum* or a wine made from *raspes*, grapes from which the seeds have been removed. *Rubus* is the Latin name for blackberries, derived from the word for red (in reference to fruits); *idaeus* means from Mt. Ida (in Crete).

WESTERN MOUNTAIN-ASH · *Sorbus scopulina*

General Erect, several-stemmed shrub, up to 5 m tall; winter buds and young growth slightly white-hairy and **sticky**.

Leaves Divided into 9-13 leaflets, usually **sharp pointed at the tip; margins sharply toothed almost entire length**.

Flowers White, small, numerous (up to 200), in flat topped to rounded clusters.

Fruits Berrylike, **orange to scarlet**, lacking a bloom.

Ecology Best vigour in openings, but also common in closed, coniferous stands. From the lowlands to subalpine elevations throughout the region.

Notes: Similar to Sitka mountain-ash, which has leaflets with rounded tips that are more finely toothed, non-sticky winter buds, and rusty hairs. • The berries of this species are very attractive to birds, especially after they have fermented. Twigs are popular food items for many ungulate species (e.g., deer, moose) as well. • The name "mountain-ash" is rather a misnomer as this is not an ash at all; however, it is thought that it acquired the name because its divided leaves resembled those of the ash. *Sorbus* is the Latin name for a mountain-ash, or the Greek name for some oak, depending on whom you believe; *scopulina* means of the rocks or cliffs.

SITKA MOUNTAIN-ASH · *Sorbus sitchensis*

General Erect shrub, with several stems, up to 4 m tall; winter buds and young growth with rusty hairs, **not sticky**.

Leaves Divided into 7-11 leaflets, **rounded at the tip; margins toothed mostly above middle**.

Flowers White, small, not more than 80, in round-topped cluster.

Fruits Berrylike, **red**, with whitish bloom; edible but extremely tart and bitter; much favoured by some birds.

Ecology Open, usually coniferous forest, streambanks, and clearings; medium to subalpine elevations. Most common at higher elevations in the moister southern and western parts of the region; absent from the northeast.

Notes: The berries were eaten occasionally by some southern interior natives and probably by the Gitksan. The bark was used in medicinal mixtures for coughs, flu, and fever. The Carrier sometimes made sidesticks for snowshoes from the wood. A cluster of berries added to canned blueberries is said to improve the flavour. • The European species (*S. aucuparia*), also called the Rowan or Service tree in Europe, is widely planted as an ornamental throughout central interior B.C. *Rowan* or *Roan* is from either the Swedish *runn* (secret) or the Old Norse *runa* (a charm), from the old belief that *S. aucuparia* has the power to avert the evil eye. It was traditionally the tree from which staves for ladders were cut, and because of the tree's magical powers, they were called *run-stafas* (mysterious staves). This appears to have given rise to "rungs" of a ladder. • This species was originally described from Sitka, Alaska (hence *sitchensis*).

RED ELDERBERRY — *Sambucus racemosa*

General Shrub to small tree, mostly 1-5 m tall, with **soft pithy twigs**; foliage with strong, characteristic odour.

Leaves **Opposite**, large, divided into **5-7 leaflets**; the leaflets lance shaped, pointed, sharply toothed, often somewhat hairy beneath.

Flowers White to creamy, in a rounded or pyramidal cluster; strong, unpleasant odour.

Fruits **Bright red berrylike drupes**; not palatable and can cause nausea.

Ecology Stream banks, swampy thickets, moist clearings, and shaded forests; up to subalpine elevations. Scattered across the southern half of the region, especially in wetter valleys; absent from the coldest, driest areas (e.g., Chilcotin and Lakes districts).

Notes: Locally abundant in our region, the berries of this plant, even though they are reputedly poisonous, were very popular with the Niska and Gitksan. They were steamed or boiled into a kind of jam. The bark and roots were boiled and the infusion was drunk as an emetic or purgative. The stems can be hollowed out to make whistles, drinking straws, blowguns, and pipestems. This should be done with caution, however, as the stems, roots, and foliage are poisonous or toxic. The berries can be made into wines and jellies. Some Thompson people soaked salmon overnight in red elderberry juice before baking it. • The flowers are popular with many insects; the fruits are eaten by a number of different bird species. • *Sambucus* is the ancient Latin name for this plant, from *sambuca* meaning harp (made from the wood of some species); *racemosa* refers to the inflorescence (called a raceme).

Key to *Ribes*

1. Stems more or less spiny and usually bristly (gooseberries).
  2. Flowers several in spreading or drooping clusters, saucer shaped; flower stalks jointed near the top just below the ovary (or berry); berries black, bristly-glandular; leaves not glandular and usually not hairy on lower surface, heart-shaped at base (a) .... *R. lacustre.*
  2. Flowers 1-2 or 3, bell-shaped; flower stalks not jointed near the top; berries bluish purple, smooth; leaves usually glandular-hairy on lower surface, squared off to slightly heart shaped at base (b) .... *R. oxyacanthoides.*
1. Stems not spiny or bristly (currants).
  3. Leaves sprinkled with yellow crystalline glands ("resin dots") on lower surface; ovaries (and berries) also usually with resin dots; fruits black and glaucous when mature.
    4. Flowers greenish with purplish tinge, several to many (15-50) in long (15-30 cm), erect to ascending clusters; leaves primarily 5 lobed more than half their length, lobes sharp pointed; plant with musky or catty odour when bruised; mostly coastal species, inland in Skeena drainage (not described in this guide) (c) .... *R. bracteosum.*
    4. Flowers white, several (6-15) in spreading, shorter (4-15 cm) clusters; leaves 3-5 lobed less than half their length, lobes rounded; mostly east of the Coast Mountains (d) .... *R. hudsonianum.*
  3. Leaves without resin dots; fruits reddish when mature (or purplish black in *R. laxiflorum*).
    5. Ovary and fruit smooth; leaves primarily 3-5 lobed, lobes rounded (e) *R. triste.*
    5. Ovary and fruit bristly with stalked glands; leaves 5-7 lobed, the lobes sharp pointed.
      6. Flowers greenish white to purplish; berries dark red, with stalked glands up to 1.2 mm long; sepals glabrous on outside, 2-2.5 mm long (f) .... *R. glandulosum.*
      6. Flowers reddish to purplish; berries purplish black, with stalked glands less than 0.7 mm long; sepals hairy on outside, 2.5-4 mm long (g) .... *R. laxiflorum.*

29

Conspectus of *Ribes* Species

	lacustre	*oxyacanthoides*	*bracteosum*
Stems	erect to spreading	erect to ascending or sprawling	erect
	armed with spines and bristles	armed with spines and usually also with bristles	unarmed
	0.5-2 m tall	0.5-1.5 m tall	1-2 (3) m tall
Leaves	without resin dots	without resin dots	with yellow crystalline glands on lower surface
	+/- glabrous, not glandular	usually glandular-hairy on lower surface	
	cordate at base	truncated-cordate at base	primarily 5-lobed for over half length, lobes sharp pointed
Flowers	several (6-20) in spreading or drooping clusters that are usually hairy & glandular	1 to 2 or 3	several to many (15 to 50) in long, erect to ascending clusters
	flower stalks jointed just below flowers	flower stalks not jointed	flower stalks jointed
	pink to reddish or purple	greenish-yellow to whitish	greenish purplish plus white
	sepals 2-3 mm long	sepals 3-5 mm long	sepals 3-4 mm long
Berries	palatable but insipid	palatable	musky or catty odour & disagreeable flavour
	dark purple	bluish	black, glaucous
	usually with stalked glands	glabrous	speckled with resin dots
	5-9 mm diam.	9-12 mm diam.	8-10 mm diam.

hudsonianum	triste	glandulosum	laxiflorum
erect	reclining to ascending	reclining to sprawling	trailing or spreading
unarmed	unarmed	unarmed	unarmed
0.5-2 m tall	up to 1 m tall	up to 1 m tall	up to 1 m tall
with yellow crystalline glands (resin dots) on lower surface	without resin dots	without resin dots	without resin dots
	glabrous or hairy below	+/- glabrous on lower surface	hairy & glandular
primarily 3-5 lobed less than half their length, lobes rounded	primarily 3-5 lobed, lobes rounded	primarily 5 lobed pointed lobes	primarily 5 lobed lobes sharp pointed
several (6-15) in ascending to spreading clusters that are hairy but not glandular	several (6-15) in drooping clusters that are often hairy & glandular	several (6-15) in erect or ascending clusters that are glandular-hairy	several (6-18) in ascending to erect clusters that are glandular-hairy
flower stalks jointed	flower stalks jointed	flower stalks jointed	flower stalks jointed
white	reddish to greenish purple	whitish or pink	reddish to purplish
sepals 3-5 mm long	sepals 1.5-2 mm long	sepals 2-2.5 mm long, glabrous on back	sepals 2.5-4 mm long, pubescent on back
disagreeable flavour	sour but palatable	skunky odour & disagreeable flavour	disagreeable flavour
black, +/- glaucous	bright red	dark red	purplish black, glaucous
speckled with a few resin dots (usually)	glabrous	hairy and with stocked glands	bristly and with stocked glands
5-12 mm diam.	6-10 mm diam.	6-8 mm diam.	6-10 mm diam.

31

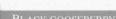

BLACK GOOSEBERRY — *Ribes lacustre*

General Erect to spreading shrub, 0.5-2 m tall, covered with numerous small sharp prickles, with larger thick thorns at leaf nodes; **bark on older stems cinnamon coloured**.

Leaves Somewhat maple-leaf shaped, mostly with 5 deeply indented lobes and heart-shaped base; margins toothed; **not glandular or hairy**.

Flowers **Reddish**, small, shallowly **saucer shaped**, in drooping cluster of **7-15 flowers**; ovary glandular-hairy; flower stalks jointed.

Fruits Dark purple berries covered with **stalked glands**; palatable and with an agreeable but insipid flavour.

Ecology Moist woods and stream banks to drier forested slopes of subalpine ridges; often on rotting wood. Throughout the region, from the lowlands to subalpine elevations.

Notes: The berries were eaten by southern and probably also by other interior native groups. They were used fresh or cooked. Today they are made into jam. • The blister rust fungus that kills *Pinus monticola* (western white pine) and other five-needle pines (such as whitebark pine) requires *Ribes* for part of its lifecycle — as the so-called alternate

host. The name gooseberry appears to be derived from the Flemish *kroes* or *kruys bezie* or the Swedish *krusbar*, a word which has two meanings – either cross-berry or frizzle-berry. The cross would refer to the 3 spines at the leaf node of *Ribes grossularia* resembling a cross. "Fizzle-berry" became translated into crisp berry or *uva-crispa* (hence *R. grossularia* may also be *R. uva-crispa* in old books).

NORTHERN GOOSEBERRY — *Ribes oxyacanthoides*

General Erect, ascending or sprawling shrub, 0.5-1.5 m tall; armed with bristles and 1-3 nodal spines up to 1 cm long; **bark on older stems whitish gray**.

Leaves Somewhat maple-leaf shaped, 5 lobed, with straight base; margins irregularly round toothed; usually **strongly glandular-hairy** beneath.

Flowers **Greenish yellow to whitish, bell shaped**, small, in small drooping clusters of **1-3 flowers**; ovary smooth; flower stalks not jointed.

Fruits Bluish purple, **smooth berries**; palatable.

Ecology Dry open woods and exposed rocky sites. Scattered at low elevations throughout the region.

Notes: Also called smooth gooseberry because the fruits are not hairy. • The berries were eaten by northern interior natives, but were not highly regarded. They make excellent jellies and pies. They have to be picked just as they are turning black; when green, they are too sour and they fall off soon after turning ripe.

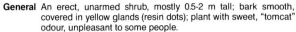

NORTHERN BLACK CURRANT — *Ribes hudsonianum*

General An erect, unarmed shrub, mostly 0.5-2 m tall; bark smooth, covered in yellow glands (resin dots); plant with sweet, "tomcat" odour, unpleasant to some people.

Leaves Maple-leaf shaped, 3-5 lobed; lobes rounded and cut less than half their own length; lower surface covered with yellow crystalline glands (**resin dots**).

Flowers *White*, small, several (6-15), in spreading to *erect clusters*; ovary with resin dots; flower stalks jointed, not glandular-hairy.

Fruits *Black* berries, with white waxy bloom, usually speckled with a few resin dots; disagreeable bitter flavour.

Ecology Moist woods, swamps, thickets, and along shaded streams. Mostly east of the Coast Mountains; common at low to medium elevations throughout the region.

Notes: The berries were eaten by several interior native groups including the Carrier, Slave, and Shuswap. Some liked them a lot, but others used them only as a last resort. The Carrier called this fruit "toadberry" but did not eat it very much.

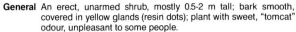

RED SWAMP CURRANT — *Ribes triste*

General Unarmed, reclining to ascending shrub, up to 1 m tall.

Leaves Broadly heart shaped, **distinctly 3 lobed** to sometimes indistinctly 5 lobed; **lobes rounded**, toothed; may be hairy below but **lacking resin dots**.

Flowers **Reddish or greenish purple**, small, several (6-15) in **drooping clusters**; ovary smooth; flower stalks jointed, often hairy and glandular.

Fruits *Bright red*, smooth berries; sour, but palatable.

Ecology Moist coniferous forest, swamps, around springs or seepage areas. From low to subalpine elevations, most commonly in the northern half of the region.

Notes: Berries good in jams and jellies. The Alaskan native people mixed them with salmon roe and stored them for winter use. They also made a medicinal tea for colds and flu from the stems and inner bark.

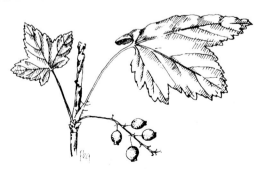

33

SKUNK CURRANT — *Ribes glandulosum*

General Unarmed shrub, up to 1 m tall; branches reclining or often trailing.

Leaves Maple-leaf shaped, deeply 5 to 7 lobed; lobes sharply pointed and toothed; fresh green, glabrous, sparsely glandular on the veins; strong skunky odour when bruised.

Flowers *Greenish white to pink*, several (6-15), in erect or ascending clusters; ovary glandular-hairy; flower stalks jointed and glandular-hairy; sepals 2-2.5 mm long, lacking hairs on outside; petals longer than broad.

Fruits *Dark red* berries, bristly, covered in stalked glandular hairs (lollipop-like); with disagreeable odour and flavour.

Ecology Moist woods, rocky slopes, clearings, roadsides; from the lowlands to subalpine elevations. An interior species common throughout the region.

Notes: Similar to the trailing black currant, *R. laxiflorum*, which has reddish purple flowers, longer hairy sepals, and purple-black berries instead. The flower and fruit stalks are jointed so that the ripe fruit falls clean away from the plant. Plant ill smelling (skunky) when bruised, hence called skunk currant or fetid currant. • The original currant was a very small grape from Corinth. The species name *glandulosum* refers to the characteristic glandular hairs on the fruit.

TRAILING BLACK CURRANT — *Ribes laxiflorum*

General Unarmed, trailing or spreading shrub, usually less than 1 m tall.

Leaves Maple-leaf shaped, usually with 5 sharp, pointed lobes and heart-shaped base; margins toothed; smooth on top, hairy and glandular beneath; strong odour when bruised.

Flowers *Reddish purple*, saucer shaped, several (6-18), in ascending to erect clusters; ovary glandular-hairy; flower stalks jointed and glandular-hairy; sepals 2.5-4 mm long, hairy on back; petals as broad as long.

Fruits *Purplish black* berries, with waxy bloom and stalked glandular hairs; disagreeable flavour.

Ecology Moist forest, slide tracks, clearings, roadsides; low to medium elevations. A mostly coastal species that also occurs scattered but locally abundant in our region.

Notes: Similar to the skunk currant, *R. glandulosum*, which has greenish white to pink flowers, shorter sepals, and dark red berries. • The Carrier and possibly the Gitksan ate the berries. They also used a decoction from boiled stems for cough medicine. • The species name *laxiflorum* means lax flowers, but the flowers are actually erect; *lax* may apply to the often trailing branches.

34

DOUGLAS MAPLE — *Acer glabrum*

General Shrub to small tree, 1-7 m tall; branches opposite; young twigs reddish, older bark grayish.

Leaves Opposite, divided into 3-5 lobes, typical maple-leaf shape, coarsely toothed, turning bright red-orange in fall.

Flowers *Greenish yellow*, small, in terminal or axillary clusters of about 10, appearing with the leaves; male and female flowers on separate or same plant; some flowers may have both sexes.

Fruits *Tan, dry pair of wings* in a V-shaped arrangement.

Ecology Dry ridges or in moist well-drained seepage sites; frequently on rocky south-facing slopes, sometimes on avalanche tracks; from lowlands to moderate elevations. More common in the interior than on the coast. Scattered throughout the southern half of our region (S of 56°), but uncommon east of the Rockies. Most abundant in relatively warm, moist to wet climates (e.g., Skeena-Nass, Rocky Mountain Trench, Quesnel Highland).

Notes: This shrub was often mistakenly referred to by interior native peoples as vine maple, *Acer circinatum*, which grows in southwestern B.C. and the southern interior wet belt. The tough, pliable wood of Douglas maple was used by central and northern interior natives for making a wide variety of goods, especially snowshoe frames. The green wood was soaked and heated before being molded into the desired shape. Other items included throwing sticks, bows, labrets, rattles, masks, and headresses. The fibrous bark was woven into mats by the Niska, and into rope by the Shuswap. • The name "maple" appears to be derived from an old Welsh word *mapwl* meaning a knob in the middle of anything and refers to the knotty burls on the trunk of the tree *Acer campestre*; *glabrum* means smooth, perhaps referring to the leaves or fruit.

HIGHBUSH-CRANBERRY — *Viburnum edule*

General Straggling to erect shrub, 0.5-2.5 m tall with smooth, reddish bark.

Leaves Opposite, shallowly 3 lobed, sharply toothed, hairy beneath, often with a pair of teeth near the junction of the blade and stem.

Flowers A small cluster of *white flowers* borne on short stems with a pair of leaves.

Fruits One-seeded, *red or orange, berrylike drupes* with large flattened stones; edible, juicy, acid, and tart; the over-ripe berries and decaying leaves impart a musty-sour odour to the woods in the fall.

Ecology Moist forest (coniferous and deciduous), seepage areas, swamps, and along streambanks; low to medium elevations. Widespread throughout our region.

Notes: Viburnum opulus (American bush-cranberry) occurs as far north as Prince George, along the Fraser River; its leaves are very deeply 3 lobed, not much toothed, and nearly glabrous. • Berries were used by all interior native groups where they were available. They were collected in the fall after they had been sweetened by the frost. Northern groups (Carrier and Niska) often mixed them with bear grease or eulachon oil. Otherwise they were eaten fresh. The large seeds were discarded. Today they are widely used in jams or jellies. The Carrier and Gitksan people made infusions of the bark and twigs which were drunk for coughs and 'blood spitting'. The Carrier also apparently smoked the bark. • "Cranberry" appears to have originally been craneberry and was the name applied to the bog cranberry. Also called squashberry. *Viburnum* is the Latin name for a species in the genus, perhaps derived from *vieo* (to tie), as European species were used to tie up bundles of things; *edule* simply means edible.

THIMBLEBERRY — *Rubus parviflorus*

General Erect shrub, ***unarmed***, 0.5-2 m tall; young growth glandular-hairy; bark shredding; usually forming dense thickets through an extensive network of rhizomes.

Leaves Large, soft, maple-leaf shaped, 3-7 lobed, toothed, with long glandular stalks; ***finely fuzzy on both sides.***

Flowers White, large, petals crinkled like tissue paper, several (3-11) in long-stemmed terminal cluster.

Fruits Shallowly domed, ***raspberrylike*** clusters of red, hairy drupelets; juicy, insipid to sweet depending on growing site.

Ecology Open forest, clearings, roadsides, and streambanks. Widespread at low to subalpine elevations in the southern half of our region.

Notes: Thimbleberries were eaten by all native groups in the central and southern interior. They were usually eaten fresh with other berries because they do not dry readily or keep well in grease. The young shoots were peeled and eaten raw or cooked with meat in a stew. The large, maple-like leaves were widely used as temporary containers, or to line baskets, to separate berries in the same basket, or as a surface on which to dry the berries. However, being tender and juicy, the berries are difficult to pick and were therefore seldom gathered in large enough  quantities to be dried for winter storage. Sometimes they were mixed in with wild raspberries or blackcaps. • *Parviflorus*, meaning few or small flowered, is a bit of a misleading name for this species.

DEVIL'S CLUB — *Oplopanax horridus*

General Erect to sprawling shrub, 1-3 m tall; stems thick, crooked, almost unbranched but often entangled, ***armed with numerous large yellowish spines***; distinctly sweetish odour to the wood.

Leaves Broad, maple-leaf shaped, with 7-9 sharply pointed and heavily toothed lobes; ***numerous spines on underside***.

Flowers Small, whitish, numerous in compact heads arranged in pyramidal terminal clusters.

Fruits ***Bright red, flattened, shiny berries*** in large, showy pyramidal clusters; not edible.

Ecology Moist woods, especially in seepage sites and along streams. Low to medium elevations (sometimes in subalpine forest) throughout the moister parts of the southern half of the region.

Notes: A fearsome plant to the outdoor hiker, as it has spines that readily break off and soon fester if embedded in the skin — hence it earns the name "devil's club." However, it is also a very handsome plant and is now gaining acceptance as a garden ornamental. • The plant was, and still is, widely used by interior native people for a vast array of ailments such as stomach ulcers, thyroid condition, tuberculosis, syphilis, diabetes; also as an emetic, cough syrup, and laxative. Various parts of the plant were ground into powders for external poultices for arthritis and rheumatism or fresh pieces were laid on open wounds. It was also used as a counter-irritant (see Turner, 1982 or Gottesfeld and Anderson, 1988). Generally the plant was believed to possess extremely strong magical powers which could be transferred to the person who used it. It was also widely used in purification rituals and for luck. Coastal groups mixed the charcoal from the burned stems with grease to make ceremonial face paint, and applied ashes to burns. • *Oplopanax* is from the Greek *hoplon* (weapon) and *Panax*, a related large-leaved genus; *horridus* needs no explanation for anyone familiar with the species.

GREEN ALDER · *Alnus viridis* ssp. *fruticosa*

General Almost always a shrub, usually 1-3 m tall; *lateral buds pointed, lacking stalks*; twigs finely hairy to smooth, reddish brown.

Leaves Oval to elliptic, sharp pointed at tip; *margins not wavy-lobed*, finely double toothed; surface usually shiny and smooth above, slightly hairy below, yellowish green on both sides; young leaves sticky beneath; secondary lateral veins not forming ladderlike pattern.

Flowers In male and female catkins, borne on current year's twigs, *appearing at same time as leaves*.

Fruits Seed cones 1-1.5 cm long, egg-shaped, borne on stalks longer than cones themselves; *nutlets with broad wings.*

Ecology Upland forested slopes and along streams; most abundant on well-drained, coarse textured soils; often forming thickets near timberline in mountains. Mainly in boreal forest east of the Rocky Mountains, but also observed in the dry, cold southwestern part of our region.

Notes: This species is also known as *A. crispa* or *A. crispa* ssp. *crispa*. • Widely used by native people as a dye, and for fuel, smoking salmon and meat, carving and basket making. Alder twigs and buds make up an important part of the winter food of the white-tailed ptarmigan. In the fall and winter the "seeds" (nutlets) are eaten by songbirds. • *Alnus* is what the Romans called alders; *viridis* means green; and *fruticosa* means shrubby, hence the shrubby green alder. • Alder appears to be from old English *alor* or old High German *elo* or *elawer* meaning reddish yellow, in reference to the bright reddish-yellow colour which develops when the timber is freshly cut.

SITKA ALDER · *Alnus viridis* ssp. *sinuata*

General Coarse shrub or small tree, 1-5 m tall; *lateral buds pointed and lacking stalks;* bark yellowish brown, scaly.

Leaves Broadly oval with somewhat rounded base and pointed tip; *margins wavy-lobed (sinuate),* double toothed; slightly sticky beneath; main lateral veins always run into projecting large teeth, secondary lateral veins forming ladder-like pattern between main laterals.

Flowers In catkins, *opening at same time as leaves.*

Fruits Seed cones 1.5-2 cm long, egg-shaped, on stalks longer than cones; *nutlets with broad wings.*

Ecology Well-drained upland forests and clearings, and seepage areas on northerly aspects; often forming thickets along logging roads or on avalanche tracks or near timberline in the mountains. Common throughout the region from lowlands to timberline, except northeast of the Rockies where it is replaced by ssp. *fruticosa*.

Notes: This species is also known as *A. sinuata*, or *A. crispa* ssp. *sinuata*, or *A. sitchensis.* • Widely used by native people as a dye, and for fuel, smoking salmon and meat, carving and basket making. May have been used for medicinal purposes by the Carrier (see mountain alder). • The subspecies name *sinuata* refers to the wavy or sinuous leaf margin that distinguishes this from green alder.

MOUNTAIN ALDER — *Alnus incana* ssp. *tenuifolia*

General Coarse shrub or small tree, 2-10 m tall, often in clumps; twigs glabrous to woolly hairy; ***buds club-shaped, with short stalks***; bark yellow-brown with distinct lenticels.

Leaves Thin, elliptical, with rounded to somewhat heart-shaped base, and rounded to blunt tip; margins thin, wavy–lobed, double toothed; pale-hairy, not sticky, below; lateral veins forming ladderlike pattern between main laterals. As with other alder species, leaves remaining green through much of the autumn.

Flowers In catkins, borne on previous season's twigs, ***appearing before the leaves***.

Fruits Seed cones with very short stalks; ***nutlets with very narrow wings***.

Ecology Along streams or at edges of ponds, lakes, swamps, or in other poorly drained sites. Widespread at low elevations throughout the region, but tends to be merely locally abundant.

Notes: The wood was considered the best by native people for smoking and drying salmon and meat because it has no pitch and does not flavour the food. It was also made into eating utensils and serving dishes. Both the wood and bark were widely used as a source of dye and to treat animal hides. The Carrier fashioned the bark into fish nets that were dyed black by boiling them in their own juice. Black nets are good because the fish cannot see them. Boiled alder bark was important medicine and was drunk to stop bleeding or "whenever the heart moved" (Carrier Linguistic Committee, 1973). • The species name *incana* refers to the whitish undersides of the leaves.

BEAKED HAZELNUT — *Corylus cornuta*

General Shrub 1-4 m tall, with many stems; twigs, leaves, and ***bud scales covered in long white hairs*** at least when young, glabrous after first season; densely clumped or spreading widely by rhizomes (suckers).

Leaves Elliptic to oval, commonly with heart-shaped base and sharp-pointed tip; margin double toothed; lower surface paler than upper surface. As with paper birch, leaves turning yellow in autumn.

Flowers Male flowers in catkins, flowering before the appearance of leaves in the spring. Female catkins very small, with protruding red stigmas.

Fruits ***Spherical, edible nuts***, enclosed in long tubular husks; husks light-green, covered with stiff prickly hairs, and projecting beyond the nut into a beak; borne in clusters of 2 or 3 at ends of branches.

Ecology Moist but well-drained sites at low elevations; in open forest, shady openings, thickets, clearings, and rocky slopes; often riparian habitats in central B.C. Scattered throughout the southern part of our region. Locally abundant along the main Fraser River valley from McBride to Prince George and Quesnel, and also along the Peace River and in the middle Skeena-Nass area.

Notes: The nuts were eaten by the Gitksan, Niska, and Shuswap and were traded to other groups. They were gathered and buried until the husks rotted away, or taken from a squirrel cache. The nuts were then eaten as is, pounded with berries, meat or animal fat into cakes, or boiled to extract the oil and used to flavour other foods. Nut milk was used to cure coughs and colds. They have largely been replaced now by commercial peanuts. The wood was made into arrows, fishing gear (traps and hooks), and spoons. The Gitksan made a type of hockey stick from bent roots and played a game with a flat rock. Young suckers, when bent and twisted, made a kind of rope. • *Corylus* is what the Greeks called hazelnuts *(korylos,* 'a helmet'); *cornuta* means beaked; both references are to the husk surrounding the nut.

SCRUB BIRCH — *Betula glandulosa* var. *glandulosa*

General Low and spreading to erect shrubs mostly 0.3-2 m tall; twigs resinous and covered with **wart-like crystalline glands** that look like octopus suckers; indistinctly fine-hairy.

Leaves **Nearly circula**r; 3 or fewer lateral veins, and 10 or fewer rounded teeth per side of leaf margin; somewhat **thick and leathery**, glandular on both surfaces; bright green, usually without hairs above, paler and often hairy below.

Flowers In small, upright catkins, flowering with the appearance of leaves in the spring.

Fruits Nutlets, slightly winged.

Ecology At low elevations typically in fens and other wetlands, and in seepage areas, on streambanks, and along margins of lakes and marshes; also on dry upland sites especially in the North and often extensively in the subalpine and alpine zones of the northern half of our region.

Notes: This variety is often difficult to distinguish from *B. glandulosa* var. *glandulifera* (=*B. pumila*, dwarf, or swamp birch). The latter has more oval-shaped leaves with 4 or more lateral veins and more than 10 teeth on each side, and is generally less glandular and more pubescent and has nutlets with broader wings than in *B. glandulosa* var. *glandulosa*. Both varieties are found in suitable habitats throughout our region. • In the fall, the northern mountains and plateaus glow with the deep orange to russet colours of scrub birch. • *Betula* is simply the ancient Latin name for birch; *glandulosa* means with glands, referring to the twigs.

BOG-LAUREL — *Kalmia microphylla* ssp. *occidentalis*

General Small, slender-branched, evergreen shrub, up to 0.5 m tall; spreading by layering and short rhizomes.

Leaves **Opposite**, narrowly lance-shaped, not drooping; margins rolled under; dark green, leathery above, **conspicuously whitish fine-hairy beneath**.

Flowers **Rose-pink, saucer-shaped**, several, in loose terminal cluster; stamens 10, the tip of each stamen tucked into a small pouch in a petal, and held under tension like a bow. At the slightest touch by an insect probing for nectar, the stamens pop out and dust the insect with pollen.

Fruits Five-valved capsules.

Ecology Bogs, muskeg, and wet mountain meadows; on peaty soils. Scattered through much of the region but apparently lacking from the extensive peatlands of the Ft. Nelson Lowland.

Notes: This species is also known as *Kalmia polifolia*. Two subspecies occur: ssp. *microphylla* is a much smaller plant not over 15 cm tall, with leaves and flowers about half the size of those of ssp. *occidentalis*, and typically occurring at higher elevations. • Check out the intricate flower in this species. Ten anthers are tucked into ten pockets on the petals, with arched filaments holding the flower open under tension. Try touching a flower and watch the pollen fly! • Contains the poison andromedotoxin (see notes under *Andromeda*). Grows together with, and is somewhat similar in appearance to, Labrador tea (*Ledum groenlandicum*) and bog-rosemary (*Andromeda polifolia*). Care must be taken when collecting Labrador tea not to confuse it with *Kalmia* and *Andromeda*, whose leaves do not have brown fuzz on the underside and don't tend to hang downwards. When in flower all three species are easy to tell apart. • Presumably it is called "bog-laurel" because the leaves of *Kalmia* are similar in shape to, and are aromatic like bay leaves. *Kalmia* is named for Peter Kalm, an 18th century student of Linnaeus; *microphylla* means "small-leaved", and *occidentalis* means "western", hence the western small-leaved bog-laurel.

39

LABRADOR TEA — *Ledum groenlandicum*

General Evergreen, much-branched shrub, 0.3-0.8 m tall; twigs with dense rusty hairs; with spicy fragrance.

Leaves *Alternate*, narrow, oblong to lance-shaped, often drooping; margins rolled under; leathery, deep green above, with *dense rusty hairs beneath* (hairs on young leaves may not be rusty).

Flowers *White*, with protruding stamens; small, numerous, in short umbrella-like clusters.

Fruits Drooping cluster of 5-part, dry, hairy capsules.

Ecology In peatlands and moist coniferous woods; indicator of wet, usually very acid and nutrient-poor organic soils. A dominant shrub in interior black spruce bogs. Widespread throughout the region at low to medium elevations.

Notes: Ledum palustre (= *L. decumbens*, northern Labrador tea) differs only in that it is smaller (up to 0.5 m tall), has shorter narrower leaves, and flower stalks with reddish (rather than white) hairs. It occurs sporadically in peatlands and in high elevation heath and tundra north of 58° in our region. • Leaves, used fresh or dried, can be boiled to make a tea with an aromatic fragrance which should be consumed in moderation to avoid drowsiness. Excessive doses are reported to act as a strong diuretic, as a cathartic, or to cause intestinal disturbances. Do not confuse with trapper's tea (*Ledum glandulosum*), bog-laurel (*Kalmia microphylla*) or bog-rosemary (*Andromeda polifolia*). All three lack the brown fuzz on the underside of the mature leaves, and *Kalmia* and *Andromeda* have pink flowers. All three contain toxic alkaloids known to be poisonous to livestock, especially sheep. • The leaves were made into tea by many native groups although there is some question as to whether or not northern groups used it as a tea aboriginally. The Gitksan and Carrier may have used it as a tonic prior to contact with Europeans. The Shuswap reportedly drank it in large amounts to counteract poison ivy. • *Ledum* is from the Greek word *ledon*, their name for another plant; *groenlandicum* refers to the fact that this species also grows in Greenland (as well as in Labrador!).

TRAPPER'S TEA — *Ledum glandulosum*

General Stout, erect, evergreen shrub, 0.4-0.8 m tall; twigs minutely hairy and glandular.

Leaves *Alternate*, narrow, oblong to lance-shaped, often drooping; margins rolled under; leathery, green and rough above, with *greenish white hairs* (not rusty brown) and resin glands underneath.

Flowers *White*, with protruding stamens; small, numerous, in umbrella-like clusters.

Fruits A drooping cluster of dry capsules.

Ecology Moist coniferous forest at moderate elevations. Locally abundant in the eastern Chilcotin.

Notes: Similar to Labrador tea (*Ledum groenlandicum*). Differs mainly in that it does not have the rusty felt of hairs on undersurface of the leaf. This plant, bog-laurel (*Kalmia microphylla*) and bog-rosemary (*Andromeda polifolia*) contain a poisonous alkaloid and are known to be toxic to livestock, especially sheep. • The species name *glandulosum* refers to the resin glands on the undersurface of the leaf.

FALSE AZALEA — *Menziesia ferruginea*

General Erect to straggly spreading shrub, up to 2 m tall, deciduous; young twigs covered with fine hairs, somewhat glandular and rusty coloured, sticky to the touch; bark scaly-shredding on older branches; with skunky odour when crushed.

Leaves In clusters along branches; dull, thin, oblong to elliptic; margins wavy, toothed; *light green to blue-green, hairy-glandular; end of mid-vein protruding at tip of leaf.*

Flowers *Salmon to greenish orange, urn-shaped*; several in drooping terminal clusters on previous year's growth.

Fruits Four-part, dry capsules.

Ecology Shady coniferous woods with acid humus, moist slopes, streambanks. In moister parts of the southern half of the region; especially abundant in some subalpine forests.

Notes: This plant is very attractive in the fall when the leaves turn a brilliant crimson-orange. Turner (1978) reports that children of the Niska used to suck the nectar from the flowers. • Called "false azalea" and "false huckleberry" because it resembles both plants. Also called "fool's huckleberry" because the flower looks so much like that of a huckleberry but the fruit is a dry, inedible capsule. *Menziesia* is named for Archibald Menzies, physician and naturalist with Captain George Vancouver; *ferruginea* means rusty, referring to the rusty hairs covering branches and leaves.

WHITE-FLOWERED RHODODENDRON — *Rhododendron albiflorum*

General Erect, slender, branched shrub, up to 2 m tall, deciduous; young twigs covered with coarse reddish hairs; bark peeling.

Leaves In clusters along branch, but especially at tip of branch; oblong to lance-shaped; *upper surface with fine rusty hairs; yellowish green*, turning beautiful shades of bronze, crimson and orange in the fall; *end of midvein not protruding at tip of leaf.*

Flowers *White to creamy*, large, showy, *cup-shaped*, in clusters of 2-3 on previous year's growth; petals fused at base.

Fruits Dry, oval capsules.

Ecology Moist coniferous forest, wet glades, and along streams, but also on relatively dry, well-drained sites. Common at mostly subalpine elevations in the southern half of our region, but mostly absent from the west-central boundary of this area (i.e., in the lee of the Coast Mountains), where it seems to be replaced by *Menziesia ferruginea* and *Vaccinium ovalifolium.*

Notes: Rhododendron lapponicum (Lapland rosebay) is a dwarf shrub (up to 30 cm tall) with purple flowers, found in the subalpine and alpine in mountains north of 58°. (There are 600 - 900 species of *Rhododendron* in the world; these are the only two occurring in our area). •Often called "mountain misery" because of its tendency to grow on shady moist mountain slopes near timberline in very thick masses. The branches tend to trail downhill making it exceedingly difficult for bushwackers to move up through it. • The Thompson people used the plant as a scent. All parts of the plant are reputed to be poisonous. • *Rhododendron* is from the Greek *rhodon* (rose) and *dendron* (tree); *albiflorum* simply means white-flowered.

41

BLACK HUCKLEBERRY — *Vaccinium membranaceum*

General Erect, spreading, coarse, densely branched shrub, 0.3 to 1.5 m tall; young branches yellowish green, somewhat angled; old branches with greyish shredding bark.

Leaves Deciduous, thin, *lance-shaped to elliptic, pointed at tip*, 2-5 cm long; *margins finely toothed*; glabrous, paler on lower surface.

Flowers Creamy pink, urn-shaped, single in leaf axil; *appearing with or after leaves*.

Fruits Purplish or reddish black berries, *without bloom*; large, edible, and with excellent flavour.

Ecology Common understory shrub in coniferous forests, on dry to moist sites, from valley bottoms to high elevations. Widespread in our region except for the northeastern and northwestern areas (Fort Nelson and Atlin districts) and uncommon in the Chilcotin.

Notes: This species is considered by many to be the tastiest huckleberry or blueberry in British Columbia. It was eaten when available by all interior groups, either fresh, dried, or preserved in grease. Today they are canned or frozen. Birds and mammals also eat these berries. • The name huckleberry is derived from whortleberry or hurtleberry, from the Anglo-Saxon *wyrtil* (a small shrub), a diminutive of *wyrt* or *wort* (plant). In B.C., at least, the fruits of *Vaccinium* shrubs tend to be called "blueberries" if they're blue, and "huckleberries" if they're any other colour (here, black). • The species name *membranaceum* refers to the thin, membranous leaves.

OVAL-LEAVED BLUEBERRY — *Vaccinium ovalifolium*

General Erect, slender, spreading shrub, up to 1.5 m tall; young twigs brownish to yellowish, or often reddish, angled, grooved; old branches greyish.

Leaves Deciduous, *oval, blunt-rounded at both ends; margins usually lacking teeth*; green above, lighter beneath.

Flowers Pinkish, globular, urn-shaped to egg-shaped 'bells' usually longer than broad; single, in axils of leaves; *appearing generally before (sometimes with) the leaves*.

Fruits Blue-black berries *with bluish bloom*; large and edible.

Ecology Moist coniferous forests and openings. Scattered at medium to subalpine elevations south of 56°; mainly on leeward slopes of the Kitimat Ranges and in the wet area of the central Rocky Mountains and Quesnel Highland.

Notes: Very similar to Alaskan blueberry (*V. alaskaense*) in which the flower is more globose, the style sticks out beyond the mouth of the flower, and the fruit stalks are enlarged just at base of berry. *V. alaskaense* is primarily a coastal species, occurring in our region only in the Skeena-Nass transitional area.

• The berries of the oval-leaved blueberry were commonly eaten fresh, dried or jammed by interior native people, but were not as popular as other types of blueberries and huckleberries. The Gitksan say they were too "seedy". • *Ovalifolium* refers to the oval leaves of this species.

VELVET-LEAVED BLUEBERRY — *Vaccinium myrtilloides*

General Deciduous, low shrub 0.1-0.4 m high, growing in dense colonies; **branches, especially young ones, velvety hairy**.

Leaves Thin, elliptic to oblong or lance-shaped, sharply pointed, up to 4 cm long in maturity; margins smooth; *softly hairy*, green.

Flowers *Greenish white or tinged pink*, cylindrically bell-shaped, 3-5 mm long; single or few, *in clusters* at ends of branches.

Fruits Blue berries with *heavy, pale-blue bloom*; edible and sweet.

Ecology Commonly on gravelly or sandy soils; open forests, clearings, and bog hummocks. Mainly in the southeastern part of the region; the Rocky Mountain Trench and Prince George to Williams Lake, also in the Peace River district.

Notes: The berries were eaten by the Carrier and other groups within the range of the species. Eaten fresh or dried in cakes for winter.
• *Vaccinium* is the Latin name for another shrub with berries, perhaps one the cows (*vacca*) ate; *myrtilloides* means the leaves are like those of myrtle (*Myrtus* spp.)

SHRUBBY CINQUEFOIL — *Potentilla fruticosa*

General Spreading to erect shrub, 0.3-1.3 m tall; young branches silky-hairy; *bark brown, shredding*.

Leaves Divided into *3-7 closely crowded, greyish green leaflets*; margins often curled; lightly hairy.

Flowers *Golden yellow, buttercup-like* (small and pale at low elevations to larger and brighter at higher elevations); solitary or few, in clusters near tip of branch.

Fruits A cluster of achenes with long straight hairs.

Ecology Open, often moist habitats, such as peat bogs, tundra, and high elevation meadows; but also dry meadows, cliffs, rocky slopes, gravelly river flats in areas with calcareous soils. Throughout the northern half of the region.

Notes: Our only truly shrubby *Potentilla* (a number of other *Potentilla* species are described on pp. 161-166). A popular garden ornamental, with many cultivars. The leaves were made into a tea by Alaskan Inuit and the dry, flaky bark was used as tinder for making friction fires by the Blackfoot of Alberta.
• *Cinquefoil* is from the Latin *quinque* meaning five and *folium* meaning leaf and refers to the fact that many *Potentilla* species have 5 leaflets and their flower parts are in 5's. *Potentilla* is from the Latin *potens*, referring to the medicinal properties of some cinquefoils; *fruticosa* means shrubby.

LEATHERLEAF — *Chamaedaphne calyculata*

General Low, ***evergreen***, branching shrub, mostly 0.2-0.6 m high; twigs hairy or scaly.

Leaves ***Alternate***; oblong, elliptic or lance shaped, with short stalks and pointed or blunt tips; margins minutely round-toothed or smooth; ***leathery with white-brown scales*** especially on lower surface.

Flowers White, small, urn-shaped to tubular, in a one-sided, elongated, leafy, terminal cluster.

Fruits Five-chambered, round, many-seeded capsules.

Ecology ***Sphagnum bogs and muskeg***; often forming dense thickets. Restricted to peatlands of the North, primarily in the Peace and Liard watersheds. A characteristic species of boreal and subarctic peatlands in Canada, Alaska, and the "Soviet Union."

Notes: The name *Chamaedaphne* means low-growing (*chamai*) *Daphne*, *Daphne* being the Greek name for the bay laurel. Sometimes called *Cassandra*, after the daughter of Priam, King of Troy.

FALSEBOX — *Paxistima myrsinites*

General Low, ***evergreen*** shrub, erect or prostrate, up to 0.6 m high; branches reddish brown, 4-ridged, otherwise smooth.

Leaves ***Opposite*** or nearly so, oval to elliptic, 1-3 cm long; ***margins toothed*** and slightly rolled under; leathery.

Flowers ***Maroon***, very small, numerous in axillary clusters all along the branches.

Fruits Small, oval, 1- to 2-seeded capsules.

Ecology Coniferous forest (mature and seral), rocky openings, dry mountain slopes. At low to medium elevations in the southeastern and southwestern parts of the region.

Notes: The genus name is spelled various ways — commonly as *Pachystima*. • Widely used by florists; picking falsebox for this market supports a cottage industry in some places. • From Old English *box* or Latin *buxus*. A box was originally a receptacle made from the boxwood tree (*Buxus sempervirens*). *Paxistima* is from the Greek words for the thick (*pachys*) stigma; *myrsinites* is the Greek word for myrrh (smell the flowers!).

PINK SPIREA, HARDHACK *Spiraea douglasii* ssp. *menziesii*

General Erect, much-branched shrub to 1.5 m tall; young growth woolly.

Leaves Oblong to oval, toothed above the middle, glabrous.

Flowers **Pink to deep rose**, numerous, in a long, narrow and **compact cluster which is several times longer than broad**.

Fruits Cluster of several small, smooth follicles.

Ecology Mesic to wet, open forests, streambanks, swamps, fens, lake margins, and damp meadows. This species often indicates sites with cold-air drainage (frost pockets). Low to middle elevations in the southern half of the region; especially common in the Bulkley Valley, Nechako Plateau, and Quesnel Highland.

Notes: The coastal *S. douglasii* ssp. *douglasii* has gray matted hairs on the lower surface of the leaf. • Twigs were used by coastal native groups as an implement to harvest dentalium shells, as well as to make hooks for drying and smoking salmon, blades, scrapers, and roasting sticks. • The name "hardhack" may be derived from the fact that early settlers and pioneers had to hack their way through dense masses of this bush which readily takes over wet land if it is not kept down. Species names *douglasii* and *menziesii* celebrate David Douglas and Archibald Menzies, the same naturalist duo honoured in naming Douglas-fir (*Pseudotsuga menziesii*).

PYRAMID SPIREA *Spiraea pyramidata*

General Spreading to erect shrub, mostly 0.5-1 m tall, usually with extensive rhizomes; usually finely hairy throughout, but especially among the flowers.

Leaves Oval-oblong to lance-shaped, coarsely toothed above middle, glabrous.

Flowers **Rose-pink**, but varying from off-white to pink, numerous, in **loose pyramid-shaped cluster approximately twice as long as broad**.

Fruits A cluster of finely hairy follicles.

Ecology Variety of wooded sites and forest edges from wet to dry, at low elevations. Scattered throughout the southern half of the region, locally abundant especially in the Bulkley Valley, Fraser Basin, Nechako Plateau, and Quesnel Highland.

Notes: *S. pyramidata* is suspected of being a hybrid between *S. betulifolia* and *S. douglasii*, and one sometimes encounters mixed populations of all three species, with a variety of intermediate individuals. • Turner (1978) notes that the Thompson made a tea by boiling the stems, leaves and flowers. • *Spiraea* is from the Greek *speiraira*, a plant used in wreaths; some garden varieties are called "bridal-wreath." The species name *pyramidata* refers to the shape of the inflorescence.

45

SHRUBS

BIRCH-LEAVED SPIREA — *Spiraea betulifolia*

General Erect shrub, strongly rhizomatous, mostly 25-60 cm tall; **not hairy**.

Leaves Oval to oval-oblong, but wider toward the tip, **leaf base tapering to stalk**; usually **coarsely double-toothed** above the middle; dark green above, pale green below.

Flowers **Dull white**, often with pale pinkish or lavender tinge; **small, numerous, in a nearly flat-topped cluster**.

Fruits A cluster of smooth, beaked **follicles**.

Ecology Typically in open, dry to moist, coniferous and deciduous forest; also on dry rocky slopes. Widespread from low to medium elevations in the southern half of the region (to 56° N).

Notes: Sometimes confused with saskatoon (*Amelanchier alnifolia*). The leaves are similar although those of *S. betulifolia* are more oblong and more coarsely toothed, whereas the more rounded leaves of *A. alnifolia* are more regularly toothed. Look for the similar *Spiraea beauverdiana* (Beauverd's spirea) in open forest and mountain thickets and meadows in far northwestern B.C., west of Atlin and in the Haines Triangle. • The species name *betulifolia* means the same thing as the common name − "birch-leaved".

SASKATOON — *Amelanchier alnifolia*

General Shrub to small tree, 1-5 m tall; stem smooth; bark dark grey to reddish; often spreading by rhizomes or stolons and forming dense colonies.

Leaves Alternate, deciduous, thin, round to oval, **regularly toothed** mostly on top half of leaf, **heart-shaped at base**.

Flowers White, **large, showy, in short leafy clusters** (drooping to erect) of 3-20.

Fruits Purple to nearly black, **berrylike pomes** (like miniature apples), with a white bloom; edible, sweet.

Ecology Dry to moist, coniferous and deciduous forests, thickets, open hillsides, roadsides; in well-drained soils. Common and widespread at low to medium elevations throughout the region.

Notes: Saskatoon provides important winter browse for ungulates (e.g., moose, deer, elk). • A highly variable species. Native people recognized up to eight different varieties based on the differences in flowering time and the size, texture, and sweetness of the fruit. The berries were an extremely important food for all the interior peoples. Berries were eaten fresh or dried in cakes or like raisins for storage and were a common trading item between interior and coastal groups. The hard, straight-grained wood was used for arrow shafts by Carrier and Gitksan people. The Carrier made it into slat armour and shields. • The name saskatoon appears to be a shortened version of the Blackfoot name for this bush "*mis-ask-a-tomina*." Also called serviceberry. Early reports of this fruit referred to it as "poire, wild pear or service berry" whose leaves and fruits were pear-like. Service tree is the old name given to *Sorbus (Pyrus) domestica* (sorb-apple) and wild service to the rowan tree, *Sorbus aucuparia*. Presumably the first explorers thought it resembled these old-world species. The fruits of the service tree reputedly were the source of a fermented liquor resembling beer.

46

PIN CHERRY — *Prunus pensylvanica*

General Shrub to small tree, 1-5 (12) m tall; bark reddish brown, peeling in horizontal strips, **lenticels prominent**.

Leaves *Oval to lance-shaped*, gradually tapering to long point at tip, with rounded base; margins round toothed; leaf stalk with 2 small glands near base of blade.

Flowers White, small, in **flat-topped umbel-like clusters**.

Fruits Small, round, bright red cherries with thin, acid flesh.

Ecology Dry to moist woods and open places; often abundant after fire. Scattered at low elevations in the southeastern part of our region and in the Skeena-Bulkley-Nechako valleys.

Notes: **Warning** – pin cherry stones and leaves, like those of other *Prunus* species, contain toxic cyanide. The flesh is not harmful, but poisoning and death have occurred in children who consumed large quantities of berries without removing the seeds. • Bitter cherry (*Prunus emarginata*) is a more coastal species which occurs infrequently south of 55° and west of the Rocky Mountains; it also has an umbel-like flower cluster, but the cherries are larger and the leaves less pointy tipped than those of *P. pensylvanica*. • The Carrier and Gitksan reportedly ate the fruit of bitter cherry, but pin cherry appears to be more abundant in their territory and probably both were used. There were never enough cherries to preserve for winter and they were unsuitable for drying. They make good jelly. Cherry bark has waterproof properties and was used for wrapping implements and decorating baskets. An infusion of the bark was a remedy against blood spitting for the Carrier. • Also called "bird cherry", aptly so as birds like them so much it is often hard to find any ripe fruit on the trees. *Prunus* is Latin for plum; *pensylvanica* indicates the wide range of this species (i.e., it's also found in Pennsylvania).

CHOKE CHERRY — *Prunus virginiana*

General Usually a shrub, sometimes a tree, 1-4 m tall; bark smooth, reddish brown to grey-brown, not peeling readily, **lenticels not prominent**.

Leaves Thin, **elliptic to oval**, with sharp pointed tip and blunt base; margin finely and sharply toothed; bright green and glabrous above, paler beneath; leaf stalk with 2 or 3 prominent glands.

Flowers White, small, numerous, in **elongated, terminal, bottlebrush-like clusters**.

Fruits Shiny, red to purple or black cherries; edible but with very astringent after-taste.

Ecology Edge of woods and thickets, often on dry and exposed sites; from open woodlands to grasslands and clearings. Scattered at lower elevations throughout the southern half of the region, locally common on warm aspects in Peace and Stikine river valleys.

Notes: Choke cherries were very popular with the Carrier and Gitksan, in spite of their astringency and large stones. They were eaten fresh as a snack or dried for winter use, although the Gitksan people say there were never enough to dry. The berries were also used by southern groups to make a tea for coughs and colds and, more recently, for wine making and pies. They make excellent jelly. The Carrier took a cold infusion of the bark internally as a stimulant. • The name "choke cherry" is very apt as it produces a choking sensation when eaten. The Gitksan name for the very astringent, black-fruited form found around Hazelton means "it makes your mouth and throat so that nothing will slip on it" (People of 'Ksan, 1980). • The species name *virginiana*, as in *P. pensylvanica*, indicates the wide distribution of this cherry. (Many North American plants bear species names such as *pensylvanica* or *virginiana* because the earliest North American botanists began collecting in the eastern United States.)

BLACK TWINBERRY — *Lonicera involucrata*

General Erect to straggly shrub, 0.5-2 m tall; *young twigs four-angled in cross-section, greenish*.

Leaves Opposite, short-stemmed, *somewhat elliptical to broadly lance shaped*, pointed, often hairy beneath.

Flowers *Yellow, tubular, in pairs, in leaf axils*, cupped by a pair of large green to purplish bracts.

Fruits Shiny, *black* "twin" berries cupped by 2 deep purplish maroon bracts; not considered palatable.

Ecology Moist forest, clearings, riparian habitats, swamps, and thickets; in fairly moist or wet soil; common at low to medium elevations in the southern half of the region.

Notes: Lonicera dioica, the red honeysuckle, occurs sporadically east of the Rockies in our region; vinelike stems and yellow to orange-red, tubular flowers characterize this species. • While some interior native groups believed the berries were poisonous and would make one crazy, others did not. However, none of them apparently thought they were edible because they are so bitter. Many interior people called them "bear berries" or "grizzly berries". The Carrier boiled the leaves and used the liquid to bathe sore eyes, or applied the crushed leaves as a poultice to open sores. • The berries are eaten by birds and other animals in large quantities. • The honeysuckle genus *Lonicera* is named for Adam Lonitzer (1528-1586), a German naturalist; *involucrata* just means with an involucre, the twin bracts surrounding the flowers and fruit.

RED-OSIER DOGWOOD — *Cornus stolonifera*

General Freely spreading stoloniferous shrub with many stems, 1-4 m tall; branches opposite, lower branches often lying on ground and rooting freely; *young stems round in cross section, usually bright red especially after a frost*.

Leaves Opposite, *oval*, mostly sharp-pointed with 5-7 prominent *parallel veins* which converge at leaf tip; filmy white threads running through veins may be seen if a leaf is split crosswise and gently pulled apart.

Flowers *White to greenish*, small, numerous, *in dense flat-topped terminal clusters*.

Fruits *White* (occasionally blue-tinged), small, berrylike drupes, with somewhat flattened stones; bitter and inedible.

Ecology Moist soil, typically in swamps and riparian forest and scrub, but also in open upland forest and thickets. Throughout the region, valley bottoms to mid-elevations.

Notes: This species is also known as *Cornus sericea*. It is extremely important moose winter browse. • The rather bitter berries were eaten by all southern interior native peoples, including the Shuswap. They were usually mixed with other sweeter berries such as saskatoons. It is possible that they were also eaten by nothern groups. The boiled inner bark was applied as a poultice to sores and swellings to kill pain or was smoked for sickness of the lungs by northern native people, especially the Carrier and Gitksan. The leaves or bark were sometimes mixed with other plants as a smoking mixture. • "Osier" appears to be from the Old French word *osiere* meaning that which grows in an osier-bed, which in turn means the bed of a river, in reference to the natural habitat of the *Salix* spp. to which the name "osier" was first applied. There are several theories as to where the name "dogwood" came from. One has it that the berries were considered unfit for even a dog to eat. Another is that it is derived from the various words (French *dague*, Spanish *daga* and Sanskrit *dag*), all meaning skewer or dagger, because the wood of the tree *C. sanguinea* was used to make skewers for butchers and other pointed instruments (*daggs*).

SOOPOLALLIE — *Shepherdia canadensis*

General An unarmed spreading shrub, 1-2 m tall; **branches brownish, covered with small, branlike scabs**; young branches with rusty spots.

Leaves **Opposite**, oval; dark-greenish on upper surface, **whitish silvery felt of hairs and rusty brown spots (scales) on the under surface.**

Flowers **Yellowish brown**, inconspicuous, 1-several in clusters on stem before leaves open out; male and female flowers on separate shrubs.

Fruits **Bright red, translucent, oval, juicy berries**; extremely bitter, soapy to touch.

Ecology Dry to moist open woods and thickets; from lowlands to mid-elevation forests throughout the region.

Notes: All interior native groups whipped up the berries with a little water into a light froth often called "Indian ice-cream." The berries were either eaten fresh or dried for later use and were an important trade item throughout the province. Today they are still valued as gifts, but are either frozen or canned. • The berries, juice, twigs, or leaves were also widely used medicinally by native people for everything from heart attacks to indigestion. Berries were also chewed by women to induce parturition. • The name "soopolallie" is Chinook jargon meaning soap (*soop*) and berry (*olallie*) − so called because the berry pulp is soapy to the touch; "soapberry" is another common name. The berries contain glucoside-saponin, which is responsible for the soapy, bitter foam produced when they are whipped. Also called "hooshum berry" in parts of the interior, the name possibly being derived from the Athapascan word for this plant. Also called "buffalo berry," either because the Great Plains bison grazed the plant heavily, or because it was eaten as a garnish for buffalo steaks and tongues in early days. • *Shepherdia* is named for English botanist John Shepherd (1764-1836).

WOLF-WILLOW — *Elaeagnus commutata*

General Deciduous shrubs from spreading rhizomes, 1-4 m tall, sometimes treelike; **twigs densely covered with rusty brown scales**.

Leaves **Alternate**, oval to oblong-elliptic, silvery, **densely silvery scaley on both surfaces**, paler beneath.

Flowers **Yellowish**, silvery on outer surface, funnel shaped, 12-15 mm long, 1-3 at base of leaves, very fragrant.

Fruits **Silvery** mealy berries, about 1 cm long, each with a single large nutlet.

Ecology Sandbars, silty cutbanks, gullies, edges of meadows, shrub-carrs, and roadsides. Scattered, locally common, at low elevations in the southeastern part of the region, also along major rivers in the north (Peace, Stikine, Liard, Dease, etc.).

Notes: Rapidly spreading in disturbed areas. Also called "silverberry." • *Wolf Willow*, by Wallace Stegner, is a collection of autobiographical and historical stories about the coulee country in southern Alberta − Saskatchewan (Cypress Hills area) where Stegner grew up and wolf-willow thrives. Highly recommended. • The tough, fibrous bark provided an important material for weaving and rope making for southern interior native groups (Thompson, Okanagan, Lillooet, and Shuswap). Bags and baskets for carrying berries, nets, mats, blankets, and rope were among the items made. The Okanagan traders believed that three five-inch-thick bundles of prepared bark were worth one blanket. The silvery fruits were strung as beads for necklaces.

CREEPING JUNIPER — *Juniperus horizontalis*

General *Prostrate*, matted, evergreen shrub, not over 25 cm tall, with long trailing branches and numerous short branches; green to bluish-green.

Leaves *Scale-like*, overlapping, closely pressed to stem, not prickly, green to grey-green or steel-blue.

Fruits Female cones berrylike, fleshy, bluish purple with a grey bloom, 2-6 seeded, hanging down, apparently maturing in one year; male and female cones on separate plants.

Ecology Dry, rocky or sandy, open slopes and forests; typically on gravelly or sandy deposits. Scattered in suitable habitats, mostly at lower elevations, in the drier parts of the region. Locally common in the North, along the Stikine, Dease, Liard, Kechika, and Peace rivers, and also rarely in the southwestern part of the region.

Notes: Hybridizes with *J. scopulorum*, especially noticeable in Grand Canyon of the Stikine River. • The name "juniper" is from the Latin *juniperus* which appears ultimately to be derived from a word which means something used for binding — in reference to the tough juniper boughs (of other species) used to bind things together in the olden days. The species name *horizontalis* refers to the creeping habit of this shrub.

ROCKY MOUNTAIN JUNIPER — *Juniperus scopulorum*

General Evergreen, *usually a small erect tree* up to 10 m tall, sometimes a sprawling shrub to 1 m tall; bark reddish brown, scaly, fibrous or stringy.

Leaves *Mostly scale-like*, overlapping, pressed close to stem; juvenile leaves needle-like, often persisting on older trees.

Fruits Female cones berrylike, bluish-purple, covered with white-grey bloom, 1-2 seeded, sweet, erect, ripening in second season; male and female cones on separate trees.

Ecology Dry grassy slopes and rocky ridges, in our region usually on sedimentary or volcanic bedrock and warm south slopes. Scattered and locally common at low elevations along the Fraser River from Hixon south, the Bulkley River, the shores of Francois, Ootsa, Babine and Stuart lakes, also on the Peace River breaks and in the Stikine River Canyon.

Notes: When in the juvenile stage with needle-like leaves, could be confused with *J. communis*, but the leaves of *J. scopulorum* are not jointed at the base as in *J. communis*. Also the berrylike cone of *J. scopulorum* has a heavy bloom whereas *J. communis* does not.• Pungent boughs of this species were used widely as a fumigant and air freshener, in sweat houses, for smoking hides, and for making deodorizing solutions. The extremely tough wood was considered by many interior groups (including the Carrier) to be the best for making bows. The Carrier made rough temporary spoons from the bark. The boughs or leaves were probably used for medicinal purposes by the Carrier in the same way as common juniper. The wood is durable and an attractive colour and hence is now used for carving and making fenceposts and pencils. • The species name *scopulorum* (of the rocks or cliffs) describes where it's often found.

COMMON JUNIPER *Juniperus communis*

General Evergreen, ***prostrate*** and trailing-branched shrub; bark very thin, reddish brown, shredding, scaly.

Leaves ***Needle-like*** to narrowly lance shaped, jointed to the branchlet, usually stiff, very prickly, dark green above, whitish below, mostly in three's.

Fruits Female cones berrylike, bluish black, very fleshy, not covered in white-grey bloom, maturing in the second season; male and female cones on separate plants.

Ecology Dry open woods, gravelly ridges, outcrops, and open rocky slopes; throughout the region from lowland forest to subalpine ridges and alpine tundra.

Notes: Juniper fruit is well known as a flavour for gin and beer, and as a culinary spice. • The berries were seldom eaten and the most common use of junipers by northern interior natives was as fumigants, deodorizers and cleansers, especially in connection with sickness. Boughs were burned or boiled and the strong pungent odour emitted was thought to purify the house and protect the inhabitants from infection and harmful spirits. The Gitksan and Carrier names suggest the plant was believed to possess supernatural powers. Branches and berries were also boiled to make a tea, taken as a medicine for numerous ailments including tuberculosis, colds, heart trouble, and respiratory problems. • The species name *communis* means common, which this species is (over much of the globe). Common juniper is the only circumpolar conifer of the northern hemisphere.

WESTERN YEW *Taxus brevifolia*

General Evergreen shrub to small tree, 2-15 m high, up to 30 cm diameter; branches drooping; trunk often twisted and fluted; **bark reddish, papery scaly to shreddy**.

Leaves **Needles flat, ending abruptly in fine point, arranged in 2 rows**.

Fruits Male and female cones inconspicuous, on separate trees; although a conifer, instead of a seedcone it produces a single bony seed almost completely surrounded by **a bright red, fleshy cup** that looks like a large red huckleberry with a hole in the end; poisonous to humans although highly attractive to birds.

Ecology Moist flats along streams. A scattered understory species of moist mature coniferous forests in the southeastern portion of our region.

Notes: Bark of this species is the source of the drug taxol, used to treat ovarian and breast cancers. The seeds are definitely poisonous and the fleshy "berries" should generally be avoided, although a wide variety of birds consume them and are responsible for seed dispersal. The foliage is reported to be poisonous to horses and cattle especially if left to rot, but it is also reported to be a preferred winter moose browse. • The Haida women used the berries as a contraceptive, but would become sterile if they ate too many. The Upper Lillooet also considered them edible only in small amounts. The heavy, close-grained wood was prized by all native people where it grew within their territory. It was also traded. Implements such as bows, wedges, clubs, paddles, digging sticks, adze handles, harpoons, etc., were made from it. • The name "yew" comes from an Anglo-Saxon word *iw*, but its exact meaning is not clear. One report suggests it is from *iua*, which in turn is an abbreviation of *aruga*, a mispelling of the Latin *abiga* which means abortion. Maybe the fruits were used to induce abortions, which agrees with the Haida use as a contraceptive. • *Taxus* is the Greek name for yews, perhaps derived from taxon (a bow), one thing yew wood was used to make; *brevifolia* means short-leaved.

COMMON SNOWBERRY — *Symphoricarpos albus*

General Erect branching shrub, rhizomatous, 0.5-1.5 m tall; twigs very fine.

Leaves *Opposite*, elliptic to oval, may be lobed on young stems; margins smooth to wavy-toothed.

Flowers *Pink to white*, bell-shaped; in short dense clusters of few flowers; mostly terminal.

Fruits *White, globose, berry-like drupes* with 2 seeds; persistent through the winter; considered poisonous by many.

Ecology Open forests, thickets, dry rocky slopes; most abundant in dry habitats but also on moist sites, especially well-drained floodplains. Common at low elevations in the southern half of the region, extending north on dry slopes to the Peace and Stikine rivers.

Notes: Symphoricarpos occidentalis (wolfberry, western snowberry) is scattered at low elevations in the North, especially along the breaks of the Peace River and the Stikine - Telegraph Creek area, in thickets on well-drained south slopes with trembling aspen, wolf-willow, and saskatoon. *S. occidentalis* has clustered sessile flowers with styles that are long and hairy near the middle and that stick out from the floral tube, whereas *S. albus* has short-stalked, single or sparsely clustered flowers with glabrous styles that do not stick out from the floral tube. The common snowberry is one of the most widespread shrubs in North America. • The berries were not eaten by any of the native peoples and many considered them poisonous or toxic. The name for them in several interior languages means corpse berries or ghost berries. Some southern groups, and probably others, made brooms out of the branches and the Gitksan hollowed out the twigs to make pipe-stems. The plants may have also been used in medicinal preparations. • Called "snowberry" either because the berries are white or because they persist through the winter. Also called "waxberry" from the waxy appearance of the berry and probably because it contains the soapy compound saponin. *Symphoricarpos* is from the Greek *syn* (together), *phorein* (to bear), and *karpos* (fruit), i.e., fruits in clumps; *albus* refers to the fruit colour.

TALL OREGON-GRAPE — *Mahonia aquifolium*

General Erect, evergreen, stiff-branched shrub, 0.2-1 m tall; bark and wood yellowish.

Leaves With 5-7 leathery leaflets, **glossy green above**; leaflets oblong to egg-shaped, *with several prominent spiny teeth along margin (leaflets resembling those of English holly)*.

Flowers Bright *yellow* in many-flowered erect clusters; flower parts in 6's.

Fruits *Blue berries* with few large seeds and a whitish bloom, in elongated clusters, edible.

Ecology Dry open forests, clearings, warm rocky hillsides. Scattered at low elevations in the southeastern part of our region, mainly in the Fraser River drainage.

Notes: Tall Oregon-grape is also known as *Berberis aquifolium*.• Coastal and southern interior native people extracted a bright yellow pigment from the inner bark of stems and roots which was used for dyeing basket materials or porcupine quills. Although tart, the berries were eaten by the Carrier and southern interior people and were considered beneficial for the blood. Leaves simmered until tender were also eaten by the Carrier. An infusion of the bark and wood was considered especially good as a general tonic and blood purifier. • This species is recommended by some as a garden ornamental. With sweet-smelling yellow flowers and "grapes" which yield delicious juice and jelly, who can dispute this?

Willows

Why so many willows? This question will no doubt be asked by many readers of this guide. For most people who are interested in plants, a willow is a willow – *Salix* sp.! There are good reasons for this. Willows are notoriously difficult to identify to species: flowers are small and inconspicuous (except *en masse*!), not particularly colourful, and present for only a very short time each year; leaf shape and species habit can be quite variable, even within one species. Keys from other areas are often very technical, relying on flower and/or fruit characters, and may contain many more (or different) species than we need to know in the north.

But willows are a very important component of the vegetation in central and northern B.C., more important the further north you go. And though the different species may appear to be very similar in many respects, the more you learn about them, the more you appreciate their ecological differences. There are alpine species and riverbar species; some form shrub-carrs in moist areas, others quickly colonize disturbed sites such as clearcuts. Some are restricted to the boreal forests and points north; others find their northern range around Prince George.

Most willow species are browsed by herbivores such as moose; while red-osier dogwood may be a preferred species, willows are a staple diet item. Several studies (e.g., Roberts 1986; Porter 1990) document moose use of willows in our region. Willows are important to a wide range of species, not only as food but also for bedding, hiding, and giving birth.

The native people in our area used willows for a variety of purposes, from weaving containers to starting fires, smoking meat, or as clothing. It's often difficult to determine exactly which species of willow was used by native groups; in all likelihood they used a wide variety of species depending on availability and abundance.

As with other sections of this book, this is a guide to the common species only. Readers are referred to Argus (1973, 1983, 1992) or Brayshaw (1976) for more complete treatments. Two keys are provided: a technical key requiring flowers and/or fruit (pages 55-57); and a less technical key which can be used without flowers or fruit (pages 59-62). Because species identification is sometimes tricky, all identifications based on the keys should be confirmed using the full species descriptions.

One final note: Don't get discouraged! Learning the willows may be an arduous and (at times) confusing task, but the rewards are considerable. Good luck!

Diagram of a female willow flower, illustrating key structures

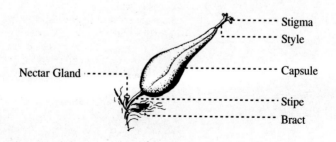

Key to the Willows

1. Plants dwarf, sometimes trailing, alpine shrubs less than 10 cm tall.
  2. Leaves green beneath; capsules uniformly or patchily pubescent .... *S. polaris*
  2. Leaves glaucous beneath; capsules glabrous or pubescent.
    3. Capsules glossy and glabrous or hairy only on beak .... *S. stolonifera*
    3. Capsules dull and pubescent.
      4. Mature leaves glabrous beneath, usually strongly reticulate above, apex rounded or obtuse.
        5. Leaves 1.5-6.6 cm long, the first leaves silky beneath; catkins with 20-40 flowers... *S. reticulata* ssp. *reticulata*
        5. Leaves 0.5-2.5 cm long, all leaves glabrous; catkins with 2-25 flowers .... *S. reticulata* ssp. *nivalis*
      4. Mature leaves usually pubescent beneath or at least with a tuft of hair at tip, not reticulate above, apex sharply pointed .... *S. arctica*
1. Plants shrubs or small trees.
      6. Leaf margins distinctly toothed.
        7. Leaves hairy at maturity, at least beneath.
          8. Leaf margin distantly toothed with short, slender projections.
            9. Leaves linear, sides parallel .... *S. exigua*
            9. Leaves narrowly elliptical, often broader toward the tip, sides not parallel .... *S. melanopsis*
          8. Leaf margin closely serrate or crenate.
            10. Leaves broadly elliptical, base rounded to obtuse ... *S. bebbiana*
            10. Leaves narrowly elliptical, base acute.
              11. Leaves glabrous or clothed on both sides with long, silky hairs, margins coarsely serrate ....*S. petiolaris*
              11. Leaves silky beneath with a coating of short, appressed hairs, margins finely serrulate .... *S. arbusculoides*
        7. Leaves glabrous, or inconspicuously hairy at maturity.
          12. Leaves green beneath, non-glaucous.
            13. Expanding leaves with rust-coloured hairs; capsules hairy; catkins robust .... *S. maccalliana*
            13. Expanding leaves glabrous or with a few white hairs; capsules glabrous; catkins slender.
              14. Young twigs glabrous; stipules minute or absent; low, trailing shrub .... *S. myrtillifolia* var. *myrtillifolia*
              14. Young twigs hairy; stipules prominent; tall shrub .... *S. myrtillifolia* var. *cordata*
          12. Leaves glaucous beneath.
            15. Leaves lance-shaped, apex long and tail-like;leaf stalk with glands at base of blade ....
              .... *S. lucida* ssp. *lasiandra*
            15. Leaves narrowly to broadly elliptic, apex acute; stalk not glandular.
              16. Capsules hairy.
                17. Leaves narrowly elliptical; catkins terminate in a leafy shoot .... *S. petiolaris*
                17. Leaves broadly elliptical; catkins sessile.
                  18. Leaves glossy above; stipes 0.5 mm long; styles 0.6-1.8 mm long........ *S. planifolia*
                  18. Leaves dull above; stipes 2-2.5 mm long; styles 0.3-0.7 mm long......... *S. discolor*

16. Capsules glabrous.
  19. Leaves lacking stipules; unfolding leaves yellowish-green, translucent ....*S. pyrifolia*
  19. Leaves with prominent stipules; unfolding leaves reddish or greenish, opaque.
    20. Catkins sessile, even lacking leafy bracts at base; unfolding leaves reddish .... *S. pseudomonticola*
    20. Catkins on leafy shoots, sometimes subsessile but with leafy bracts at base; unfolding leaves reddish or greenish.
      21. Stipes 1.8-4.2 mm long; stipules ovate, apex round; unfolding leaves mainly reddish; branches mainly glabrous .... *S. prolixa*
      21. Stipes 0.3-1.5 mm long; stipules elliptic, apex acute, sometimes rounded; unfolding leaves greenish; branches mainly spreading hairy .. *S. barclayi*
6. Leaf margins entire or indistinctly toothed.
  22. Leaves smooth at maturity, not hairy.
    23. Leaves narrowly elliptic to narrowly oblanceolate, acute at tip and base .... *S. melanopsis*
    23. Leaves elliptic to broadly so, tip and base various.
      24. Stipules prominent.
        25. Stipules usually smaller (1.5-15 mm long), ovate to narrowly elliptic, not persistent; catkins terminating a leafy shoot .... *S. barclayi*
        25. Stipules larger (6-25 mm long), linear to ovate with a broad base, often persistent for several years; catkins sessile .... *S. lanata* ssp. *richardsonii*
      24. Stipules inconspicuous or absent.
        26. Catkins sessile, flowering in early spring.
          27. Leaves glossy above; stipes 0.5 mm long; styles 0.6-1.8 mm long............................ *S. planifolia*
          27. Leaves dull above; stipes 2-2.5 mm long; styles 0.3-0.7 mm long .... *S. discolor*
        26. Catkins terminating short, leafy shoots, flowering in summer.
          28. Unfolding leaves hairy with white and rust-coloured hairs, a few of which may be permanent; capsules partly hairy ...... *S. athabascensis*
          28. Unfolding leaves glabrous or with a few white hairs; capsules glabrous .... *S. pedicellaris*
  22. Leaves distinctly hairy at maturity.
    29. Leaf underside densely and opaquely hairy.
      30. Leaf hairs appressed, appearing shiny and silky.
        31. Branchlets usually pruinose (with a whitish waxy bloom); catkins sessile .... *S. drummondiana*
        31. Branchlets not pruinose; catkins terminating a short, leafy shoot .... *S. sitchensis*

56

30. Leaf hairs wavy and erect or spreading, appearing dull and woolly.
   32. Branchlets glabrous and pruinose with a waxy bloom.
      33. Stipules 4-20 mm long, linear .... *S. alaxensis* var. *longistylis*
      33. Stipules 0.2-7 mm long, elliptic .... *S. drummondiana*
   32. Branchlets woolly, lacking a waxy bloom.
        34. Petioles velvety with erect hairs; stipules minute, lobes to half-ovate .. .. *S. scouleriana*
        34. Petioles woolly with matted hairs; stipules narrow.
          35. Stipules narrowly ovate, 2-3 mm long; leaves with tufts of hairs above .... *S. candida*
          35. Stipules linear, 4-20 mm long; leaves without tufts of hair above .... *S. alaxensis* var. *alaxensis*
29.   Leaves hairy beneath but leaf surface visible.
      36. Leaves green, non-glaucous beneath.
        37. Leaves narrowly elliptic, base acute; floral bracts falling after flowering .... *S. melanopsis*
        37. Leaves elliptic to broadly so, base rounded; floral bracts persistent .... *S. commutata*
      36. Leaves glaucous beneath.
        38. Leaf hairs including some matted, rust-coloured hairs; velvety with short, erect hairs .... *S. scouleriana*
        38. Leaf hairs white; petioles not velvety.
          39. Catkins sessile.
            40. Buds oily; stipules narrowly ovate, inconspicuous, 2-3 mm long .... *S. barrattiana*
            40. Buds dry; stipules conspicuous, linear to ovate, 6-25 mm long .... *S. lanata* ssp. *richardsonii*
          39. Catkins terminating short, leafy shoots.
            41. Leaves impressed reticulate above, long silky beneath .... *S. vestita*
            41. Leaves plane above, short hairy beneath.
              42. Capsules on long stipes; catkins loosely flowered .... *S. bebbiana*
              42. Capsules sessile or on short stipes; catkins compact.
                43. Capsules sessile or on very short stipes; petioles less than 3 times length of buds.
                  44. Catkins short-cylindrical to subglobose ..... *S. brachycarpa* ssp. *brachycarpa*
                  44. Catkins long-cylindrical .... *S. brachycarpa* ssp. *niphoclada*
                43. Capsules on distinct stipes; petioles more than 3 times length of buds
                  45. Underside of leaves nearly glabrous or sparsely shaggy; stipules 0.3-4 mm long, pistillate catkins 16-55 mm long ..... *S. glauca* var. *villosa*
                  45. Underside of leaves with long straight hairs; stipules 4-13 mm long; pistillate catkins 35-80 mm long .... *S. glauca* var. *acutifolia*

 **WILLOWS**

Distinguishing characteristics of some *Salix* species

Dwarf shrubs: *arctica, polaris, reticulata, stolonifera.*
Trees: *bebbiana, lucida* ssp. *lasiandra, scouleriana, sitchensis.*
Shrubs: all others.

Twigs brittle at base: *drummondiana, lucida* ssp. *lasiandra, sitchensis.*
Twigs flexible at base: all others.

Twigs coated with waxy bloom ("pruinose"): *alaxensis* var. *longistylis, drummondiana, planifolia* (rarely), *polaris, stolonifera.*

Buds oily: *barrattiana.*

Leaves entire: *alaxensis, arctica, athabascensis, barrattiana, brachycarpa, candida, commutata* (variable), *glauca, lanata* ssp. *richardsonii, pedicellaris, polaris, scouleriana, stolonifera.*
Leaves toothed: all others.

Leaves with rust-coloured hairs: *arbusculoides, athabascensis, discolor, drummondiana, lucida* ssp. *lasiandra, maccalliana, planifolia, scouleriana.*

Leaves green beneath (lacking whitish wax): *barrattiana, commutata, exigua, melanopsis, maccalliana, myrtillifolia, polaris, sitchensis.*
Leaves densely hairy beneath (surface obscured): *alaxensis, barrattiana, candida, drummondiana, sitchensis.*
Leaves with a whitish wax beneath: all others.
Leaves glaucous on both sides: *pedicellaris.*

Leaf base heart-shaped: *pseudomonticola, pyrifolia, vestita* (rarely).

Leaves leathery: *maccalliana, pedicellaris, reticulata* ssp. *reticulata, vestita.*

Leaf stalks with glands near base of blade: *lucida* ssp. *lasiandra, pyrifolia, vestita.*

Catkins appear before leaves (sessile on branch): *alaxensis, barrattiana, discolor, drummondiana, lanata* ssp. *richardsonii, planifolia, prolixa* (variable), *pseudomonticola, scouleriana.*
Catkins appear with the leaves (terminating a leafy twig): all others.

Capsules glabrous: *barclayi, commutata, exigua* (variable), *lanata* ssp. *richardsonii, lucida* ssp. *lasiandra, myrtillifolia, pedicellaris, prolixa, pseudomonticola, pyrifolia.*
Capsules hairy: all others.
Capsules with some rust-coloured hairs: *athabascensis, maccalliana, reticulata.*

Floral bracts deciduous after flowering: *exigua, lucida* ssp. *lasiandra, melanopsis.*

Stamens 4-7: *lucida* ssp. *lasiandra.*
Stamens 1: *sitchensis.*
Stamens 2: all others.

Picture-Key to Common Willows Using Mature Leaves

Leaves Long and Narrow

leaf very narrow, with parallel margins .... coyote willow
S. exigua page 65

leaf shiny above, with toothed margins .... Pacific willow
leaf tapers to a long tip   *S. lucida* ssp *lasiandra* page 65

leaf densely hairy below, appearing shiny and silky .... Drummond's willow
branchlets with a waxy bloom   *S. drummondiana* page 67

leaf densely white-woolly below .... hoary willow
twigs white-woolly   *S. candida* page 69

Low-growing, Trailing Shrubs

leaf leathery with a network of veins
leaf oval or round; pale below
shrub less than 10 cm tall ..... net-veined willow
S. reticulata page 64

leaf small, green on both sides
shrub less than 10 cm tall .... polar willow
S. polaris page 63

leaf broad, roundish
leaf deep green above, pale below
shrub less than 10 cm tall ... stoloniferous willow
S. stolonifera page 63

leaf broadly elliptical
leaf greyish green above, pale below
shrub usually trailing (may be up to
    50 cm tall) .... arctic willow
S. arctica page 64

59

Short Shrubs (usually under 1 m tall)

leaf slender, leathery in texture
waxy bloom on leaf surface gives a bluish green
   colour .... bog willow
                    S. pedicellaris page 71

leaf small, less than 3 cm long
leaf usually sparsely covered with hair
leaf stalk greater than 3 mm   Athabasca willow
          S. athabascensis page 71

leaf wrinkled, leathery (veins on upper side deeply impressed)
   underside or leaf covered with hairs .... rock willow
                    S. vestita page 77

leaf pale greyish-green
leaf hairy when young, less so when mature
shrub height variable from 0.5 - 4 m grey-leaved willow
              S. glauca page 75

leaf pale greyish-green, small (less than 3 cm)
leaf hairy when young, less so when mature
short leaf stalk (1-3 mm) .... short-fruited willow
             S. brachycarpa page 75

leaf and twig with long, straggly hairs
shrub height variable, from 0.2-3 m
leaf base rounded .... variable willow
       S. commutata page 74

twigs black, stout, oily or sticky
leaf grey, with long hairs on both sides ....
....,............................... Barratt's willow
             S. barrattiana page 69

leaf smooth, green on both sides
margins with small teeth
leaf with a blunt tip and base .. blueberry willow
    S. myrtillifolia var. *myrtillifolia* page 70

Tall Shrubs (usually over 1 m tall)
Leaf Margin With Obvious Teeth, Regularly Spaced

leaf tapers to a sharp tip
young leaves reddish
distinct leafy appendages at base of leaf stalk
.... Mackenzie's willow
S. prolixa page 66

leaf thin, lower surface with a network of veins
no appendages at base of leaf stalk ....
.... balsam willow
S. pyrifolia page 66

leaf narrow, with rounded tip
leaf green on both sides
young leaves reddish .... tall blueberry willow
S. myrtillifolia var. *cordata* page 70

leaf usually broad
young leaves greenish
prominent appendages at base of leaf
stalk .... Barclay's willow
S. barclayi page 72

leaf broad, base indented
young leaves reddish
small rounded appendages at base of leaf
stalk .... mountain willow
S. pseudomonticola page 72

leaf long, with a narrow base and tip
leaf firm and leathery
glossy green on both sides Maccall's willow
S. maccalliana page 70

leaf slender, shiny above
leaf silky, with short hairs, below
narrow appendages at base of leaf stalk
.... little-tree willow
S. arbusculoides page 74

Tall Shrubs (usually over 1 m tall)
Leaf Margin Smooth (sometimes with very fine teeth, or with irregularly spaced, coarse teeth)

leaf broad, tapering to a narrow base
large shrub to tree
leaf sparsely hairy below
twigs coated with short hairs Scouler's willow
S. scouleriana page 76

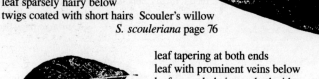

leaf tapering at both ends
leaf with prominent veins below
leaf sparsely hairy on both sides
twigs covered with wavy, tangled hairs .. Bebb's willow
S. bebbiana page 76

leaf slender; glossy above
leaf with parallel, closely spaced
side veins .... tea-leaved willow
S. planifolia page 73

large shrub or tree
leaf broad, pointed at both ends
  margins often wavy .... pussy willow
S. discolor page 73

twigs covered with woolly, white hairs
leaf sparsely hairy on both sides .... woolly willow
S. lanata ssp. *richardsonii* page 68

leaf slender, tapering to a narrow base
leaf densely white-woolly below
leaf dark green above   felt-leaved willow
S. alaxensis page 68

shrub or small tree
leaf broad, tapering to base
lower side of leaf with a distinct satiny
lustre .... Sitka willow
S. sitchensis page 67

leaf pale greyish-green
leaf hairy when young, less so when mature
  shrub height variable from 0.5 - 4 m ....
.... grey-leaved willow
S. glauca page 75

leaf and twig with long, straggly hairs
shrub height variable from 0.2 - 3 m
leaf base rounded .... variable willow
62   *S. commutata* page 74

POLAR WILLOW   *Salix polaris*

General ***Dwarf*** shrub spreading by underground stems; branches reddish brown, glaucous; twigs short and erect.

Leaves Obovate to narrowly elliptic, apex rounded, margins entire, ***glabrous*** or rarely with long hairs, ***green and glossy beneath***.

Flowers Catkins on short, leafy shoots; pistils hairy; floral bracts brown.

Fruits Reddish, glossy, ***sparsely hairy*** capsules; styles long (0.7-1.6 mm long); stipes 0.2-0.7 mm long, much shorter than the nectary.

Ecology Alpine tundra, especially late snow bed and snow flush areas, also scree slopes. Common throughout the region north of 55°.

Notes: Polar willow reaches the highest elevation of any willows in our region; its dwarf stature is an adaption for surviving the rigours of life in the alpine. It has disproportionately large pistils.
• *Salix* is the ancient Latin name for willows.

STOLONIFEROUS WILLOW   *Salix stolonifera*

General ***Dwarf*** shrub trailing on the surface or with underground stems; branches dark reddish brown; twigs greenish brown, ***glaucous*** or sometimes glabrous and glossy beneath.

Leaves Broadly obovate to broadly elliptic, apex rounded, margins entire, ***sparsely hairy***.

Flowers Catkins on leafy shoots; pistils glabrous or sparsely hairy; floral bracts dark brown.

Fruits ***Glabrous*** capsules, sometimes with a few hairs on the beak; styles 0.8-1.6 mm long; stipes 0.2-0.8 mm long.

Ecology Alpine tundra and heath. Scattered in the northwestern part of the region (north of 55°, west of the Rockies).

Notes: This species hypridizes with arctic willow and Barclay's willow. • The specific name *stolonifera* means with stolons (horizontal stems or runners).

NET-VEINED WILLOW (ssp. *reticulata*) *Salix reticulata*
DWARF SNOW WILLOW (ssp. *nivalis*)

General *Dwarf* shrub 1-10 cm tall, rooting along stems; branches light brown with short internodes; twigs greenish brown, glabrous.

Leaves Elliptic-circular to oblong, *apex rounded*, margins entire, *upper side with deep veins and a rough surface*, the *lower side glaucous and glabrous* or sometimes with long silky hairs; leaf stalk 10-25 mm long.

Flowers Most shoots bearing typical foliage terminate in a catkin; catkins with 20 to 50 or more flowers; pistils densely silky; floral bracts dark.

Fruits Sparsely silky capsules; short styles; stipes absent or short (to 0.8 mm long).

Ecology Moist to dry alpine tundra and subalpine seepage areas (ssp. *reticulata*); moist to dry alpine tundra (ssp. *nivalis*). Common and abundant at high elevations throughout our region, often the dominant plant.

Notes: The more southerly (south of 55°) ssp. *nivalis* differs from the more northerly ssp. *reticulata* in having only 2-22 flowers per catkin, and smaller leaves that lack long silky hairs beneath. *Salix reticulata* could be confused with some species of *Pyrola* (which are unbranched) or with *Arctostaphylos rubra* (more difficult, but *Arctostaphylos* has leaves that are green beneath, and lacks the single bud-scales of a willow).
• *Reticulata* means net-veined, referring to the leaves.

ARCTIC WILLOW *Salix arctica*

General *Dwarf to suberect* shrub usually prostrate or trailing but sometimes up to 50 cm tall; branches stout, brown; twigs glabrous or sparsely hairy.

Leaves Narrowly to broadly elliptic or obovate, *apex pointed*, margins entire, *glaucous beneath, sparsely hairy beneath usually with a tuft of hairs at tip*.

Flowers Catkins on a prominent leafy shoot; pistils hairy; styles red in life; floral bracts dark to blackish.

Fruits Sparsely hairy capsules; styles 0.6-2.2 mm long; stipes 0.6 mm long or less.

Ecology Alpine tundra to open subalpine ridges on various substrates and moisture regimes. Common at high elevations throughout the region.

Notes: Sometimes difficult to distinguish from stoloniferous willow, especially where the two species grow together, as in northwestern parts of our region. *S. arctica*, *S. glauca*, and *S. brachycarpa* are all related and could also be confused. • The species name means, simply, of the arctic, describing its preference for cooler climes.

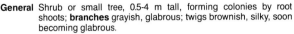

COYOTE WILLOW · *Salix exigua*

General Shrub or small tree, 0.5-4 m tall, forming colonies by root shoots; **branches** grayish, glabrous; twigs brownish, silky, soon becoming glabrous.

Leaves *Linear, margins with distant teeth*, glabrous or sparsely silky, *not glaucous beneath*; stalks short (0.8-5 mm long); stipules small.

Flowers Catkins on long, leafy shoots, sometimes branched; pistils sparsely hairy, long-beaked; floral bracts pale, deciduous after flowering.

Fruits Glabrous capsules; style very short; stigmas deciduous after flowering.

Ecology *Pioneer on sandy or gravelly floodplains.* Common at low elevations along major rivers east of the Rockies, and also along the Fraser and Liard Rivers.

Notes: Sometimes named *S. interior.* May be confused with *S. petiolaris*, which has glaucous, closely toothed leaves, unbranched catkins, and hairy capsules. The similar *S. melanopsis* has narrowly elliptic leaves (i.e., sides of leaves not parallel as in *S. exigua*), evident styles, and nectaries longer than stipes. Both of these species also occur in riparian thickets. • The bark and twigs were made into a type of twine and used for tying house walls together by the Tahltan and for small bows by the Sekani. The Carrier used it for making fish nets and made a decoction from the bark that they applied to running sores and ulcers. Turner (1982) notes that this willow was used by interior native people for basket-weaving. • The species name *exigua* means small or very small, though this is a fair-sized willow.

PACIFIC WILLOW · *Salix lucida* ssp. *lasiandra*

General Tall shrub or tree, 1-9 m tall; branches brown, glabrous; *twigs glossy, with yellow, duckbill-shaped buds*, usually glabrous, *brittle at base*; bark fissured on older trees.

Leaves *Lance shaped, tapering to a long tip, margins toothed*, young leaves reddish and densely hairy with white and rust-coloured hairs, *older leaves glabrous, glaucous beneath*; stipules prominent and glandular; *stalks glandular at base of leaf*.

Flowers Catkins on long, leafy shoots; pistils glabrous; floral bracts pale and deciduous after flowering.

Fruits Glabrous capsules; styles 0.4-0.8 mm long; stipes 0.9-1.2 mm long.

Ecology River banks, floodplains, lakeshores, and wet meadows; often standing in quiet river backwaters. Scattered throughout the region at low elevations along major rivers.

Notes: One of our largest native willows. • Pacific willow is one of the willow species used by interior native people (see Bebb's willow). The Lillooet people called it the "match plant" and made fire drills from it. They also made a twine from the bark and rope by twisting bark and twigs together. Poorer people wove shredded bark and incorporated it into their clothing. • *Lucida* means clear or shiny, probably in reference to the twigs.

65

BALSAM WILLOW — *Salix pyrifolia*

General 1-3 m tall; branches dark reddish brown; twigs glabrous; ***buds and leaves with a balsam-like fragrance***.

Leaves Elliptic or egg shaped, base rounded or heart shaped, margins toothed; ***young leaves translucent*** yellow-green and often purplish while expanding, older leaves ***glabrous, net veined and glaucous beneath***; stalks glandular at base of blade.

Flowers Catkins on leafy shoots; pistils glabrous; floral bracts pale.

Fruits ***Glabrous capsules***; styles 0.3-1 mm long; stipes 2.5-4 mm long.

Ecology Muskegs, fens, swamps, stream and wetland margins, and moist clearings. Scattered, locally abundant at low elevations in the south-central (north of Williams Lake up the Fraser and Nechako-Bulkley drainages) and northeast portions of the region.

Notes: The balsam-like fragrance is suggestive of *Populus balsamifera*, and persists in dried specimens.

MACKENZIE'S WILLOW — *Salix prolixa*

General 1.5-5 m tall; branches reddish brown; twigs usually glabrous, sometimes hairy.

Leaves ***Narrowly oblong-obovate to lance shaped, tapering to a sharp tip***, margins finely toothed. ***Young leaves reddish***, hairy above; ***older leaves glabrous, glaucous beneath, stipules large, egg or kidney shaped***.

Flowers Catkins on short, leafy shoots or sessile; pistils glabrous; floral bracts dark brown.

Fruits ***Glabrous capsules***; styles 0.3-0.6 mm long; stipes 1.2-3.2 mm long.

Ecology Sand and gravel bars along rivers, fens, swamps, clearings, open forest. Fairly common at low elevations throughout the region.

Notes: Sometimes known as *S. rigida* or *S. mackenzieana*. Related to mountain willow from which it differs in its narrower leaves and shorter styles, and to Barclay's willow from which it differs in its narrower leaves and reddish petioles. One of our sandbar willows. • This is one of the willow species used by interior native groups for a variety of purposes (see comments under *S. bebbiana* and *S. scouleriana*). • The common name and the synonym *S. mackenziana* both honour famed explorer Alexander Mackenzie.

SITKA WILLOW — *Salix sitchensis*

General Shrub or small tree 1-8 m tall; branches dark brown to gray, sparsely hairy; *twigs densely velvety, brittle at base.*

Leaves Narrowly *obovate* to narrowly elliptic, margins entire or glandular dotted, the upper side bright green and sparsely silky, the *lower side satiny with short appressed hairs, not glaucous*; stalks yellowish, velvety; stipules half ovate.

Flowers *Catkins on short leafy shoots*; stamens one; pistils densely silky; floral bracts brown.

Fruits *Silky capsules*; styles 0.4-0.8 mm long; stipes 0.5-1.4 mm long.

Ecology Riparian thickets, lakeshores and wetland margins, forest edges and wet openings, clearings, avalanche tracks. A more typically coastal species that also occurs east of the Coast Mountains occasionally at low to (in the south) subalpine elevations, uncommonly in the North.

Notes: Vegetative specimens may be distinguished from Scouler's willow by their brittle twigs and non-glaucous leaves.
• The species name *sitchensis* means of Sitka (Alaska).

DRUMMOND'S WILLOW — *Salix drummondiana*

General 1-3 m tall; branches reddish brown to blackish; *twigs* yellowish green to brown, *usually with a conspicuous white bloom, slightly hairy, brittle at base*.

Leaves *Narrowly elliptic to obovate*, margins entire and undulating to coarsely toothed, young leaves densely silky with white and rust-coloured hairs, *older leaves dark green and sparsely hairy above, densely to sparsely silky beneath*; stalks 2-12 mm long; stipules narrowly elliptic, 3-8 mm long.

Flowers *Catkins* appear before the leaves, *sessile* on branches of previous year; pistils densely silky; floral bracts black or dark brown.

Fruits *Capsules sparsely silky*; styles 0.7-1.3 mm long; stipes 0.6-1.4 mm long.

Ecology Riparian thickets, swamps, shrub fens, gravelly floodplains, and moist clearings. Common and often abundant, at low to moderate elevations throughout the region.

Notes: The bloom on the twigs is most noticeable in the spring.
• It may be separated from the similar *S. alaxensis* var. *longistylis* by its shorter stipules, shorter catkins, shorter styles, longer stipes, and leaf hairs that are silky rather than woolly.
• A major component of the willow flora of our region, and frequently heavily utilized by moose. • *Drummondiana* recalls Thomas Drummond, an early Canadian (and Texan) botanist.

67

FELT-LEAVED WILLOW — *Salix alaxensis*

General Shrub or small tree, 1-8 m tall, erect, sometimes gnarled and decumbent; branches densely and persistently hairy; *twigs densely white to gray hairy*.

Leaves Elliptic to obovate, margins entire, *densely white woolly beneath*, dark green above; *stipules long and narrow*, 4-15 mm long.

Flowers Catkins appear before the leaves, sessile on branches of previous year, large; pistils densely woolly; floral bracts dark brown.

Fruits *Sparsely woolly*, subsessile capsules 1.3-2.8 mm long.

Ecology Alpine and subalpine wet meadows and thickets (var. *alaxensis*); gravel bars, lakeshores, fresh morainal deposits, and openings in spruce-subalpine fir forests (var. *longistylis*). Scattered throughout the northern half of our region, from lowlands to alpine.

Notes: The twigs of var. *alaxensis* are densely woolly, those of var. *longistylis* are sparsely hairy and covered with a white waxy bloom (like that of Drummond's willow). • One of the "diamond willows," so called because of the striking diamond-shaped depressions on their stems. These markings can also occur on Bebb's willow, mountain willow, little tree willow, and Scouler's willow. A fungus (or fungi) appears to cause the lesions. The wood is used for making decorative canes, lamps, rustic furniture, and that essential fashion item, bolo ties. • *Alaxensis*, of course, means Alaska, a good name for this truly northern species.

WOOLLY WILLOW — *Salix lanata* ssp. *richardsonii*

General 0.6-3 m tall; branches reddish brown, covered with persistent coarse hairs; *twigs densely white woolly*.

Leaves Elliptic or broadly elliptic to narrowly egg shaped, margins entire to blunt toothed, young leaves sometimes covered with rust-coloured hairs, *older leaves sparsely hairy on both sides, glaucous beneath*; stalks 5-18 mm long; *stipules* linear to egg shaped, apex tapering, *base broad and often irregularly toothed, persistent for several years*.

Flowers Catkins stout, appearing before the leaves, sessile on previous years branches; pistils glabrous; floral bracts dark brown.

Fruits *Glabrous* capsules; styles 1.2-1.6 mm long; stipes 0.2-0.5 mm long, nectaries often twice as long as the stipes.

Ecology Riparian thickets, gravelly lakeshores, shrub fens, wet meadows, and open forests. Scattered from low elevations to alpine talus slopes north of 56°.

Notes: Woolly willow can be separated from Barclay's willow by its sessile catkins, long nectaries, and more prominent, persistent stipules. Barratt's willow is also similar. • The species name *lanata* means woolly; both this and the common name refer to the twigs. *Richardsonii* is named for John Richardson, botanist with John Franklin's early l9th century Canadian expedition.

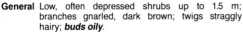

BARRATT'S WILLOW · *Salix barrattiana*

General Low, often depressed shrubs up to 1.5 m; branches gnarled, dark brown; twigs straggly hairy; **buds oily.**

Leaves Narrowly to broadly elliptic, margins entire to sometimes finely toothed, **upper side gray hairy**, lower side hairy becoming sparsely so; **leaves crowded on the twig with short internodes**; **stipules broadly egg shaped, glandular, and oily.**

Flowers Catkins appearing with or just before the leaves, sessile on branches of previous year; **pistils densely gray-white silky**; floral bracts black to dark brown.

Fruits **Sparsely hairy to glabrous** capsules; styles 0.6-1.6 mm long; stipes 0.2-0.6 mm long.

Ecology Gravelly stream channels, fluvial fans and terraces along high elevation streams, shrub fens, timberline thickets, wet meadows, and tundra. Common at high elevations in the northern half of our region and sporadically south along the Rocky Mountains.

Notes: Related to woolly willow from which it differs in its oily buds and stipules, pistils with densely gray-white, silky hairs, and in its more hairy leaves. Hybridizes with Barclay's willow, variable willow, and tall blueberry willow. • The oily substance on the buds and stipules has a balsamic fragrance like that of balsam willow and *Populus balsamifera.*

HOARY WILLOW · *Salix candida*

General 0.3-1.5 m tall; branches dark brown, sparsely hairy; **twigs densely white-woolly.**

Leaves **Narrowly elliptic**, margins entire to subentire, upper side dark green and sparsely woolly, **lower side densely dull white-woolly**; stalks 3-9 mm long; stipules narrowly elliptic.

Flowers Catkins on short, leafy, shoots; **pistils densely white-woolly**; floral bracts brownish.

Fruits **Sparsely hairy** capsules; styles 0.8-1.6 mm long, bright red in life; stipes 0.5-1.2 mm long; nectaries red in life.

Ecology Fens, lakeshores, and riparian thickets, usually where calcareous or alkaline. Scattered at low elevations in the North, and on the lower Fraser Plateau.

Notes: Hoary willow is an uncommon but locally abundant species.

69

MACCALL'S WILLOW — *Salix maccalliana*

General 1-3 m tall; branches dark reddish brown, glossy; twigs brown to yellowish, glabrous to sparsely hairy.

Leaves *Leathery*, narrowly lance shaped to oblong, *margins coarsely toothed*, young leaves silky with white and rust coloured hairs, *older leaves glossy and green on both sides*; stipules usually small.

Flowers Catkins large, on long leafy shoots; pistils densely hairy; floral bracts pale.

Fruits Large (6-8 mm long), *persistently hairy capsules*; styles 0.8-1.2 mm long; stipes 1-2 mm long.

Ecology Muskegs and fens, riverbanks. Common, locally abundant at low to moderate elevations on Fraser and Nechako plateaus and Quesnel Highland, apparently rare in the North.

Notes: In early spring, Maccall's willow stands out with the bright red of the previous year's growth.

BLUEBERRY WILLOW — *Salix myrtillifolia*

General 0.1-1.5 m tall; branches grayish, soon glabrous; twigs greenish to reddish brown, sparsely hairy with short, curved hairs.

Leaves Narrowly elliptic to narrowly obovate, 2-5 cm long, apex broad and acute, *margins with blunt rounded teeth, glabrous, green on both sides*; stipules 0.2-2 mm long, narrowly elliptic.

Flowers Catkins on short, leafy shoots; pistils glabrous; floral bracts light brown with a dark tip.

Fruits *Glabrous capsules*; styles 0.3-0.5 mm long; stipes 0.6-1.6 mm long.

Ecology Deep moss in muskegs, fens, and lake and river shores (var. *myrtillifolia*); upland forests, shores of lakes and rivers, floodplain forests, scrub birch thickets, and rarely muskegs (var. *cordata*). Both varieties common and abundant at low to moderate elevations in the North, var. *cordata* scattered in the southeastern portion of the region and also in the Chilcotin.

Notes: Blueberry willow differs from tall blueberry willow (*S. myrtillifolia* var. *cordata*, sometimes named *S. novae-angliae*) in being a small decumbent shrub with short-hairy twigs, minute stipules, and shorter styles. Tall blueberry willow is 1-4 m tall, has leaves that are hairy at least on the upper midrib and are paler beneath, has 1-5 mm long stipules, and 0.5-1 mm long styles. The two varieties also occupy different habitats.

Bog Willow — *Salix pedicellaris*

General Small erect shrub, 0.2-1.5 m tall, decumbent and rooting in the moss; branches grey-brown, glabrous; twigs reddish to yellowish brown, sparsely hairy with short erect hairs.

Leaves *Leathery*, narrowly elliptic, *apex usually rounded*, *margin entire*, *glabrous from the start*, often *glaucous on both sides*; foliage often has a bluish-green appearance.

Flowers Catkins on short leafy shoots; pistils glabrous; floral bracts pale.

Fruits *Glabrous capsules*; styles very short; stipes 2-3 mm long.

Ecology Fens and bogs. Scattered, locally abundant at low to moderate elevations in the southern half of the region, scattered in the northeast, apparently absent from much of the northwestern portion of the region.

Notes: Hybrids with Athabasca willow have patches of hairs on the pistils, and pubescent leaves.

Athabasca Willow — *Salix athabascensis*

General 0.5-1 or 2 m tall; branches and twigs grayish to reddish brown, glossy, densely to sparsely hairy.

Leaves Elliptic to narrowly so, *apex acute*, *margins entire*, *young leaves silky* with white and rust-coloured hairs, *becoming glabrous in age*.

Flowers Catkins on short, leafy shoots; pistils densely silky (with some rust-coloured hairs); floral bracts pale.

Fruits *Sparsely silky* capsules; styles 0.5-1 mm long; stipes 0.8-1.2 mm long.

Ecology Fens, muskegs, and bogs. Scattered, locally abundant, at low to medium elevations in the northern two thirds of the region. Most frequent in the Liard River drainage.

Notes: Athabasca willow is a relatively uncommon peatland shrub.

71

BARCLAY'S WILLOW · *Salix barclayi*

General Usually 1-3 m tall; branches dark reddish brown; *twigs yellow-green, glossy, densely to sparsely hairy.*

Leaves *Elliptic to obovate*, apex acute, base rounded to somewhat heart shaped, *margins toothed*, young leaves *greenish*, sparsely hairy, *older leaves usually glabrous*, sometimes sparsely hairy, *glaucous beneath; stipules prominent, glandular above.*

Flowers *Catkins on short, leafy, flowering shoots*; pistils glabrous; floral bracts dark.

Fruits *Glabrous* capsules; styles 0.5-2.5 mm long; stipes 0.5-1.5 mm long, nectaries short, half as long as the stipe.

Ecology Alpine and subalpine thickets, lake and river shores, open forests, clearings, muskeg, fens. Common at moderate to high elevations throughout the region.

Notes: A common and variable species, related to blueberry willow and variable willow, from which it differs in its glaucous leaves. Hybridizes with Barratt's willow and variable willow. See woolly willow, Mackenzie's willow, and mountain willow for comment. • Farr's willow (*Salix hastata* var. *farrae*) is a related species of similar higher elevation habitats, but has non-glaucous or thinly glaucous leaves with more or less entire margins, and shorter styles (0.2-0.4 mm long). Farr's willow is uncommon but locally abundant in the Haines Triangle and south of 55°.

MOUNTAIN WILLOW · *Salix pseudomonticola*

General 1-4 m tall; branches dark reddish brown; *twigs lighter and glabrous.*

Leaves Narrowly to broadly *elliptic*, apex acute, base more or less heart shaped, *margins toothed*, young leaves *reddish*, older leaves glabrous, glaucous beneath; stipules egg shaped.

Flowers *Catkins sessile*; pistils glabrous; floral bracts dark brown.

Fruits *Glabrous* capsules; styles 0.7-1.2 mm long; stipes 0.9-2 mm long.

Ecology Fens, moist forest edges and openings, and riparian thickets. Scattered, locally abundant, at low to moderate elevations, throughout the region (except the Nass Basin).

Notes: Similar to Barclay's willow from which it differs in its reddish young leaves, reddish leaf stalks, glabrous or sparsely hairy twigs, and sessile, early flowering catkins. Forms big thickets in some valley bottoms.

WILLOWS

PUSSY WILLOW — *Salix discolor*

General Tall shrub or sprawling tree, 2-6 m tall; branches dark brown to yellowish, usually lacking hairs; twigs moderately hairy, soon glabrous.

Leaves Elliptic to obovate, margin entire and undulate to coarsely toothed, young leaves densely silky with white and rust-coloured hairs, *older leaves becoming glabrous, lower side glaucous*.

Flowers *Catkins* appearing before the leaves, *sessile* on branches of previous year; pistils sparsely silky; floral bracts dark brown to black.

Fruits *Sparsely silky* capsules; styles 0.3-0.7 mm long; stipes 2-2.5 mm long.

Ecology Riparian thickets, swamps, shrub fens, fringes of marshes and lakes, open forest, and moist clearings. Common and abundant at lower elevations in the northeast; common but less abundant at low to moderate elevations in the south-central part of the region.

Notes: Can be separated from the similar *S. planifolia* (see below) by its shorter styles, longer stipes, and duller upper leaf surface. • The species name means two-coloured, perhaps in reference to the glabrous/glaucous leaves.

TEA-LEAVED WILLOW (ssp. *planifolia*) — *Salix planifolia*
DIAMOND-LEAVED WILLOW (ssp. *pulchra*)

General 0.5-4 m tall; branches dark brown to reddish brown, glabrous, sometimes glaucous; twigs glabrous to densely hairy.

Leaves Elliptic to narrowly so, mostly subentire to remotely toothed, young leaves sparsely hairy with short silky hairs some of which are rust-coloured, *older leaves glabrous and shiny above, sparsely silky and glaucous beneath*; stipules short.

Flowers *Catkins* appearing before the leaves, *sessile* on previous year's branches; pistils densely silky; floral bracts dark brown to blackish.

Fruits *Sparsely silky* capsules; styles 0.6-1.8 mm long; stipes 0.5-0.6 mm long.

Ecology Shrub thickets in fens, swamps, forest openings, clearings, edges of lakes and streams, at *low to moderate elevations* (ssp. *planifolia*); *high elevation* thickets, subalpine woodland, alpine tundra (ssp. *pulchra*). Common and locally abundant (both subspecies) from low to high elevations in the northern part of the region, scattered (ssp. *planifolia*) in the southern part.

Notes: The diamond-leaved willow occurs in northernmost British Columbia. It differs from ssp. *planifolia* in its prominent, linear stipules (3-14 mm long) that persist on the plant for several years, and leaves that tend to be rhombic (equally but obliquely 4-sided, angularly oval) in shape.

VARIABLE WILLOW — *Salix commutata*

General 0.2-2 m tall; branches dark brown, sometimes remaining hairy; *twigs densely woolly*.

Leaves Elliptic to broadly so, apex acute, margins entire to finely toothed, young leaves densely hairy, *older leaves persistently hairy on both sides, not glaucous beneath*, stalks 1.5-7 mm long.

Flowers Catkins on leafy shoots; *pistils* glabrous, *reddish*.

Fruits *Glabrous* capsules, brownish; styles 0.5-1 mm long; stipes 0.3-1.5 mm long.

Ecology Riparian, wetland, and high elevation thickets, lakeshores, gravelly benches, fresh alluvial and morainal materials, open forests. Scattered at alpine and subalpine elevations throughout the region.

Notes: Characteristically a late-flowering species with non-glaucous leaves clothed with distinctive straggly hairs, short leaf stalks, and reddish pistils. Hybridizes with Barclay's willow and Barratt's willow.

LITTLE-TREE WILLOW — *Salix arbusculoides*

General Shrubs to small trees, 1-4 (up to 6) m tall; branches slender, reddish brown and glossy; twigs sparsely velvety.

Leaves *Narrowly elliptic* to very narrowly so, *margins finely toothed, upper side glossy and glabrous, lower side glaucous and silky* with short hairs; stalks 5-8 mm long; stipules linear.

Flowers Catkins appearing with the leaves, sessile or on short shoots. Pistils densely silky with short hairs (some rust-coloured).

Fruits *Sparsely silky* capsules; styles 0.3-0.5 mm long; stipes 0.6-0.9 mm long.

Ecology Fens, swamps, muskeg, openings in spruce forests, mountain thickets, streambanks, and lake shores. Common at low to subalpine elevations in boreal and subalpine forest in the North; occasional in the Bulkley, Nechako, and Fraser valleys in the southern half of our region.

Notes: Salix petiolaris (also know as *S. gracilis*) resembles little-tree willow in its long, narrow, usually finely toothed leaves that are glaucous and somewhat silky beneath, and in its sparsely silky capsules. However, *S. petiolaris* has yellowish to brown, glabrous twigs, and its stipes are 1.5 mm or more long. It is an occasional tall shrub of riparian thickets at low to medium elevations in the North. • *Arbuscula* means a low shrub, so *arbusculoides* should be so as well, though this "bush willow" can occasionally exceed 5 m in height.

GREY-LEAVED WILLOW — *Salix glauca*

General Up to 3 m (usually 0.5-1.5 m) tall; branches reddish brown to grayish, usually hairy; twigs densely to sparsely hairy.

Leaves Elliptic to obovate, apex acute to obtuse, **margins entire; hairy on both sides, especially the underside, which is also glaucous**.

Flowers Catkins on short, leafy shoots, **cylindrical**, persistent; pistils densely hairy; styles greenish, drying brown.

Fruits **Sparsely hairy** capsules; styles 0.5-0.8 mm long; stipes 0.5-1.6 mm long.

Ecology Swamps, fens, bogs, shrub-carrs, streambanks, dry to wet open forest, high elevation thickets. Common and abundant from valley bottoms to alpine in the North, common and locally abundant in the south-central part of the region.

Notes: The shaggy-leaved willow (var. *villosa*) is much more common and widespread, but the sharp-tipped willow (var. *acutifolia*), with prominent, long stipules and longer leaves and catkins, occurs in northwestern parts of our region. • The species name *glauca* and its common equivalent, "grey-leaved willow," both refer to leaves of this species.

SHORT-FRUITED WILLOW (ssp. *brachycarpa*)
SNOW WILLOW (ssp. *niphoclada*) — *Salix brachycarpa*

General Low, erect, **usually less than 1 m tall**, but up to 2 m; twigs slender, densely and coarsely white to gray hairy.

Leaves Narrowly elliptic to strap-shaped, apex obtuse, **margins entire; densely hairy on both sides, glaucous beneath**; stalks short (0.5-3 or 4 mm long).

Flowers Catkins short and **subglobose to cylindrical**, on short leafy shoots; pistils densely white-woolly; floral bracts pale.

Fruits **Densely woolly** capsules; styles 0.5-1.2 mm long; stipes absent or very short.

Ecology Open forests, shrub-carrs, sedge fens, gravel floodplains, and lake margins (ssp. *brachycarpa*); dry, stony alpine slopes, limestone talus, subalpine thickets (ssp. *niphoclada*). Scattered, locally abundant, at moderate to high elevations, in the northern half of the region, and in the Chilcotin.

Notes: Snow willow, which occurs in northwestern British Columbia, differs from short-fruited willow in leaves less hairy above, long-cylindrical catkins, and shorter styles (0.2-0.5 mm long). • *Brachycarpa* means the same thing as the common name, "short-fruited."

General Tall spindly shrub or multi-stemmed small tree 2-12 m tall; branches dark brown to yellowish brown, often velvety; twigs densely velvety.

Leaves Obovate to narrowly elliptic, base tapering, margins entire to coarsely toothed, *young leaves densely velvety, older leaves dark green above, the lower side sparsely hairy* with short appressed hairs (*some rust-coloured*), or densely hairy with wavy hairs, *glaucous beneath*.

Flowers Catkins appear *well before* the leaves, sessile on previous year's branches; pistils densely silky; *floral bracts dark* brown to black.

Fruits *Silky* capsules; styles 0.2-0.6 mm long; stigmas often twice as long as the styles; *stipes 0.8-2 mm long*.

Ecology Upland thickets, riparian areas, clearings, edges of forests and wetlands, open forests (deciduous and coniferous). Common and abundant at low to moderate elevations throughout the region.

Notes: When lacking catkins, Scouler's willow and Bebb's willow can be difficult to distinguish, especially with young leaves early in the growing season. • See Sitka willow for comment. Scouler's willow is one of our larger willows. • The wood was used for drying meat and fish, smoking hides, making barbeque sticks, berry-drying racks, packboards, fishing weirs, and snowshoes. The Carrier say that willow snowshoes get fuzzy when they are worn and hence they do not slip backwards. The Carrier peeled inner willow bark in the spring and twisted it into a twine which was strong when wet, but brittle when dry. It was used for tying a variety of objects and for making fishing nets which had to be folded wet and then soaked before using again so they would not break. Shredded bark was used as diapers, wound dressings, and sanitary napkins. • This common species is named for Dr. John Scouler, an associate of David Douglas.

General Shrub or small tree 0.5-5 m tall; branches reddish brown; twigs densely to straggly hairy.

Leaves Elliptic to obovate, margins entire to coarsely toothed, upper side dull green, *lower side gray and glaucous with prominent venation, sparsely hairy on both sides*; stalks 2-9 mm long; stipules small, falling early.

Flowers Catkins appearing *just before or with the leaves*, on leafy shoots or sometimes subsessile. The female catkins loosely flowered; pistils finely silky; *floral bracts pale*.

Fruits *Sparsely hairy* capsules; *on long stipes (2-5 mm long)*; styles short.

Ecology Upland forests and lowland thickets, riparian zones, swamps, muskeg, and on disturbed sites. Common throughout the region at low to moderate elevations.

Notes: Probably the most frequent source of diamond willow (see felt-leaved willow) in our region. This common species was probably one of

the willows used by interior native people for a variety of purposes; some of the uses are described under Scouler's willow (above). Willows were often used for smoking or drying fish and meat. For more information on native use of willows, see Turner (1979).

ROCK WILLOW · *Salix vestita*

General Low, sometimes stunted shrub, up to 1.5 m tall; stems crooked; branches gray-brown, bark leathery, often with numerous internodes.

Leaves Elliptic, obovate, or narrowly elliptic, *leathery, wrinkled (veins deeply impressed above)*, apex round to obtuse, base round to somewhat heart shaped, margins apparently subentire, *upper side dark green, lower side densely to sparsely hairy, glaucous*; stalks 2-8 mm long, glandular dotted on margins.

Flowers Catkins on prominent 3-leaved shoots; pistils silky; floral bracts dark.

Fruits *Silky* capsules; styles very short; stipes 0.4-1.2 mm long, usually surrounded by several linear nectaries.

Ecology Open subalpine forest, rocky streamsides, timberline ridges, rarely in alpine. Uncommon but locally abundant (especially on limestone), *primarily in the Rocky Mountains south of 55°.*

Notes: This species is related to *S. reticulata*. A beautiful willow, perhaps useful as an ornamental species.

77

Dwarf Shrubs

Dwarf shrubs are woody plants that are less than 30 cm tall when mature. They've been separated from the shrubs because people often have difficulty recognizing these plants as "shrubs." A few willows commonly found above or just below timberline (e.g., polar willow, stoloniferous willow, net-veined or dwarf willow, and arctic willow) might well be placed here, but instead they're included with the other willows (p. 54).

The category of "Dwarf Shrubs" is admittedly an artificial one, as many of the species in this section are closely related to those in "Shrubs" (e.g., *Vaccinium* spp. and *Rubus* spp.). As well, a disproportionate number of species in this section live in alpine or bog habitats, where the dwarf habit is advantageous for survival and growth.

As with the shrubs, we've tried to group similar species to aid in identification. And don't underestimate the "dwarfs" in our northern flora: the group contains some fragrant flowers, some delicious berries, and even a few tobacco substitutes!

DWARF SHRUBS

CROWBERRY — *Empetrum nigrum*

General Low-creeping, matted, freely branching, **evergreen** shrub; stems up to 15 cm tall, with long woolly hairs.

Leaves Linear, needle-like, **3-7 mm long**, minutely glandular-hairy, spreading, in whorls of 4 or alternate on branch; margins somewhat rolled under; **leaves grooved beneath**.

Flowers **Purplish crimson, inconspicuous**, 2-3 **in leaf axils**, appearing in very early spring.

Fruits Juicy, **black, berrylike drupes**, with large white seeds.

Ecology Swamps, muskeg, cold coniferous forest, rocky mountain slopes, subalpine parkland, and alpine tundra. In suitable habitats throughout the region, from low to high elevations.

Notes: See Alaskan and pink mountain-heathers, which look like crowberry when not in flower or fruit. • The Carrier, Slave, and probably other Athapaskan groups ate the berries fresh, mixed with bear grease, or boiled, mashed and dried in cakes for winter use. The Slave gathered them all winter from under the snow. The berries are somewhat acid tasting and are better with sugar. They make excellent pies and jellies. Beer and sparkling wine can also be made from the juice. • A favourite food of bears. • The name crowberry is thought to come either from the black colour of the fruit, because crows feed on it, or because it is only good for crows, not humans. Also called curlew berry and crakeberry (*crake* is an Old Norse word for crow). *Empetrum* is from the Greek *en petros*, or on rock, the common alpine and rocky slope habitat for this species; *nigrum* means black.

PINK MOUNTAIN-HEATHER — *Phyllodoce empetriformis*

General Low **evergreen** shrub, much branched, matted; stems erect, 10-40 cm tall; young stems glandular-hairy, becoming glabrous with age.

Leaves Needle-like, linear, **5-10 mm long**, glabrous except for minute glands along margins; **groove present on lower surface**.

Flowers **Showy, pink to deep rose**, bell shaped, erect to nodding, few to many, in a **terminal cluster**.

Fruits Erect **capsules**.

Ecology Subalpine and alpine heath, sometimes down into cold coniferous forest on rocky sites or seepage areas. At high elevations throughout the region except the northeast; often very abundant and co-dominant with *Cassiope mertensiana*, but usually so in the snowier western parts of the region. Distribution parallels that of *Luetkea pectinata*.

Notes: *Phyllodoce glanduliflora* (yellow mountain-heather) is very similar to *P. empetriformis,* but has yellowish green, urn-shaped flowers and very sticky-glandular flowers and flower stalks. These two species often share the same high-elevation habitats and frequently hybridize. Here is what Lewis Clark (1976) has to say about this species: "These cheerful bells ring an invitation to high places above the timber line, to those serene and lofty slopes where peace and quiet enter our souls." • Called heather because, superficially, it resembles the true heather (*Calluna vulgaris*) of Europe. It also resembles crowberry, but has longer leaves and larger, showy flowers. • *Phyllodoce* was a sea-nymph in Greek mythology; *empetriformis* refers to the resemblance of this plant to *Empetrum nigrum* (crowberry)

79

WHITE MOUNTAIN-HEATHER — *Cassiope mertensiana*

General Tufted *evergreen* shrub, forming widespread mats; stems up to 30 cm tall, nearly completely hidden by leaves, smooth or finely hairy, four angled.

Leaves Opposite, small, scale-like, egg to lance shaped, arranged in 4 rows, pressed flat against stem, sessile; lower side rounded and *grooved only at extreme base*.

Flowers White, with reddish sepals, bell shaped, more or less nodding, several, near branch tips.

Fruits Erect capsules.

Ecology Alpine heath and subalpine parkland. A dominant species of alpine heath communities throughout much of our region, but absent from the northeast. In our northern interior climates, tends to occur in snowbed habitats, or on northern aspects where snow lies deeper and longer.

Notes: Resembling and related to the true Scottish heather (*Calluna vulgaris*). Branches reputedly produce a golden brown dye. • Individual plants of mountain-heather may be 20 years old or more — they are very slow growing. So, admire them where they grow, but leave them there. • *Cassiope* was the mother of Andromeda (see *Andromeda polifolia*); *mertensiana* refers to F. C. Mertens (1764-1831), a German botanist.

FOUR-ANGLED MOUNTAIN-HEATHER — *Cassiope tetragona*

General Low-spreading *evergreen* shrub; stems 5-30 cm tall, stout, leafy, four angled.

Leaves Opposite, small, thick, scale-like, egg to lance shaped with *deep groove on lower surface*, arranged in 4 rows, pressed flat against stem, sessile.

Flowers White to pink tinged, bell shaped, more or less nodding, one to few, near branch tips.

Fruits Erect capsules.

Ecology Dry alpine heath and rocky tundra. Widespread at high elevations in the northern two-thirds of the region, and along the length of the Rockies. Tends to occupy windswept habitats in moister, snowy climates, and snow-accumulation sites in drier climates.

Notes: Often confused with white mountain-heather. Using a hand lens, the deep groove on the back of the leaves of *C. tetragona* can easily be  seen. The leaf of *C. mertensiana* is not grooved except at its extreme base. • In Alaska this plant is much used by Inuit as a fuel during the summer. • The species name *tetragona* means the same thing as the common name (four-angled) and refers to the shoots.

ALASKAN MOUNTAIN-HEATHER — *Cassiope stelleriana*

General Low-spreading, matted, **evergreen** shrub; stems up to 15 cm tall, minutely hairy.

Leaves Alternate, spreading, needle-like (not pressed close to stem), linear to lance shaped, flat on top, rounded below, **not grooved.**

Flowers **White** or tinged pink, with reddish sepals, broadly bell shaped, more or less nodding, mostly single at branch tips.

Fruits Erect capsules.

Ecology Alpine heaths and seepage areas, rocky slopes, and gravelly creek-beds, at and above timberline. Restricted to snowy, western portions of our region, in Hazelton, Skeena, and Cassiar Mountains and on leeward flanks of the Coast Mountains.

Notes: Similar in appearance to crowberry and pink mountain-heather which, however, have leaves that are grooved underneath. • *Loiseleuria procumbens* (alpine azalea) is also a matted, evergreen, dwarf shrub that often grows with this and the other mountain-heathers and can be locally abundant, especially in the northwestern part of the region. The clusters of upright, bell-shaped pink flowers and much-branched stems with tiny, opposite, elliptic, leathery leaves are unmistakeable (but see *Saxifraga oppositifolia* and *S. tolmiei*).

PARTRIDGEFOOT — *Luetkea pectinata*

General Prostrate, mat-forming, **evergreen** semi-shrub; flowering stem up to 15 cm tall, leafy.

Leaves Numerous, mostly crowded in **thick basal tufts, fan shaped**, two- to three-times 3-**dissected**, withering and persistent for many years; stem leaves alternate.

Flowers **Small, white**, in a dense terminal **cluster** on an upright leafy, flowering stem.

Fruits Several-seeded follicles.

Ecology Moist heaths, tundra, meadows, and mossy seepage areas. At high elevations throughout the region except the northeast; more common in moist, snowy areas; indicator of late snow-melt patches.

Notes: The common name "partridgefoot" refers to the finely divided leaves that somewhat resemble the footprint of a partridge or ptarmigan. Also called creeping or mountain spiraea and formerly known as *Spiraea pectinata*. • *Luetkea* commemorates Count F.P. Lütke, a 19th century Russian sea captain and explorer; *pectinata* means pectinate (like the teeth of a comb) and here refers to the leaves.

RED BEARBERRY — *Arctostaphylos rubra*

General ***Deciduous***, prostrate or tufted shrub up to 15 cm tall; branches brittle, with slender branchlets; bark shredding, papery.

Leaves Oval, leathery, with ***deep veins and rough surface***, green on the underside; margins round toothed; turning scarlet in fall.

Flowers White to green-pink, small, urn shaped, nodding, several in terminal cluster.

Fruits ***Juicy, bright red berries***.

Ecology Bogs, swamps, peaty seepage areas, moist cold subalpine forest and heath, moist alpine tundra. Fairly common, widespread ***north of 55°*** from low to high elevations.

Notes: Do not confuse with *Salix reticulata*, which is pale glaucous on the underside of the leaves. • The berries are rather insipid but were collected with blueberries by Inuit people; the flavour is improved by cooking. • *Arctostaphylos* is from the Greek *arktos* (bear) and *staphylos* (a bunch of grapes), i.e., bearberry; *rubra* means red and refers to the berries. It is generally thought that the common name "bearberry" is given to kinnikinnick (*A. uva-ursi*) because the berries are a favourite food of bears.

KINNIKINNICK — *Arctostaphylos uva-ursi*

General Trailing ***evergreen*** shrub, often forming mats with long flexible rooting branches; bark brownish red.

Leaves ***Alternate***, oval to spoon shaped, ***entire margins***, leathery, to 2.5 cm long; dark green and somewhat shiny above, paler beneath.

Flowers ***Pinkish white***, small, urn shaped, drooping, several in a few-flowered terminal cluster.

Fruits ***Bright red berries*** like miniature apples; edible but with ***mealy*** and rather tasteless pulp.

Ecology Sandy and well-drained exposed sites, dry rocky slopes, dry forest and clearings. Common and widespread, from low elevations to alpine tundra throughout the region.

Notes: The berries were eaten by most central and northern interior native groups (including the Shuswap, Niska, Gitksan, and Carrier). Gathered in the fall or even from under the snow, they were fried in oil or boiled in soups with meat or fish. They were too dry to eat fresh. The Niska preserved them in oil for winter use. The dried or toasted leaves were used in smoking mixtures by southern interior natives, but apparently not by the Carrier people until after contact with white men. The leaves were also made into a tea by some southern groups and the Gitksan, and used as a beverage, tonic, and diuretic. The Carrier sprinkled ground leaves and stems on sores. • The name "kinnikinnick" is an eastern native word meaning mixture and was applied originally to any smoking mixture. The name was brought to the Pacific Coast by employees of fur companies and applied to this plant. The coastal native name for this plant was *sacacomis*. The French constructed a pun around this name calling it "sac-a-commis" from the words *sac* (a bag) and *commis* (a clerk) because the clerks of the Hudson's Bay Company were fond of smoking it and habitually carried around a pouch full of dried leaves. • Also called bearberry, from the Latin *uva* (grape), *ursus* (bear).

TWINFLOWER — *Linnaea borealis*

General Trailing, semi-woody *evergreen* shrub; short (less than 10 cm tall), erect, leafy stems from long runners, more or less hairy.

Leaves *Opposite*, firm, broadly elliptic, with a *few shallow teeth along the upper half*.

Flowers *Pink, trumpetlike, nodding; in pairs*, borne on a thin Y-shaped stalk; fragrant.

Fruits Dry fruits with *hooked bristles* that readily catch onto the fur of mammals or feathers of birds.

Ecology Open or dense, mossy forest or shrub thickets at various elevations up to timberline. Common throughout the region on a wide range of sites from dry ridges to swamps and bogs where it occurs on mossy hummocks.

Notes: The beautiful twin flowers of *Linnaea* produce one of the most fragrant perfumes of the northern woods. • The Kootenay formerly made a tea from the leaves of this plant (Turner, 1978). • This species was supposedly the favourite flower of Linnaeus and, therefore, was named after him by his benefactor Gronovius; *borealis* just means northern.

LINGONBERRY — *Vaccinium vitis-idaea*

General Low, mat-forming, *evergreen* shrub, 10-20 cm tall; branches creeping or trailing, tufted, hairy.

Leaves *Alternate*, leathery, narrowly elliptic to egg shaped, rounded at tip; *margin entire*, rolled under; shiny, dark green above, pale and dotted with *dark glands beneath*.

Flowers Pinkish, with *4 short lobes*, bell shaped, nodding, few, in short terminal clusters.

Fruits Red berries; edible but somewhat sour.

Ecology Muskegs, rocky barrens, moist to dry coniferous woods, and above timberline among shrubs and in tundra. Common from low to high elevations in the North (N of 55°), uncommon in southern part of region.

Notes: Lingonberry is a good indicator species for boreal climates. It might be mistaken for kinnikinnick — look for the dark glands (like bristles) under the leaves in lingonberry. • The berries were eaten by the Niska and Carrier and probably by the Slave and other Athapaskan native groups as well. They were gathered in the fall along with bog cranberries, or in the spring as soon as the snow disappeared. Lingonberries are hard and tart until they are exposed to frost. They were eaten fresh or mixed with oil for storage. The Niska whipped them up with snow for a wintertime dessert. Today the Carrier make them into jam. • The name "lingonberry" (or lingenberry) is Scandinavian; the berries are in great demand in Sweden and Norway for pies, jellies, and cranberry sauce. *Vitis-idaea* literally means vine of Mt. Ida (a mountain in Crete now called Mt. Idhi) where this plant grew.

GROUSEBERRY — *Vaccinium scoparium*

General Low, matted, broomlike *deciduous* shrub, 10-25 cm tall; branches numerous, slender, *strongly angled*, greenish or yellowish green.

Leaves Lance shaped to oval, *widest at or near middle*, sharp pointed, *toothed*, light green, thin, small (less than 12 mm long).

Flowers Pearly pink, with 5 lobes, urn shaped, nodding, single, in axils of leaves.

Fruits Bright *red* (occasionally purplish) sweet berries.

Ecology Dry to moist, open coniferous forest and slopes at medium to high elevations; often forms a dense ground cover near timberline. Common, often abundant *in the southwest part of the region* south of 54°.

Notes: "Grouseberry" is a good common name for this species, as grouse eat all parts of the plant — twigs, flowers, fruit, leaves. Apparently some hunters locate good grouse habitat by searching out this shrub! • Southern interior native people gathered the berries in the same manner as *V. caespitosum* — i.e., with a comb — because the berries are so small. In fact, the Kootenay name for them means comb. They were usually eaten fresh. • The species name *scoparium* means broom and refers to the often broomlike clustering of stems.

DWARF BLUEBERRY — *Vaccinium caespitosum*

General Low-spreading, matted, dwarf *deciduous* shrub, up to 30 cm tall; twigs *rounded*, yellowish green to reddish, often hairy.

Leaves Oblong to lance shaped, *widest above middle*, pointed or blunt, *distinctly toothed*, bright green on both sides, less than 3 cm long, with pronounced *network of veins beneath*.

Flowers Small, whitish to pink, narrowly urn shaped, with 5 lobes, single, in axils of leaves.

Fruits *Blue* berries with a pale grey bloom; edible and sweet.

Ecology Dry to moist, usually mossy, coniferous forest, clearings, wet meadows, mountain slopes, moist rocky ridges, and alpine tundra; common throughout the region from low to high elevations.

Notes: The berries were extremely popular with the northern and central interior natives and were commonly traded. They were usually gathered using a comb made of wood or a salmon backbone. Alternatively, the gatherer would lie on the ground, place one hand under the bush and wriggle the fingers of the other hand in the bush until the berries dropped off. Then they would have to be cleaned and sorted to remove twigs and leaves. The berries were eaten fresh or dried in cakes for winter use. • Blueberry comes from *blaeberry*, from the 15th century word *blae* meaning blue-black. *Caespitosum* means tufted and refers to the growth habit of the species.

BOG BLUEBERRY — *Vaccinium uliginosum*

General Low, erect, freely branched **deciduous** shrub 0.1-0.3 m tall; young branches prostrate, yellowish green, hairy, not angled; old branches greyish red.

Leaves Firm, lance shaped to oval, but **broadest above middle**, with rounded but minutely pointed tip and **no teeth**, 1-3 cm long, green above, pale beneath; network of **veins strongly pronounced on lower surface**.

Flowers Pink, urn shaped with **4 lobes**, 1-4 per leaf axil, sepals persistent on mature fruit.

Fruits **Blue berries**, covered in fine waxy powder; edible and sweet.

Ecology Dry to moist, rocky alpine tundra, also in low elevation muskegs and peat bogs. Abundant in the mountains of the North, not generally found in the southern half of our region.

Notes: This is one of the few fruits available to northern native groups such as the Tahltan, Kaska, and Slave. The Slave ate them only fresh, but native people in the Northwest Territories also boiled them in grease and stored them for winter.

BOG CRANBERRY — *Vaccinium oxycoccos*

General Low-creeping, vinelike, **evergreen** shrub; stems very slender, up to 40 cm tall, finely hairy to smooth; bark brown to black.

Leaves Alternate, **widely spaced,** leathery, small, 6-10 mm, sharp pointed, with edges rolled under; grey-waxy beneath, dark green above.

Flowers Deep pink, nodding, with **petals sharply bent backwards** and stamens protruding (like miniature shooting stars); often solitary or 2-3, each on slender, long stem.

Fruits **Pale-pink to dark red**, juicy berries; small, but appearing oversized on the plant.

Ecology Restricted to muskegs and peat bogs, always in association with *Sphagnum* moss. Throughout the region, at low to medium elevations.

Notes: These tart berries are closely related to our commercial cranberries. They were gathered by all native groups in the interior and eaten raw or boiled with meat. The Carrier dried them for winter use. The Niska preserved the berries by boiling them and mixing them with oil. Then they would whip them up with some oil and snow for a dessert in winter. The Carrier applied a mash of berries to cutaneous erruptions ("pimples") in children. • "In the valleys and low land close by the River and facing the Sun are plenty of Cranberries, can gather those of last Year and those of this upon the same Shrub ..." (Journal of Alexander Mackenzie, July 18, 1798) • The name "cranberry" may be a corruption of "craneberry," which in turn may be because the flower resembles the neck and head of a crane. Or it may be because the plant grows in wet places where cranes (or herons) were to be found. A third explanation suggests it is because the fruit supposedly ripens in the Spring when the cranes return. • Sometimes treated as a separate genus, *Oxycoccus*, which is differentiated into two species – *O. microcarpus* (= *V. microcarpum*), in the northern part of the province only, and *O. quadripetalus*, restricted to the central and southern parts. • The species name *oxycoccos* is from the Greek *oxys* (bitter) and *kokkos* (berry), though they are more tart than bitter.

Conspectus of *Vaccinium* Dwarf Shrub Species

	microcarpum	*oxycoccos*	*vitis-idaea*
Habit	creeping, vinelike	creeping, vinelike	low, mat forming with creeping branches dwarf shrub up to 20 cm tall
Leaves	evergreen, thick, leathery, with entire, strongly inrolled margins oval-elliptic, broadest near the base 2-6 mm long; 1.5-2 mm wide shiny dark green above, glaucous below	evergreen, thick, leathery with entire, slightly inrolled margins broadest near the middle 6-10 mm long; 2-5 mm wide shiny dark green above, glaucous below	evergreen, thick, leathery with entire, inrolled margins shiny green above, pale beneath and dotted with dark stalked glands
Flowers	like miniature shooting stars solitary or in small clusters, nodding on long, slender, +/−glabrous stalks petals 4, pink, united only at base, bent backwards, about 5 mm long	like miniature shooting stars solitary or in small clusters, nodding on long slender, hairy stalks petals 4, pink, united only at base, bent backwards, 5-7 mm long	few in short terminal clusters, on short glandular stalks bell shaped, pink with 4 short lobes
Fruit	pale-pink berry to 7 mm diam.	dark red berry 8-12 mm diam.	bright red berry up to 10 mm diam.

scoparium	caespitosum	uliginosum
low, broomlike shrub with many fine, erect, strongly angled, greenish branches to 25 cm tall	low or dwarf shrub, tufted or mat forming up to 30 cm tall	
deciduous, thin, pointed at top, glabrous, light green, margins finely toothed	deciduous, thin, rounded at top, light green, margins finely toothed along upper half	deciduous, firm, green above, lighter below, with conspicuous veins, rounded tip, margins entire
lance shaped to narrowly egg shaped	inversely egg shaped, widest above middle, net veined on lower surface	inversely lance to egg shaped, usually thickest above middle
small, less than 12 mm long, usually	10-25 mm long	10-20 mm long, margins entire
single in axils of leaves	single in axils of leaves	1-4 from ends or side branches
urn shaped, pale pink, with 5 lobes small (up to 4 mm long)	narrowly urn shaped, pink or whitish, with 5 lobes, 6-8 mm long	urn shaped with 4 lobes, pink, 3-5 mm long
bright red berry 5 mm diam.	blue berry, 6-8 mm diam., with a whitish bloom	blue to black berry with whitish bloom, 6-8 mm diam.

CREEPING-SNOWBERRY · *Gaultheria hispidula*

General Delicate, low-creeping, matted, **evergreen** shrub; stems slender, covered with brownish, flattened hairs.

Leaves Alternate, **closely spaced**, small, leathery; margins rolled under; **brown scale-like hairs** pressed to underside like whiskers.

Flowers Pinkish, **bell shaped**, nodding, mostly solitary in axils of leaves, on short stalks.

Fruits *White* berries with hairs; juicy with a mild wintergreen flavour and smell.

Ecology In bogs or upland coniferous (frequently black spruce) forest; on *Sphagnum* hummocks or on decaying wood. Scattered in suitable habitats across the southern half of the region at low to medium elevations.

Notes: If not in flower or fruit, it could be mistaken for *Vaccinium vitis-idea,* which also has leathery leaves with dark hairs beneath, but the leaves of *Gaultheria hispidula* are generally smaller and much more closely spaced along the stem. • Closely related to *Gaultheria procumbens* from which oil of wintergreen was originally obtained. Care should be taken not to eat too many of the berries, which taste of wintergreen, as they contain methyl salicylate (essence of wintergreen) which is closely related to aspirin and can be toxic in large doses. Children should avoid eating them. Leaves were used to make a tea by eastern native peoples. • *Gaultheria* is named for Dr. Hugues Jean Gaultier (1708-1756), a French Canadian naturalist; the genus also contains the coastal salal (*Gaultheria shallon*). • Called snowberry because of white fruits; other common names are maidenhair plum, moxie berry, and capillaire.

BOG-ROSEMARY · *Andromeda polifolia*

General Low-spreading **evergreen** shrub; stems erect, 10-50 cm tall, from creeping rhizomes.

Leaves *Alternate*, leathery, narrowly lance shaped to oblong, sharp pointed; margins rolled under; lower surface with a fine, waxy powder, **not hairy**; upper surface dull green, with sunken veins.

Flowers Pinkish, small, **urn shaped**, 2-6 in terminal clusters; flower stems somewhat curved downwards at tip.

Fruits Roundish, erect, 5-valved capsules.

Ecology Bogs, fens, and swamps, at low to medium elevations. Scattered throughout, but seems to be lacking in many apparently suitable wetland habitats in the southwestern portion of our region.

Notes: Similar appearance and habitat to bog-laurel, but *Andromeda* has alternate leaves, while *Kalmia*'s are opposite. Both species contain the poison andromedotoxin, which causes watering of eyes, nose, and mouth, loss of energy, respiratory problems, vomiting, etc., and progressive paralysis until death. • Named after Andromeda, the beautiful daughter of Cepheus of Ethiopia; when her mother Cassiope boasted that Andromeda was more beautiful than the Nereids (nymphs of the Mediterranean), Poseidon (Greek god of the sea) sent a monster to punish the land; Andromeda was chained to a rock as a sacrifice to the monster but was rescued by Perseus, whom she married. • The leaves and twigs were used in some parts of Russia for tanning. • Rosemary comes from the Latin *rosmarinus* or *ros maris* meaning dew of the sea − a name given originally to a Mediterranean plant, *Rosmarinus officinalis*, because it grew near, and smelled like, the sea.

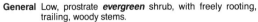

YELLOW MOUNTAIN-AVENS   *Dryas drummondii*

General Low, prostrate *evergreen* shrub, with freely rooting, trailing, woody stems.

Leaves *Oblong to elliptical, broadest above the middle*; leathery, wrinkly; *margins scalloped*; dark green above, densely covered in white hairs below.

Flowers *Pale yellow*, single, on leafless stem (15-25 cm tall), nodding; petals never fully opened; sepals broadly oval.

Fruits Numerous achenes, each with a silky, golden-yellow, feathery plume which becomes twisted around others; later opens up to a fluffy mass and each seed is eventually carried off by its own "parachute" in the wind.

Ecology A common pioneer on gravelly river bars, rocky slopes, and roadsides from the lowlands up into the alpine tundra. Scattered throughout our region and particularly abundant in the North, especially on calcium–rich soils.

Notes: Roots of the mountain-avens have nitrogen-fixing nodules, useful on the rocky, gravelly, nitrogen-poor sites where yellow mountain-avens commonly grows. • The name "avens" appears to be derived from several words all of which have an obscure origin, but which may mean antidote since species of *Geum* (also called avens) were supposed to ward off the devil and evil spirits, venomous serpents, and wild beasts (see *G. macrophyllum*). The scientific name *Dryas* means wood-nymph; *drummondii* is named for Thomas Drummond (1780-1835), an early Canadian (and Texan) botanist.

SMOOTH-LEAVED MOUNTAIN-AVENS   *Dryas integrifolia*

General Perennial, matted *evergreen* from trailing, woody stems.

Leaves *Narrowly oblong to somewhat lance shaped, broadest below the middle*, leathery; *margins entire or with few teeth*, often rolled under; slightly wrinkled to smooth, dark green and shiny above, densely white-hairy below.

Flowers *Creamy white* (rarely yellow), single, on leafless, hairy stem; sepals almost lance shaped.

Fruits Numerous achenes with long, feathery styles.

Ecology Alpine tundra and heath, also a pioneer on rocky or gravelly sites. At high elevations throughout the northern half of the region (north of 55°); especially abundant on calcium-rich soils.

Notes: Dryas octopetala (white mountain-avens), another white-flowered alpine species, occurs in our region only near the Yukon boundary, and has scalloped leaf margins. The very similar *D. hookeriana* (Hooker's mountain-avens) occurs in the southernmost part of the region, in the southern Chilcotin Mountains and in the Rockies. • As Clark (1973) notes, "these dryads are superbly adapted to the rigours of their exposed and airy homes." Note especially the thick, leathery leaves which are low to the ground, curled under, and hairy beneath. • The flowers and seed plumes produce a vivid green dye.

89

PRINCE'S-PINE — *Chimaphila umbellata*

General Stout, slightly woody, ***evergreen*** shrub, with creeping rhizome; stems up to 35 cm tall, simple or branched, greenish, without hairs.

Leaves ***Whorled;*** narrowly oblong, sharply toothed mostly above the middle, bright green and shiny above.

Flowers Whitish pink, ***waxy***, fragrant, saucer shaped, nodding, several (3-10) in a small, loose cluster; flowering stem with fine hairs; plump green ovary surrounded by ten reddish stamens.

Fruits Roundish, erect capsules.

Ecology Mossy, well-drained sites in open or dense coniferous forests, and in clearings; in humus and on rotting wood. Scattered at low to moderate elevations in the southern half of the region; seems to be most common in drier forests of moist climates.

Notes: Some southern interior natives were known to boil the leaves, stems, and roots to make a tea for a beverage, or for colds and sore

throats. It may also have been used by some groups as a wet dressing for swellings and sores, or for rheumatism and kidney problems. • Also called "pipsissewa" — an adaptation of the Cree name *pipisisikweu*, meaning it-breaks-into-small-pieces, because the leaves contain a substance that was supposed to dissolve kidney stones. • *Chimaphila* comes from Greek *cheima* (winter) and *philos* (loving) and refers to its evergreen habit. Prince's-pine presumably refers to its appearance — a miniature pine tree fit for a prince, perhaps?

Rubus Silhouettes

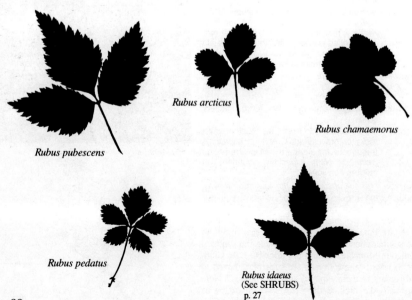

Rubus arctica

Rubus chamaemorus

Rubus pubescens

Rubus pedatus

Rubus idaeus
(See SHRUBS)
p. 27

TRAILING RASPBERRY — *Rubus pubescens*

General Unarmed perennial, with slender trailing **runners**, often rooting at nodes; flowering stems erect, up to 30 cm tall, with soft long hairs.

Leaves **Divided into 3** oval to diamond-shaped, toothed, pointed leaflets.

Flowers **White**, rarely pink, erect, 1-3, on short lateral branches; stalks covered with stalked glands.

Fruits Cluster of **dark red** drupelets **(a small raspberry)**; edible.

Ecology Moist to wet forests, swamps, and bogs. Low to medium elevations throughout the region except the far northwest.

Notes: Leaves resemble those of red raspberry which, however, is an erect shrub; as well, leaflets of red raspberry are toothed to the base, while those of trailing raspberry are often not. • The berries were eaten fresh by the Carrier and probably by other Athapaskan groups. They sometimes refer to it incorrectly as salmonberry (*Rubus spectabilis*). It makes good jelly. When Carrier women had "sickness in their womb" they drank an infusion of boiled raspberry stems (Carrier Linguistic Committee, 1973). • Originally (16th century) raspberries were called *rasps, raspis,* or *raspises*. The exact origin of these names is not clear but may have come from the 15th century word *raspis* (a fruit from which a drink could be made); from *vinum raspatum* (a sweet red French wine) or a wine made from *raspes* (grapes with seeds removed); or from *resp* which means shoot or sucker.

DWARF NAGOONBERRY — *Rubus arcticus*

General Unarmed perennial, from extensively creeping **rhizomes**; flowering stems erect, several, up to 10 cm tall, finely hairy.

Leaves Round to heart shaped in outline, **3 lobed; lobes rounded** and coarsely toothed; more or less hairy.

Flowers **Pink to reddish pink**, showy, usually solitary.

Fruits A cluster of several **red** fleshy drupelets (**a small raspberry**).

Ecology Bogs, swamps, wet forest and thickets, meadows, peaty seepage areas. Throughout the region, from the lowlands to high elevations.

Notes: This species is called *Rubus acaulis* by some taxonomists. • The berries have an excellent flavour and can be eaten raw or made into jams, jellies, or for flavouring liquor. The Shuswap people called them false wild strawberries and probably ate them. • *Rubus* means red and refers to the colour of the fruits of many species (including this one!). The origin of the common name "nagoonberry" remains a mystery.

CLOUDBERRY — *Rubus chamaemorus*

General Unarmed perennial with extensively creeping rhizome; flowering stems erect, unbranched, up to 20 cm tall.

Leaves *Not divided into leaflets*, 1-3 per stem, *round to kidney shaped*, more or less 5 lobed, somewhat leathery, coarsely saw toothed.

Flowers *White*, with spreading petals; solitary, terminal, unisexual with male and female flowers on different plants.

Fruits A *raspberry-like* collection of drupelets, at first reddish, then *amber to yellow* when mature; edible with baked-apple taste.

Ecology Muskegs and peat bogs; in association with *Sphagnum* moss. Widespread at low to medium elevations in the North, scattered but locally abundant south of 55°.

Notes: Cloudberry plants are either male or female, but not both — a most unusual situation. Female plants have flowers with dwarf male parts; male plants have flowers with dwarf female parts. • The berries are very high in Vitamin C content and were undoubtedly used by the inland Tlingit, Tahltan, Kaska, and Slave, among other groups. The Gitksan recognize this berry, which they called frogberry. The berries have a baked-apple taste which, once acquired, is delicious. They were highly prized by Inuit and were eaten fresh or frozen for winter use. Alaskan natives say the juice is good for hives. • "Cloudberry" comes from the Old English *clud* meaning rocky hill. In the 16th century it was called knottberry from the English *knot* (rocky hill) or the Norse *knott*. According to folk tales it grew on the top of "two of the highest mountains in all England where the clouds are lower than the mountain tops all winter long." •*Chamaemorus* means the mulberry (*Morus* spp.) that grows along the ground (*chemai*).

FIVE-LEAVED BRAMBLE — *Rubus pedatus*

General Unarmed perennial with creeping stems (*runners*); rooting at the nodes and producing short, erect stems bearing 1-3 leaves; flowering stems erect, short (2 cm or less).

Leaves Usually *divided into 5 leaflets* or oval-shaped lobes, coarsely toothed.

Flowers *White*, the petals spreading or bent backwards; solitary on very slender stalks.

Fruits A small cluster of bright *red* small drupelets, sometimes with just one drupelet per fruit; juicy and flavourful.

Ecology Moist, mossy, usually coniferous forest, from the lowlands to subalpine parkland, but most abundant at middle elevations. Throughout the region, but rare in the northeast and absent from the southern part of our region on the Fraser Plateau and in the Chilcotin.

Notes: The five-leaved bramble is a good example of why local plant guides are often superior to those from other areas: a field guide from southern British Columbia would describe this species as predominantly subalpine; a guide from Alaska might describe it as a lowland species! • The berries, although very small, are very tasty and were probably eaten by hunters and travellers of several interior native peoples. They were definitely eaten by Haida and other coastal groups. • The name "bramble" is from the Old English *braembel*, from *brom* meaning wiry or thorny shrub, and originally referred to the blackberry *Rubus fruticosus*. • The species name *pedatus* means foot and refers, perhaps, to the 5 leaflets as 5-toed prints in the moss.

Wildflowers

The Wildflower section includes all non-woody flowering plants except the Grasses, Sedges and Rushes. It is divided into 12 parts. Eleven of these represent major plant families, and the twelfth includes flowers from all other (smaller) families.

Plants representing the eleven major plant families are illustrated on the following page. If the leaves, flowers and/or fruit of your "unknown plant" resemble one of those shown, then you're probably in the right family. If not, your plant may belong to a smaller family and might be found in "Other Families."

More detailed descriptions of some of these various plant families can be found in the following Royal B.C. Museum publications:

Family	Reference
Sunflower (composites)	Douglas (1982)
Lily	Taylor (1966)
Orchid	Szczawinski (1959)
Buttercup	Brayshaw (1989)
Rose	Taylor (1973b)
Pea	Taylor (1974b)
Heath	Szczawinski (1962)
Figwort	Taylor (1974a)

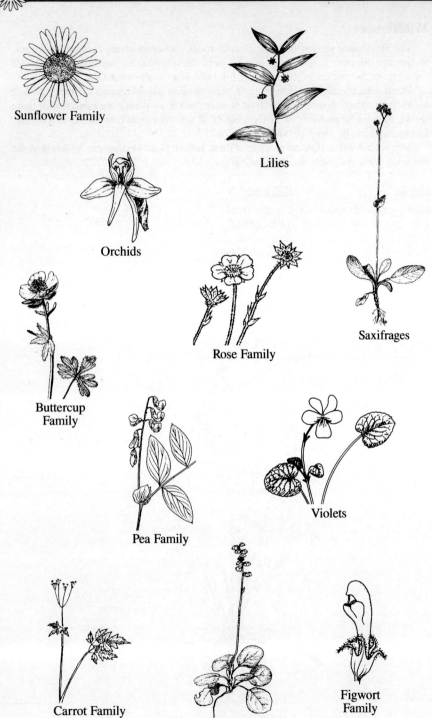

Sunflower Family

Lilies

Orchids

Saxifrages

Rose Family

Buttercup
Family

Pea Family

Violets

Carrot Family

Heath Family

Figwort
Family

Sunflower Family

The composites, or sunflower family (the plant family Asteraceae, also known as Compositae) are one of the largest plant families in the world, with over 20,000 species. B.C. alone has over 350 species, with many of these occurring in our region.

Composites are easily recognized by their inflorescence, which is often mistaken for a single large flower, but is actually made up of numerous individual flowers on the broadened top of the stem. These flowers can be of two forms — tubular and sitting on the broadened stem top (**disk** flowers) or strap-shaped and arranged around the edges of the stem top (**ray** flowers). (When you play "loves me, loves me not" you're plucking ray flowers). A plant may have ray flowers only, disk flowers only, or both. Other flower parts are commonly modified into hairs (collectively called the **pappus**) attached to the single-seeded fruits (**achenes**), to assist in wind-dispersal (as in the downy parachute of a dandelion), or less commonly into hooks to help seeds cling to passing animals (and your clothing!). Attached to the rim of the head is an **involucre**, consisting of scale-like or somewhat leaf-like bracts, called **involucral bracts**.

Keys are provided to genera, and to species within some of the larger genera. Many more species occur in northern B.C. than are covered in this guide. The best additional reference is Douglas (1982), but this only covers part of the family (including the genera *Arnica*, *Petasites* and *Senecio*); additional volumes in the series are expected to be published very soon by the Royal B.C. Museum, to cover the rest of the composites.

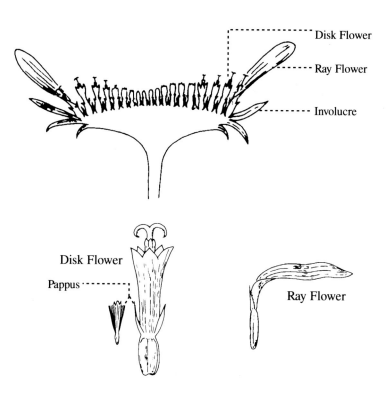

Disk Flower

Ray Flower

Involucre

Disk Flower

Pappus

Ray Flower

Key to Asteraceae Genera

1. Flowers all strap–shaped ray flowers; plants with milky juice
  2. Leaves all basal; heads solitary
    3. Leaves deeply toothed or lobed; achenes roughened with tiny spines .... *Taraxacum*
    3. Flowers entire to few-lobed; achenes ribbed but not spiny .... *Agoseris*
  2. Stems leafy; heads several.
    4. Leaves with prickly margin; achenes flattened .... *Sonchus arvensis*
    4. Leaves without prickly margin; achenes not flattened .... *Hieracium*
1. Flowers not all ray flowers; plant juice usually watery
  5. Heads of disk flowers only
    6. Leaves compound, deeply divided into narrow segments .... *Artemisia*
    6. Leaves simple, entire to deeply lobed
      7. Leaves spiny; involucral bracts with prickly tips .... *Cirsium*
      7. Leaves not spiny
        8. Basal leaves large, long stalked, deeply lobed to sharply or shallowly toothed .... *Petasites*
        8. Basal leaves relatively small, entire (not lobed)
          9. Basal leaves conspicuous; stem leaves much reduced upwards ..... *Antennaria*
          9. Basal leaves withering early; stem leaves conspicuous, not much reduced .... *Anaphalis*
  5. Heads with both ray and disk flowers
    10. Leaves compound, deeply disected into linear segments (fernlike) .... *Achillea millefolium*
    10. Leaves simple, entire to deeply lobed
      11. Basal leaves large, long stalked, deeply lobed to sharply or shallowly toothed .... *Petasites*
      11. Basal leaves various, not as above
        12. Ray flowers yellow or orange
          13. Heads small, numerous in fairly tight clusters .... *Solidago*
          13. Heads larger, fewer
            14. Leaves, at least the lower, opposite .... *Arnica*
            14. Leaves alternate .... *Senecio*
        12. Ray flowers pink, purple, red, or blue
            15. Involucral bracts in 3 or more rows and overlapping like shingles on a roof, or with 1 or more green, leafy outer rows; ray flowers relatively broad; plants often with rhizomes .... *Aster*
            15. Involucral bracts in a single equal row, ray flowers mostly very narrow; plants seldom with rhizomes (except in *E. peregrinus*) .... *Erigeron*

COMMON DANDELION — *Taraxacum officinale*

General Perennial herb with **milky juice**, with a simple or branched stem base and a thick, often blackish **taproot**; flowering stems solitary to several, naked, 5-60 cm tall, rarely taller.

Leaves **All basal**, oblong to spoon shaped, **toothed or, more usually, pinnately lobed or divided**, tapering to more or less winged stalks.

Flowers Heads **yellow, solitary**, made up of ray flowers only; involucral bracts glabrous, **the inner bracts not horned**.

Fruits Achenes beaked, ribbed, spiny above.

Ecology A weedy species of disturbed sites at low to moderate elevations throughout our region.

Notes: This plant was unintentionally imported to North America on the *Mayflower*. The young leaves make a good vegetable green. The cooked roots can be eaten as a vegetable or dried and ground as a coffee substitute. The flowers make dandelion wine and the whole plant can be brewed to make beer. • Since its introduction by Europeans, the Carrier have eaten the boiled spring leaves as greens. • *Taraxacum* (from the Greek *tarassein*, "to stir up") and *officinale* (medicinal) both refer to the use of this plant as medicine.

HORNED DANDELION — *Taraxacum ceratophorum*

General Perennial herb with **milky juice**, with a simple or branched stem-base and a thick, often blackish, **taproot**; flowering stems solitary to several, naked, 3-10 cm tall.

Leaves **All basal**, lance shaped, **toothed or more usually pinnately lobed or divided**, the terminal lobe often wider than the others, tapering to more or less winged stalks.

Flowers Heads **yellow, solitary**, made up of ray flowers only; involucral bracts glabrous to finely hairy, **the inner bracts usually horned**.

Fruits Achenes beaked, ribbed, spiny above.

Ecology Moist to dry subalpine and alpine meadows; high elevation tundra, scree, and gravelly ridges. Common but rarely abundant at high elevations throughout our region.

Notes: The horned dandelion is a native species; *T. officinale* (common dandelion) is an introduced, aggressive weedy species. • In similar, high elevation habitats be on the look-out for *Crepis nana* (dwarf hawksbeard), a striking plant with a rounded, cushionlike tuft of long-stalked, elliptical or spoon-shaped leaves, surmounted by a dense mass of small, yellow, dandelion-type flower heads. • "Dandelion" is from the French *dent-de-lion*, or lion's tooth, in reference to the leaves; horned is in reference to the involucral bracts. • *Cerato* means horn shaped, again in reference to the involucral bracts.

ORANGE AGOSERIS · *Agoseris aurantiaca*

General Perennial herb with *milky juice*, from a taproot and simple or branching stem-base, mostly 10-30 cm tall.

Leaves *All basal*, narrowly to broadly lance shaped, entire to few lobed, long stalked, glabrous or somewhat hairy.

Flowers Heads *burnt orange*, often becoming pink or purplish with age, *solitary*, large, consisting only of ray flowers.

Fruits Achenes *long-beaked*.

Ecology Dry to moist grasslands, meadows, thickets, and forest openings from low to high elevations throughout our region.

Notes: A less common species, *Agoseris glauca* (pale agoseris), may also be encountered in the region. It, however, has yellow ray flowers and unbeaked or short-beaked achenes. • The leaves, and especially the latex of some *Agoseris* and *Hieracium* species were chewed for pleasure by some southern interior native groups.

ORANGE HAWKWEED · *Hieracium aurantiacum*

General Plant *hairy in all parts*; stems 15-40 cm tall, basal rosettes of leaves connected by rapidly spreading *stolons and rhizomes*; stems exuding *milky juice* when broken.

Leaves Narrowly elliptic to lance shaped, entire, hairy, confined to a *basal rosette*.

Flowers *Red-orange*; heads of ray flowers only, to 2 cm broad, several crowded into a flat- to round-topped cluster; involucral bracts *blackish hairy*.

Fruits Achenes narrowed at both ends, ribbed.

Ecology Disturbed sites; roadsides, gravel pits, pastureland. Scattered, locally abundant along major transportation corridors in the southern half of our region.

Notes: Orange hawkweed is another weedy introduced European species, commonly occurring on roadsides and other disturbed sites. • A very aggressive weed that only recently has invaded but is making rapid progress in the settled parts of the region. • This species is also called "devil's paintbrush" and is our only orange-flowered hawkweed; all others have yellow or white heads. • *Aurantiacum* means orange coloured.

NARROW-LEAVED HAWKWEED   *Hieracium umbellatum*

General Perennial herb with **milky juice**, with a **short woody rhizome**; stems solitary or few, glabrous or nearly so below, commonly having **starlike hairs** above.

Leaves **Basal leaves few** and soon deciduous, stem leaves small and soon deciduous below and strongly reduced above, the middle ones lance shaped, sessile, entire or somewhat toothed, with starlike hairs.

Flowers Heads **yellow**, few to many in a flat-topped cluster, consisting only of ray flowers; involucral bracts graduated, **glabrous or nearly so**.

Fruits Ribbed achenes.

Ecology Fairly dry, open forests and meadows, clearings, and roadsides, scattered at low to moderate elevations in the southern half of the region.

Notes: The name "hawkweed" comes from a belief by the ancient Greeks that hawks would tear apart a plant called the *hieracion* (from the Greek *hierax* meaning hawk) and wet their eyes with the juice to clear their eyesight.

SLENDER HAWKWEED   *Hieracium gracile*

General Perennial herb with **milky juice**, with a **slender, horizontal rhizome** and short stem base; stems few to several, unbranched, 8-25 cm tall.

Leaves **Mostly basal**, broadly lance to spoon shaped, narrowed below to a stalk, entire or toothed, glabrous or sometimes inconspicuously hairy and glandular on both surfaces; stem leaves absent or few and much reduced.

Flowers Heads **yellow**, few to several in small cluster, all of ray flowers; involucral bracts subequal, **with fine blackish hair and black glandular hairs**, these on the stalk as well.

Fruits Nerved achenes.

Ecology Subalpine and alpine meadows, heath, and snowbed tundra; common at high elevations throughout our region.

Notes: This species could be mistaken for the closely related *Hieracium triste* (woolly hawkweed). The latter, however, has larger heads and longer, grayish-black hairs (heads and stalks look quite shaggy), but no glands. *H. triste* is common only in the western part of the region, along the Coast Mountains and adjacent ranges. • The species name *gracile* means slender, as in the common name.

99

WHITE-FLOWERED HAWKWEED — *Hieracium albiflorum*

General Perennial herb with **milky juice**, from fibrous-rooted and commonly unbranched, short stem-base; stems solitary, 30-100 cm tall.

Leaves **Mostly basal**, oblong to broadly lance shaped, narrowed to a stalk or upper ones sessile, **bristly with short, rigid hairs on the upper surface**; margins entire or wavy toothed.

Flowers Heads **white**, made up of only ray flowers, several to many in open cluster; involucral bracts in one row.

Fruits Several-nerved achenes.

Ecology Relatively dry, open forests, meadows, clearings, and roadsides at low to moderate elevations mostly in the southern half of the region.

Notes: According to Elsie Steedman in *Ethnobotany of the Thompson Indians of British Columbia* (1929), the Thompson chewed the leaves and coagulated latex of two or three species of *Hieracium* (probably *H. albertinum*, *H. cynoglossoides* and/or *H. scouleri*), at least one species of *Agoseris* (*A. glauca*), and an introduced species, common salsify or oyster plant (*Tragopogon porrifolius*). The leaves and stems of these plants were broken, allowing the milky latex to exude. When it had hardened, it was collected in a little ball and chewed for pleasure and to cleanse the mouth; later it was swallowed. The Okanagan, Spokane, and Kalispel chewed the latex of *Agoseris glauca*. The Spokane called it "Indian bubblegum." They often dried the leaves, then chewed them to extract the gum. The Okanagan, Shuswap, Flathead, and perhaps some other groups chewed the latex of milkweed (*Asclepias speciosa*) in a similar manner.

PERENNIAL SOW-THISTLE — *Sonchus arvensis*

General Perennial herb with **milky juice** and with deep roots and extensive, creeping rhizomes, 40 cm-2 m tall; stems hollow, with yellow glands.

Leaves Pinnately lobed with **very prickly margins**, clasping the stem, 6-40 cm long, 2-15 cm wide, upper leaves smaller and less lobed.

Flowers **Dark yellow, ray flowers only**; heads 3-5 cm wide; several heads in loose, flat- or round-topped inflorescence; involucral bracts with gland-tipped hairs.

Fruits Flattened, ribbed, cross-wrinkled achenes

Ecology Cultivated fields, pastures, roadsides, clearings, meadows, thickets; common from low to medium elevations in settled parts of our region, mostly in the southern half.

Notes: Sow-thistles can be separated from the true thistles (*Cirsium* spp.) by breaking their stems. Sow-thistles have milky latex; true thistles don't. The young leaves of sow-thistle can be eaten raw in salads or cooked as a vegetable. • The thistles of Canada are described in Moore and Frankton (1974). • This is a very widespread and annoying weed introduced from Europe. • *Sonchus* is from the Greek word for spongy, in reference to the stems; *arvensis* means of the fields, where this weedy species grows. Apparently pigs like to eat them, hence the common name "sow-thistle."

CANADA THISTLE — *Cirsium arvense*

General Perennial from ***deep, wide-spreading roots and creeping rhizomes***; stems rather thin, green, ***without spiny wings***, 30 cm - 2 m tall, highly branched above.

Leaves Alternate, lance shaped, irregularly lobed, spiny toothed; glabrous or green above, densely white-hairy beneath.

Flowers ***Pink-purple***, 1-2 cm high, disk flowers only; several to many heads in an open inflorescence; involucral bracts tipped with weak prickles; plants are unisexual (male or female, but not with flower parts of both); the male heads tend to be showier.

Fruits Achenes, oblong, flattened, ribbed, 3 - 4 mm long.

Ecology Fields, pastures, meadows, clearings, roadsides. Common and often abundant at low to medium elevations, primarily in the settled or agricultural portions of the region.

Notes: Canada thistle is the only thistle with male and female flowers on separate plants. It is distinguished from other thistles by the combination of green stems without spiny wings, small almost spineless heads, and creeping rhizomes. The bull thistle (*Cirsium vulgare*) has much larger heads, spiny-winged stems, and a deep, fleshy taproot. We also have a very handsome taprooted native species, *C. edule* (edible thistle), that has big, fat, woolly, purplish pink and nodding heads and grows at medium to high elevations. • Peeled stems and roots of most thistles are edible and can provide nutritious food in an emergency. • The thistle (probably not this species) is the national flower of Scotland, adopted as far back as the eighth century A.D. Legend has it that an invading Danish army was creeping, barefoot, towards a Scotish encampment when a soldier stepped on a thistle. He yelled so loud that the Scots awoke and defeated the Danes. The thistle was thereafter considered to be the guardian of Scotland and acquired the motto *nemo me impune lacessit* ("no-one shall provoke me with impunity," or in Scottish "wha duar meddle wi me") as the emblem of that dour land.

OXEYE DAISY — *Chrysanthemum leucanthemum*

General Perennial from a well-developed, woody rhizome, ***typically smelling strongly of sage***; stems 20-80 cm tall, simple or once branched, glabrous to slightly hairy.

Leaves Basal leaves broadly or narrowly spoon shaped, with rounded teeth and lobes on the margin; ***stem leaves oblong, toothed to lobed***.

Flowers ***Ray flowers white, 1-2 cm long***; disk flowers yellow, 1-2 cm wide across the disk; heads solitary.

Fruits Achenes black, with about 10 white ribs.

Ecology Fields, meadows, roadsides, clearings. Primarily at low elevations in the settled portions of the southern half of the region.

Notes: This species is also known as *Leucanthemum vulgare*. • This introduced weed (of European origin) is widespread and often very abundant in disturbed places, especially roadsides. It also invades fields and meadows where it competes aggressively, especially under grazing pressure, to form dense and extensive populations. • *Chrysanthemum leucanthemum* means the white-flowered (*leucanthemum*) gold flower (*chrysos* and *anthos*)! The common name (incorrectly) emphasizes the yellow flower (day's eye, or daisy − i.e., the sun) which looks like the eye of an ox (presumably white).

101

PEARLY EVERLASTING — *Anaphalis margaritacea*

General Perennial herb from rhizomes; stems usually unbranched, leafy, white-woolly, 20-80 cm tall.

Leaves Alternate, narrowly lance shaped with a conspicuous mid-vein, **greenish above, white-woolly beneath**; margins often rolled under.

Flowers Small heads all of yellowish disk flowers; heads in dense flat-topped clusters; involucral bracts **pearly white** with a dark triangular base.

Fruits Very small, roughened, glabrous to sparsely hairy achenes.

Ecology Rocky slopes, open forest, clearings, meadows, fields, pastures, roadsides. Weedy native species common and widespread throughout the region, from low to subalpine elevations.

Notes: Pearly everlasting is related to the pussytoes (*Antennaria* spp.) but has small, withering basal leaves and stem leaves not much reduced in size upwards on the stem. • The common name derives from the pearly white involucral bracts that retain their colour and shape when dried, making attractive dry bouquets. The plants usually don't bloom until mid-summer, but the flowers can last until the first snows of winter.

Antennaria silhouettes

Antennaria racemosa

Antennaria neglecta

Antennaria microphylla

Antennaria pulcherrima

SUNFLOWER FAMILY

RACEMOSE PUSSYTOES — *Antennaria racemosa*

General Perennial herb, *mat forming* with creeping, leafy stolons, 10-40 cm tall.

Leaves Basal leaves elliptic to rounded, short stalked, *white-woolly beneath, less hairy above and becoming green and glabrous*; stem leaves more linear and sessile, becoming reduced above.

Flowers *Heads greenish white to pale brown*, made up only of disk flowers, *several in an open, elongate cluster*; involucral bracts pale greenish below, colourless or pale brownish to reddish above.

Fruits Achenes.

Ecology Open, dry to moist forests, openings, rock slides and gravelly ridges, roadsides, at low to subalpine elevations. Widely distributed south of 57° but rarely abundant.

Notes: Flowers of pussytoes picked and dried soon after blooming will provide lovely bouquets throughout the winter; some people dye the blossoms as well. • *Antennaria* is from the Latin *antenna*, because tips of the pappus hairs of male flowers apparently resemble insect antennae; *racemosa* refers to the inflorescence (a raceme).

FIELD PUSSYTOES — *Antennaria neglecta*

General Perennial herb, *mat forming* with well-developed stolons, 5-30 cm tall.

Leaves Basal leaves spoon shaped to broadly lance shaped or elliptic, persistently *white-woolly below, thinly so or glabrous and green above*; stem leaves linear to lance shaped, reduced upwards.

Flowers *Heads greenish white*, made up only of disk flowers, *several in a compact, crowded cluster*; involucral bracts whitish above.

Fruits Roughened achenes.

Ecology Open, dry to moist, well-drained forest and openings at low to moderate elevations. Fairly widespread south of 57°, less common north of that latitude.

Notes: Many species of *Antennaria* have distinct male and female plants, and males may be rare or even absent from some areas. In these species, seed is often produced without fertilization, producing offspring genetically identical to their mother.

103

SUNFLOWER FAMILY

ROSY PUSSYTOES	*Antennaria microphylla*

General Perennial herb, *mat forming* with numerous leafy stolons, 5-40 cm tall.

Leaves Basal leaves *spoon or broadly lance shaped, grey-woolly above and below*.

Flowers *Heads reddish pink to white*, consisting only of disk flowers, 3-20 in a small cluster; involucral bracts woolly below, bright or pale pink to white above.

Fruits Achenes, usually glabrous.

Ecology Relatively dry, grassy slopes, meadows, clearings, and open forests at low to subalpine elevations, fairly common throughout our region.

Notes: This species is often confused with three other Antennarias which occur in the region. *A. alpina* (alpine pussytoes) and *A. umbrinella* (umber pussytoes) are very similar to each other (and to *A. microphylla*) except for middle and outer involucral bract colour; dark or brownish green in the former and brownish in the latter. *Antennaria monocephala* (one-headed pussytoes) has leaves that are green and lightly hairy above, white-woolly below, and has solitary heads. All three of these other species are fairly common at subalpine to alpine elevations throughout the region.

SHOWY PUSSYTOES	*Antennaria pulcherrima*

General Perennial herb, from a short branched or rhizomatous base, 10-55 cm tall, *often multiple stemmed but not mat forming*.

Leaves Basal leaves *narrowly lance shaped*, tufted and persistent, stalked, *white-woolly above and below*; stem leaves becoming linear and strongly reduced upwards.

Flowers *Heads greenish black*, with disk flowers only, several to many in dense, crowded cluster; involucral bracts brown to blackish (sometimes white-tipped) in aspect, densely hairy at the base.

Fruits Glabrous achenes.

Ecology Moist to dry open forest, meadows, river terraces, and shrub-carrs at low to moderate elevations. Scattered throughout the northern half of the region and south along the Rockies; apparently absent from the southern half except in the Rockies and also in the Chilcotin.

Notes: Some taxonomists include *A. anaphaloides* in *Antennaria pulcherrima*. • The species name *pulcherrima* (beautiful) echoes the common name "showy pussytoes" in emphasizing the beauty of this plant. • *Antennaria* species are called "pussytoes" because the flowering heads, especially in fruit, resemble furry cat's paws.

MOUNTAIN SAGEWORT — *Artemisia norvegica*

General Perennial herb, from a branching stem-base, stems single or a few together, 20-50 cm tall, with short runners and sterile rosettes.

Leaves *Glabrous to finely hairy*; basal leaves stalked, *pinnately divided*, the ultimate segments linear; *stem leaves few*, sessile, progressively reduced upwards.

Flowers Yellowish, often tinged with red; marginal flowers female, 6-12; central flowers bisexual, 30-50; heads of disk flowers only, *up to 1 cm wide*, often nodding, several to many in a narrow, often spikelike cluster; *receptacles* (expanded portion of the stalk to which the flowers are attached) *glabrous*; involucre 3-7 mm high, with glabrous to slightly hairy, greenish, brown-margined bracts.

Fruits Glabrous achenes.

Ecology Alpine tundra, subalpine and alpine meadows, grassland, heath; subalpine thickets and open forest. Common and widespread, from medium to high elevations, throughout the region.

Notes: Also known as *Artemisia arctica*.
• Most Artemisias are aromatic, but this species does not have the typical sage smell. • *Artemisia* is perhaps after Artemis, the goddess who represents the variable energies of women. She was the Lady of Wild Things, Huntswoman-in-chief to the gods.

MICHAUX'S MUGWORT — *Artemisia michauxiana*

General Perennial herb, from a woody stem-base, often rhizomatous; stems several, 20-70 cm tall.

Leaves *Primarily along the stem, white-woolly below* at least when young, generally glabrous and green above, *pinnately twice divided*, the short, linear ultimate segments often toothed again.

Flowers Yellowish or purplish; marginal flowers female, 9-12; central flowers bisexual, 15-35; heads of disk flowers only, *3-5 mm wide*, nodding at first, becoming erect, numerous, in a long, fairly tight cluster; *receptacles glabrous*; involucre 3-4 mm high, with glabrous, greenish or yellowish bracts.

Fruits Glabrous achenes.

Ecology Rocky slopes, outcrops, meadows, and open dry forest at low to subalpine elevations. Scattered throughout the region, except apparently absent east of the Rocky Mountains, and less frequent in the North.

Notes: The name mugwort comes from the old Saxon word *muggia* meaning midge and was the name for the European species *A. vulgaris*, which was used for attracting and killing insects. Bunches of the plants were hung in the house and would attract hundreds of insects. The bunches were then placed in a bag and the insects were beaten to death.

SUNFLOWER FAMILY

PASTURE SAGE — *Artemisia frigida*

General Perennial herb, **mat forming** with a stout stem-base or woody crown, often shrubby at the base, more or less matted, with several short, leafy offsets, 10-40 cm tall.

Leaves *Silvery-silky hairy*, small, short stalked below, nearly sessile above, *2-3 times divided in 3's* into linear segments.

Flowers Yellow, often tinged reddish; marginal flowers female, 10-15; central flowers bisexual, 25-50; heads of disk flowers only, 4-6 mm wide, nodding, several to many in a simple or branched, narrow cluster; *receptacles with numerous long hairs* between the flowers; involucres 2-3.5 mm high, with cottony-hairy, brown-margined bracts.

Fruits Glabrous achenes.

Ecology Dry, rocky slopes and south-facing grasslands, sandy terraces. Widespread at low to medium elevations throughout the region.

Notes: *Artemisia campestris* ssp. *borealis* (northern wormwood) occupies similar habitats but has glabrous receptacles and leaves that are not as divided as those of *A. frigida*. • Several species of *Artemisia* were highly valued for their pungent, aromatic fragrance by southern interior native groups, including the Shuswap. Pasture sage was burned to drive away mosquitoes and other biting insects. Pieces of the plant would be placed in bedding to get rid of bedbugs, fleas and lice. In sweathouses the Carrier sat over steaming rocks with sage leaves on them. The fragrant steam would alleviate local pains and 'nervous shooting' (Morice 1892). • The genus *Artemisia* includes several well-known, pungently aromatic species used as vermifuges, stimulants, and culinary herbs, e.g., *Artemisia tridentata* (big sagebrush), *A. absinthium* (absinthe — a harmful liqueur), *A. dracunculus* (tarragon), *A. tilesii* (Aleutian mugwort — has medicinal properties like codeine). The latter two species occur on rocky slopes and riverbars in our region. *A. tilesii* is also reported to be an anti-tumour agent still used by northern groups such as the Tahltans.

YARROW — *Achillea millefolium*

General Perennial herb, aromatic, usually rhizomatous, 10-100 cm tall.

Leaves *Fernlike, pinnately dissected*, the divisions again dissected, stalked below and sessile above.

Flowers Ray flowers usually about 5, **white to sometimes pink or reddish**; disk flowers 10-20, yellowish; heads numerous, in a short, *flat or round-topped cluster*.

Fruits Glabrous, flattened achenes.

Ecology On dry to moist, well-drained, open sites at low to high elevations, often weedy at lower elevations; meadows, rocky slopes, gravel bars, roadsides, clearings, sometimes in open forest. Common and widespread throughout the region.

Notes: Taxonomically this is one of the most complex species in our flora and has been the subject of extensive studies. It is probably best, at least for ecological purposes in the northern interior of British Columbia, to recognize a single, variable species. • *Achillea sibirica* (Siberian yarrow) has sharply toothed, not compoundly dissected, leaves, and can be found on gravelly river banks and lake shores and meadows in the northeastern part of the region. • Yarrow was, and still is, widely used in a variety of herbal remedies. The Carrier placed washed and crushed roots in their teeth to stop toothache, bathed in infusions of leaves and stems for rheumatism, or used decoctions as a tonic or astringent. To ease sore throats, the Gitksan gargled with decoctions of all but the roots of this plant. • According to legend, *Achillea* was used by Achilles to stop the bleeding of his soldiers' wounds and for this reason it is sometimes called "military plant." (It contains the alkaloid achilleine, which nowadays is sometimes used to suppress menses.) The specific name *millefolium* is French for thousand leaves, referring to the highly divided leaves.

Senecio silhouettes

Senecio lugens

Senecio pauperculus

Senecio triangularis

ARROW-LEAVED GROUNDSEL *Senecio triangularis*

General Perennial herb, with a fibrous-rooted stem-base or rhizome; stems clustered, 30-150 cm tall.

Leaves Basal ones thin, broadly to narrowly *triangular* to triangular heart shaped, squared-off at the base, *strongly toothed*, stalked, more or less glabrous above, often short-hairy on the veins below; stem leaves similar, larger, gradually reduced upwards, becoming sessile.

Flowers Ray flowers *yellow*, usually about 8; disk flowers yellow; heads few to numerous in a short, flat-topped cluster; involucres 8-12 mm high, the bracts greenish, with black and tufted-hairy tips, otherwise glabrous to sparsely hairy.

Fruits Glabrous achenes.

Ecology Moist to wet, well-drained meadows, streambanks, slide tracks, thickets, open forest. Typically a subalpine-alpine species, but also in seepage areas in medium-elevation forests; common and often abundant throughout the region.

Notes: The large, triangular, saw-toothed leaves make identification of *S. triangularis* almost foolproof, but in northwestern B.C. (e.g., Haines Triangle) watch out for *Saussurea americana* (American sawwort), which also grows in lush meadows and has similar leaves, but purplish flowers. • Another common name is triangle-leaved, or arrowleaf butterweed. • *Senecio* is from *senex*, meaning an old man, because the receptacle lacks hairs or bristles like the bald head of an old man. • With over 1500 species throughout the world, *Senecio* is one of the largest genera of flowering plants.

BLACK-TIPPED GROUNDSEL   *Senecio lugens*

General Perennial herb, with a fibrous-rooted, short, thick, ascending or horizontal rhizome; stems solitary, 10-80 cm tall.

Leaves Basal leaves relatively *thick*, lance shaped to elliptic, *more or less round toothed*, stalked; stem leaves linear to lance shaped, reduced upwards, sessile; glabrous or sparingly woolly.

Flowers Ray flowers *yellow*, 7-15 mm long; disk flowers yellow; heads few to several, in a compact cluster; involucres 5-9 mm high, the *inner bracts greenish, with black, dark-hairy tips*, otherwise mostly glabrous.

Fruits Glabrous achenes.

Ecology Tundra, heath, meadows, thickets, streambanks and lake shores, fens, open forest. Common from moderate to high elevations in the northern half of the region.

Notes: The common name "groundsel" was originally applied to the well-known garden weed *Senecio vulgaris* – an introduced European species. "Groundsel" appears to have been derived from an old English word *grundeswylige* meaning ground-swallower – an apt name for such a rampant weed. *S. vulgaris* was, however, also used by early herbalists as a treatment for inflammation or watering of the eyes. It may be that the name was mistakenly transcribed to *gundeswelge* from *gund* meaning matter discharged from eyes and *swelge* meaning swallower.

CANADIAN BUTTERWEED   *Senecio pauperculus*

General Perennial herb, with a fibrous-rooted, short, simple or slightly branched stem-base; stems solitary, 15-60 cm tall.

Leaves Basal leaves *thin*, broadly lance shaped to elliptic or oblong, *toothed throughout*, stalked, glabrous; stem leaves lance shaped, *toothed or lobed*, progressively reduced upwards, sessile.

Flowers Ray flowers *yellow*, 5-10 mm long; disk flowers yellow; heads few to several in an umbel-like cluster; involucres 3-8 mm high, the *bracts green or tinged with purple at the tip*.

Fruits Glabrous or sometimes finely hairy achenes.

Ecology Moist forest, meadows, streambanks, lakeshores, and marshes at low to moderate elevations. Scattered throughout the region but less common on Nechako and Stikine plateaus.

Notes: This species is easily confused with *S. pseudaureus* (streambank butterweed) or *S. streptanthifolius* (Rocky Mountain butterweed). *S. streptanthifolius* is distinguished by its numerous basal leaves which are toothed only above the middle while *S. pseudaureus* is recognized by its rounded or heart-shaped basal leaves. *S. streptanthifolius* also prefers fairly dry, rocky habitats, while *S. pseudaureus* is a species of moist meadows and streambanks. Two other species (*S. indecorus*, rayless mountain butterweed; and *S. pauciflorus*, rayless alpine butterweed) have leaves similar to *S. pauperculus* but lack ray flowers. They are separated mainly by their purple (*S. pauciflorus*) or green (*S. indecorus*) involucral bracts, and *S. pauciflorus* has bright orange rather than yellow flowers.

SPIKELIKE GOLDENROD *Solidago spathulata*

General Perennial herb, with a short stout rhizome or stem-base, 10-60 cm tall.

Leaves Basal and lower leaves large, broadly lance to spoon shaped, usually toothed (at least on the upper half), glabrous; stem leaves similar to the basal but few and *progressively reduced upwards*.

Flowers Ray flowers *yellow*, usually 8; disk flowers yellow, about 13; heads numerous, in *long, narrow, branched cluster*; involucres 3-6 mm high, *5-7 mm broad, the bracts overlapping and often sticky*.

Fruits Densely hairy achenes.

Ecology Open, fairly dry forest, riverbanks, gravel bars, terraces, and meadows at low to moderately high elevations. Widespread throughout the region but often merely sporadic.

Notes: Also known as *Solidago decumbens*. • Goldenrods may be confused with yellow-flowered species of *Hieracium* or *Senecio*, but can be separated by their numerous small (usually less than 1 cm wide) heads. • All goldenrods contain small quantities of natural rubber in their latex. • *Solidago* is another medicinal plant; the name comes from the Latin *solidus* (whole) and *ago* (to make) — i.e., to make whole (or cure).

NORTHERN GOLDENROD *Solidago multiradiata*

General Perennial herb, with a short or rarely elongate rhizome or branching stem-base; stems usually solitary, hairy towards the flowers, 5-30 cm tall.

Leaves Basal and lower leaves large, broadly lance to spoon shaped, usually toothed, glabrous except *conspicuously hairy-margined on the leaf stalks*; stem leaves similar to the basal but *becoming reduced above*.

Flowers Ray flowers *yellow*, 12-18; disk flowers yellow, 15-21; heads several to many, in *dense, short-branched cluster*; involucres 5-8 mm high, *7-14 mm broad, the bracts not obviously overlapping, not sticky*.

Fruits Short-hairy achenes.

Ecology Tundra, rocky ridges, grassy slopes, gravel bars, meadows, sometimes in dry open forest. Widespread throughout the region from medium to high elevations.

Notes: One of the most common and widespread species of our alpine tundra.

CANADA GOLDENROD — *Solidago canadensis*

General Perennial herb, with long, creeping rhizomes, *30-100 cm tall*.

Leaves Basal leaves lacking, lower ones soon deciduous, stem leaves *numerous, crowded, only gradually reduced upwards*, lance-linear to narrowly elliptic, tapering to a sessile base, *saw toothed to entire*, from essentially glabrous to rough-hairy on both sides.

Flowers Ray flowers *yellow*, 10-17; disk flowers yellow; *heads numerous, in dense pyramidal clusters*; involucres 3-4 mm high, 3-6 mm broad, the bracts overlapping and sometimes sticky-glandular.

Fruits Short-hairy achenes.

Ecology Roadsides, meadows, thickets, forest openings or edges, sometimes in open forest, often in disturbed areas. Scattered throughout the region in appropriate habitats at low to moderate elevations.

Notes: Okanagan native children pulled the plants up and played with them like whips. • Goldenrod was reputedly carried into battle during the Crusades and was commonly used as a substitute for the highly taxed English tea during the American Revolution.

Key to *Arnica*

1. Pappus hairs themselves have side-hairs, somewhat like the plume of a feather, tawny or straw-coloured (a) .... *Arnica mollis*

1. Pappus hairs with short stiff side-hairs, usually white or nearly so.

  2. Leaves narrow, basal ones 3-10 times as long as wide (b) ....
  .... *Arnica angustifolia*

  2. Leaves broad, basal ones 1-2.5 (rarely 3) times as long as wide.

    3. Achenes short-hairy throughout; involucre often densely white-hairy; leaves often heart shaped (c) .... *Arnica cordifolia*

    3. Achenes glabrous below, or glabrous throughout; involucre with few or no long hairs; leaves various, stem leaves seldom heart shaped (d) .... *Arnica latifolia*

SUNFLOWER FAMILY

ALPINE ARNICA — *Arnica angustifolia*

General Perennial herb, from an ascending, fibrous-rooted rhizome or stem-base, 10-50 cm tall.

Leaves Basal leaves lance shaped to narrowly elliptic, hairy and often glandular, stalked, entire to toothed, stem leaves opposite, 2-4 pairs (rarely 1 or 5), reduced and becoming sessile and entire upwards.

Flowers Ray flowers *yellow*, 10-16, toothed at the squared-off tips; disk flowers yellow; heads 1 or 3-6, *on densely white-hairy stalks*; involucres 10-18 mm high, the bracts lance-shaped, hairy, and usually glandular.

Fruits Uniformly densely hairy and often glandular achenes; *pappus hairs white with short stiff side-hairs*.

Ecology Moist to dry meadows, tundra, and forest openings. Scattered throughout the region, typically at high elevations but down to lower slopes and valley bottoms in the North.

Notes: Also known as *Arnica alpina*. Species of the genus *Arnica* are the only composites in B.C. with opposite leaves. • An extremely variable species; four subspecies have been recognized in B.C. and all four occur in this region. One of these, *A. angustifolia* ssp. *tomentosa*, is a small, single-headed alpine plant that could be confused in the North with *A. frigida* (northern arnica). *A. frigida* has a single nodding (rather than erect) head and glabrous or sparsely hairy achenes. • Although *Arnica* species were widely used in Europe and parts of North America in herbal remedies, especially for the external treatment of bruises and swellings, there are no written reports of their use by aboriginal people in B.C. • The name *Arnica* translates as lamb's skin, presumably in reference to the soft woolly bracts (involucre) beneath the flower head.

HAIRY ARNICA — *Arnica mollis*

General Perennial herb, from a freely rooted rhizome, 15-60 cm tall; stems solitary, sometimes branched above.

Leaves Basal leaves elliptic, often produced on separate shoots, often deciduous by flowering time; stem leaves 2-4 pairs, opposite, lance shaped to elliptic, reduced above, glabrous to glandular and hairy, stalked below, sessile above, entire to coarsely toothed.

Flowers Ray flowers *yellow*, 14-20, toothed at the tips; disk flowers yellow; heads 1-5, *on hairy and glandular stalks*; involucres 10-18 mm high, the bracts lance-shaped, hairy, and with stalked glands.

Fruits Usually moderately hairy and sometimes glandular achenes; *pappus hairs brownish, somewhat feathery with side-hairs*.

Ecology Moist meadows and open forests at moderate to high elevations. Scattered, merely locally abundant, throughout the region.

Notes: Arnica chamissonis (meadow arnica), another species which may have a brownish pappus, also occurs in the region; however, it has 5-10 pairs of leaves and a distinctive tuft of hairs on the tips of the involucral bracts and tends to grow at lower elevations than *A. mollis*.

MOUNTAIN ARNICA — *Arnica latifolia*

General Perennial herb, from a horizontal rhizome, 10-50 cm tall; stems solitary or occasionally a few clustered together.

Leaves Basal leaves rounded to lance-elliptic, *rarely heart shaped*, usually withered by flowering time, often produced on separate short shoots; stem leaves opposite, 2-4(5) pairs, rounded to lance-elliptic, often becoming narrower and smaller above, thinly hairy and usually sparsely to densely glandular, stalked below, sessile above, usually toothed.

Flowers Ray flowers *yellow*, 8-12, conspicuously toothed at tips; disk flowers yellow; heads usually 1-5, on hairy and sometimes glandular stalks; involucres 7-18 mm high, the bracts lance shaped, sparsely (usually) to densely long-hairy and often glandular.

Fruits *Glabrous or sparsely hairy achenes; pappus hairs white*, with short stiff side-hairs.

Ecology Moist, open forest, meadows, streambanks, and rocky slopes. Fairly common at moderate to high elevations throughout the region.

Notes: Arnica latifolia can be confused with *A. cordifolia*, especially when not in flower or fruit. The involucral bracts and achenes of *A. cordifolia* are generally much hairier than those of *A. latifolia*, which also has stem leaves that are seldom heart-shaped. • Taken internally, arnicas cause a rise in body temperature; applied externally, they are antiseptic.

HEART-LEAVED ARNICA — *Arnica cordifolia*

General Perennial herb, from a long, branching rhizome, 10-60 cm tall; stems solitary or occasionally a few clustered together.

Leaves Basal leaves *heart shaped*, often produced on separate short shoots; stem leaves opposite, 2-4 (5) pairs, larger than the basal ones, heart shaped, becoming lance shaped above, glandular to hairy, stalked below, sessile above, coarsely toothed to entire.

Flowers Ray flowers *yellow*, 9-16, conspicuously toothed at tip; disk flowers yellow; heads usually 1-3, sometimes as many as 7, on hairy and often glandular stalks; involucres 13-22 mm high, the bracts lance shaped, sparsely to densely long-hairy and often glandular.

Fruits *Moderately to densely short-hairy achenes; pappus hairs white*, with short stiff side-hairs.

Ecology Moist to dry, open or dense forests, openings, meadows, and clearings. Common and abundant at low to moderate elevations throughout the region.

Notes: Hybrids between *A. cordifolia* and *A. latifolia* are frequently encountered in our range. These are intermediate in leaf characters but usually have achene characters of only one of the parents. • This is the region's most common arnica, and one of the most common showy-flowered species of the northern forests. It's also one of several species (like fireweed and showy aster) that thrive in the first few years after a stand-destroying disturbance like wildfire or clearcutting and slashburning.

Petasites silhouettes

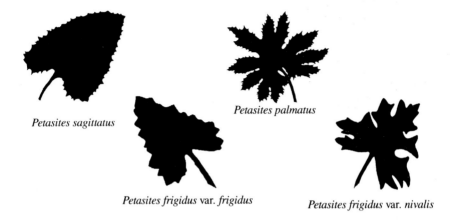

Petasites sagittatus

Petasites palmatus

Petasites frigidus var. frigidus

Petasites frigidus var. nivalis

ARROW-LEAVED COLTSFOOT	*Petasites sagittatus*

General Perennial herb, with **slender** creeping rhizomes, stems many, 10-50 cm tall; flowering stems precede leaves.

Leaves Basal leaves arising directly from rhizome, large, **triangular** to heart shaped, **toothed (with 20 or more teeth per side)** or sometimes nearly entire, green and thinly hairy above, densely white-woolly below, stalked; stem leaves reduced to alternate bracts.

Flowers Ray flowers **whitish**, female; disk flowers **whitish**, bisexual; heads several to many, on glandular or white-woolly stalks; involucres 7-12 mm high, the bracts lance-shaped, with glandular hairs at the base.

Fruits Glabrous achenes.

Ecology Bogs, fens, swamps, and marshes, wet ditches, often in standing water. Scattered at low to moderate elevations throughout the region.

Notes: The leaves of *P. sagittatus* could be confused with those of *P. frigidus* var. *frigidus*, but those of *P. sagittatus* are more arrowhead-shaped and have more teeth (usually more than 20 per side) − compare leaf silhouettes. • Some Alaskan natives chew coltsfoot root or soak it in hot water and drink the tea for tuberculosis, chest problems, sore throat, and stomach ulcers. • *Petasites* is from the Greek *petasos* (a broad-brimmed hat), referring to the large basal leaves characteristic of this genus. • Another common name for species of *Petasites* is "butterbur."

113

SWEET COLTSFOOT   *Petasites frigidus*

General Perennial herb, with **thick**, creeping rhizome, stems numerous, 10-50 cm tall, either with mostly female or mostly male flowers; flowering stems precede leaves.

Leaves Basal leaves **triangular to heart shaped**, large, **with 5-8 broad teeth or deeply lobed into 3-5 coarsely toothed segments**, green and thinly hairy to glabrous above, sparsely to densely white-woolly below, stalked; stem leaves reduced to alternate, reddish bracts.

Flowers Ray flowers **whitish or pink to purplish**; disk flowers **pink to purplish**; heads several, in elongating flat-topped cluster, on glandular and often white-woolly stalks; involucres 6-12 mm high, the bracts lance shaped, with hairs at the base.

Fruits Glabrous achenes.

Ecology Wet to moist meadows, seepage areas, streambanks, and lakeshores. Common from subalpine to alpine elevations throughout the region.

Notes: Petasites frigidus var. *frigidus* (below left) is distinguished by its merely coarsely toothed or shallowly and obscurely lobed leaves; whereas, *P. frigidus* var. *nivalis* (= *P. hyperboreus*) has deeply lobed leaves. • The name "coltsfoot" was originally given to the closely related European species – *Tussilago farfara* – because the leaves supposedly resemble the foot of a colt.

PALMATE COLTSFOOT   *Petasites palmatus*

General Perennial, with **slender**, creeping rhizomes; stems numerous, 10-50 cm tall, either with mostly female or mostly male flowers; flowering stems precede leaves.

Leaves Basal leaves **heart or kidney shaped, deeply divided (to more than two-thirds toward base) into 5-7 toothed lobes**, green and glabrous above, white-woolly below; stem leaves reduced to alternate bracts.

Flowers Ray flowers **creamy white**; disk flowers **whitish to pinkish**; heads several to many, on glandular and often white-woolly stalks; involucres 7-16 mm high, the bracts lance shaped, with hairs at the base.

Fruits Glabrous achenes.

Ecology Moist to wet forest, thickets, swamps, openings, clearings. Common and widespread at low to moderate elevations throughout the region.

Notes: The Quinault Indians in Washington State used the leaves to cover berries in steam-cooking pits. • The coltsfoots are unusual in that the flowering stems come up before the leaves.

Key to Asters

1. Involucre and leaf stalks glandular.
   2. Leaves thick, round to elliptic, usually sharp toothed .... *Aster conspicuus*
   2. Leaves thin, lance shaped, remotely toothed .... *Aster modestus*
1. Involucre and leaf stalks without glands.
      3. Involucral bracts usually with purple tips and margins; disk flowers with the tube (basal part) equalling or longer than the width of the slender limb (the upper expanded part of the flower, including lobes); leaves rough beneath or on both sides .... *Aster sibiricus*
      3. Involucral bracts without purple tips and margins (except occasionally in some forms of *A. foliaceus*); disk flowers with tube shorter than the limb; leaves not rough beneath.
         4. Basal or lower stem leaves heart shaped and distinctly stalked .... *Aster ciliolatus*
         4. Basal or lower stem leaves not heart shaped and usually sessile or nearly so.
            5. Plants slender, leaves less than 1 cm wide; rhizomes slender, less than 2 mm thick; plants of wetlands and lake margins .... *Aster borealis*
            5. Plants differing in one or more respects from the above.
               6. Involucral bracts, at least the outer, loose or spreading, with minutely spiny tips; ray flowers white, rarely pinkish to purplish .... *Aster ericoides*
               6. Involucral bracts appressed to spreading, without spiny tips; ray flowers usually blue to purple .... *Aster foliaceus*

American botanist Asa Gray (1810-1888) had this to say of *Aster*: "Never was so rascally a genus! . . . [they] may reduce me to blank despair." (cited in Clark 1973). This is surely an apt description of this difficult genus. Here we describe 7 species (of the approximately 11 which occur in our region).

GREAT NORTHERN ASTER   *Aster modestus*

General Perennial herb, with creeping rhizomes; stems single, simple or branched, 30-100 cm tall, sparsely to densely hairy and glandular up towards the flowers.

Leaves Basal leaves somewhat smaller than the others, usually withered by flowering time; stem leaves **lance shaped, sessile**, more or less clasping, glabrous above, sparsely hairy beneath; **margins smooth to few toothed**.

Flowers Ray flowers **violet or purple**, 20-45; disk flowers yellow; heads few to many, on glandular stalks; involucres 7-11 mm high, the bracts narrowly lance shaped, **glandular**, greenish.

Fruits Sparsely hairy achenes; pappus hairs whitish or yellowish.

Ecology Moist to wet forests, openings, swamps, stream and river banks, and clearings. Common throughout the region at low to moderate elevations.

Notes: Aster modestus and *A. conspicuus* are the only species of *Aster* in this region with glandular involucral bracts. • *Aster* is the Greek, Latin, and English name for a star and describes the appearance of the flower heads.

SHOWY ASTER — *Aster conspicuus*

General Perennial herb, with creeping rhizomes; stems usually single and unbranched, **30-100 cm tall**, glandular and sometimes also hairy up towards the flowers.

Leaves Basal and lower leaves small and soon withering; stem leaves egg shaped **to elliptic**, clasping, **mostly sessile, thick, sharp toothed, with "sandpapery" surface** when mature.

Flowers Ray flowers **blue to violet**, 12-35; disk flowers yellow; heads few to many, on glandular stalks; involucres 9-12 mm high, the bracts lance shaped, **densely glandular**, green at the tip, whitish at the base.

Fruits **Glabrous** achenes; pappus hairs whitish.

Ecology Moist to dry, open forests, thickets, meadows, and clearings. Common and often abundant in the southern half of the region (south of 57°) at low to medium elevations; also in the Peace River district.

Notes: Aster conspicuus can be distinguished from *A. modestus* on the basis of thicker, wider, and sharply toothed leaves, as well as usually drier habitats. • Much like fireweed and heart-leaved arnica, showy aster has the ability to maintain and extend itself, by

means of spreading rhizomes, in sterile condition under a closed forest canopy. After removal of the canopy by fire or other disturbance, these species respond with vigorous growth and profuse flowering.

ARCTIC ASTER — *Aster sibiricus*

General Perennial herb, simple or few branched, with slender, creeping rhizomes; stems arising singly or a few together, simple or few branched, **5-45 cm tall**, more or less hairy.

Leaves Basal leaves small, usually withered by flowering time, firm, sessile; stem leaves progressively reduced upwards, **lance shaped to oblong or elliptic, mostly sessile**, sparsely to copiously short-hairy on the lower surface; **margins smooth** or with a few small teeth.

Flowers Ray flowers **purple**, 10-25; disk flowers yellow; heads 1-20, on hairy, not glandular, stalks; involucres 7-15 mm high, the bracts oblong to lance shaped, somewhat hairy but **not glandular**, the outer green, the inner purplish or purple tipped.

Fruits **Hairy** achenes; pappus hairs brown or yellowish.

Ecology Moist to dry alpine meadows and rocky slopes down to sandy or rocky streambanks and terraces at lower elevations. Distributed primarily in the North at all elevations and south at higher elevations along the Rockies; also in the Chilcotin Mountains.

Notes: The purplish or purple-tipped involucral bracts are distinctive. *Aster alpinus* (alpine aster) is a somewhat similar alpine species of the North, but has only one flower head, entire leaves, and white or pink ray flowers. • All of the asters are browsed by a number of wildlife species, especially ungulates such as deer and moose.

LEAFY ASTER — *Aster foliaceus*

General Perennial herb, with creeping rhizomes or a stem base; stems single or several together, simple or branched, 10-60 cm tall, sparsely hairy to glabrous.

Leaves Extremely variable; basal and lower leaves broadly lance to egg shaped, usually stalked, often deciduous; middle stem leaves *lance shaped to rounded, sessile, and often clasping*, glabrous to soft-hairy, with *mostly smooth margins.*

Flowers Ray flowers *blue to purplish*, 15-60; disk flowers yellow; heads solitary to many in a flat-topped to rounded cluster, on hairy stalks; involucres 7-10 mm high, the bracts graduated in size, *often large and somewhat leafy, green with white margins at the base, glabrous.*

Fruits Glabrous to grey-hairy achenes; pappus hairs white or straw coloured to occasionally reddish.

Ecology Moist meadows, open forests and clearings, at all elevations. Throughout our region south of 56° and in the extreme northwest corner of the province.

Notes: Sometimes difficult to separate from *Aster subspicatus* (Douglas' aster). The latter has outer non-leafy involucral bracts with yellowish or brownish margins at the base and slightly if at all clasping leaves, and is a more typically coastal species. • Could also be confused with *Erigeron peregrinus* (subalpine daisy), especially when both species grow together in subalpine meadows. *E. peregrinus* has equal-sized, non-graduated involucral bracts.

FRINGED ASTER — *Aster ciliolatus*

General Perennial herb, with long creeping rhizomes; stems single or several together, usually unbranched, 20-80 cm tall, hairy or glabrous.

Leaves Basal and lower leaves *long stalked, heart shaped,* sharply toothed, and often soon deciduous, often produced on separate short shoots; middle and upper stem leaves *egg shaped*, becoming sessile, fewer toothed, the *stalks broadly winged and with long-hairy margins.*

Flowers Ray flowers *pale blue*, 12-25; disk flowers yellow; heads several to numerous in an open cluster; involucres 5-8 mm high, the bracts lance-oblong, *glabrous except for the sometimes long-hairy margins, green at the tip and whitish at the base.*

Fruits Mostly glabrous achenes.

Ecology In dry to moist, open to closed forests, openings, and clearings. Widespread at low to moderate elevations south of 55°; also common east of the Rockies north of 55°.

Notes: The long, hairy-margined stalks of the lower leaves are characteristic for this species. • Asters are often confused with species of *Erigeron*, but the Erigerons bloom earlier in the year, the Asters later. A good way to remember this is that *Aster* spp. are sometimes called "Michaelmas" or "Christmas" daisies, because they sometimes bloom as late as Christmas (further south).

RUSH ASTER — *Aster borealis*

General Perennial herb, with a *long slender rhizome*, stems arising singly, unbranched, 15-80 cm tall, hairy in lines from the upper leaf bases and somewhat glandular on upper part.

Leaves Basal leaves short stalked, reduced and soon deciduous; *stem leaves linear to oblong*, sessile with rounded and sometimes clasping bases, glabrous, with entire margins.

Flowers Ray flowers *white to pale blue*, 20-50; disk flowers yellow; *heads relatively small, few to several in rather short compact cluster*, on hairy stalks; involucres 5-7 mm high, the bracts oblong, overlapping in several series, *greenish and often whitish near the base, often purple tipped, glabrous*.

Fruits Hairy achenes.

Ecology Marshes, fens, bogs, wet meadows, and lakeshores. Scattered at low to moderate elevations mostly north of 57°, but also in the south-central part of the region.

Notes: Also known as *Aster junciformis*.

TUFTED WHITE PRAIRIE ASTER — *Aster ericoides* ssp. *pansus*

General Perennial herb, with a *stem-base or short rhizome*, fibrous-rooted; stems clustered, branched above, rough-hairy, 30-80 cm tall.

Leaves *Mostly along stem, numerous, firm, linear,* sessile, rough margined, somewhat hairy, *often spiny tipped*.

Flowers Ray flowers *white*, 12-30; disk flowers yellow; *heads numerous, small*, in a *large branched cluster*; involucres 3-5 mm high, the bracts lance shaped, overlapping in three series, *the outer bracts loose and with green spiny tips, glabrous*.

Fruits Achenes.

Ecology Dry open forests, grasslands, and meadows; tolerant of alkaline soil. East of the Rocky Mountains, south of 58°; also in the dry south-central part of the region (Cariboo – Chilcotin); sporadic at low to moderate elevations.

Notes: Also known as *Aster pansus*. • *Aster falcatus* (little grey aster) is another white-rayed, narrow-leaved species of dry sites in the Northeast, but has been separated from *A. ericoides* on the basis of long rhizomes, stems not clustered, and solitary or few heads.

ARCTIC DAISY — *Erigeron humilis*

General Perennial herb, with a short taproot or short, brittle stem-base and often some fibrous roots; **stems single, 3-20 cm tall, hairy with greyish or dark hairs**.

Leaves Basal leaves broadly lance shaped to spoon shaped, commonly glabrous or nearly so by flowering time; stem leaves linear to lance shaped, reduced, sessile; leaves with entire margins.

Flowers Ray flowers **white to purplish**, numerous (about 50-150); disk flowers yellow; **heads solitary**; involucres 6-9 mm high, the bracts lance-oblong, purplish black or greenish, **with long multicellular hairs with purplish black crosswalls**.

Fruits Hairy achenes; pappus hairs white to tan.

Ecology Tundra, snowbeds, seepage sites, rocky ledges, and scree. In moist to wet alpine sites, also sometimes in bogs at lower elevations. Widely distributed throughout the region, usually at high elevations.

Notes: At least 20 species of *Erigeron* occur within the area covered by this guide; we've described only four of the most common. For more information, please consult Douglas *et al.* (1989). •*Erigeron purpuratus* (purple daisy) is a similar dwarf alpine species, but has reddish-purple pappus hairs and occurs only in the far North (north of 58° in this region).

BITTER FLEABANE — *Erigeron acris*

General Biennial or perennial herb from a simple or branched stem-base and a taproot; stems solitary to several together, **10-70 cm tall**, hairy or glabrous.

Leaves Basal leaves broadly lance to spoon shaped, stalked, usually entire; stem leaves ample or reduced, lance shaped to linear, becoming sessile, entire.

Flowers Ray flowers **pink to purplish or white**, numerous, of two kinds (the outer with a long narrow tube and narrow rays, the inner tubular but rayless); disk flowers yellow; **heads few (occasionally solitary) to many** in a long cluster; involucres 5-11 mm high, the bracts narrowly lance shaped, **glandular or hairy or both**.

Fruits Hairy achenes; **pappus hairs straw coloured**.

Ecology Gravel bars, river terraces, wetlands, streambanks, lakeshores, clearings and roadsides, moist meadows and open forests, at low to moderate (var. *asteroides* and var. *elatus*) or high (var. *debilis*) elevations. A very variable species widespread throughout the region, often weedy.

Notes: The common name fleabane was first applied to European species of *Erigeron*. It was believed that bunches of the dried plants hung in the house would drive out the fleas. •*Erigeron* comes from the Greek *eri* meaning spring and *geron* meaning an old man — in reference to the hairy seed heads or possibly to some hairy spring-flowering species.

PHILADELPHIA FLEABANE *Erigeron philadelphicus*

General *Biennial or short-lived perennial*, with stem-base and a taproot or fibrous roots; stems 20-70 cm tall, with long spreading hairs or glabrous.

Leaves Basal leaves broadly lance shaped, coarsely toothed, hairy, short stalked; stem leaves progressively reduced in size, lance shaped, clasping at base, often toothed, sessile.

Flowers Ray flowers *pink to pinkish purple or white, numerous (over 150), very narrow*; disk flowers yellow; *heads few to many*; involucres 4-6 mm high, the bracts lance-oblong, *with broad clear margins, hairy on midvein or glabrous*.

Fruits Sparsely hairy achenes; *pappus hairs whitish*.

Ecology Open forests, thickets, streambanks, roadsides, clearings. Scattered at low to moderate elevations throughout the region except in the far northwest.

Notes: Erigeron speciosus (showy fleabane) is another species with numerous, narrow ray flowers, but it has smaller, entire stem leaves and occurs only in the southeastern part of the region. • Unlike W.C. Fields, on the whole we would never rather be in Philadelphia, especially when visiting Liard Hotsprings, where you can find nice populations of this species.

SUBALPINE DAISY
Erigeron peregrinus ssp. *callianthemus*

General Perennial herb, from a rhizome or short stem-base; stems single, unbranched, 10-60 cm tall, hairy or glabrous.

Leaves Basal leaves narrowly or broadly lance to spoon shaped, tapering to the stalk, variable in size, 1-20 cm long, essentially glabrous, often hairy margined; stem leaves similar to lower ones, sometimes clasping, ample or greatly reduced.

Flowers Ray flowers *pink, lavender, or reddish purple, sometimes whitish, 30-80*; disk flowers yellow; *heads mostly solitary*; involucres 6-12 mm high, the bracts lance-oblong, *sticky-hairy*.

Fruits Hairy achenes; *pappus hairs white to tan*.

Ecology Moist to wet meadows and open forests from moderate to high elevations. Common in suitable habitats throughout; one of the most typical species of subalpine meadows in the southern half of the region, less abundant in the North.

Notes: The Thompson Indians of the southern Interior called this plant "star-flower" and used the flower heads as a pattern in basketry.

Lilies

Lilies are members of the plant family Liliaceae. As with the orchids, northern naturalists might not immediately recognize our local species as relatives of the large, showy lilies available at flower shops. Closer examination reveals the characteristic traits of the lily family: parallel-veined leaves and (except for *Maianthemum*) flower parts in 3's. Many of the lilies occur only in the southern parts of our region, and are uncommon or absent from boreal forests.

Though the family contains some poisonous species (e.g., mountain death-camas and Indian hellebore), other species were used extensively for food or medicine by native groups in the north.

A key to the lilies of northern B.C. is provided. As well, we have designed a conspectus to assist in separating the species of fairybells, false Solomon's-seals and twistedstalks in our region − without flowers, they are very difficult! Taylor (1966) provides further information about B.C.'s lilies.

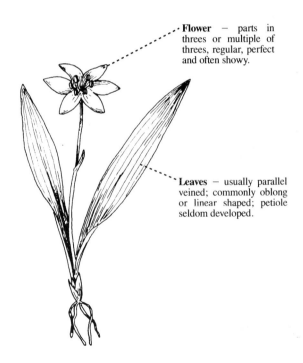

Flower − parts in threes or multiple of threes, regular, perfect and often showy.

Leaves − usually parallel veined; commonly oblong or linear shaped; petiole seldom developed.

 **LILIES**

Conspectus of *Disporum, Smilacina, Streptopus* (Lily Family)

	Disporum hookeri	*Disporum trachycarpum*	*Streptopus amplexifolius*	*Streptopus roseus*
Rhizomes	slender	slender	thick, short, covered with fibrous roots	slender
Stems	erect, sparingly branched, up to 100 cm tall; usually with irregularly curled hairs	erect, sparingly branched, 30-70 cm tall; with irregularly curled hairs, at least when young	erect, freely branched (usually from below the middle), 40-100 cm tall; glabrous at least above; nodes glabrous	erect, usually unbranched, 15-30 cm tall; hairy-fringed at nodes, otherwise glabrous
Leaves	lance to egg shaped, usually somewhat clasping at base, 5-13 cm long; lower surface somewhat rough hairy, upper surface sparsely so or glabrous	egg shaped to oblong, somewhat clasping at base, 3-9 cm long; lower surface moderately hairy with flattened hairs, upper surface glabrous	egg to broadly lance shaped, clasping at base, 5-14 cm long; glabrous on lower surface	egg shaped to elliptic, not clasping at base, 5-10 cm long; glabrous on surfaces, not glaucous below
	margins with forward-pointing hairs	margins with long spreading (not forward-pointing) hairs	margins entire or with irregularly spaced minute teeth (not evident)	margins with irregularly spaced hairs
Flowers	1-3, at tips of stems; narrowly bell shaped, 10-15 mm long, creamy white; ovary football shaped, distinctly pointed; style usually hairy; stigma not 3-cleft	1-2 at tips of stems; narrowly bell shaped, 8-12 mm long, creamy white; ovary egg shaped, distinctly rounded; style glabrous; stigma usually 3-cleft	usually 1 (sometimes 2) on sharply bent stalk from leaf axils; bell shaped with flaring tips, 8-11 mm long, greenish white	single on curved stalks from leaf axils; bell shaped; usually rose coloured with white tips, sometimes greenish yellow streaked with reddish purple
Fruit	lemon-yellow & finally orange-red, egg shaped, often hairy, 4-6 seeded	orange to red, subglobose, usually warty-roughened, velvety in appearance, 6-12 seeded	yellow to red, oval-oblong, 10-15 mm long (sometimes turning dark purple)	red, globose to somewhat oblong, 5-7 mm long

| | Zigzag stems sometimes | | |
Streptopus streptopoides	*Smilacina racemosa*	*Smilacina stellata*	*Smilacina trifolia*
very slender	stout, fleshy, brownish, knotty	slender, pale	very slender, scaly, whitish
erect to spreading, unbranched, 5-15 cm tall; coarsely hairy, fringed at nodes	erect (stiffly arched), unbranched, 30-100 cm tall; finely hairy at least above	erect to arching, unbranched, 20-40 cm tall; finely hairy	erect, but slender and weak, 5-20 cm tall
egg to lance shaped, not clasping at base, 3-5 cm long; glabrous on surfaces	egg shaped to oblong-elliptic, often somewhat clasping at base, 5-15 cm long; finely hairy; often in two ranks on stem	lance shaped to oblong, abruptly narrowed and +/- clasping at base, 5-17 cm long; often finely hairy on lower surface; flat or folded, often in two ranks	oval to oblong, lance shaped, tapering to a somewhat sheathing base, 3-13 cm long; glabrous; leaves 2-4, usually 3
margins with closely crowded, regular teeth			
single on curved stalks from leaf axils; saucer shaped, with flaring, curved-back tips; rose coloured or greenish with strong purple tinge; yellowish green tips	small, numerous in branched, egg- or pyramid-shaped, 5- to 15-cm-long terminal cluster; 1.5-3 mm long, white, on very short stalks	small, few (usually 5-10) in short, unbranched, 2- to 5-cm-long, terminal cluster (sessile); 3-6 mm long, creamy white; flower stalks as long or longer than flowers	small, few (2-10) in an unbranched terminal cluster (long-stalked); about 3 mm long, white to greenish white; flower stalks longer than flowers
red, globose, about 5 mm in diameter	red (sometimes dotted with purple), globose, about 5 mm in diameter	greenish yellow, 6-striped with purple becoming dark blue or reddish black, globose, about 8-10 mm in diameter	dark red, about 5 mm in diameter

Key to Lilies

1. Leaves grasslike, linear
  2. Petals pink to rose-purple; growing in dry places; entire plant smelling strongly of onion .... *Allium cernuum*
  2. Petals greenish or white; growing in wetter places; plant not smelling of onion
    3. Plant growing from a bulb; stem not sticky; commonly occurring in grassy alpine meadows and tundra, or in the Liard Plain (near Cassiar) in dry pine forests with kinnikinnick on coarse-textured soils; flowers smelling foul .... *Zygadenus elegans*
    3. Plant growing from a rhizome; stems sticky; usually in wet, boggy, or marshy habitats; flowers not with any particular smell .... *Tofieldia glutinosa*
1. Leaves not grasslike
    4. Leaves occurring in whorls of 6-9 on the stem; flowers large, bright orange .... *Lilium columbianum*
    4. Leaves not in whorls; flowers not bright orange
      5. Leaves basal, tongue shaped to lance shaped, 2-3; fruit a shiny blue berry .... *Clintonia uniflora*
      5. Principal leaves not basal, occurring on stem; fruit not a shiny blue berry
        6. Stem branched
          7. Flowers axillary (arise between stem and leaf); leaf bases nearly encircling stem; stem usually not hairy .... *Streptopus amplexifolius*
          7. Flowers at the tips of the branches of the main stem; leaf bases not surrounding stem; stem hairy
            8. Leaves not hairy on the upper surface, the marginal hairs irregular, spreading, flattened, not pointing forward (use hand lens) ...... *Disporum trachycarpum*
            8. Leaves usually hairy on the upper surface, the marginal hairs pronounced,not flattened, distinctly pointing forward (use hand lens) .... *Disporum hookeri*
        6. Stem not branched
          9. Flowers axillary (arising between stem and leaf)
            10. Flowers bell shaped; marginal hairs on leaves coarse and visible; usually 15-30 cm tall .... *Streptopus roseus*
            10. Flowers saucer shaped with petals and sepals spreading; marginal hairs on leaves microscopic; usually 5-15 cm tall ... *Streptopus streptopoides*
          9. Flowers in terminal clusters
            11. Flowers on stalks attached directly to a main stem axis; plants 5-40 cm tall
              12. Petals and sepals 4; leaves 1 or 2, distinctly stalked, broadly arrow shaped with rounded lobes ..... *Maianthemum canadense*
              12. Petals and sepals 6; leaves sessile
                13. Leaves 2-4 (usually 3), oval; in bogs and fens .... *Smilacina trifolia*
                13. Leaves more than 4, lance shaped; not usually in bogs and fens .... *Smilacina stellata*
            11. Flowers on stalks attached to branches off a main axis; plants 30-200 cm tall
              14. Flower cluster usually less than 10 cm long; stem somewhat arched, not hairy; leaves 2 ranked, not pleated .... *Smilacina racemosa*
              14. Flower cluster more than 20 cm long; stem erect, very stout, hairy but sometimes sparsely so; leaves spirally arranged, pleated .... *Veratrum viride*

NODDING ONION — *Allium cernuum*

General Perennial, from oval, **tapering, faintly pink coated**, usually **clustered bulbs**; stems slender, somewhat angled, up to 50 cm tall; **smelling strongly of onion**.

Leaves Several per bulb, linear, grasslike, flat or channelled; remaining green during flowering.

Flowers **Pink to rose-purple**, bell shaped, numerous; arranged in nodding, umbrella-shaped cluster.

Fruits Three-lobed capsules.

Ecology Dry open woods and exposed grassy places, rocky crevices and sandy soils, often with Douglas-fir. Scattered but locally common, at low elevations in the southern part of the region, north to 55°.

Notes: If you are in the alpine tundra and you find small, very narrow, onion-like leaves that don't smell of onions and aren't attached to a bulb, most likely it is the alp lily (*Lloydia serotina*), which has a creamy white, purple-lined flower, but blooms very soon after snow melt. • *Allium* is the genus which contains not only onions but also garlic, leeks, and chives. The bulbs were used widely by all interior natives. Harvested before flowering, they were eaten raw (together with the leaves), steamed, boiled, or roasted or were used for flavouring other foods such as salmon and meat. The bulbs were also dried for later use. The Gitksan name for this plant literally means Raven's underarm odour. The Gitksan say that moose meat from the upper Kispiox valley is automatically flavoured with wild onion. • **CAUTION: Wild onion bulbs can be confused with those of death-camas (*Zygadenus* spp.; see below) but the latter do not have an onion odour.**

MOUNTAIN DEATH-CAMAS — *Zygadenus elegans*

General Perennial from oval **bulbs covered with blackish scales**; stems 30-50 cm tall with 1 or 2 leaves, glaucous, often pinkish.

Leaves Mainly basal, glaucous, grasslike becoming smaller up the stem.

Flowers Greenish to yellowish white, with **green glands at the base of the petals**, foul smelling, few to several in loose, spreading terminal sprays, lily-like.

Fruits Three-lobed capsules.

Ecology Open forests, damp meadows, and rocky or grassy slopes. Frequent at low to alpine elevations, mainly in the northern part of our region.

Notes: *Z. venenosus* var. *gramineus* (meadow death-camas) is a similar species, with smaller petals (less than 8 mm long, vs. greater than 10 mm for *Z. elegans*), which occurs primarily from Williams Lake south. • This is a very poisonous plant. The bulb and leaves are poisonous to humans and grazing animals. Symptoms include vomiting, lowered body temperature, difficult breathing, and finally coma. • The interior native peoples recognized its poisonous nature and were careful to distinguish between its bulb and those of other bulbs and roots regularly harvested for food. The safest distinction for most is that the bulb does not have an onion odour. • Okanagan people used the mashed bulbs as arrow poison.

125

Sticky false asphodel — *Tofieldia glutinosa*

General Perennial from fairly stout, vertical rhizome covered with fibrous remains of old leaf bases; stems up to 40 cm tall, smooth below, very **glandular-hairy (sticky) on upper part of stem**.

Leaves Basal (2-4), sheathing, *irislike*, half the length of stem; with 1 or 2 smaller ones on stem.

Flowers Small, white, or greenish white (anthers often **purplish and conspicuous**); several in dense, terminal clusters.

Fruits Large, erect, **reddish purple capsules**.

Ecology Bogs, fens, wet meadows, streambanks. Uncommon but sometimes locally abundant, from valley bottoms to the alpine, throughout the region.

Notes: T. pusilla (common false asphodel) and *T. coccinea* (northern false asphodel) are similar species occurring in the area covered by this guide. Both have smooth (not glandular-sticky) stems; *T. pusilla* is occasional on very wet sites in northern B.C., with a leafless stem and greenish white flowers, and *T. coccinea* is very rare (collected only in the northern Rockies and around Fort Nelson), with one or more leaves on the stem, and purplish flowers. • The origin of the name "asphodel" is obscure, but ancient. It is the flower of the Elysian Fields – Homer's meadows of asphodel inhabited by the souls of the dead. This would fit with one possible origin – from the Greek *a* meaning not and *spodos* meaning ashes. Another source says it is from the Greek *a* (not) and *sphallo* (I surpass) – meaning a stately plant of great beauty.• In medieval England the name was somehow corrupted to the now widely used Daffodil (*Narcissus* sp.). • *Tofieldia* is named for English botanist Thomas Tofield (1730-1779).

Tiger lily — *Lilium columbianum*

General Perennial, from deep-seated oval white bulb with thick scales; stems slender, to 1 m tall.

Leaves **Narrowly lance shaped**, usually arranged in several **whorls** of 6-9 on stem; upper stem leaves may be scattered.

Flowers **Large, showy, bright orange**, with deep red or purple spots near centre, petals curved backwards; few to many, nodding at top of stem.

Fruits Barrel-shaped capsules.

Ecology Meadows, thickets, open forest, and clearings. Common at low to subalpine elevations in the southeast, north to 54°.

Notes: L. philadelphicum is similar, with erect (not drooping) flowers; it is uncommon, and occurs (in our range) only in the southeastern part of the region, in and east of the Rocky Mountains. • The bulbs were eaten by interior native peoples whenever they were available; they are reported to be strong tasting, peppery, and bitter. For this reason they were never eaten raw, but cooked by boiling or steaming, or used to flavour other foods. Called "beaver-stick" by the Carrier and Chilcotin Indians, they were believed to be a good health food. The bulbs of *L. philadelphicum* were also eaten by interior groups where available. • The name tiger probably comes from the spots on the petals. Also called Columbia lily and Oregon lily. The spots also give rise to the superstition that smelling the tiger lily will give you freckles!

HOOKER'S FAIRYBELLS · *Disporum hookeri*

General Perennial from slender rhizome; stems with few branches, to 1 m tall, with irregularly curled hairs; very similar to *D. trachycarpum*.

Leaves Oval to lance shaped with pointed tips, somewhat clasping at base, slightly hairy on upper surface, 5-13 cm long; **margins with forward pointing hairs**.

Flowers Creamy white, narrow, **bell shaped**, 1-3 (usually 2) at tip of branch; **style usually hairy**.

Fruits Lemon yellow to orange-red (ultimately), egg-shaped berries, often hairy, 4-6 seeded.

Ecology Wooded areas, usually where moist, often in deep shade. Scattered at low elevations in the southern part of the region (below 55°) except for the southwestern plateau area.

Notes: The pointed leaf tips of Hooker's fairybells, sometimes called "drip tips," provide a way for the leaves to shed the ample moisture which falls where this species often grows. The leaves of *D. trachycarpum*, which occurs in drier climates as well, are not nearly so well designed for shedding water. • Not generally eaten by interior native people, although the Thompson ate the berries raw. • *Disporum* means 2 seeded, probably in reference to the arrangement of flowers and fruit at branch tips; *hookeri* is named for European botanist John Hooker. "Fairybells" refers to the beautiful flowers of *Disporum* spp.

ROUGH-FRUITED FAIRYBELLS · *Disporum trachycarpum*

General Perennial from slender creeping rhizome; stems with few branches, 30-60 cm tall, slightly hairy when young; very similar to *D. hookeri*.

Leaves Oval to oblong with somewhat pointed tips, somewhat clasping at base, with crinkly edges, not hairy on upper surface, 3-10 cm long; **long spreading hairs on margins not all pointing forward**.

Flowers Creamy white, narrowly **bell shaped**, 1-2 at tip of branch; **style glabrous**.

Fruits At first green, becoming orange to red, rounded berries, triangular in cross-section, with **warty-velvety roughened surface**; 6-12 seeded.

Ecology Moist to dry, coniferous and deciduous forest, forest edges and clearings. Scattered at low elevations in the region south of 56°, except absent on the southwestern plateau.

Notes: Distinguished from Hooker's fairybells by close examination of the hairs on the leaf margins, and by the rough, warty surface of the fruits. • The berries were not generally eaten by interior native peoples. Kootenay called them "grizzly bear's favorite food" but did not consider them edible. However, the Shuswap ate the berries raw and called them "false raspberries." • The species name *trachycarpum* means "rough-fruited;" this and the mildly suggestive common name refer to the warty surface of the berries.

CLASPING TWISTEDSTALK — *Streptopus amplexifolius*

General Perennial from thick, short, horizontal rhizome covered with fibrous roots; stems 0.4-1.0 m tall, smooth, **branched**, sometimes bent at nodes (zig-zag).

Leaves 5-14 cm long, oval to oval-lance-shaped, pointed, **clasping the stem at base**, glaucuous beneath; **leaf margins may have inconspicuous, irregularly spaced teeth**.

Flowers Greenish white, bell shaped with flaring tips, 1-2 hanging from each leaf axil along stem, **on thin kinked stalk**.

Fruits Yellow to red, oval-oblong berries (sometimes turning dark purple).

Ecology Moist rich forest, streambanks, avalanche tracks, subalpine thickets, clearings. Widespread throughout the region except in the alpine.

Notes: The branched stem separates this species from other twistedstalks; the flower attachment separates it from fairybells (which also have branched stems). • Although some southern native people reportedly ate the berries in large quantities, most groups considered them inedible or poisonous and referred to the berries as "snake berries" or "grizzly bear's favourite food." The berries are used by natives in the Bristol Bay area of Alaska. The young tender shoots are eaten as a salad vegetable in Alaska. They have a cucumberlike flavour, earning the plant the local names "cucumber plant" or "cucumber root." Some interior tribes used the roots or whole plants, tied to their clothes or hair, as a scent. • The name twistedstalk probably refers to the zig-zag stem, though in this species the flower stalks are also strongly bent. • The scientific and common names are the same here; *Streptopus* is from the Greek *streptos* (twisted) and *podus* (foot), and *amplexifolius* is from the Latin *amplexor* (to surround) and *folius* (leaf), hence the "clasping twistedstalk."

SMALL TWISTEDSTALK — *Streptopus streptopoides*

General Perennial from creeping, very slender rhizome; **stems unbranched**, 5-15 cm tall, with a fringe of coarse hairs at the nodes.

Leaves Leaves small (3-5 cm long), oval to lance shaped, **not clasping at base**, sharp pointed at tips; **margins with tiny, closely crowded teeth**.

Flowers **Rose coloured to greenish purple**, saucer shaped with curved-back yellowish green tips, hanging solitary from leaf in axils.

Fruits Red, round berries.

Ecology Shady, coniferous forests with western hemlock and subalpine (or sometimes amabilis) fir, especially in areas with heavy snowfall. Scattered at low to medium elevations in wetter parts of the region south of 56°.

Notes: Recognizable by its small size and rose-coloured, flat, saucer-shaped flowers with their curved-back tips. • As with *S. amplexifolius*, berries of small twistedstalks were considered by natives to be good food for grizzly bears, but not humans. The berries are eaten by chipmunks and grouse. • *Streptopus streptopoides* means the *Streptopus* that's like *Streptopus*, or the redundant twistedstalk!

ROSY TWISTEDSTALK — *Streptopus roseus*

General Perennial from slender rhizome; ***stems usually unbranched,*** not conspicuously bent (zig-zag), 15-30 cm tall, with a sparse fringe of hairs at the nodes (where leaves arise).

Leaves Mostly oval to ***elliptic,*** 5-9 cm long, ***not clasping at base***; margin with irregularly spaced hairs.

Flowers Usually ***rose coloured with white tips,*** (sometimes greenish yellow streaked with reddish purple), bell shaped, single from leaf axils, on curved (***not kinked***) stalks.

Fruits Red, round to oblong berries.

Ecology Moist forest, forest openings, streambanks, clearings, and meadows. Fairly common at low to high elevations in wetter parts of the region south of 56°.

Notes: Distinguished from clasping twistedstalk by the unbranched stem, rose-coloured flowers, the non-clasping leaves, the fringe of hairs at each node, and the shiny underside of the leaves.

STAR-FLOWERED FALSE SOLOMON'S-SEAL — *Smilacina stellata*

General Perennial from slender, pale rhizome; stems erect, arching, unbranched, ***20-40 cm tall,*** finely hairy.

Leaves Alternate in 2 rows, narrowly ***lance shaped,*** 5-10 cm long, flat, sometimes folded down centre, with prominent veins and somewhat clasping bases; ***margins without hairs.***

Flowers Creamy white, starlike, few (5-10) in ***short, unbranched, terminal cluster.***

Fruits Round greenish yellow berries with 6 blue-purple stripes, changing to ***dark blue or reddish black*** at maturity.

Ecology Moist (less commonly dry) forest, often abundant in alluvial or deciduous forest, also in clearings and meadows. Common from valley bottoms to (occasionally) timberline, throughout the region.

Notes: A very variable species. For comments on edibility see *S. racemosa.* Roots or whole plants of *S. stellata, S. racemosa,* and *Streptopus amplexifolius* were tied to clothes, hair, or the body as a scent by the Shuswap Indians. • The name Solomon's-seal (originally given to *Polygonatum multiflorum*) is traditionally thought to refer to the rhizomes of this species. They bear surface scars, or show markings when freshly cut, which resemble the seal of Solomon – a 6-pointed star. However, Grigson (1974) claims the original medieval Latin refers to one of the flowers hanging like a seal on a document. *S. racemosa* resembles *P. multiflorum* – hence "false" Solomon's-seal.

129

LILIES

FALSE SOLOMON'S-SEAL *Smilacina racemosa*

General Perennial from stout, fleshy rhizome; stems erect to stiffly arched, ***0.3-1.0 m tall***, unbranched, finely hairy above, often growing in clumps.

Leaves ***Broad, elliptical***, 7-20 cm long, alternating along the stem in 2 rows, with strong parallel veins and somewhat clasping bases; ***margins without hairs***.

Flowers Creamy white, small, ***numerous, in branched, egg- or pyramid-shaped terminal cluster***, flower stalks very short; strongly perfumed and showy.

Fruits ***Red*** (sometimes dotted with purple), fleshy, round berries; showy.

Ecology Moist forests, streambanks, meadows, and clearings; widespread at low to subalpine elevations south of 56°, except in the southwestern plateau area.

Notes: Berries of *Smilacina* spp. are edible but not especially palatable. Interior native people classed them together with

fairybells and twistedstalks as "grizzly-bear food" and did not consider them edible. • The Gitksan people report eating them, but because they were so hard to collect, they were only served to chiefs. They were served in oolichan oil and called "Indian glads." The Gitksan also made a decoction from boiled rhizomes which was considered very strong medicine for rheumatism or as a purge, or it was applied to wounds and cuts.

THREE-LEAVED FALSE SOLOMON'S-SEAL *Smilacina trifolia*

General Perennial from very slender, creeping, scaly, whitish rhizome; stems erect but slender and weak, ***5-20 cm tall***.

Leaves ***2-4 (usually 3)***, 3-13 cm long, oval to oblong lance shaped, ***tapering to a somewhat sheathing base, not hairy***.

Flowers White to greenish white, few (2-10) in an ***unbranched terminal cluster*** that has a long stalk.

Fruits Dark red, round berries.

Ecology ***Bogs and fens***. Low elevations throughout the northern part of our region (except Haines Triangle).

Notes: Might be mistaken for *Maianthemum*, but the latter has its floral parts in 4's, not 6's, and is not a species of bogs and fens. Distinguished from *S. stellata* especially by leaves (2-4 for *S. trifolia*, more than 4 for *S. stellata*), the long-stalked inflorescence, and habitat. • For comments on edibility see *S. racemosa* above.

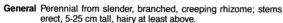

WILD LILY-OF-THE-VALLEY — *Maianthemum canadense*

General Perennial from slender, branched, creeping rhizome; stems erect, 5-25 cm tall, hairy at least above.

Leaves 2-3, broadly heart shaped to oval with pointed tip, smooth on top, **hairy below, with short stalks**, on flowering stem, 3-12 cm long.

Flowers Small, white in terminal cluster, with **flower parts in 4's** (unlike usual 6's of most species in the lily family).

Fruits Small, round berries; at first hard, green, mottled with brown, finally becoming red and soft.

Ecology Moist to dry, usually shady woods, clearings (especially in the south). Common at low to medium elevations in the northeast boreal forest (north of 55°), less common south where it extends along the Fraser River to about Quesnel, absent in the west.

Notes: Although coastal native people gathered and ate the berries of the similar *M. dilatatum*, there are no reports of berries of *M. canadense* being eaten by interior groups. There is evidence that they are a strong purgative, and one author suggests that they may contain glycosides (heart stimulants)! • This species is called "wild lily-of-the-valley" because of its similarity to the true lily-of-the-valley, the European *Convallaria majalis*. Sometimes called "mayflower" from *Maianthemum* (meaning, literally, May flower), though our northern plant blooms considerably later.

QUEEN'S CUP — *Clintonia uniflora*

General Perennial from slender, creeping rhizome; stems mostly underground, short, to 15 cm tall.

Leaves **2-3 in basal rosette**, 15-25 cm long, oblong or elliptic with sheathing base, slightly fleshy and shiny; noticeably hairy margin.

Flowers **Large, white, cup shaped**, erect; solitary (rarely 2).

Fruits Single bright **metallic blue berries**.

Ecology Moist forest, forest openings, clearings. Widely distributed and often abundant at low to subalpine elevations, north to 56°.

Notes: The beautiful pure white cup-shaped flower with a crown of golden stamens deserves the name queen's cup. Another common name, "blue-bead lily," refers to the single blue berry. The berries, however, are considered unpalatable, although grouse reportedly eat them sometimes. • Turner (1978) notes that queen's cup "was not generally recognized by contemporary native peoples, but both the Lower Lillooet and Lower Thompson believed the berry to be inedible. The former used it as an eye medicine, the latter as a blue dye." • *Clintonia* is named in memory of New York State Governor, and botanist, DeWitt Clinton (1769-1828).

INDIAN HELLEBORE · *Veratrum viride*

General Perennial from short, stout, erect, rhizome; stems simple, robust, *0.7-2.0 m tall*, leafy and hairy throughout.

Leaves *Large* (10-25 cm long), *broad*, oblong to elliptic, pointed at tip, clasping at base, prominently ribbed (*accordion pleated*), hairy beneath, gradually getting narrower above.

Flowers *Star shaped, yellow-green* with dark green centres, numerous in thin, branched, *drooping terminal tassels*; with musky odour.

Fruits Oblong or oval capsules, straw coloured to dark brown.

Ecology Wet thickets, moist to wet, usually open forests, lowland to alpine meadows. Most abundant at subalpine elevations, in wet meadows and late snowmelt patches in the forest. Widespread and often abundant, throughout our region, except absent at low elevations in the southwest.

Notes: This is one of the most violently poisonous plants in B.C.; plants of this genus are powdered to form the garden insecticide "hellebore". The native people recognized its poisonous nature, and *Veratrum* was, and still is, treated with great respect. It is considered to have great spiritual values and is used for purification as well as healing. The Gitksan and others sliced and dried the rhizomes and then burned them as a fumigant to drive away evil spirits. The grated roots were added to bath water for skin and scalp conditions, or added to laundry to purify or cleanse clothing, and to remove human smell for better hunting. Inhaled smoke assists sleepwalkers to return to the body properly and acts as a decongestant. • It is rarely taken internally and only in greatly diluted form and with caution. • People drinking water in which Indian hellebore is growing have reported stomach cramps. Other symptoms of hellebore poisoning include frothing at the mouth, blurred vision, "lock-jaw", as well as vomiting and diarrhoea. • *Veratrum* presumably refers to the dark flowers or blackish rhizome (*vera*, "true;" *atrum*, "black"). The origin of the name "hellebore" is obscure; true hellebores are species of *Helleborus* and do not bear much similarity to *Veratrum* species.

Orchids

Orchids are members of the plant family Orchidaceae, a very large family distributed primarily in the tropics. B.C. has a fair number of orchids, but (with a few exceptions such as *Calypso* and *Cypripedium*) our orchids are not particularly showy. Still, they're beautiful in their own modest way — their flowers are intricate, complex, and often wonderfully scented. The orchid flower is distinctive: three sepals, one usually modified, and three petals, the lower one usually modified into a **lip** (sometimes inflated into a pouch) which may have a **spur** extending from it. It's important to remember that many of our orchids have established an intimate relationship between their roots and fungi growing in the soil. This makes them very difficult to transplant, and are therefore best left in the wild to be enjoyed.

A key to the orchids of northern B.C. is provided. Further information about B.C.'s orchids is provided in Szczawinski (1959).

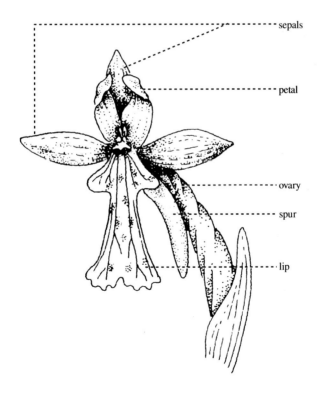

133

Key to Orchids

1. Plants saprophytic, without green leaves; roots coral-like (the coral-roots)
  2. Plants generally less than 20 cm tall; flowers yellowish to nearly white, sometimes lightly red-spotted .... *Corallorhiza trifida*
  2. Plants generally more than 20 cm tall; flowers with either wine red spots, or purplish stripes
    3. Flowers pinkish, with wine red spots .... *Corallorhiza maculata*
    3. Flowers pink to yellowish pink, with purplish stripes .... *Corallorhiza striata*
1. Plants with green leaves; roots not coral-like
    4. Lip of flower inflated, pouch-shaped
      5. Flower rose-purple, 2-3 cm long; leaf solitary, basal .... *Calypso bulbosa*
      5. Flower white (yellow in *C. calceolus*), 3-5 cm long; leaves several, extending up the stem .... *Cypripedium montanum*
    4. Lip of flower not inflated
      6. Lip of flower spurred at the base (the rein-orchids)
        7. Leaves 1 or 2, basal
          8. One leaf .... *Platanthera obtusata*
          8. Two leaves .... *Platanthera orbiculata*
        7. Leaves more than 2, on the stem
          9. Lip notched or 2 or 3 toothed; spur sac-shaped; flowers scentless .... *Coeloglossum viride*
          9. Lip widened at the base, not toothed; spur cylindrical; flowers sweetly scented .... *Platanthera dilatata*
      6. Lip of flower spurless
        10. Leaves 1-2, either basal or borne near the midlength of the stem (the twayblades)
          11. Lip deeply cleft into linear pointed lobes; heart-shaped leaves .... *Listera cordata*
          11. Lip rectangular or ear shaped at the base, provided with a pair of lateral teeth; leaves egg to lance shaped, pointed at the tip .... *Listera borealis*
        10. Leaves more than 2, basal (the rattlesnake-plantains)
          12. Flowering stem 25-40 cm tall; leaves mottled or striped with white, especially along the midrib, 3-7 cm long .... *Goodyera oblongifolia*
          12. Flowering stem 10-15 cm tall; leaves 1.5-3 cm long, midrib not white .... *Goodyera repens*

FAIRYSLIPPER — *Calypso bulbosa*

General Perennial from a round or oval, **bulb-like corm**; stems delicate, yellow-purple to brown-purple; covered in membranous sheathing bracts, 10-25 cm high.

Leaves **Single, dark-green leaf** produced at top of corm in fall and persistent through winter, withering in summer; broadly egg shaped, mostly 3-6 cm high.

Flowers **Rose-purple, large, showy, and solitary**; 3 sepals and 2 petals (narrow, pointed, and twisted) sit erect above the upper lip; lower lip is large, slipper-like, wide, yellow to whitish, streaked and spotted with purple and with a cluster of golden hairs; a spotted double spur below the lip; with sweet fragrance.

Fruits Erect capsules.

Ecology Mostly in forests, often in soil rich with leaf mould. Common from lowlands to middle elevations, throughout our region except the Fort Nelson Lowland.

Notes: This beautiful (and deliciously perfumed) little orchid, although widespread, is rapidly being exterminated in populated areas due to trampling and especially picking. The corms are attached by means of delicate roots that are easily broken even by the lightest touch or tug on the stem. Hence, when the flower is picked, the plant usually dies. • The corms were peeled and eaten raw by the lower Lillooet and the Haida. Haida girls ate them raw to enhance their bustline. • *Calypso*, the goddess daughter of Atlas, was Homer's beautiful nymph hidden in the woods and found by Ulysses when he was wrecked on the island of Ogygia. *Calypso*'s name means concealment, apt for a flower often found in mossy, shady hideaways. Other common names include Cytherea, Venus slipper, hider-of-the-north, pink slipper-orchid, and false ladyslipper. Cytherea is another name for Aphrodite − the goddess of love, beauty, and marriage.

MOUNTAIN LADYSLIPPER — *Cypripedium montanum*

General Perennial, somewhat rhizomatous herb; stems **20-70 (-100) cm tall**, glandular to somewhat hairy, branched or simple.

Leaves Elliptic to egg shaped, alternate, to 12 cm long, 5 cm wide; **all along the stem**, with the bases of the lower ones wrapped around (sheathing) the stem.

Flowers White with purple veins, fragrant, the lip inflated into a **showy pouch**, other petals and sepals copper-coloured, long and twisted; usually 2 flowers per stem.

Fruits Ascending, oblong capsules, 2-3 cm long.

Ecology Dry to moist, usually fairly open woods, often deciduous or with a deciduous component, commonly on rich humus; also on disturbed sites such as roadsides; scattered but locally abundant, at low to medium (and sometimes subalpine) elevations along major river systems in the south, less common further north but distributed throughout the region.

Notes: The flowers of the mountain ladyslipper and the yellow ladyslipper (*C. calceolus*) somewhat resemble the fairyslipper in that their lip has been expanded into a pouch. The flowers differ from *Calypso*'s in colour (white for *C. montanum*, yellow for *C. calceolus*) and size (*Cypripedium* has larger flowers, also known as "moccasin flowers"). In addition, the mountain and yellow ladyslippers have numerous leaves, and are much larger than the fairyslipper. • *Cypripedium passerinum* (sparrow's-egg ladyslipper) also occurs in the region, in moist, shaded, mossy, coniferous forest, in swamps and fens, on gravelly outwash, and on streambanks and pond margins; usually on calcium-rich sites, and mostly north of 58°, but also south along the Rockies. *C. passerinum* is only 15-30 cm tall and usually has a single, relatively small flower with a creamy white pouch that is purple spotted inside. • All three ladyslippers are threatened by overcollecting; would-be growers should be aware these orchids reportedly take 15 years to flower.

135

SPOTTED CORALROOT   *Corallorhiza maculata*

General Perennial **saprophyte** from branched, coral-like rhizomes; **stems** 20-30 cm tall, **purplish to reddish brown**, or often light yellow to tan.

Leaves Reduced to thin, semi-transparent sheaths.

Flowers *Reddish purple and pink, with wine-red spots*; lip white and spotted with purple; flowers 10-30 in a loose terminal cluster.

Fruits Nodding, oval capsules.

Ecology Rich humus in moist to fairly dry coniferous or mixed forest. Widespread at low elevations in the southern part of the region, extending north to 56°.

Notes: The less common *C. mertensiana* is similar, but its lip is reddish purple and unspotted. • Although non-albino plants more commonly have spotted than unspotted flowers, the two kinds often occur together and differ in no other obvious way. "Albino" plants are also fairly common, being pale yellowish throughout except for the white, always unspotted petals. • Members of the genus *Corallorhiza* are saprophytic orchids − that is, they derive their nutrients from decaying organic matter, unlike most plants which make their own food. Because of this, the coralroots lack the green colour that is characteristic of most plants. • This species is called spotted coralroot because of the spots on the flowers and the coral-like roots. (*Corallorhiza* literally means coral-like root and *maculata* means spotted.)

STRIPED CORALROOT   *Corallorhiza striata*

General Perennial **saprophyte** from branched, coral-like rhizomes; **stems purplish tinged**, 15-40 cm tall.

Leaves Thin, semi-transparent, sheathing scales.

Flowers *Pink to yellowish pink with 3 purplish stripes* on the sepals; lip tongue shaped, not lobed, stripes on lip merging to solid brown-purple; flowers 7-25 and drooping in fairly loose terminal clusters.

Fruits Nodding, elliptic capsules.

Ecology Moist humus in shady coniferous and deciduous forests; streambanks, ravines. At low elevations, mainly in the southern part of the region; not collected north of 55°.

Notes: As in other species of coralroot, an occasional "albino" specimen is pale yellow throughout. • Common names, while often descriptive, are also often botanically incorrect. The "bulb" in *Calypso bulbosa* is actually a corm, a swollen underground stem; the "coral-roots" are actually coral-rhizomes (rhizomes are horizontal underground stems). • Called striped coralroot because of stripes on sepals. Also called madder-stripes in reference to the flower colour, sometimes described as madder-purple. The coralroots are also sometimes called "chicken toes."

136

YELLOW CORALROOT   *Corallorhiza trifida*

General Perennial **saprophyte** from branched, coral-like rhizome; **stems** slender, **pale yellow to greenish yellow**, 10-25 cm tall.

Leaves Thin, semi-transparent sheaths.

Flowers **Yellow or greenish yellow to nearly white**; lip nearly white, sometimes lightly red-spotted, three lobed; 3-15 flowers in loose terminal clusters.

Fruits Drooping, elliptic capsules.

Ecology Moist to dry forest, also in bogs, swamps, and along streambanks. Widespread from low to middle elevations throughout the region.

Notes: The species name *trifida* refers to the 3-lobed lip, similar to that of *C. maculata* but quite different from the unlobed lip of *C. striata*. • This is a common, but often overlooked, coralroot, sometimes found in spectacular combination with *Calypso bulbosa*. These two species are among the first to flower in the spring.

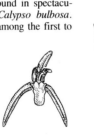

Picture Key to *Platanthera/Coeloglossum*

1. Leaves basal, stems leafless but with sheathing bracts

    2. Plants 8-20 cm tall, with a single basal leaf (a) *Platanthera obtusata*

    2. Plants 20-40 cm tall, with two basal leaves (b) *Platanthera orbiculata*

1. Leaves arranged along the stem

    3. Plants to 70 cm tall; flowers white to greenish tinged, very fragrant; spur long, slender .... *Platanthera dilatata*

    3. Plants to 30 cm tall; flowers green, tinged with bronze; spur short, sac-like (c) .... *Coeloglossum viride*

137

ORCHIDS

ONE-LEAVED REIN-ORCHID   *Platanthera obtusata*

General	Perennial from slender, fleshy-tuberous roots; stems 8-20 cm tall, smooth, leafless, but with 1 or 2 sheathing bracts.
Leaves	**Single**, basal sheathing leaf, **narrowly elliptic to oblong** but broadest above middle, blunt-tipped; **5-15 cm long**.
Flowers	**Pale green or yellowish green**, lip and petals sometimes whitish; lip narrowly lance shaped, straight to slightly curved upwards; spur slender, tapering, as long as lip; 3-12 flowers in loose terminal clusters.
Fruits	Erect capsules.
Ecology	Swamps, fens, bogs, and cold, moist to wet forest sites. Common at low to medium elevations throughout our region.

Notes: Another one-leaved orchid of boggy sites in our region is *Amerorchis rotundifolia* (round-leaved orchid), which has showy, white, purple-spotted flowers. • This genus of orchids is referred to in some guides as *Habenaria*, e.g., *Habenaria obtusata*, *H. orbiculata*, etc. Do not confuse *Habenaria* with "Habanera", a sultry Spanish dance made famous by Bizet's "Carmen". Carmen was intrigued by Jose's initial indifference to her charms. The flowers of rein-orchid may initially appear indifferent, but they are curiously contrived and intriguing. • The name "rein" orchid comes from the Latin *habenas* meaning a strap or rein and refers to the thong like shape of the lip and spur. Also called the blunt-leaved orchid (*obtusata* = blunt) because of its single, blunt-tipped leaf. This species is regularly cross-pollinated by mosquitoes.

ROUND-LEAVED REIN-ORCHID   *Platanthera orbiculata*

General	Perennial from fleshy tuberlike roots; stems 20-40 cm tall, smooth, with 1-5 lance-shaped bracts.
Leaves	**Usually 2**, basal, **round**, opposite, clasping at the base, **glossy**, somewhat fleshy, lying on the ground, to 10 cm in length.
Flowers	Pale to deep **whitish green**; lip straight, linear or strap-shaped; spur long, cylindrical, tapering and curved upward at tip; flowers small, 5-25 in a loose, elongated terminal cluster.
Fruits	Erect, curved capsules.
Ecology	In moist to dry, mossy, coniferous forests; also in swamps and bogs. Fairly common at low to medium elevations throughout the southern part of our region, north to 56°.

Notes: Platanthera unalascensis (Alaska rein-orchid) is another rein-orchid with two leaves, but its leaves are lance shaped and don't lie flat on the ground. • The species name *orbiculata* means round and refers to the large, round leaves; hence, round-leaved rein-orchid. Other common names are "moon-set" and "heal-all."

WHITE BOG-ORCHID — *Platanthera dilatata*

General Perennial from fleshy tuberlike roots; stems erect, to 70 cm tall, smooth, leafy.

Leaves Gradually getting smaller up the stem, sheathing, oblong to broadly lance shaped; *stem leafy throughout*.

Flowers *White to greenish tinged*, waxy, small but very fragrant, 5-30 in loose to densely packed terminal clusters; *spur long, slender*, cylindrical, curved, longer than lip.

Fruits Elliptic capsules.

Ecology Swamps, bogs, fens, marshes, wet meadows, moist seepage slopes, along streams and lake edges, also in subalpine meadows, swampy coniferous forests, and clearings. Throughout our region at low to high elevations except absent in the northeast.

Notes: P. saccata (slender bog-orchid) and *P. hyperborea* (northern bog-orchid) somewhat resemble white bog-orchid, but they have green flowers and fewer leaves, which are more rounded at the tip. • Some interior natives believed the plant to be poisonous to humans and animals. The Shuswap used extracts as poison to sprinkle on baits for coyote and grizzlies. Other sources report that the tuber-like roots are edible. Care should be taken until the exact poisonous nature of this plant is clarified. • This is a very fragrant species, often smelled before being sighted. Another common name for this species is "scent-candle." Szczawinski (1959) describes the perfume as a mix of cloves, vanilla, and mock-orange! The species name *dilatata* means expanded, in reference to the lower lip of the flower.

FROG-ORCHID — *Coeloglossum viride*

General Perennial from fleshy thickened rhizome; *stems leafy*, smooth, to 30 cm tall.

Leaves The lower of the 2-5 leaves oblong to lance shaped and blunt, the upper smaller, narrower, and pointed at the tip; all sheathing.

Flowers Green tinged with bronze; lower lip oblong, 2-3 times longer than the *short sac-like spur*, and with 2-3 teeth at its tip; flowers numerous in loose to dense terminal cluster, *each flower* in axil of and *almost hidden by very large*, lance-shaped leafy *bract*.

Fruits Elliptic capsules.

Ecology Open forest, grassy streambanks, meadows, and lakeshores. Scattered at low to medium elevations throughout the region; most common in Bulkley, Nechako, and Blackwater drainages.

Notes: Formerly called *Habenaria viridis* var. *bracteata*. A highly variable species. • Often called long-bracted orchid because of the long bracts that stick out between the flowers. The plant may have acquired the name "frog-orchid" because it grows in places often inhabited by frogs. *Coeloglossum* means hollow tongue, *viride* means green.

139

HEART-LEAVED TWAYBLADE — *Listera cordata*

General Perennial from slender creeping rhizome; stems 6-15 cm tall, smooth to glandular-hairy above leaves.

Leaves A single pair near mid-length of stem, broad, *heart shaped*, opposite, clasping.

Flowers *Pale green to purplish brown*; lip divided into *2 linear or lance-shaped lobes* and with a pair of horn-like teeth at base; 5-16 flowers in terminal elongated cluster.

Fruits Egg-shaped capsules.

Ecology Moist to wet, mossy coniferous forests, along streams, or in bogs. Widespread from low to subalpine elevations, throughout our region except in the drier southwestern parts.

Notes: Heart-leaved twayblade is by far our most common *Listera*. • The intricate pollination mechanisms of *Listera* species fascinated Darwin who studied them intensively. The pollen is blown out explosively within a drop of viscous fluid that glues the pollinia to unsuspecting insects (or to your finger if you touch the top of the column!) • The genus *Listera* is

named for English naturalist M.Lister (1638-1712); *cordata* means heart shaped and refers to the leaves, as does the common name. Also called mannikin twayblade; "mannikin" means a dwarf or little man.

NORTHERN TWAYBLADE — *Listera borealis*

General Perennial from fleshy fibrous roots; stems 7-20 cm tall, 4 sided, smooth below becoming glandular among flowers.

Leaves In single pair, nearly opposite to 1 cm apart, slightly above the middle of the stem, lacking stalks, *oval-elliptic*, 2-5 cm long.

Flowers *Pale green to yellowish green*, small, 3-15 in an open to densely packed terminal cluster; lip rectangular to oblong, broadest and *shallowly 2-cleft* at tip, with earlike flanges at its base, hairy.

Fruits Oval capsules.

Ecology Moist to wet forest, along streams, also in fens and swamps. Uncommon and scattered at low to medium elevations throughout the region.

Notes: *L. caurina* (northwestern twayblade) and *L. convallarioides* (broad-leaved twayblade) also occur in the southern half of our region; both have wedge shaped, not bilobed (cleft at the tip) lips. The northwestern twayblade and

the broad-leaved twayblade are difficult to distinguish from each other; a key is provided in Szczawinski (1959). • *Listera* species earn the name "twayblade"(two blade) because of the two small leaves found on the flowering stem. Also called "big ears"(!) — maybe because the two leaves resemble a pair of large ears. • The species name *borealis*, so common in our northern plants, simply means of the north.

General ***Evergreen*** perennial from short creeping rhizome, with fibrous roots; stems 20-30 cm tall, stout and stiff, glandular hairy; spreads very rapidly by vegetative multiplication.

Leaves In ***basal rosette***, thick, dark green, ***mottled or striped with white, especially along midrib***, oval or oblong to narrowly elliptic, ***3-10 cm long***.

Flowers Dull white to greenish, numerous in long dense, downy, terminal spike; most of the flowers oriented to one side; petals and one of the sepals form a hood over the lip.

Fruits Capsules.

Ecology On humus among mosses in dry to moist coniferous forest. Fairly common from lowlands to subalpine elevations, mainly south of 56°.

Notes: According to the "Doctrine of Signs" it was believed by early settlers that, because the markings on the leaves of the rattlesnake-plantain resembled snakeskin markings, this plant could be used in treatment of (rattle) snake bites. Presumably, it was also thought to resemble a plantain (*Plantago* spp.) because of the similarity of the flattened basal leaf rosettes of the two genera. • Apparently the leaf, if crushed by a sideways motion between thumb and forefinger, divides and can then be applied to cuts and bruises — the raw side of the leaf being placed next to the wound. • Originally named after Goodyer, a 17th century botanist.

General ***Evergreen*** perennial from slender creeping rhizome; 10-15 cm tall, generally less robust than *G. oblongifolia*.

Leaves In ***basal rosette***, narrowly oval, ***1.5-3 cm long***; green with darker green veins; ***midrib not white***.

Flowers White or pale green, in spikelike terminal cluster; all the flowers oriented to one side; petals and a sepal form hood.

Fruits Capsules.

Ecology Dry to moist, coniferous and mixed forest. Scattered at low to medium elevations throughout the region.

Notes: The lack of white mottling on the leaves and the generally smaller size of this plant distinguish it from *G. oblongifolia*. • *Spiranthes romanzoffiana* (ladies' tresses) is another fairly small orchid with creamy white to straw-coloured flowers, but it has narrow, linear to lance-shaped leaves part-way up the stem, and a spike of spirally arranged, hooded flowers. It is widespread at low to medium elevations throughout all but the northeastern part of our region, and occupies a wide variety of habitats, including open forest, clearings, meadows, gravelly-sandy shores and banks, moist swales, bogs and fens, dry open slopes, old gravel pits, and roadside ditches. • The *Goodyera* spp. represent some of the most common, least showy orchids in central interior B.C. In addition to spreading by seeds, they multiply vegetatively, and can very rapidly cover a large piece of ground. • The species name *repens* refers to the creeping habit of the rhizome.

PURPLE MOUNTAIN SAXIFRAGE	*Saxifraga oppositifolia*

General Densely or loosely matted perennial with *condensed, crowded, or trailing branches.*

Leaves Very small (1-4 mm long), oblong to oval, *leathery, bristly-hairy,* overlapping and scale-like, *arranged in four rows.*

Flowers Showy, *lilac or purple* (rarely white), single at branch tips. One of the earliest flowering species of the alpine zone.

Fruits Follicles, with slender spreading tips.

Ecology Moist, but well-drained, alpine cliffs, ledges, gravelly ridges and scree, and exposed tundra; most abundant on calcareous substrates; high mountains throughout the region.

Notes: Saxifrage comes from the Latin *saxum* (rock) and *frangere* (to break), as these plants were thought to break the rocks upon which they grow. Because of this, plants were ground up and fed to patients with gallstones as a supposed cure. Hence saxifrages may also be called "breakstone."
• An old belief is that the fresh roots of saxifrages are supposed to remove freckles and relieve toothaches.

TOLMIE'S SAXIFRAGE	*Saxifraga tolmiei*

General Low, mat-forming perennial with numerous sterile leafy shoots; flowering stems 2-8 cm tall, with stalked glands.

Leaves *Entire,* glabrous or the bases sparsely long-hairy, *fleshy* and slightly rolled over on the edges, 2-10 mm long, *club shaped to spoon shaped.*

Flowers White, one to three, saucer shaped, with 5 well-separated, spreading petals.

Fruits Two-lobed, oval capsules, usually purplish mottled.

Ecology In moist talus, scree, or rock crevices, typically watered by melting snow, or near streams in the alpine zone. In our region, primarily along the western mountain ranges (the species is most abundant in the Coast Mountains).

Notes: See comment on common name under *S. oppositifolia.* • The sausage-like, fleshy leaves give *S. tolmiei* the look of a *Sedum* or stonecrop.

THREE-TOOTHED SAXIFRAGE *Saxifraga tricuspidata*

General Loose to densely matted perennial, *often forming large cushions*; 5-25 cm tall; *branches closely covered with withered leaves.*

Leaves *Evergreen, leathery,* overlapping and often reddish tinged along the densely crowded branches, oblong to wedge-shaped, with *3 prickly teeth at the tips.*

Flowers Creamy *white and usually orange-dotted*; few to several in a somewhat flat-topped group.

Fruits Two-beaked capsules.

Ecology Dry, sandy, gravelly, and rocky places; cliffs, crevices, ridges, dunes, well-drained river terraces; usually non-forested habitats. Common throughout from medium to high elevations.

Notes: S. bronchialis (spotted saxifrage) is similar, but its leaves are not three toothed at the tip, rather are coarsely hairy along the margin. The species occupies much the same habitats as does *S. tricuspidata* and is widespread in western North America, but in northern B.C. *S. tricuspidata* seems to be much more common, except in the Haines Triangle.

STOLONIFEROUS SAXIFRAGE
Saxifraga flagellaris

General Perennial with several long, narrow, glabrous, brown or *red stolons or runners* that end in buds; flowering stems erect, sticky-hairy, 5-15 cm tall, from a basal rosette.

Leaves Mostly basal, oblong to spoon shaped, with *coarse spiny hairs along their margins.*

Flowers *Showy, bright golden yellow,* one to few.

Fruits Two-beaked capsules.

Ecology Alpine tundra, scree slopes, gravelly ridges; almost always alpine in our region, where it is scattered along the high mountain ranges, more commonly in the North.

Notes: Stolons (like those of garden strawberry) radiate out from the central rosette, giving the plant a spiderlike appearance and another common name, "spider plant."

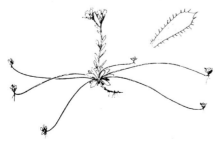

RED-STEMMED SAXIFRAGE *Saxifraga lyallii*

General Perennials from basal rosettes and rhizomes; flowering stems leafless, glabrous to hairy, reddish to purplish.

Leaves *Fan or wedge to spoon shaped, coarsely toothed, abruptly narrowing into long stalks*, glabrous to hairy.

Flowers White, few to several in open groups.

Fruits Two- to three- or four-beaked capsules.

Ecology Streambanks, seepage areas, snowbeds, and other wet places in the mountains; mostly in the alpine zone, but also along creeks in ravines in subalpine forest. Widespread throughout the region.

> *Notes: Saxifraga mertensiana* (wood saxifrage) and *S. nelsoniana* (also known as *S. punctata*, brook saxifrage) are similar to *S. lyallii* in habitat and general appearance, but *S. mertensiana* has circular, semi-fleshy leaves that are both lobed and toothed, whereas *S. nelsoniana* also has circular to kidney-shaped leaves that are heart shaped at the base but have only one set of teeth.

LEATHERLEAF SAXIFRAGE *Leptarrhena pyrolifolia*

General Perennials with robust, wide-spreading rhizomes and unbranched, glandular-hairy flowering stems that are 20-40 cm tall.

Leaves Mostly basal, oval-oblong, glabrous, *leathery, glossy green, rough and deeply veined above*, pale green below; margins round-toothed; 1-3 smaller leaves on flowering stem.

Flowers White, small, in a tight cluster at the stem tip; in fall, *flowering stem purplish red*.

Fruits Consist of two follicles that are *bright purplish red*, as is the fruiting stem.

Ecology Streambanks, flushes, and wet ground, in subalpine and alpine thickets and meadows. Widespread in suitable habitats at high elevations throughout our region, although more abundant in snowier mountain ranges.

> *Notes:* Hitchcock *et al.* (1977) note that leatherleaf saxifrage "takes well to cultivation and, because of its deep green leathery leaves and usually reddish follicles, is well worth a place in the native garden or in a moist spot in the rockery." • The brightly coloured fruiting cluster is very showy.

SAXIFRAGE FAMILY

COMMON MITREWORT   *Mitella nuda*

General Rhizomatous and usually stoloniferous perennial; the erect flowering stems 3-20 cm tall, leafless or with a reduced, sessile leaf near the base, finely glandular-hairy.

Leaves *Few*, heart shaped to kidney shaped, *1-3 cm long*, round toothed; scattered, stiffly erect hairs on upper surface.

Flowers Greenish yellow, small, **saucer shaped**, inconspicuous, in **few-flowered clusters;** petals dissected into four pairs of threadlike lateral divisions (much like a television antenna); stamens 10.

Fruits Capsules, which shed their top halves to expose the shiny black seeds in a shallow cup.

Ecology Moist forests and thickets, along streambanks, in bogs and swamps. Common at low to medium elevations throughout our region.

Notes: The only species of *Mitella* in B.C. with 10 stamens (all others have 5). Seed dispersal is (at least partly) by a "splash-cup" mechanism, as also for *M. pentandra* and *Chrysosplenium tetrandrum* (see notes under *Chrysosplenium*). • The common and Latin names come from the diminutive of *mitra*, which means cap or mitre. Presumably the seed capsule was thought to resemble a bishop's mitre, though one reference suggests that it looks more like "a tattered French-Canadian toque!"

FIVE-STAMENED MITREWORT   *Mitella pentandra*

General Perennial, occasionally with creeping shoots; flowering stems 20-30 cm tall, generally leafless, glandular-hairy to glabrous.

Leaves *Few*, oval to heart shaped, *4-8 cm long*, shallowly 5-9 lobed, round toothed, stiffly erect hairs on both surfaces.

Flowers Greenish, small, **saucer shaped**, in an elongated cluster of *6-25*; petals dissected into 2-5 pairs of threadlike segments; stamens 5, located opposite the petals.

Fruits Capsules, much like those of *M. nuda*.

Ecology Moist woods, especially along streams, and in wet meadows, to forest glades, clearings, and avalanche tracks. Lowland forests to subalpine parkland throughout, but probably most common at subalpine elevations.

Notes: Two other species of *Mitella* occur in the southern half of our region. *Mitella breweri* is similar in appearance and habitat to *M. pentandra*, but has more or less orbicular leaves and stamens alternate with the petals. *M. trifida* has whitish flowers with 3-cleft petals, and is scattered in low to medium elevation forests (primarily deciduous or mixed stands), thickets, and clearings. • Without flowers, it can be very difficult to distinguish among several genera and species of the Saxifragaceae with similar foliage (e.g., *Mitella, Heuchera, Tellima, Tiarella*). Refer to the key and silhouette diagrams (p. 146) for help.

SAXIFRAGE FAMILY

| MEADOW ALUMROOT | *Heuchera chlorantha* |

General Robust perennial with a branching crown and short thick rhizomes; flowering stems densely hairy (hairs brownish when dry) in lower part to glandular-hairy above, 40-100 cm tall.

Leaves *Numerous,* all basal, heart or egg shaped to kidney shaped, with 5-9 broadly rounded shallow lobes that are round toothed; *leaf stalks also densely hairy.*

Flowers Greenish to cream coloured, small, *top shaped to bell shaped,* strongly perfumed, *numerous* in narrow, dense, terminal clusters.

Fruits Many-seeded capsules; seeds small, dark brown, covered with rows of tiny spines.

Ecology Moist to dry thickets, open woods, rocky slopes and crevices, meadows and disturbed areas (especially gravelly roadsides); scattered but locally abundant at low to medium elevations in the southern part of the region.

Notes: Heuchera glabra (smooth alumroot) has sparsely hairy, more sharply toothed leaves and looser clusters of flowers. It inhabits rocky meadows, mossy talus slopes, moist slabs and boulders (as in the spray zone near waterfalls), at medium to high elevations in the southern half of the region and on up to the Yukon along the Coast Mountains. *H. cylindrica* (round-leaved alumroot) looks much like *H. chlorantha* but is smaller (15-50 cm tall) and less hairy, and is a species of dry, rocky, sunny sites at low elevations in the southernmost part of the region. • The pounded, dried root of several *Heuchera* species are reputed to have been used by North American native people and herbalists as a poultice applied to cuts and sores to stop bleeding and promote healing.

Key to Saxifrages and Relatives

1. Flowering stems leafless or with bracts, foliage-leaves in a basal rosette 2
   2. Petals dissected into threadlike segments or three-cleft. .... *Mitella*
   2. Petals entire .... *Heuchera*
1. Flowering stems distinctly leafy 3
   3. Petals oblong and deeply fringed laterally (frilly); basal leaves triangular or oval heart shaped, with up to seven shallow lobes .... *Tellima*
   3. Petals very narrow (linear) but entire; fruit opening by two unequal parts; basal leaves broadly heart shaped with 3-5 lobes, to heart shaped in outline with three leaflets .... *Tiarella*

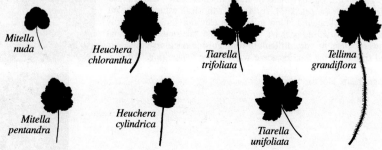

Mitella nuda   Heuchera chlorantha   Tiarella trifoliata   Tellima grandiflora

Mitella pentandra   Heuchera cylindrica   Tiarella unifoliata

THREE-LEAVED FOAMFLOWER — *Tiarella trifoliata*

General Perennial with slender rhizomes; stems erect or ascending, glandular-hairy, 15-50 cm tall.

Leaves The main leaves basal, with long stalks and **three leaflets** that are irregularly lobed and coarsely toothed, sparsely hairy; the **stem leaves (1-few) reduced in size** and with shorter stalks.

Flowers **Tiny delicate white** flowers at the end of short wirelike stalks, several to many in elongate clusters.

Fruits Few-seeded capsules that are borne horizontally and open by splitting between the small upper valves and the larger lower valves to form structures that **resemble sugar scoops**.

Ecology Moist, shady coniferous forests, especially along streambanks; also in clearings. Widespread at low to subalpine elevations in the moister parts of the southern half of the region.

Notes: Often found growing beside *T. unifoliata* (one-leaved foamflower). The two species are very similar in general appearance, floral characters, and habitat and some taxonomists think that they are two varieties of the same species. The leaves of *T. unifoliata* are simple – merely shallowly 3-5 lobed (maple leaflike: see circled leaf at right).

• *Tellima grandiflora* (tall fringecup) has leaves much like *Tiarella unifoliata* and some of the Heucheras and Mitellas (see silhouettes). However, *Tellima* has larger, fragrant, greenish white to pink flowers with frilly petals. It inhabits seepage sites in the forest, avalanche tracks, thickets, and clearings, in the moister parts of the southern half of the region, and on up to 60° along the Coast Mountains.

• Presumably they are called foamflowers because the flowers appear like specks of foam. The plant is sometimes called "sugar-scoops" in reference to the unusual shape of the opened capsules. The capsule is also thought to resemble a little tiara (hence *Tiarella*).

NORTHERN WATER-CARPET — *Chrysosplenium tetrandrum*

General Weak, mostly glabrous perennial with stolons (runners); stems ascending to erect, simple or branched, 1-15 cm tall; **foliage typically yellowish green**.

Leaves **Round to kidney shaped, with 3-5 broad rounded teeth**; leaf stalks 1-3 cm long.

Flowers Mostly **green**, sometimes purple dotted, **small, inconspicuous**, top shaped, relatively few (3-10) in loose clusters; sepals 4.

Fruits **Flattened, saucer-shaped capsules (splash-cups)**.

Ecology Moist to wet, often shaded habitats such as along streams, in seepage areas, swamps, and clearings; scattered throughout the region, but more common in the North and at low elevations – usually only locally abundant.

Notes: The shallow cups of the fruiting capsules are well suited to **splash-cup dispersal**, whereby raindrops scoring direct hits eject the small, smooth seeds. • The flower parts are in 4's – hence *tetrandrum*. The plant forms mats in wet areas – hence the common name. Northern golden-saxifrage is another common name.

FRINGED GRASS-OF-PARNASSUS   *Parnassia fimbriata*

General Glabrous perennial from short rhizomes; flowering stems 1-several, 15-30 cm tall, with a *clasping leaf about halfway or more up on the stem*.

Leaves Mostly basal, *broadly kidney shaped*, glossy green.

Flowers White, with greenish or yellowish veins, showy, solitary on stem; petals (5) nearly twice as long as sepals; lower margins of *petals fringed with hairs* in a comblike arrangement; fertile stamens (the 5 with anthers) alternating with broad, glandular-tipped sterile stamens that are divided into 5-9 segments or fingerlike lobes.

Fruits Capsules, with numerous seeds.

Ecology In damp meadows, along streams, and in open and forested seepage areas. Common; generally at medium to alpine elevations in the southern part of our region, more commonly at low elevations in the North.

Notes: There are four species of *Parnassia* in B.C. and in our region; *P. fimbriata* is the only one with fringed petals. *Parnassia palustris* (northern grass-of-Parnassus) and *P. parviflora* (small-flowered grass-of-Parnassus) are about the same size but *P. palustris* has leaves that are heart shaped at the base, whereas *P. parviflora* has leaves that are narrowed to the base. *Parnassia kotzebuei* (Kotzebue's grass-of-Parnassus) is a smaller plant (about 10 cm tall), has leafless flowering stems, and has petals about as long as the sepals. All four species occupy similar wet, spongy habitats. • For common name, see *P. palustris*.

NORTHERN GRASS-OF-PARNASSUS   *Parnassia palustris*

General Glabrous perennial from short rhizomes; flowering stems solitary or clustered, 10-40 cm tall, with a heart-shaped, *clasping leaf usually from below the middle of the stem*.

Leaves Mostly basal, *egg shaped* or elliptic, but more or less heart shaped at the base.

Flowers White, with greenish or yellow veins, showy, solitary on stem; *petals entire (no fringe)*, up to twice as long as sepals; fertile stamens 5, alternating with broad, 7-15 segmented, gland-tipped, sterile stamens.

Fruits Capsules, with numerous seeds.

Ecology Wet, open, seepy places; river flats and riparian thickets, lakeshores, swamps and fens, roadside ditches, wet clearings, deep skidder tracks; sometimes in moist forest glades. Widespread at low to medium elevations in the North, less common in the southern part of the region.

Notes: Dioscorides described a grasslike plant growing on the side of Mount Parnassus. When the Greek description was translated, this "grass" was taken to be *P. palustris*. Obviously, this was a mistake because *Parnassia* species are not even remotely grasslike, but the name stuck.

CUT-LEAF ANEMONE — *Anemone multifida*

General Hairy, tufted perennial with one to many stems from a thickened, commonly branched stem base; 15-50 cm tall.

Leaves Basal leaves long stalked, numerous, divided into three leaflets that themselves are divided 2 or 3 times; leaves that cradle the flower stems short stalked but dissected similarly to basal leaves.

Flowers Fairly showy, ***creamy white, yellowish, or pinkish*** and tinged with red, blue, or purple, particularly on outer surface; ***sometimes bright red-pink***. Single or less commonly in clusters of up to four, long-stalked.

Fruits ***Silky-woolly achenes***, borne in egg-shaped or globose clusters about 1 cm wide.

Ecology From dry, rocky, exposed slopes and open forest in the foothills and valleys to timberline; very common in grasslands, dry open woods, scrub, and rocky meadows ***throughout the region except in wetter climates***.

Notes: Two other species of anemone are superficially similar to *A. multifida*. *A. richardsonii* (yellow anemone) is a small (5-15 cm tall) delicate herb with simple, palmately-lobed basal leaves and solitary, bright yellow flowers. It is a plant of higher elevation thickets, creekbanks, seepage areas, and tundra, generally where wet. *A. parviflora* (northern anemone) is a 10-30 cm tall plant with basal leaves that have 3 wedge-shaped, broadly-lobed leaflets, and solitary, frosty white flowers that are often tinged with blue on the outside. It also inhabits upper elevations, but is more typically an alpine species, in moist tundra, heath, seepage areas, snow beds, and scree. Both *A. richardsonii* and *A. parviflora* are widespread at subalpine to alpine elevations in the northern half of the region, but decrease in abundance further south. • A strong decoction of the plant was used to kill fleas and lice. Smith (1926) reported that the Gitksan placed a handful in their sweatbath for rheumatism and even drank a weak concoction for the same purpose but warns that it burns the throat like whiskey. This has not been confirmed by modern sources.

NARCISSUS ANEMONE — *Anemone narcissiflora*

General Perennial from woody base; stems erect, 5-60 cm tall, glabrous to spreading-hairy.

Leaves Basal, divided into three broad lobes that are themselves deeply divided into narrow pointed segments; stem leaves clustered just below flowers.

Flowers ***Creamy white*** with bluish tinge on back, showy, ***roughly twice as large as those of A. multifida***. Flowers one per stem, in terminal clusters of 1-5.

Fruits ***Glabrous achenes***.

Ecology Grassy glades in subalpine willow-birch scrub, heathlands and snowbeds in alpine tundra, and sometimes in forest openings; scattered but locally abundant ***in northern (south to 55°) part of region***, except for the northeast.

Notes: Alaskan and Siberian native people ate the early spring growth on the upper end of the root. It has a waxy, mealy texture and taste. The leaves were eaten like cress and "Eskimo ice cream" was made from greens and oil beaten to a creamy consistency. Anemone roots were considered to have powerful healing properties and were used for treating wounds. • *Pulsatilla (Anemone) patens* (prairie crocus) can be found in grassland and on dry slopes at low elevations in the North (N of 58°), especially on limey soils. The foliage is very similar to that of *A. narcissiflora* although much more silky-hairy. The flowers of *P. patens* are large and strongly coloured, blue to deep purple. Its achenes are strongly plumose. • *P. patens* is also known as "pasque flower" because it flowers at Easter, and "prairie smoke" because the feathery tails of the fruits give the illusion of smoke crossing the prairie.

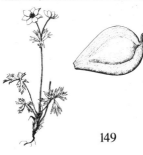

ALPINE WHITE MARSH-MARIGOLD — *Caltha leptosepala* var. *leptosepala*

General Fleshy, glabrous perennial, 5-40 cm tall, from short, erect rootstock.

Leaves Basal, *oblong-oval*, longer than broad with somewhat heart- or arrowhead-shaped base, to 6 cm long, *nearly smooth edged to blunt toothed, waxy green*.

Flowers Showy, *white or greenish, often tinged with blue on back* (outside) and with a greenish-yellow center; usually one per stem.

Fruits Clusters of almost sessile follicles.

Ecology Wet meadows, seepage areas, streambanks, and snow-beds at subalpine and alpine elevations throughout our region.

Notes: The leaves and flower buds were eaten raw or cooked by Alaskan native people. They also boiled the long, white roots which look like sauerkraut when cooked. • Soaked in saltwater and vinegar, the flower buds apparently make an acceptable substitute for capers. • The related *C. palustris* was also eaten, but it contains the poison helleborin which must be destroyed by cooking. • The common name marigold appears to come from the Anglo-Saxon *meargealla*, which means horse-gall, because the unopened buds presumably resembled galls. Marsh because it grows in wet places.

GLOBEFLOWER — *Trollius laxus*

General Glabrous perennial with strong fibrous roots arising from short rootstock; stems erect, 1-several, 10-40 cm tall.

Leaves Basal with broad membranous stipules, the blade *palmately divided* into 5, oval-shaped main segments, which are further divided and toothed; all leaves with stalks except the uppermost stem leaves.

Flowers Showy, *greenish white to creamy white* sometimes with pinkish tinge; single, long stalked.

Fruits Fruiting heads cone shaped, composed of several, many-seeded follicles.

Ecology Wet meadows, seepage areas, streambanks, and snowbeds at high elevations, down into the subalpine zone along streams and in seepage areas, usually blossoming just as the snow recedes. Occurs *only in the southern part of this region* (south of Nechako/McGregor River drainages); commonly in areas of wet climates, less so in the southwest.

Notes: Should not be confused with *Caltha* or white anemones, which usually have a bluish tinge on the outside of the flowers. • The common name, "globeflower," is derived from the globular shape of the flower, at least of the European species *T. europaeus*.

150

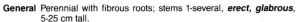

SUBALPINE BUTTERCUP — *Ranunculus eschscholtzii*

General Perennial with fibrous roots; stems 1-several, **erect, glabrous,** 5-25 cm tall.

Leaves Basal leaves on slender stalks, kidney shaped to oval in outline, **usually 3 lobed and then divided again**; stem leaves lacking or sessile; all leaves glabrous.

Flowers Yellow, one to three, terminal, **15-30 mm wide**; sepals and petals 5; sepals **glabrous or with yellowish or brownish hairs**, dropping off soon after flower opens.

Fruits Smooth achenes, essentially glabrous, with **short, slender, straight to somewhat curved beaks**; 20-50 or more in an elongate cluster.

Ecology Mountain meadows, avalanche tracks, talus slopes, into subalpine forest along streambanks, often blooming at edges of melting snowbanks or along streams; a subalpine-alpine species, common throughout.

Notes: Three species in our region somewhat resemble *R. eschscholtzii*. *Ranunculus nivalis* (snow buttercup) can be distinguished by its densely brown-hairy sepals; the hairs are much darker than those on the sepals of *R. eschscholtzii*. *R. nivalis* grows in wet alpine tundra, along creeks and in moist meadows, seepage areas, and snowbanks, north of 57°. *Ranunculus occidentalis* (western buttercup) is more typically a coastal species but has penetrated inland to the upper Skeena, Nass, and Stikine drainages. In our region it usually grows in lush moist subalpine meadows; it is quite hairy on the leaves and also often the stems. *Ranunculus cooleyae* (Cooley's buttercup) has glabrous basal leaves that are circular in outline, no stem leaves, and a single flower with 8-15 narrow petals. It is a species of snowbeds, rocky gullies, and moist scree at high elevations in the Coast Mountains, but also extends inland much like *R. occidentalis*.

SHORE BUTTERCUP — *Ranunculus cymbalaria*

General Glabrous to hairy, tufted perennial **with strawberry-like runners** that root at the nodes.

Leaves Basal, **undivided**; egg, heart, or kidney shaped; **margin scalloped with blunt teeth**; leaf stalks relatively long.

Flowers Yellow, **small (5-12 mm wide)**, few per plant; sepals and petals usually 5; sepals greenish, glabrous, dropping off soon after flowering; petals yellow, as long or slightly longer than sepals.

Fruits Numerous achenes, small, glabrous, **longitudinally ribbed**, forming cylindrical clusters; each achene with a **short, straight beak**.

Ecology Muddy, often trampled areas along streams, ponds, or in marshes; near fresh, brackish, or alkaline water; widespread but scattered at low elevations, most commonly in the southwestern part of our region.

Notes: Ranunculus cymbalaria is one of a group of amphibious or aquatic buttercups (also called water−crowfeet) common in or around our northern wetlands. These plants often have strikingly different floating vs. submerged leaves. *R. aquatilis/trichophyllus* (white water-buttercup) has white flowers and is truly aquatic (usually in shallow water). *R. flammula* (lesser spearwort; long narrow leaves from nodally rooting runners), *R. gmelinii* (small yellow water-buttercup), and *R. hyperboreus* (far-northern buttercup; very small leaves) are amphibious species of pools, muddy shores, and muddy depressions. *Ranunculus lapponicus* (Lapland buttercup), an essentially terrestrial species of black spruce bogs, swamps, and wet forests, is scattered in suitable habitats in the southern part of the region but common in the North. It has long-creeping rhizomes, long-stalked basal leaves, no stem leaves, and solitary, long-stalked flowers with 3 sepals and 6-8 petals.

MEADOW BUTTERCUP — *Ranunculus acris*

General Tall, *hairy* perennial with slender fibrous roots; *stems 1 to several, erect, branched*, hollow, 30-80 cm tall.

Leaves Basal leaves with long stalks, the blades broadly pentagonal or heart shaped in outline, deeply 3 lobed; the lateral segments again divided nearly to base, so that the *whole leaf blade appears 5 lobed in outline*; the whole again divided 2-3 times into narrow, sharp-pointed segments, so that the leaves have a ragged appearance; stem leaves alternate, transitional to 3- to 5-lobed bracts.

Flowers Glossy yellow, *15-30 mm wide*, with hairy stalks, several in loose cluster; sepals greenish, hairy, quickly dropping off; 5 petals.

Fruits Glabrous, smooth achenes with tiny, *flattened and curved beaks*; 25-40 in globular clusters.

Ecology Moist to well-drained soil at lower elevations; moist meadows, hay pastures, clearings, roadsides. *A weedy, European species widely established*, more so in the southern part of the region.

Notes: Many members of the Ranunculaceae, including this species, contain chemicals that can cause severe irritation and blistering of skin, or inflammation of tissues of mouth, throat and digestive tract when swallowed. However, *R. acris* is considered to be harmless in hay because the poisonous material is volatile and "evaporates" when the hay is cured. • Thompson Indians rubbed flowers or whole plant of *R. glaberrimus* (sagebrush buttercup) or other buttercup species on arrow tips as a poison. *R. glaberrimus* is scattered on dry rocky ridges and sandy-gravelly benches in the drier parts of the southern (S of 55°) part of the region, and is one of our earliest spring-blooming wildflowers.

LITTLE BUTTERCUP — *Ranunculus uncinatus*

General Annual or perennial; *stems single, erect, hairy to glabrous, usually unbranched*, hollow, 20-60 cm tall.

Leaves Mostly basal with long stalks; blades simple, heart to kidney shaped in outline, deeply divided into three lobes, which are again divided into toothed lobes, hairy below; *somewhat similar to those of R. acris but not as finely or deeply divided*; stem leaves 1-2, alternate, with lobes more lance shaped and transitional between basal leaves and the bracts at top of stem.

Flowers Yellow, *very small (3-8 mm wide), single at ends of several stalks clustered together above large, lance-shaped leafy bracts*; petals 5.

Fruits Achenes small, 5-30 in rounded clusters; each achene with *small hooked beak*.

Ecology *Native species* common at low to middle elevations throughout the region; often in shady moist soil in woodlands, thickets, meadows, glades, beaches, and along streams; also in disturbed, trampled areas.

Notes: Although this is not the best buttercup for the purpose (because of its small flowers) any buttercup can be used to determine if a person likes butter. Just hold the flower under a person's chin — a yellow reflection means that he or she likes butter!

BUTTERCUP FAMILY

SMALL YELLOW WATER-BUTTERCUP
Ranunculus gmelinii

General Perennial *creeping on mud or floating in water; stems freely rooting at nodes*, glabrous to hairy.

Leaves Mainly on stem, more or less circular in outline, *small (1-3 cm long), deeply divided into 3 lobes, each lobe divided again into linear, elongated lobes*; lobes of submerged leaves delicate and often finer than floating leaves (sometimes almost threadlike).

Flowers Small *(6-15 mm wide)* with yellow petals.

Fruits Achenes with *short beaks*.

Ecology Mudflats, shallow water in ponds, ditches, drained beaver ponds, and along lake shores, throughout the region at lower elevations.

Notes: Another common name for this species is "yellow water-crowfoot," from the supposed resemblance of the leaf to the foot of a crow.

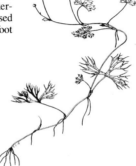

MOUNTAIN MONKSHOOD   *Aconitum delphiniifolium*

General Perennial herb from *tuberous roots*, 0.1 to 1.2 m tall; *stems single, unbranched, hairy above*.

Leaves Mostly from the stem, alternate, deeply palmately 5 lobed; lobes themselves incised and toothed; glabrous.

Flowers Large, showy, *usually dark blue-purple*, but sometimes tinged with green, yellow, or white; *upper part of each flower hoodlike*; single or several in terminal clusters.

Fruits Three to five, glabrous to sparsely hairy follicles.

Ecology Moist, open, often deciduous forest, moist thickets, glades, meadows, streambanks, and tundra; from lowlands to alplands; widespread, but generally uncommon in closed coniferous forest, and more common and over a wider elevational range in the North.

Notes: The species exhibits wide variation in size. Alpine plants are often dwarfed (less than 10 cm tall) and have but a single flower, in contrast to robust, valley-bottom individuals that exceed 1 m in height and have 10 or more flowers. • General leaf shape is similar to that of *Delphinium glaucum*, some species of *Ranunculus*, and *Geranium* spp. – compare their leaf silhouettes. *A. delphiniifolium* typically has narrower leaf lobes. • All parts of the plant are highly poisonous, especially to livestock. The tubers contain aconitin, an ester alkaloid that paralyses the nerves and lowers body temperature and blood pressure. • *Aconitum* is called monkshood because the upper part of the flower resembles the cowl of a monk.

153

TALL LARKSPUR   *Delphinium glaucum*

General Stout perennial, from **thick, tough, short rootstock; stems usually several**, unbranched below flowers, (0.3) 1-2 m tall, usually glabrous and glaucous.

Leaves Numerous, alternate, gradually smaller up the stem, palmately 5-7 lobed with each lobe 2-3 times sharply lobed or toothed, glaucous and glabrous to sparsely hairy.

Flowers *Deep purple* (pale blue within), **with prominent, straight spurs**; numerous in simple to branched, elongate and loose, terminal clusters.

Fruits Erect, glabrous to slightly hairy follicles.

Ecology Open, deciduous or mixed forest, aspen parkland, forest edges, moist thickets, glades, meadows, subalpine parkland, and tundra; from valley bottoms to alpine; widespread, but uncommon to lacking in closed coniferous forest, and uncommon in the southernmost parts of our region.

Notes: Poisonous to cattle (contains delphinine); apparently not toxic to sheep, which can be used to eradicate it from rangeland in restricted areas. Plants are very toxic in spring, less so at flowering and maturity, but the seeds are highly toxic. Burning, clearing of trees, or overgrazing of range containing tall larkspur can lead to great increases in the density of the species. Highly toxic to humans; symptoms of poisoning are abdominal pain, nausea, depressed respiration, and eventually asphyxiation. • A blue dye used in dying cloth or colouring arrows was extracted from the flowers by the Thompson and Okanagan Indians. In recent times small Shuswap girls have scattered the flowers in the Corpus Christi procession in church. • The name larkspur is derived from French *pied d'alouette* meaning foot of the lark or *eperon d' alouette* meaning spur of the lark and refers to the projecting spur of the flowers. "Delphinium" (also used as a common name) is derived from *Delphinus* meaning dolphin.

BLUE COLUMBINE — *Aquilegia brevistyla*

General Perennial from taproot; stems simple, erect, to 70cm tall, glabrous below, sparsely spreading-hairy and somewhat glandular above.

Leaves Mainly basal, twice divided in threes, blades glabrous to long-hairy, *often bluish tinged*, paler and glaucous below.

Flowers *Blue and cream* with bluish, *hooked spurs*; usually 2-3, *relatively small (12-18 mm long)*, spreading to nodding.

Fruits Usually five erect, hairy follicles.

Ecology Gravelly or shaley soil, in open deciduous or mixed forest, thickets, meadows, glades, and along streams; from valley bottoms to near timberline, *sporadically throughout the North, rarely in the southern part of our region*.

Notes: Leaves of *Aquilegia* and *Thalictrum* are similar in general appearance; compare their silhouettes. • The common name is derived from the Latin *columbina* meaning dove-like. The arched petals and spurs of the flowers resemble a quintet of doves (pigeons) arranged in a ring around a dish (a favourite device of ancient artists).

RED COLUMBINE — *Aquilegia formosa*

General Perennial herb from taproot; stems simple, erect, to 1 m tall, glabrous below, sparsely hairy and somewhat glandular above.

Leaves Mainly basal, twice divided in threes; blades glabrous to hairy, *green above*, paler and glaucous beneath.

Flowers *Red and yellow* with 5 long, *straight, reddish spurs with bulbous, glandular tips*; central tuft of stamens and styles protruding. Usually 2-5, sometimes more numerous in vigourous plants, drooping.

Fruits Usually 5 erect follicles with hairy, spreading tips.

Ecology Moist, partly shaded roadsides, rocky slopes, meadows, and forest glades; subalpine meadows, clearings. *Throughout the region* from the lowlands to timberline.

Notes: The flowers are a strong attraction for hummingbirds and butterflies. • Some sources report that the leaves and flowers of columbine are edible; however, care should be taken when trying them, considering the toxic nature of so many plants in this family. • Although there are no reports of columbine being used in traditional native medicines for B.C., Smith (1926) reports that the Gitksan name for the plant means good for bleeding nose. Natives in other parts of North America used various parts in medicinal preparations for diarrhoea, dizziness, aching joints, and possibly venereal disease.

155

WESTERN MEADOWRUE — *Thalictrum occidentale*

General Rhizomatous perennial; *stems glabrous*, 0.4-1.0 m tall; *young stems purplish*.

Leaves Mostly from the stem, glabrous, *bluish green, delicately divided* 3-4 times in threes; each leaflet 3 lobed, on thin stalk.

Flowers Small, in loose clusters at top of plant. *Male and female flowers on separate plants; female flowers with inconspicuous greenish-white sepals (no petals), male flowers purplish with prominent pendant stamens*.

Fruits Short-stalked *achenes with three prominent nerves on each side*.

Ecology Open woods, thickets, meadows, slide tracks, and clearings; from the lowlands to timberline throughout, but most common in the southern half of the region.

Notes: Thalictrum sparsiflorum (few-flowered meadowrue) and *T. venulosum* (veiny meadowrue) are similar to *T. occidentale*. *T. sparsiflorum* has male and female flowers on the same plant, has long-stalked achenes, and is more common in the north. *T. venulosum* has prominent, much-raised veins on the lower surface of the leaflets, and is more common in northeastern B.C. *T. alpinum* (alpine meadowrue) is a dwarf, high elevation species with glossy, mostly basal leaves. • Smith (1926) reported that some Gitksan people may have swallowed the juice of a small piece of the plant for headaches, eye trouble, and sore legs and to clear the throat. This has not been confirmed. • Turner (1979) notes that the Flathead of Montana "dried seeds [of western meadowrue], chewed them until pulverised then rubbed them on the hair and body as perfume."

BANEBERRY — *Actaea rubra*

General Rhizomatous, glabrous to sparsely hairy perennial with 1 to several, erect, branched, leafy stems, 0.4-1.0 m tall.

Leaves Few, all from stems, *large, crinkly*, 2-3 times divided in threes, *the segments coarsely toothed and lobed*.

Flowers *Small, white, and numerous, in rounded clusters*, on long stalks.

Fruits Smooth, *glossy red or white berries*; the red form is more common.

Ecology Moist shady forest, streambanks, and clearings; throughout the region at low to subalpine elevations.

Notes: The berries, foliage, and roots are all highly poisonous. As few as six berries can induce vomiting, bloody diarrhoea, and finally paralysis of respiration. The rootstock is a violent purgative and emetic. • "The Lillooet name for this plant means sick. They used it sparingly as a physic and tonic boiled in water. Anyone taking it had to suffer the consequences of being severely ill." (Turner 1978) • The common name "baneberry" obviously refers to the plant's severely poisonous nature and comes from the Anglo-Saxon word *bana* meaning murderous. • The leaf shape is similar to that of *Osmorhiza* species; compare their silhouettes.

Silhouettes

Aconitum delphiniifolium

Delphinium glaucum

Ranunculus acris

Ranunculus uncinatus

Geranium erianthum

Geranium viscosissimum

Geranium richardsonii

157

Silhouettes

*Thalictrum
occidentale*

*Thalictrum
venulosum*

*Thalictrum
sparsiflorum*

*Thalictrum
alpinum*

*Aquilegia
formosa*

*Aquilega
brevistyla*

*Osmorhiza
chilensis*

158

GOAT'S BEARD — *Aruncus dioicus*

General Robust perennial; stems several, glabrous, from stout short-creeping rhizomes, *1-2 m tall.*

Leaves Lower leaves large, usually three times compound, the leaflets sharply toothed and pointed, the upper leaves smaller and less compounded; green and usually glabrous above, hairy and paler below.

Flowers *White, tiny, densely packed in elongated, terminal, much divided cluster; the branchlets spikelike.* Male and female flowers on separate plants.

Fruits Small, erect follicles, 3 mm long, with divergent tips.

Ecology Moist forest, slide tracks, streambanks, roadsides, and clearings. More common in coastal areas, but can be found in the wetter, southern parts of our region in moist, usually open sites at low to subalpine elevations.

Notes: The name "goat's beard" refers to the large, fluffy, white flower clusters. Also known as "spaghetti flower".

SITKA BURNET — *Sanguisorba canadensis* ssp. *latifolia*

General Perennial, glabrous, freely rhizomatous; flowering stems 25-100 cm tall.

Leaves *Mostly basal, with attached membranous stipules;* blades 10-30 cm long, *divided into 9-17 egg-shaped to oblong, coarsely toothed leaflets;* leaves of flowering stems 1-3, reduced, with leaflet-like stipules.

Flowers *Greenish white or yellowish white*, numerous and small, arranged *in dense cylindrical heads*.

Fruits Achenes, slightly winged on the four angles.

Ecology Fens, swamps, shrub-carrs, streambanks, thickets, forest openings, seepage areas, and moist subalpine-alpine meadows; generally grows in the open, and sometimes thrives in wetter parts of recent clearcuts. From low to high elevations throughout the region although, as with *Aruncus dioicus*, most abundant towards the coast.

Notes: Known as *Sanguisorba sitchensis* or *S. stipulata* by some taxonomists. • Herbalists recommend the leaves be made into an herbal tea and root decoctions may be used for internal and external bleeding, for dysentery, or for genital discharges. • The name *burnet* comes from the old French word *brunette* meaning brown, and is applied to European species of *Sanguisorba* because their flowers are a rich red-brown colour.

159

LARGE-LEAVED AVENS — *Geum macrophyllum*

General Hairy perennial with short rhizome, stems *to 1 m tall*.

Leaves *Basal leaves long stalked, with heart- to kidney-shaped terminal segment many times larger than the several smaller leaflets below*; stem leaves few, sessile or nearly so, deeply 3 lobed or 3 parted.

Flowers *Bright yellow, saucer shaped*, at the tips of the branches, single or in a few-flowered cluster.

Fruits Clusters of *short-hairy achenes that have elongate styles with a distinctive S-shaped bend near tip*. These fruits cling to any rough surface, hence have a "stick-tight" mode of dispersal by animals, including humans wearing wool socks.

Ecology Moist woods, openings, roadsides, clearings, or along stream banks, from low to subalpine elevations throughout the region.

Notes: Geum macrophyllum has several subspecies, two of which (ssp. *macrophyllum* and ssp. *perincisum*) some taxonomists consider separate species. We have both these taxa in our region; ssp. *macrophyllum* is more typically a coastal plant, whereas ssp. *perincisum* (which has the terminal segment of the basal leaves deeply cleft rather than shallowly lobed) is the more frequent form in most of the region. • The related *Geum rivale* (water avens) is scattered at low elevations in wet, often shaded habitats (swamps, streambanks, wet meadows, and thickets) south of about 57°. The individual leaflets are lyre shaped rather than heart shaped. The flowers have yellow-flesh-coloured petals with purple veins and stand upright rather than spreading as in *G. macrophyllum*. The sepals of *G. rivale* are reddish purple and the achenes lack the S-shaped curve on the beak (style). • The name "avens" apears to come from the old French *avence* or medieval Latin *avancia*. They in turn may have derived from the Greek word for antidote because species of avens were supposed to ward off "the devil and evil spirits, venomous serpents and wild beasts."

OLD MAN'S WHISKERS — *Geum triflorum*

General Perennial with thick ascending rhizome, *covered in old leaf bases; stems up to 40 cm tall*, softly hairy.

Leaves Basal leaves divided into *9-19 crowded leaflets* divided again into narrow, toothed segments; stem leaves 2-4, small, usually divided into linear lobes.

Flowers Sepals *purplish, urn shaped*, enclosing 5 pinkish to yellow petals (*flowers appear to be partially closed*). Clusters of 1-5, usually 3, *usually nodding*.

Fruits Elongated achenes with long, slender, plumelike, bronze to purplish styles; *in erect, feathery clusters*.

Ecology Open, dry, often calcareous habitats, gravelly soils, grasslands, foothills, dry open forest, and into subalpine meadows. Locally common in the southernmost part of region (to about 54°), and also in the Peace River district.

Notes: The Thompson and Okanagan people boiled and steeped roots to make a tea which was used as a beverage or appetizer as well as a medicine for colds, flu, and fever. The Blackfoot of Alberta reportedly used the crushed seeds as a perfume. • Also known as "prairie smoke;" both common names refer to the feathery styles on the fruits. When there are many plants growing together the colour and "plumage" of the fruits suggest a haze of low-lying smoke.

Potentilla Key

1. Shrub; flowers yellow; leaves numerous, pinnate .... *P. fruticosa*
   (see section on SHRUBS)
1. Herbs (or, woody at base)
   2. Flowers reddish purple; semiaquatic with long, often floating, more-or-less woody rhizomes (a) .... *P. palustris*
   2. Flowers yellow or white
      3. Plant with long, strawberry-like runners; flowers solitary on leafless stalks (b) .. .. *P. anserina*
      3. Plants without runners; flowers few to many on more-or-less leafy stems, if solitary the plant dwarf and tufted
         4. Plants glandular-hairy; petals white, cream, or pale yellow; style from near the base of the ovary; leaves pinnate (c) .... *P. arguta**
         4. Plants generally not glandular-hairy; petals bright yellow; style from the tip of the ovary or nearly so
            5. Principal leaves divided in 3's or palmate with 5-9 leaflets
               6. Principal leaves mostly divided in 3's
                  7. Lower surface of leaves without matted white wool, but often hairy
                     8. Plants annual or biennial (usually); flowers numerous in leafy clusters; petals about as long as sepals .... *P. norvegica**
                     8. Plants perennial; stem bases reddish-brown scaly; flowers one to few; petals longer than sepals (d) ....,,,,,,,,,,,,,........ *P. hyparctica**
                  7. Lower surface of leaves distinctly white-woolly
                     9. Plants generally with long soft (not matted) hairs throughout; scales on stem base very dark (dark brown); leaflets somewhat leathery, dark grayish green above, strongly ribbed beneath; flowers usually more than 2 cm in diameter (e) .... *P. villosa*
                     9. Plants generally not with long soft hairs throughout; stem base scales lighter (reddish-brown); leaflets not leathery or strongly ribbed beneath; flowers usually less than 2 cm in diameter
                        10. Stem (at least the lower part) and leaf stalks cobwebby-woolly but lacking soft spreading and long straight hairs (f) .... *P. nivea**
                        10. Stem and leaf stalks not matted-woolly, with soft spreading or long straight hairs
                           11. Plants usually dwarf, less than 7-10 cm tall; stem and leaf stalks with short spreading hairs beneath the longer outer hairs; flowers usually 1-2, often over 1.5 cm wide (g) .... *P. uniflora*
                           11. Plants often taller (10-45 cm tall), less tufted and matted; stem and leaf stalks without short spreading hairs beneath the longer outer hairs; flowers two to few-several, mostly less than 1.5 cm wide (h) .... *P. hookeriana**
               6. Principal leaves palmate with 5-9 leaflets
                  12. Leaflets usually greenish above, grayish-woolly beneath; plants usually more than 30 cm tall (i) ... . *P. gracilis*
                  12. Leaflets usually greenish or grayish-green on both surfaces, never woolly; plants usually less than 30 cm tall, relatively few-flowered (j) .... *P. diversifolia*
            5. Principal leaves pinnate
               13. Leaves green above and below, or white-woolly only on lower surface
                  14. Leaves green or equally grayish-green on both surfaces, the 5-7 leaflets irregularly toothed in upper part, entire in lower portion (j) .... *P. diversifolia*
                  14. Leaves green above and below, or white-tomentose below, the 5-11 leaflets toothed or lobed to near the base (k) .... *P. pensylvanica*
               13. Leaves silky hairy to white-woolly on both surfaces (l) .... *P. hippiana**

* Not described in detail in this guide, but see the conspectus of *Potentilla*.

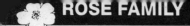

Conspectus of Common Species of *Potentilla*

	palustris	fruticosa	anserina	arguta	norvegica	diversifolia	gracilis
Habit	semiaquatic perennial	shrubby perennial	perennial	perennial	annual or biennial	perennial	perennial
Rhizomes	long-creeping, +\- woody, often floating	lacking	lacking	lacking	lacking	lacking	lacking
Stems	prostrate to ascending, 10-100 cm long; glabrous below, glandular-hairy above, often reddish	up to 1.5 m tall; branches hairy when young, soon becoming glabrous in age with brown, shreddy bark	long, hairy, strawberry-like runners	25-80 cm tall; glandular-hairy	simple or branched, up to 60 cm tall; hairy	slender, mostly unbranched 15-40 cm tall; glabrous	stout, 30-80 cm tall; hairy
Leaves	lower leaves pinnate with 5-7 leaflets; green above, paler and hairy below	numerous, pinnate with (3) 5-7 leaflets; green and sparsely hairy above, greyish and silvery hairy below.	all basal, with 5-17 main leaflets interspersed by smaller ones; green and glabrous to silky above, silky hairy below	basal leaves pinnate, with 7-9 leaflets; green and glandular hairy on both sides; upper leaflets larger than lower	mostly along stem with 3 leaflets	mostly basal, palmate or pinnate, with 5-7 leaflets; green and mostly glabrous above, green (though often paler) and hairy below	basal and along stem; basal leaves palmate, with 5-7(9) leaflets; green and hairy to glabrous above, usually paler and hairier below
Flowers	few to several, intensely reddish purple	solitary (usually single in leaf axils), or in small terminal clusters; yellow, showy	showy, yellow, single on long (5-30 cm) stalks	several to many in compact, narrow, +\- flat-topped cluster; petals pale yellow to cream or whitish	few to several in compact +\- leafy clusters; petals yellow, shorter than sepals	few to several in open cluster; showy, yellow	several to many in open +\- flat-topped cluster; showy, yellow
Habitat	marshes, fens, bogs, stream-banks, and lakeshores; low to medium elevations	usually moist open woods, thickets, swamps, and bogs	open damp areas; streambanks lakeshores, meadows, mudflats;	open, often dry and rocky areas; meadows, grassy ridges, open deciduous forest	damp, disturbed ground; roadsides, gravel pits, landings, other waste areas	open montane to alpine areas; grassland, meadows, heath, tundra	lowland meadows, grassland, thickets, and open deciduous woods

hyparctia	villosa	nivea	hookeriana	uniflora	pensylvanica	hippiana
dwarf, tufted perennial	tufted perennial (often dwarfed in our region)	perennial	perennial	dwarf, tufted perennial	tufted, perennial	perennial
lacking; stem bases reddish brown scaly	lacking; stem bases brown-scaly	lacking	lacking	lacking; stem bases reddish brown	lacking	lacking
3-20 cm (usually less than 10 cm) tall; stems and leaf stalks long-hairy, not at all white-woolly	5-30 cm (in our region usually less than 20 cm) tall; stems and leaf stalks with long spreading hairs but not woolly	7-30 cm tall; stems and leaf stalks cobwebby-woolly	8-30 cm tall; stems and leaf stalks with long spreading hairs, not at all matted-woolly	3-15 cm tall (usually less than 7 cm); stems and leaf stalks with long spreading hairs, usually not woolly, but commonly with short hairs beneath the long outer hairs	10-45 cm tall; one to several; sparsely to densely hairy and usually woolly; stipules of stem leaves cleft	30-50 cm tall; one to several, white silky or woolly; stipules of stem leaves +\- entire
mostly basal, with 3 leaflets; green and sparsely hairy to glabrous above, paler and hairier below	mostly basal, with 3 leaflets; dark green and silky hairy above, white or greyish woolly below; strongly ribbed below	mostly basal with 3(-5) leaflets; green and silky-hairy above, distinctly white woolly below	mostly basal with 3 (-5) leaflets; green and hairy above, densely white woolly below	mostly basal, with 3(-5) leaflets; green and sparsely to densely hairy above, densely white woolly below	basal and along stem; pinnate with 5-9 leaflets, deeply divided into narrow segments; grey-green and hairy to glabrous above, grayish woolly below	mostly basal; pinnate with 7-11 leaflets, white or greyish-silky on both surfaces
one to few; showy (1-2 cm diam.), yellow; petals 6-8 mm long	one to several; showy (2-3 cm diam.), yellow; petals 8-12 mm long	one to several in loose cluster; showy, yellow; petals 4-7 mm long	two to few flowered; showy, yellow; petals 4-7 mm long	1 or 2 flowered; showy, yellow; petals 6-11 mm long	few to many in +\- compact cluster; showy, yellow; petals 5-8 mm long	several to many in open cluster; showy, yellow; petals 6-8 mm long
alpine scree and tundra	in our region, gravelly or rocky alpine tundra	montane grassy slopes, gravelly ridges and outcrops; alpine scree and tundra, often calcareous	gravelly, often calcareous soil and rock outcrops; montane meadows and grassland to (usually) alpine zone	alpine tundra, scree, outcrops, ledges	dry rocky slopes, grasslands; mostly in southern part of our region (Chilcotin) but also in Peace District and Stikine drainage.	dry rocky slopes and grasslands; mostly in southern part of the region but also in Peace district and Telegraph Creek area

SILVERWEED — *Potentilla anserina*

General Perennial from ***thick fleshy roots***; with long, ***strawberrylike runners***, rooting and forming leaf-clusters at nodes; ***grayish, silky hairs on leaves***.

Leaves Basal, tufted, deeply divided with ***7-12 oval to oblong, coarsely toothed leaflets***, interspersed with smaller leaflets lacking teeth, varying from silky-gray hairy on both surfaces to green-glabrous above.

Flowers ***Yellow, single flower on long leafless stem***.

Fruits Corky achenes, grooved on back and top.

Ecology Open damp places, streambanks and pond margins, alkaline mudflats, depressions in meadows. Scattered at low to medium elevations, locally common primarily on the Fraser Plateau, in the Peace River district, and in the northwest part of the region (Atlin area).

Notes: P. anserina is sometimes also referred to as "Indian sweet potato" because the long fleshy roots were eaten cooked or raw by many interior tribes (Thompson, Lillooet, Shuswap, and Okanagan). The roots are said to have a pleasant, slightly bitter taste. • "The Blackfoot of Alberta used the runners as ties for leggings and blankets" (Turner 1979). • The common name, "silverweed," describes the silky-grey, hairy appearance of the plant.

MARSH CINQUEFOIL — *Potentilla palustris*

General Perennial with ***long-creeping, often floating, more or less woody rhizomes***; stems frequently reddish below, to 1 m tall.

Leaves Mainly on flowering stems, ***lower ones palmately divided into 5-7 leaflets, oblong, coarsely toothed***, pale green above, glaucous to finely hairy on the underside; upper leaves smaller.

Flowers Strikingly ***reddish purple***, about 2 cm wide, arranged in loose terminal clusters.

Fruits Numerous, plump, oval to egg-shaped achenes.

Ecology In marshes and bogs, wet meadows, and lake margins from low to medium elevations, ***usually at least partly submerged***. Common throughout the region.

Notes: The name "cinquefoil" literally means five leaves and refers to the fact that many species of *Potentilla* have leaves divided into five leaflets. • The reddish purple flowers emit a fetid odour that attracts carrion-feeding insects as pollinators.

GRACEFUL CINQUEFOIL — *Potentilla gracilis*

General Perennial with several erect stems from a thick, scaly, woody base, *40-80 cm tall*; highly variable in degree of hairiness.

Leaves Basal leaves numerous, variable, long stalked, *palmately divided into 5-9 leaflets; hairy to glabrous above, usually paler and more densely hairy (often woolly) below*; 1-2 stem leaves.

Flowers Yellow, showy, with notched petals; *several to many*, in terminal clusters.

Fruits Numerous small achenes.

Ecology Grassland, scrub, open woods, and meadows. Also roadsides and waste places. At low to medium elevations and usually on relatively dry and warm aspects; mostly in the southern half of our region, occasionally in the Northeast.

Notes: A highly variable species. • *Potentilla arguta* (white cinquefoil) grows in similar habitats throughout the region, but is easily distinguished by pinnately compound leaves (7-9 leaflets) that are sticky-hairy but not white-woolly beneath, sticky-hairy stems, and pale yellow to whitish flowers.

ONE-FLOWERED CINQUEFOIL — *Potentilla uniflora*

General *Densely tufted, silvery-green* perennial; stems from short branched rhizome, *2-10 cm tall, grayish-hairy* throughout, the leaf-stalks and often the lower stems with wavy to nearly straight, scarcely tangled hairs, the stems densely woolly above.

Leaves Leaves *white-woolly beneath, hairy and somewhat greenish above*, the basal leaves divided into *three, oval-shaped, deeply toothed leaflets*, 1-2 cm long; stem leaves few and small.

Flowers Yellow, showy, *single, rarely 2-3*; petals with shallow notch at tip.

Fruits Several to many achenes.

Ecology Rocky alpine slopes, ridges, ledges, and crevices, gravelly soils. Common throughout at high elevations.

Notes: P. uniflora can be mistaken for puny versions of *P. villosa* (violous cinquefoil) or *P. nivea* (snow cinquefoil). *P. villosa* has generally larger flowers with narrower calyx bracts than *P. uniflora*. A lack of tomentum (woolly matted hairs) on the leaf petiole distinguishes *P. uniflora* from *P. nivea*. Another species, *P. hookeriana*, bears enough similarities to *P. uniflora* that their relationship must be close, although *P. hookeriana* is larger and has a branched inflorescence (and therefore two or more flowers). • *P. hyparctica* (arctic cinquefoil) is another low-growing species found in alpine habitats. Its leaflets are less hairy on the undersurface than those of *P. uniflora* and its stems and leaf stalks are hairy but not densely woolly. Refer to the key and conspectus of *Potentilla* for more details.

165

| DIVERSE-LEAFED CINQUEFOIL | *Potentilla diversifolia* |

General Tufted perennial from stout, branched rhizome, stems slender, usually several, spreading to erect, 15-35 cm tall.

Leaves Mostly basal (usually a few stem leaves), long stalked, **deeply divided into 5(-7) leaflets**, strongly toothed above the middle, glabrous to slightly hairy on upper surface, generally hairy on under surface.

Flowers Yellow, showy, few to several, in open cluster on long stalks; petals 5-9 mm long, notched at tip.

Fruits Cluster of achenes.

Ecology Common throughout the region in subalpine meadows and alpine tundra; in the Chilcotin, descends to medium elevations in dry open forest; in the North also occurs at low elevations in grasslands, and on rocky ridges and gravel bars.

Notes: Some plants in some areas have a distinct bluish green or grayish green appearance.

| PRAIRIE CINQUEFOIL | *Potentilla pensylvanica* |

General Tufted, grayish-green perennial from stout woody base; 1-several flowering stems 15-40 cm tall, reclining to erect, sparsely to thickly hairy and **usually densely woolly** as well.

Leaves Basal leaves **twice divided, very hairy, usually greenish above but nearly white on the lower surface; leaflets 5-11**, the lower ones often smaller, the upper 3 the largest, more or less oblong and further divided halfway to midrib, 1-4 cm long.

Flowers Yellow, showy, few to many; petals 4-7 mm long, notched at tip.

Fruits Cluster of achenes.

Ecology Dry rocky slopes, grassland, scrub, open woods. Occasional at low elevations, mostly in the southwestern part of our region, but also in dry boreal areas like the Peace River breaks and the Stikine Canyon.

Notes: Potentilla hippiana (woolly cinquefoil) is similar but its leaves are only once divided and tend to be white-hairy all over. It occurs in very dry open habitats (much like those of *P. pensylvanica*) but is known from our region only along the Fraser River south from Quesnel and along the Peace River.

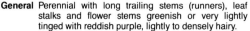

WOOD STRAWBERRY   *Fragaria vesca*

General   Perennial with long trailing stems (runners), leaf stalks and flower stems greenish or very lightly tinged with reddish purple, lightly to densely hairy.

Leaves   Basal, compound, divided into 3 leaflets, strongly toothed, the **terminal tooth projecting beyond the adjacent lateral ones**, silky-hairy underneath, **yellow-green on upper surface**.

Flowers   White, 3-15 **on stems that are usually longer than leaves at maturity**.

Fruits   Small achenes buried in fleshy red berries that are juicy and delicious; **fruit stems longer than leaves**.

Ecology   Dry to moist open woods, stream banks, and sandy meadows; at low elevations mostly in south central part of the region.

Notes: The fruit of both *F. vesca* and *F. virginiana* were highly prized by all interior native people. They were usually eaten fresh, although some people mashed them and dried them, uncooked, in cakes for winter use. • The leaves were steeped for a type of tea or used to flavour cooked roots. The Carrier drink a decoction of boiled stems "when they have bleeding in their stomach" (Carrier Linguistic Committee 1973). • Three or four runners of strawberries were plaited together by Lillooet girls to make belts or headbands. • In folk medicine, the tea from leaves is a remedy for diarrhoea and a gargle for sore throats. Linnaeus was reported to have eaten lots of strawberries to keep himself free of gout. • For common name, see *F. virginiana*.

WILD STRAWBERRY   *Fragaria virginiana*

General   Perennial with rhizome usually from a single crown, with several trailing stems (runners); leaf stalks and flowering stems sparsely hairy but usually not reddish tinged.

Leaves   Basal, **glaucous bluish green above**, naked to silky-hairy beneath, compound, divided into three leaflets with toothed edges; **terminal tooth less than 1/2 as wide and shorter than the adjacent teeth**.

Flowers   White, 2-15 in open clusters **on stems that are usually shorter than the surrounding leaves at maturity**.

Fruits   Small strawberries, juicy, delicious, and much richer in flavour than domestic species; **fruit stem shorter than leaves**.

Ecology   Open, often disturbed places (clearings, landings, roadsides), also in open forest, from the lowlands to subalpine elevations throughout the region.

Notes: This species is the original parent of nine-tenths of all the cultivated strawberries now grown. The related coastal species, *F. chiloensis*, is the original parent of the remaining cultivars. • A tea made from the leaves may also be used as a cure for diarrhoea. • The name strawberry from the Anglo-Saxon *streowberie* could derive from the dried runners being strewed on the ground, or from the Old English word for straw, which also meant mote or chaff — here in reference to the small achenes embedded in the surface of the berry. • Also sometimes called the blue-leaf strawberry because the leaves have a glaucous blue-green colour.

167

Pea family silhouettes

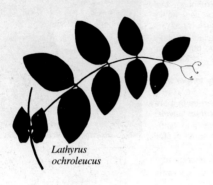

Lathyrus ochroleucus

Lathyrus venosus

Lathyrus nevadensis

Vicia americana

CREAMY PEAVINE — *Lathyrus ochroleucus*

General Perennial with creeping rhizome and climbing, somewhat angled stems; 30-100 cm tall; glabrous.

Leaves *Leaflets in 3-4 pairs*, to 7 cm long, *without hairs*, with well-developed, usually branched tendrils; *stipules broad, oval shaped, often half as long as the leaflets*.

Flowers *White to yellowish white*, "pealike," in terminal clusters of *6-15*.

Fruits Hairless pods.

Ecology Moist to dry, open woods (more abundant in deciduous and mixed stands than coniferous stands), rocky slopes, and clearings. Widespread and often abundant at low to medium elevations mostly in the southern half of the region, and also in the Peace River district. Has a similar habitat to, and often occurs with *L. nevadensis*.

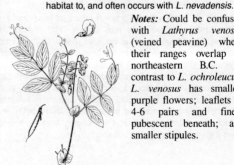

Notes: Could be confused with *Lathyrus venosus* (veined peavine) where their ranges overlap in northeastern B.C. In contrast to *L. ochroleucus*, *L. venosus* has smaller, purple flowers; leaflets in 4-6 pairs and finely pubescent beneath; and smaller stipules.

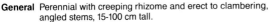

PURPLE PEAVINE — *Lathyrus nevadensis*

General Perennial with creeping rhizome and erect to clambering, angled stems, 15-100 cm tall.

Leaves With *4-10 leaflets*, 2-12 cm long, **hairy on under surface**, tendrils present; **stipules narrow, linear to lance shaped**.

Flowers *Bluish purple to mauve-red*, pealike, in *2-7* flowered terminal clusters.

Fruits Hairless pods.

Ecology Moist to dry, open woods, clearings, open rocky slopes. A typically low to medium elevation species that dominates the understory in many aspen or mixed-wood stands in the southern half of the region.

Notes: Often confused with *Vicia americana* because both have purple flowers. Where they grow together, *Lathyrus nevadensis* generally appears more robust and has fewer and larger leaflets than *V. americana*. The stipules of *Lathyrus* have smooth or inconspicuously toothed margins, whereas *Vicia* stipules have jaggedly toothed margins. Another reliable way of telling them apart is by looking at the style. The hairs at the tip of the style of *Lathyrus* are arranged on one side so that they resemble a toothbrush. The hairs of the style of *V. americana*, however, are all around the very tip like a bottle-brush. • *Lathyrus venosus* has stems that are more ridged than those of *L. nevadensis*, and leaflets that are markedly veiny underneath.

AMERICAN VETCH — *Vicia americana*

General Perennial, trailing or climbing, often in tangled masses; glabrous to hairy stems, 15-100 cm tall.

Leaves With simple or forking tendrils; *8-18 leaflets* that are about 3.5 cm long and glabrous or hairy; **stipules small, narrow, and sharply toothed**.

Flowers *Bluish purple to reddish purple*, pealike; *3-9* flowers in loose terminal cluster.

Fruits Glabrous pods.

Ecology Fields, thickets, and open deciduous or mixed forest, at low to medium elevations. Similar in range and habitat to the peavines, but more widespread.

Notes: Often confused with *Lathyrus nevadensis* (see Notes above). • Several species of vetch have been reported to be toxic to livestock and children. The seeds in the pods in particular may attract a child's curiosity. • The name vetch is from the Latin *vicia*, which is thought to be derived from the Latin verb *vincio* (to bind), in reference to the climbing habit of these plants.

PEA FAMILY

ARCTIC LUPINE — *Lupinus arcticus*

General Perennial with several stems from a branched rhizome; stems to 60 cm tall, slender, hollow, long-hairy.

Leaves Mostly arising from near the base, with long stalks; **palmately compound with 6-8 leaflets** mostly with sharp, pointed tips, hairy on under surface. **Stalks of basal leaves 4-6 times as long as leaflets**.

Flowers Bluish, several in an elongated cluster; typical "pea-like" flower.

Fruits Hairy pods.

Ecology Mostly open ground; common throughout. Most abundant in high elevation meadows and open subalpine forests, but also on roadsides and in open, successional forest (e.g., pine stands) down to medium elevations.

Notes: Two similar species are *Lupinus polyphyllus* (large-leaved lupine) and *L. nootkatensis* (Nootka lupine). *L. polyphyllus* has large leaves with 10-17 leaflets and the lower stem leaves, at least, have stalks that are 3-6 times as long as the longest leaflet. In *L. nootkatensis* (a more typically coastal species), all the leaves are on the stem, the leaf stalks are rarely more than twice the length of the longest leaflet, and the tips of the leaflets are rounded to blunt with a slight point as opposed to the sharply pointed ones of *L. arcticus*. • *L. polyphyllus* is a native species that has been widely cultivated. Where it escapes it spreads into new areas and can be seen on disturbed sites, especially roadsides north of Quesnel in the Fraser River drainage. • Several lupines are known to have caused fatal poisoning in animals. All species should be considered poisonous.

ALPINE MILK-VETCH — *Astragalus alpinus*

General Matted perennial with widespread rhizomes; stems slender, **leafy**, creeping at base but becoming erect, 5-25 cm long.

Leaves Compound leaves 5-15 cm long, hairy; mostly **8-11 pairs of leaflets**, oval to oblong-elliptic, 5-20 mm long, rarely as much as 10 mm broad.

Flowers **Two-toned bluish or pinkish purple, pale to white at base; 5-17** flowers in crowded terminal cluster up to 4 cm long.

Fruits Black-hairy pods.

Ecology Alpine tundra, heath, meadows, scree slopes; moist thickets, open woods, glades, gravel bars, floodplain thickets and forests. From the lowlands to the alpine zone, scattered throughout the region but most common in the North.

Notes: Also found in our region in low elevation riparian habitats, *Astragalus americanus* (American milk-vetch) is a more robust plant with stout stems and leaflets that are bigger and broader than those of *A. alpinus*. The flowers of *A. americanus* are white, the flowering stems are usually shorter than the leaves, and the pod is not hairy and becomes inflated like a bladder. • Several species of *Astragalus* are known to be toxic to livestock. The symptoms of poisoning include staggering and loss of muscle control, hence some species are called "locoweeds." The symptoms could be caused by either locoine or the accumulation of large amounts of selenium, which is known to cause blind staggers. Whether or not the above two species of *Astragalus* are toxic is not known for sure. • For derivation of "vetch," see *Vicia americana*. Species of *Astragalus* have the name "milk-vetch" from the belief that the milk supply of goats was increased when they ate these plants.

170

ALPINE SWEET-VETCH — *Hedysarum alpinum*

General Perennial from woody taproot; stems several, 10-90 cm tall, declining to erect, branched above, sparsely hairy.

Leaves Compound with 9-21 leaflets that are oblong to lance shaped with pointed tips and **prominent veins**, and are sparsely gray-hairy underneath.

Flowers *Reddish purple at tip, paler at base*; pea shaped, 10-18 mm long, several to many, somewhat drooping in compact to elongated, terminal clusters.

Fruits *Flattened pods with constrictions* between each of 2-5 seeds, *glabrous*; look *like short strings of flattened beads*.

Ecology Rocky slopes, open woods, spruce forests, roadsides, gravel bars to alpine tundra. From low to high elevations throughout the region north of 55°.

Notes: Typically occurs at low elevations as a tall plant with numerous flowers, but grades into smaller plants with fewer flowers at higher elevations or on harsher sites. Can form large colonies on grassy slopes or moist gravel flats; a marvellous sight when in flower. • Also called "Eskimo potato," "licorice root," "bear root," and "Indian potato," the roots of this species were very important to northern peoples. Inuit and interior Alaskan natives collected them in fall or spring and ate them raw, boiled, or roasted. • Do not confuse with northern sweet-vetch, the root of which is considered to be poisonous to humans. Roots of both species are a favourite food of grizzly bears.

NORTHERN SWEET-VETCH — *Hedysarum boreale* ssp. *mackenzii*

General Perennial from woody taproot, stems several to many, 25-60 cm tall, branched above, gray-hairy.

Leaves Compound with 9-15 small leaflets, linear-oblong to elliptic, densely hairy on both sides to glabrous above; *veins of leaflets inconspicuous*.

Flowers *Rose to red-purple*, very showy and fragrant, 16-22 mm long, in elongated clusters.

Fruits *Flat pods constricted* between each of 1-4(6) enclosed seeds, *hairy*.

Ecology Dry hillsides and open slopes, gravel bars, at low to middle elevations mostly north of 55°.

Notes: H. boreale ssp. *mackenzii* (= *H. mackenzii*) can be distinguished from *H. alpinum* by its thicker leaflets that have inconspicuous lateral veins, and by its generally larger, showier flowers. • The roots are extremely poisonous and are known to have caused severe illness in members of Sir John Richardson's Arctic Expedition, who mistook it for the edible *H. alpinum*. • It is a favourite food of grizzly bears, who make large excavations to get at the roots. • Also known as wild sweet pea.

FIELD LOCOWEED — *Oxytropis campestris*

General Densely tufted, hairy perennial; many **basal leaves** arising from a much-branched woody crown with stout taproot below; very variable in size and hairiness.

Leaves Compound, with 7 to numerous leaflets that are scattered, opposite, and narrowly elliptic.

Flowers **Yellowish white**, small, arranged in terminal cluster on a leafless stem.

Fruits Pods up to 16 mm long, **with black and white hairs, membranous but becoming thin and papery when dry**.

Ecology Gravel bars, rocky outcrops, roadsides, dry open woodland and meadows, and up into alpine tundra. Widespread throughout the region except in areas of wet climate, from valley bottoms to the alpine zone.

Notes: Oxytropis campestris is the name traditionally given to a complex that includes at least 3 segregate species in this region: *O. monticola*, *O. varians*, and *O. jordalii*. See Welsh (1974) and Douglas *et al.* (1989) for details. • *Oxytropis campestris* can be  confused with two other species, *O. sericea* (silky locoweed) and *O. splendens* (showy locoweed). *O. sericea* has pale yellow flowers but is generally more gray silky-hairy all over than *O. campestris* and has fewer leaflets. The pods of *O. sericea* are leathery and become hardened and bony when dry. *O. splendens* has numerous showy purple flowers. When not in flower, it can be distinguished from the other two species because its leaflets are arranged in whorls of 2 to 6. This species is also densely silvery-silky all over. It grows mainly in low elevation grasslands and on rocky south slopes in the North.

BLACKISH LOCOWEED — *Oxytropis nigrescens*

General Dwarf perennial from stout taproot, in **dense tufts or clumps** from branched woody base; stems flat on ground to erect; **usually densely covered in shiny hairs**.

Leaves Divided into 5-15 oval to elliptic, very hairy leaflets.

Flowers **Bright purple**, showy, **usually only 1-2 on hairy stems**; sepals covered in black hairs.

Fruits Stalkless, **sausage-shaped pods, covered in gray-black hairs**, pointed at both ends and three times longer than broad, turning **bright red when mature**.

Ecology Windswept ridges, rocky places, often among lichens and mosses in alpine tundra; fairly common north of 57°.

Notes: Very similar to two other purple-flowered species, *O. huddelsonii* (Huddelson's locoweed), and *O. podocarpa* (stalked-pod locoweed), which grow in the same type of habitat. • The pod of *O. podocarpa* differs from both other species in that it has a short stalk, is oval to elliptic in shape, and has papery, thin walls that are strongly inflated like a bladder. • The stalkless pod of *O. huddelsonii* is similar in shape to that of *O. nigrescens*, but is shorter, being only two times (or less) as long as broad. It has a hooked beak and is scarcely hairy, whereas the *O. nigrescens* pod is black-hairy with a straight beak. • "Locoweed" refers to the symptons of staggering and loss of muscle control observed in livestock that have grazed on these plants.

WHITE SWEET-CLOVER — *Melilotus alba*

General *Tall annual* (occasionally biennial) from a taproot, up to 1-2 m; stems erect, *much branched*.

Leaves Small, *in 3's* (like clover); *leaflets oblong*, toothed, 1-2 cm long.

Flowers *White*, small (4-5 mm long), typical pea flowers; numerous and crowded in long, slender, tapering, *spikelike clusters*.

Fruits Glabrous, one- or two-seeded pods; *surface veined, black when ripe*.

Ecology Waste places, roadsides, cultivated fields. Scattered throughout the region at low to medium elevations essentially wherever roads and settlement occur.

Notes: Melilotus officinalis (yellow sweet-clover) is similar but has yellow flowers, wider oblong-elliptic leaflets, and pods that are yellowish-brown and not strongly net-veined when ripe. Both species are weedy, introduced as forage crops from Europe (white sweet-clover) and the Mediterranean (yellow sweet-clover). *Medicago sativa* (alfalfa) can often be found growing with the sweet-clovers, and has a similar growth form and three leaflets. However, alfalfa has short clusters of bluish purple flowers and coiled pods. • The sweet-clovers are often responsible for the overwhelmingly sweet fragrance noticed while driving some roads in our region on hot summertime days. The sweet smell comes from coumarin, which also imparts a very pleasant smell to sweetgrass (*Hierochloe* spp.) and fresh-cut hay. If allowed to degrade (e.g., through rotting of hay), the coumarin can break down into compounds which prevent blood from clotting, leading to death of hay-fed animals from even minor injuries. • In some areas, as in the Peace district, they are important nectar plants for honeybees.

RED CLOVER — *Trifolium pratense*

General Taprooted, short-lived perennial, somewhat hairy, with several erect stems 20-50 cm tall.

Leaves With *3 leaflets* (rarely and luckily 4) 2-4 cm long, often with a white, crescent-shaped spot near the base; stipules egg shaped to oblong, 1-3 cm long, conspicuously greenish veined.

Flowers *Pinkish purple*, petals about 17 mm long, fused sepals forming a tube; numerous in a *dense head* that is *sessile or with a very short stalk*.

Fruits Small pods, containing 2 seeds.

Notes: This introduced species is one of several clovers which occur in our area. All have leaves with 3 leaflets and flowers in dense heads and occur most commonly on disturbed sites, as agricultural escapes or (sometimes) deliberately seeded for erosion control or to increase soil fertility. *Trifolium repens* (white clover) and *T. hybridum* (alsike clover) are the two most common species. White clover has creeping stems and white to pinkish flower heads on long stalks. Alsike clover has ascending stems and pinkish white, stalked flower heads; it is a hybrid between red and white clover. • Plants in the pea family commonly harbor nitrogen-fixing bacteria (*Rhizoctonia* spp.) in their roots. These bacteria pull nitrogen out of the air and "leak" it into the soil in a form that plants can use. Nitrogen is the nutrient in most limited supply in most soils in this region. For this reason, species such as clovers, alfalfa, sweet-clovers, and lupines increase soil fertility where they grow.

173

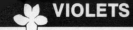

Conspectus of *Viola*

	adunca	langsdorfii	canadensis	glabella
Aerial stems	absent early in season, but later present; short, to 10 cm tall	present but may be poorly developed (usually at least one internode apparent); 2-10 cm tall	present, 10-40 cm tall	present, 5-30 cm tall; leafless except on upper section
Rhizomes	slender, short to long	thick, short to widely spreading	thick, short	thick, fleshy scaly, widely spreading
Stolons	lacking	lacking	may be present, slender, creeping	lacking
Leaves:				
Shape	heart-egg	kidney to egg-heart, rounded at tip	heart, long stemmed, sharply pointed at tip	kidney to egg-heart, sharply pointed at tip
Hairiness	glabrous or hairy	generally glabrous	glabrous or hairy	nearly glabrous
Width	1-3 cm	2-5 cm	2-10 cm	3-6 cm
Other				
Stipules	linear lance shaped, entire or toothed, 5-10 mm long	egg to lance shaped, entire to glandular-toothed, 5-17 mm long	lance shaped, entire, 10-20 mm long	egg shaped, entire to finely glandular-toothed, 5-10 mm long
Flowers			occurring on upper part of stem	occurring mostly on upper part of stem
Length	5-15 mm	15-25 mm	10-20 mm	8-15 mm
Spur	slender, over half the length of blade of lowest petal	thick, sac-like, much less than half as long as blade of lowest petal	short	very short
Petals	blue to violet	violet	white with yellow base	clear yellow on both surfaces
	lower 3 often whitish based, lateral pair white bearded	lower 3 whitish based, lateral pair white bearded	lower 3 purplish pencilled, lateral pair bearded, purplish tinged on back	lower 3 purplish pencilled within, lateral pair well bearded
Style head	bearded	glabrous or bearded	sparsely bearded	heavily bearded
Habitat	variable, but usually well drained, dry to moist meadows, grassland, thickets, open woods; from lowlands to near timberline	moist turfy sites; in our area mostly in subalpine bogs and fens and along streams	moist to fairly dry forest and woodland (usually deciduous or mixed), floodplain forests; mostly low elevations	moist forest and along streams; lowlands to middle elevations, sometimes in subalpine meadows

174

orbiculata	macloskeyi	palustris	renifolia	selkirkii	nephrophylla
lacking or very short (to 5 cm tall)	lacking	lacking	lacking	lacking	lacking
short, scaly	slender	slender, widely spreading	lacking	slender, short to long	thick, fleshy, long
lacking	present, threadlike	present, slender, creeping	lacking	lacking	lacking
egg-heart to nearly circular, rounded at tip	egg-heart	heart to kidney	heart-circular to kidney, rounded or blunt tipped	heart-egg	egg-heart to kidney, rounded or obtuse at tip
usually glabrous	glabrous	glabrous	hairy at least beneath	hairy above, glabrous below	glabrous to minutely hairy, hairy on veins of upper surface
2-4 cm	1-3 cm	2-4 cm	2-5 cm	1-3 cm	2-7 cm
dark green, thin in texture but persistent over winter, often lying flat on ground		delicate	clustered in basal rosette	delicate	
	lance shaped, glandular-toothed	lance shaped, entire, 4-9 mm long	lance shaped, toothed, 3-10 mm long	glandular-toothed, 6-15 mm long	linear lance shaped, entire, 5-12 mm long
			on stalks shorter than leaves		
5-15 mm	5-10 mm	10-15 mm	8-15 mm	8-13 mm	10-22 mm
short, sac-like	fairly prominent	conspicuous, sac-like	very short	long (more than 4 mm long)	short (2-3 mm long), sac-like
yellow	white	white (to lavender)	white	pale violet	bluish violet
lower 3 purplish pencilled, lateral pair yellow bearded	lower 3 generally purplish pencilled, lateral pair bearded	lower 3 purplish pencilled or tinged with violet, lateral pair sparsely bearded	lower 3 purplish pencilled, all beardless	all beardless	lower 3 whitish at base and bearded
short bearded	not bearded	not bearded	not bearded		not bearded
usually in mid-elevations and subalpine coniferous forests, occasionally in higher elevation meadows	swampy spots in lowland to middle elevation forests	wetlands (swamps, fens, marshes, bog margins), wet seepage areas in forest, streambanks; low to middle elevations	moist cool coniferous forests, forested bogs, and swamps; lowland to subalpine	moist rich woods, thickets, swamps, and fens; uncommon, primarily lowlands to middle elevations	moist places in forests, glades, meadows, and along streams; usually at low elevations

Violets are tricky to identify reliably. As often as not, you will find them without flowers or in fruit. Try the key, but it may not work satisfactorily because of its reliance on flower colour. If so, the species can be identified using vegetative characters, as summarized in the conspectus, and the illustrations provided. The key and conspectus include all 10 species likely to be encountered in our region. Detailed descriptions are provided only for the six most common species.

Key to the Violets

1. Plants lacking stems, the leaves and flower stalks arising from a thickened stem base or from stolons (runners)
  2. Flowers yellow; leaves broadly rounded at tip, dark green, often lying flat on the ground (a) .... *Viola orbiculata*
  2. Flowers not yellow
    3. Plants with stolons.
      4. Petals white (tinged violet or blue on the back) or pale violet, mostly 10-13 mm long; leaves 2-4 cm wide (b) ..... *V. palustris*
      4. Petals white, the lower three with purplish pencilling; leaves generally narrower (1-3 cm wide) (c) .... *V. macloskeyi**
    3. Plants without stolons
      5. Petals white; leaves usually soft-hairy on lower surface; flowers on stalks shorter than leaves (d) .... *V. renifolia*
      5. Petals bluish-violet; leaves glabrous on lower surface
        6. Rhizome slender; leaves hairy above; spur more than 4 mm long (e) .... *V. selkirkii**
        6. Rhizome thick; leaves glabrous above; spur less than 4 mm long (f) .... *V. nephrophylla**
1. Plants with leafy, aerial stems; flowers arise from leaf axils
      7. Petals partially or wholly yellow
        8. Petals all clear yellow on both surfaces, lower three petals purplish-pencilled on the inside (g) *V. glabella*
        8. Petals white with yellow bases, upper petals (especially) purplish tinged on back (h) *V. canadensis*
      7. Petals not yellow
        9. Petals white to pale violet; stipules entire; aerial stems well developed (h) .... *V. canadensis*
        9. Petals deep violet to purple; stipules toothed; aerial stems shorter than flower stalks
          10. Flowers large (15-25 mm long); head of style not bearded; spur thick, much less than half as long as the blade of the lowest petal (i) .. .. *V. langsdorfii**
          10. Flowers smaller (5-15 mm long); head of style bearded; spur slender, to half as long as blade of lowest petal (j) .... *V. adunca*

* Not described in detail in this guide, but see the conspectus of *Viola*.

EARLY BLUE VIOLET — *Viola adunca*

General Perennial with short to long, slender rhizomes, **usually stemless (and starts to flower) in early part of season, later developing aerial stems** to 10 cm tall.

Leaves Generally oval and heart shaped at base, margin finely round toothed; hairy or glabrous; stipules narrowly lance shaped, margins smooth to slender toothed.

Flowers Petals **blue to deep violet**, the lower three often white at base; **flowers 5-15 mm long**, with slender spur half as long as lowest petal.

Fruits Small capsules opening by three valves.

Ecology Variable but including dry to moist meadows, open woods, grasslands and open, disturbed ground, from lowlands to near timberline throughout the region.

Notes: Could be confused with the blue-flowered *Viola langsdorfii* (Alaska violet). *V. langsdorfii* differs from *V. adunca* in that it has larger flowers (l5-25 mm long) with bearded styles, and spurs that are thicker and less than half as long as the lowest petal. • The leaves and flowers of all violet species can be eaten raw in salads, used as potherbs, or made into a tea. Candied violet flowers are used for cake decorations. In the southern U.S. the leaves are often added to soups as a thickening agent. • Flowers and leaves have long been used in various herbal remedies as poultices, a laxative for children, and to relieve coughs and lung congestion. • The name violet comes from the latin *viola*, which may in turn have been the diminutive of the word *via* meaning love.

V. langsdorfii (inset)

KIDNEY-LEAVED VIOLET — *Viola renifolia*

General Perennial from short ascending rhizomes; **horizontal rhizomes and stolons lacking; no leafy aerial stems.**

Leaves Stipules lance shaped, toothed; leaf blades **heart shaped to kidney shaped, round toothed, hairy at least beneath**; clustered in basal rosette.

Flowers Petals **pure white**, lower 3 purple-pencilled, all beardless; flowers with very short spurs, on stalks shorter than the leaves.

Fruits Purplish capsules.

Ecology Moist, cool, coniferous forests and forested bogs and swamps. Scattered throughout the region, from the lowlands to medium elevations.

Notes: • This species blooms very early after snowmelt. • Pansies are violets; the name pansy is from the French *pensée*, meaning a thought or remembrance *à la* Proust (a notion similar to forget-me-not). • The species name *renifolia* means kidney leaved.

177

VIOLETS

CANADA VIOLET — *Viola canadensis*

General Perennial with **short, thick rhizomes and often with slender, creeping stolons; stems leafy**, 10-40 cm tall.

Leaves **Heart shaped, long stemmed, sharply pointed at tip**, usually hairy on one or both surfaces, margin saw toothed.

Flowers **White with yellow base**; lower 3 petals with purple lines, upper 2 petals purplish tinged on back, lateral petals bearded; flowers occur on upper portion of the stem.

Fruits Capsules.

Ecology In moist to fairly dry woodland and forest (usually mixed or deciduous), often on floodplains, clearings. Mostly at low to medium elevations in the southern half of our region, also in the Peace River district.

Notes: • Easily transplanted and often invasive in a garden setting. • The first, showy blossoms of violets don't generally produce seed. Greenish flowers, borne later in the season either underground or right at the soil surface, don't open and are self-fertilized, ensuring seed production.

MARSH VIOLET — *Viola palustris*

General Perennial with **slender spreading rhizomes and creeping stolons, but without aerial stems**.

Leaves Arising directly from rhizomes or stolons, **delicate, heart to kidney shaped, not hairy**; stipules lance shaped, with smooth margins.

Flowers Petals **white to lavender, generally tinged with violet or blue on back**, lateral pair sparsely bearded; flowers fairly large (10-15 mm), with conspicuous sac-like spur.

Fruits Small capsules.

Ecology Wetlands (swamps, fens, marshes, bog margins), wet seepage areas in forests, and along streambanks. Usually at low to medium elevations, throughout the region.

Notes: A similar species, *V. macloskeyi* (small white violet), has smaller flowers (generally less than 8 mm long) that are white with purple lines on the 3 lower petals. The leaves of *V. macloskeyi* are usually narrower than those of *V. palustris*. The leaves and flowers are edible and may be used in many ways (see *V. adunca*).

STREAM VIOLET — *Viola glabella*

General Perennial with spreading, **scaly, fleshy rhizome; flowering stem leafless except on uppermost section**, 5-30 cm tall.

Leaves Somewhat **kidney-shaped to heart-shaped, sharply pointed at tip**, toothed, without or more commonly with hairs; basal leaves stalked.

Flowers **Yellow**; 3 lower petals with purple lines, lateral pair bearded; flowers occur mostly on upper portion of stem.

Fruits Capsules.

Ecology Moist forests, glades, clearings, or along streams. Lowlands to middle elevations, and often to subalpine meadows, primarily in the southern part of our region.

Notes: • Some violets (usually those with flowers held higher than the leaves) have sort of an explosive seed dispersal mechanism, in which the drying capsule walls fold in on themselves, eventually expelling the seeds under pressure, catapulting them into the air. Some violet seeds also have outgrowths called oil-bodies. Ants eat the oil-bodies after carrying the seeds off and leaving them at some distance from the parent plant.

ROUND-LEAVED VIOLET — *Viola orbiculata*

General Perennial with **flowering stems lacking or less than 5 cm tall**, from short scaly rhizomes.

Leaves Dark green, not hairy, **oval to nearly circular, heart shaped at base, toothed, often remaining green through the winter, lying flat on the ground**.

Flowers **Lemon yellow to gold**, 3 lower petals purplish pencilled, lateral pair yellow bearded; spur short, sac-like.

Fruits Capsules.

Ecology Usually in mid-elevation coniferous forests, occasionally in montane and subalpine meadows. Only in southern part of the region.

Notes: See *Viola adunca*.

179

MOUNTAIN SWEET-CICELY *Osmorhiza chilensis*

General Perennial with well-developed *taproot*; stems solitary or sometimes 2-3, slender, 0.3-1 m tall, branched above.

Leaves *Twice divided into 3 for total of 9 leaflets, coarsely toothed, more or less hairy*, thin; basal leaves several, long stalked; stem leaves 1-3, short stalked.

Flowers *Greenish white, inconspicuous*, in loose umbrella-shaped clusters.

Fruits *Black, needle-like, narrowing (constricted) below tips, broadening into beaks, bristly-hairy*, often catching on one's clothing.

Ecology Open forests (often deciduous or mixed), openings, meadows, and clearings. Common at low to medium elevations throughout the southern half of our region, uncommon in the North.

Notes: Very similar to *O. depauperata* (blunt-fruited sweet-cicely). The two can be distinguished by close examination (with hand-lens) of the mature fruits. In *O. depauperata*, fruits are club or baseball bat shaped with no subapical constrictions. In *O. chilensis*, the fruit is conspicuously constricted below the apex. *O. depauperata* also tends to be smaller all over. • The plant is called "sweet-cicely" because of the licoricelike odour of the root when crushed. Also called "sweet root" and "dry land parsnip" by lower Lillooet and Thompson who ate the thick aromatic roots. Dug in early spring, the roots were steamed or boiled in stews and were known for their delicate sweet flavour. It was called "dry land parsnip" to distinguish it from water-parsnip, *Sium suave*. There are no written reports of it being eaten by northern natives, but it is abundant in the area. • Cicely is from the Greek word *seseli* meaning a carrot family plant used in medicine. It has been confounded with the girl's name *Cicely*.

PURPLE SWEET-CICELY *Osmorhiza purpurea*

General Perennial, slender from stout, branched taproot, stems 20-70 cm tall.

Leaves *Twice divided into 3, the 9 sharp-pointed leaflets* coarsely toothed and *usually hairless*, thin, yellowish green.

Flowers *Small, pink to purplish* (sometimes greenish white) in umbrella-shaped clusters.

Fruits *Spindle shaped, 8-13 mm long, with constriction below the beaked apex*, the beak cone shaped and broader than tall.

Ecology Generally coniferous forests or openings, along streambanks, river flats, and in meadows and clearings. Scattered at mostly medium to subalpine elevations in the southern half of the region, and northwards along the Coast Mountains.

Notes: Easily confused with *O. chilensis* and *O. depauperata*, both of which have hairy leaves, however. It also differs from *O. depauperata* in that the fruit has a constriction or narrowing below the apex and the flowers tend to be pink-purplish (though not always). Apart from flower colour, it can be distinguished from *O. chilensis* by close examination of the fruit. In *O. purpurea*, the fruit is generally smaller and the cone-shaped beak is broader than it is tall, whereas in *O. chilensis* the beak is as broad as it is tall. Overall, *O. purpurea* is smaller. • Smith (1920-23) reports that Ulkatcho Carrier called a plant "wild carrot" which may have been this species, but use by northern groups has not been confirmed.

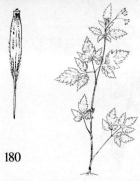

COW-PARSNIP — *Heracleum lanatum*

General **Very large, hairy**, single-stemmed perennial from **stout taproot or cluster of fibrous roots, 1-3 m tall**; stems hollow with strong pungent odor when mature.

Leaves Large, broadly oval leaves, **divided into 3 large segments, each coarsely toothed and palmately lobed; base of leaf conspicuously inflated and winged.**

Flowers Small, white, numerous, in a large, flat-topped, terminal, umbrella-like cluster with 1-4 secondary clusters from side shoots of the main stem.

Fruits Egg to heart shaped, flattened, with or without hairs; one seeded, **aromatic, sunflower-seedlike** mericarps.

Ecology Streambanks, moist slopes, roadsides, moist low ground, clearings, deciduous forest, and woodland openings. Throughout the region from lowlands to moderate elevations in mountains, sometimes higher in subalpine meadows and along avalanche tracks.

Notes: Also known as *H. sphondylium*, "Indian celery," and "Indian rhubarb," it was and still is widely used as a green vegetable. Virtually every native group reports harvesting young stalks and leaf stems, peeling the fibrous outer layer off, and eating them raw. Sometimes the stems were boiled, steamed, or roasted. Traditionally, they were eaten with eulachon grease or fish, but now are dipped in sugar. The taste is reminiscent of celery with a texture like rhubarb. • Several groups made toy flutes and moose whistles out of the dry hollow stems. • Mashed fresh roots were applied as a poultice for rheumatism by Carrier and Gitksan native people. • **CAUTION:** Time must be taken to correctly identify the plant to avoid confusion with the violently poisonous, but similar, *Cicuta douglasii* (water-hemlock) and *Conium maculatum* (poison-hemlock).

KNEELING ANGELICA — *Angelica genuflexa*

General Perennial with stout, leafy, glabrous, hollow, often purplish stem arising from erect, tuberous, chambered stem base; **often more than 1 m tall; stem commonly covered in a fine, waxy powder**.

Leaves Compound with 3 major divisions that are in turn divided again once or twice, the **primary divisions bent back (not directed forward as in other species), leaf stalk also bent (above the first pair of primary leaflets)**; ultimate leaflets egg-shaped to lance-shaped, coarsely toothed, **veins tending to end at the points of the teeth**; leaf stems with inflated bases sheathing main stem.

Flowers Small, white or pinkish flowers in numerous small clusters, all arranged together in large umbrella-shaped clusters.

Fruits Circular, single-seeded, **with broad lateral wings**, no hairs.

Ecology Moist thickets and forest openings, swamps, along streams, wet ditches; frequently abundant in wet places in clearcuts. Common at low to subalpine elevations in the southern half of the region, especially in areas of wetter climates; uncommon in the North.

Notes: Angelica lucida (sea-coast angelica, sea-watch) is similarly stout but has a tighter arrangement of leaflets and the primary leaflets are not reflexed. It is typically a coastal species but extends inland into our region, in meadows and thickets from low to subalpine elevations along eastern flanks of the Coast Mountains. • The hollow stems were used as children's whistles or blowguns by Kootenay peoples. Bella Coola used the stems as breathing tubes when hiding under water in times of trouble. • Care must be taken not to confuse this species with the poisonous water-hemlock *(Cicuta douglasii)*. Both have tuberous-thickened and chambered stem bases, so pay close attention to the leaves; the kink in the leaves of *A. genuflexa* is a giveaway.

181

CARROT FAMILY

DOUGLAS' WATER-HEMLOCK — *Cicuta douglasii*

General Perennial, *stout, 0.5-2 m tall*; stems solitary or few together *from a tuberous-thickened and chambered base*; several roots generally tuberous-thickened as well.

Leaves *Divided several times producing many lance-shaped to oblong leaflets*, sharply pointed and toothed; *lateral veins end at the base of the teeth*.

Flowers Small, numerous, white to greenish in several flat-topped, umbrella-like clusters.

Fruits *Egg shaped to circular, with corky-thickened unequal ribs*.

Ecology Marshes, edges of streams and ditches, and in other low wet places; from the lowlands to middle elevations, scattered throughout the region but relatively uncommon north of 58°.

Notes: **WARNING: extremely poisonous.** Even small amounts could be deadly. *Cicuta douglasii* is highly poisonous to humans as well as to livestock. It causes many deaths of cattle, especially in early spring when the shallow root is easily pulled up along with the young tops by cattle hungry for green feed. All parts of the plant are poisonous, but the tuberous-thickened roots and stem base are especially so. The basal parts of one plant are enough to kill a cow. • *C. bulbifera* (bulbous water-hemlock) has bulblets in the axils of its upper leaves, and the leaflets are narrowly linear. It occupies habitats similar to those of *C. douglasii*, and is uncommon but scattered throughout our region. • An important feature that aids in identification of *C. douglasii* and serves to distinguish it from similar plants (e.g., *Angelica*, *Heracleum*) is the arrangement of the leaf veins. The lateral veins of its leaves end at the base of the marginal teeth rather than at the points. Also the thickened stem-base when cut lengthwise clearly reveals the chambers (not found in *Heracleum*, *Sium*, *Osmorhiza*; but see *Angelica genuflexa*). • The powdered roots were used as an arrow poison by Okanagan people. Fresh roots were applied as a poultice for rheumatism by Carrier Indians.

WATER-PARSNIP — *Sium suave*

General *Semiaquatic* perennial from a *very short, erect stem base (not chambered) with fibrous roots*; stout, hollow, *strongly ridged stem, mostly 50-120 cm tall*, generally branched above.

Leaves Emergent leaves *once-divided into 7-13 leaflets that are lance shaped to linear, finely toothed*; leaf stalks with sheathing base.

Flowers Small, white, numerous in dense umbrella-like heads.

Fruits *Oval to elliptic, with prominent ribs*.

Ecology Swampy places and in shallow water, marshy edges of lakes and ponds. Throughout the region in suitable, usually low-elevation habitats.

Notes: Also called "swamp-parsnip," "wild carrot," and "wild saccharin," the sweet, fingerlike roots were eaten by many interior and some coastal groups. Dug in Spring, they are either eaten raw or steam-cooked and have a distinct carrot flavour. • CAUTION: The **young** shoots are also edible, but older plants and flowers should be avoided because they could be toxic, and have been implicated in livestock poisonings. • All care should be taken to correctly identify this plant because of its similarity to the poisonous *Cicuta douglasii*. In contrast to *C. douglasii*, the base of the stem of *S. suave* is **not** swollen or chambered and its leaves are only once compound. • The Carrier and Shuswap, and possibly other northern interior groups, ate the long fleshy roots raw or cooked, but they took great care to distinguish it from water-hemlock.

SINGLE DELIGHT *Moneses uniflora*

General Perennial, ***delicate, evergreen***, arising from a very slender creeping rhizome, ***up to 10 cm tall***; a very distinctive and attractive plant when in flower.

Leaves ***In basal rosette, small, oval to circular***, thin, veiny, and ***toothed***.

Flowers ***White, waxy***, fragrant; ***solitary, terminal, and nodding on a leafless stem*** with one or two bracts; large prominent style and stigma.

Fruits Spherical, erect capsules that split lengthwise into five parts when dry.

Ecology Open to dense, usually moist coniferous forests with moss ground cover, in humus or on rotting wood. Common throughout the region at low to moderate elevations.

Notes: Formerly *Pyrola uniflora*. When lacking flowers, single delight might be confused with one-sided wintergreen, whose leaves are less veined.
• This plant was considered to be powerful medicine by the Haida. A weak tea made from the whole plant was drunk for many ailments including diarrhoea, smallpox, cancer as well as for "power" and good luck. Alaskan natives drank tea made from leaves for sore throats and a few drops were given to babies.
• The delicate, waxy-white, fragrant, solitary flowers justly deserve the name "single delight." The Latin name *Moneses* derives from the Greek *monos*, meaning one, and *hesia*, meaning delight.

ONE-SIDED WINTERGREEN *Orthilia secunda*

General Perennial ***evergreen***, with a slender much-branched rhizome; ***stem single, leafy and often woody towards base, up to 20 cm tall***.

Leaves ***Evergreen, numerous, oval-elliptical, toothed***, dark green above, paler beneath.

Flowers ***Pale green to white, bell shaped, nodding, 6-20 in elongated cluster with flowers directed to one side***; style straight, projecting.

Fruits Spherical, erect capsules.

Ecology Dry to moist, usually mossy, coniferous or mixed forests; also persists in unburned clearcuts. Widely distributed and very common throughout, from the valley bottoms to subalpine parkland.

Notes: Formerly *Pyrola secunda*.
• The common name "wintergreen" appears to have originally been applied to ivy, because it stayed green throughout the winter. The name has subsequently been applied to Pyrolas because they are also evergreen. • The Pyrolas are true wintergreens and are not the plants from which oil of wintergreen is obtained. The oil comes from an eastern North American plant, *Gaultheria procumbens* (false wintergreen); see also *G. hispidula*.

183

GREEN WINTERGREEN   *Pyrola chlorantha*

General Perennial *evergreen* with long slender rhizomes and leafy sterile shoots, *flowering stems to 25 cm tall.*

Leaves *One to few in basal rosette. Circular to broadly oval, leathery,* pale green on top, darker beneath, **slightly round toothed**; leaf stalks longer than blades.

Flowers *Pale yellowish to greenish white, in a long cluster of 3 to 10 flowers; style bent downward.*

Fruits Spherical capsules.

Ecology Humus in dry to moist coniferous and mixed forest. Common throughout the region at low to medium elevations.

Notes: Also called *P. virens.* May be confused with *Pyrola minor.* • The leaves contain acids which are effective in the treatment of skin erruptions, and mashed leaves of several *Pyrola* species have traditionally been used by herbalists as skin salves or poultices for snake and insect bites. • The Latin name *Pyrola* comes from the word *pyrus* meaning pear, because *Pyrola* leaves are often pear shaped.

LESSER WINTERGREEN   *Pyrola minor*

General Perennial **evergreen** with slender rhizomes; *flowering stem single, to 25 cm tall.*

Leaves Several *in basal rosette, broadly elliptic or round,* rounded to heart shaped at base, dark green and thin, *with small, rounded teeth.*

Flowers *White, flesh coloured or pink; 5-20 in elongated cluster with flowers not directed to one side; style short and straight.*

Fruits Sperical capsules.

Ecology Humus in mesic to moist, mossy, coniferous or mixed forest. Scattered throughout the region at low to moderate elevations, but more common in the North.

Notes: Similar to *P. chlorantha*, which has greenish-white flowers with styles bent downward and sticking out beyond the petals. • Chewed or mashed leaves may be used as emergency skin salves or poultices.

HEATH FAMILY

PINK WINTERGREEN — *Pyrola asarifolia*

General Perennial **evergreen** with long, creeping, branched rhizome; *flowering stem up to 40 cm tall* and with a few papery bracts.

Leaves *Numerous, in basal rosette, circular to elliptic, leathery, shiny, slightly toothed*, dark green on top, purplish beneath, leaf stalks as long as blades.

Flowers *Pinkish to purplish red*, 10-25 in a long loose cluster, open or saucer shaped; *style long, curved and bent downwards*.

Fruits Spherical capsules.

Ecology Moist usually wooded sites, chiefly in coniferous forest but also common in deciduous (birch-aspen) and mixed-wood stands, including cottonwood-spruce floodplain forests; also in thickets and meadows. Widespread throughout, from valley bottoms to near timberline.

Notes: The largest and most handsome wintergreen in our forests. • Though some of the other wintergreens may have flowers tinged with pink, only pink wintergreen has truly pink to red flowers.

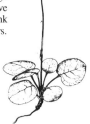

ARCTIC WINTERGREEN — *Pyrola grandiflora*

General Perennial **evergreen** from slender rhizomes with *single flowering stem, 5-15 cm tall*, with brown papery bracts.

Leaves *Basal, round to oval, stiff, leathery, shiny, often whitish along veins, with wavy margins*.

Flowers *Creamy white or tinged with pink*; large, 4-11 in loose elongate cluster; *style long, curved at base*.

Fruits Spherical capsules.

Ecology Moist turf in alpine shrublands, heath, and tundra; also in moist, mossy, mostly coniferous forest. Scattered, locally abundant in the North (mostly north of 57°) from floodplain forest to alpine ridges.

Notes: A very showy species of *Pyrola*; the species name *grandiflora* (large flowered) reflects this.

INDIAN-PIPE — *Monotropa uniflora*

General **Saprophytic** (growing on decomposed vegetable matter), **fleshy, waxy-white or pinkish, blackening with age**, appearing in clusters of flowering, unbranched stems, 5-25 cm tall.

Leaves Linear or lance shaped to oval shaped, **scale-like**, up to 10 mm long.

Flowers **White, single, narrowly bell shaped, at first nodding or curved to one side**; petals sac-like and broadened at base.

Fruits Erect, oval to circular capsules, brown and splitting open when mature.

Ecology In humus in shaded, usually mature, coniferous forests at low elevations. Primarily coastal; seems to be uncommon in the southern half of our region, and rare or lacking in the North.

Notes: Roots of Indian-pipe are connected via fungi to the roots of nearby coniferous trees. In this manner Indian-pipe, which lacks chlorophyll and so cannot make its own food, obtains nutrition from the efforts of another plant (the conifer). • The common name "Indian-pipe" refers to the pipelike flowers. Also called "ghost-flower", "corpse plant", and "ice plant" - names inspired by the unusual colour and texture of the plant. • Note that while the flower hangs down, the fruit eventually points up!

PINESAP — *Hypopitys monotropa*

General **Fleshy saprophyte** to 30 cm tall, unbranched, **yellowish to pinkish, drying black, usually hairy**; from dense mass of fleshy roots.

Leaves Small, **scale-like**, lance-shaped to linear, thick, crowded near base of stem, lacking green colour.

Flowers **Yellowish to pinkish, several to many**, in terminal cluster, **at first nodding**, more or less bent to one side; petals hairy on one or both surfaces, somewhat sac-like at base.

Fruits Erect, oval to round capsules, brown and splitting when dry.

Ecology In humus in coniferous forests at low to medium elevations. Relatively infrequent in the southern half of our region although locally common, especially in areas of wetter climates (especially the Interior Cedar-Hemlock zone). Not known north of 57°, at least in the interior.

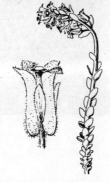

Notes: The related *Pterospora andromedea* (pinedrops) is also a fleshy saprophyte but is tall (30-100 cm), reddish brown, sticky-hairy all over, and has numerous, nodding, urn-shaped flowers. It also grows in humus in coniferous forests, often on drier sites, and is uncommon in our region south of 56°. • Common name, "pinesap", refers to the fact that it often grows under pines and perhaps because the colour and texture of the nodding flowers resemble congealed pine resin. • *Hypopitys* comes from the Greek *hypos* (beneath) and *pitys* (tree).

COMMON RED PAINTBRUSH — *Castilleja miniata*

General Perennial with few, erect or ascending stems from a woody base, to 60 cm tall.

Leaves Narrow, sharp pointed, linear to lance shaped, *usually entire*, but sometimes upper ones with three shallow lobes; without or with fine hairs.

Flowers Greenish, tubular, inconspicuous, mostly concealed by several, showy, *bright red to scarlet*, toothed and hairy bracts.

Fruits Capsules.

Ecology Open woods and meadows, thickets, grassy slopes, clearings, gravel bars, roadsides; at low to high elevations throughout the region.

Notes: This is the most common species of *Castilleja* in the area. The genus is complex and highly variable. • *C. unalaschcensis* (Unalaska paintbrush) differs from *C. miniata* in that it has yellowish bracts and the lobes of the calyx are blunt or rounded (whereas those of *C. miniata* are lance-linear). Otherwise, if not in flower, these two species can be confused where found together. *C. unalaschcensis* occurs mostly north of 54°. • Carrier people report that long ago parents forbade children to pick it because it was considered sacred (Carrier Linguistic Committee 1974). • The species name *miniata* has nothing to do with size; instead, it's a reference to the scarlet-red colour "minium."

SMALL-FLOWERED PAINTBRUSH — *Castilleja parviflora*

General Perennial from woody base; stems clustered, erect or ascending to usually not more than 30 cm tall, unbranched, hairy above; whole plant becoming black when dry.

Leaves Oval to lance shaped, all except few lowest ones *divided into 3-5 lobes*; somewhat hairy.

Flowers Greenish, tubular, with two lips; upper lip edged with violet-purple; inconspicuous, hidden among *rose-pink to crimson (magenta)* leafy bracts, (sometimes white); bracts lobed and hairy.

Fruits Capsules.

Ecology Subalpine and alpine meadows, heath, and streambanks; high elevations throughout the region.

Notes: Note that the "brush" is not the flowers themselves, but the leafy bracts surrounding the greenish flowers. The showy red, leafy bracts resemble a brush dipped in paint, hence the common name. • *Castilleja* species are partial root parasites, i.e., they are parasitic on the roots of other plants; therefore, they are extremely difficult to transplant.

Conspectus of Common Species of *Pedicularis*.

	racemosa	*groenlandica*	*ornithorhyncha*	*labradorica*	*parviflora*
Stature	20-50 cm	20-50 cm	5-30 cm	15-25 cm	10-40 cm
Habit	perennial	perennial	perennial	biennial or short-lived perennial	short lived (annual?)
Stems	unbranched, usually clustered, +/-glabrous	unbranched, often clustered, glabrous, often reddish purple	unbranched, glabrous, often reddish purple	single, often much branched, hairy	single, simple or (usually) branched
Leaves	mostly along stem; not lobed but margins toothed	basal and along stem; lobed	mostly basal; lobed	basal and along stem; lobed	basal and along stem; lobed
Flowers	few in open spike or in upper leaf axils	dense spike	short, compact spike or cluster	few in small clusters or in upper leaf axils	few in small clusters or in upper leaf axils
	creamy white (sometimes pink to purplish)	pinkish to reddish purple	purple	yellow, reddish, or yellow with red spots	purple
	12-15 cm long; galea strongly arched and beaked, sickle shaped	10-25 mm; galea strongly beaked and curved, resembling head and trunk of elephant	10-17 mm; galea strongly arched, extended into a straight, 2-4 mm long beak	10-13 mm; galea hooded, beakless, but with a pair of long slender teeth near the tip	11-14 mm; galea beakless, toothless at tip
Habitat	subalpine meadows and open, subalpine and timberline forest	wet turfy meadows, fens, and swamps; generally at high elevations but also in low elevation wetlands of the North	subalpine and alpine meadows and heath	lowland coniferous and mixed forest to subalpine thickets and meadows	bogs, swamps, wet meadows

	langsdorfii	sudetica	kanei	oederi	bracteosa	capitata
	5-30 cm	5-50 cm	5-25 cm	5-20 cm	30-100 cm	5-15 cm
	perennial	perennial	perennial	perennial	perennial	perennial
	unbranched, often clustered, glabrous to hairy (especially towards the top)	unbranched, single or clustered, glabrous to hairy, dark purple	stout (from thick yellow taproot), unbranched, mostly single, densely hairy towards the top	unbranched, single, glabrous below, hairy towards the top	unbranched, clustered, glabrous except in inflorescence	unbranched, single, sparsely hairy
	basal and along stem; lobed	mostly basal; lobed	basal and along stem; lobed	mostly basal; lobed	basal and (mostly) along stem; lobed	mostly basal; lobed
	dense spike	spirally arranged in a dense hairy spike	thick dense white-woolly spike	dense spike	dense spike	short, compact 1- to 8-flowered spike
	purple to pinkish purple	reddish purple, pink, or bicoloured	rose	yellow with brownish red tips	yellowish, sometimes tinged with red or purple	pale yellow (cream), often tinged with rose or purple at tips
	20-25 mm; galea hooded, beakless, but with a pair of slender teeth near the lip	15-25 mm; galea hooded, twisted, beakless, but with a pair of teeth near the tip	15-20 mm; galea hooded, beakless, toothless	15-25 mm; galea hooded, beakless, toothless	13-20 mm; galea hooded, beakless or short beaked	25-35 mm; galea strongly arched and hooded, short beaked with a pair of short teeth near tip
	alpine tundra	alpine tundra, subalpine meadows and parkland, often in turfy seepage areas	alpine tundra	alpine tundra and heath	open subalpine forest, parkland, and meadows	alpine tundra and heath; in our region often on cool moist slopes

Key to *Pedicularis*

1. Leaves merely toothed; calyx lobes 2 .... *P. racemosa* *
1. Leaves, or many of then, deeply lobed
  2. Stems branched; plants relatively short-lived; flowers in leaf axils as well as in terminal spikes.
    3. Flowers purple; bracts of flowers leaf-like, dissected; galea usually without a pair of subapical teeth .... *P. parviflora* *
    3. Flowers yellow or reddish; bracts of flowers toothed, but not dissected; galea with subapical teeth .... *P. labradorica*
  2. Stems unbranched; plants longer-lived perennials; flowers mostly in terminal clusters
    4. Leaves mostly along stem, basal leaves (if present) not markedly larger than stem leaves .... *P. bracteosa*
    4. Leaves mostly basal, stem leaves (if present) reduced in size
      5. Galea clearly beaked, the beak 2 mm or more long
        6. Beak straight, usually 2-4 mm long; flowers purple; leaves mostly basal .... *P. ornithorhyncha* *
        6. Beak strongly curved, more than 4 mm long; flowers pink to reddish purple; leaves basal and along stem .... *P. groenlandica*
      5. Galea essentially beakless, sometimes with a point not more than 1 mm long
        7. Flowers yellow or yellowish-white, sometimes tinged or marked with red or purple
          8. Galea with pair of long slender subapical teeth; flowers 10-14 mm long .... *P. labradorica*
          8. Galea with pair of short subapical teeth; flowers 25-35 mm long, in very short, sparsely hairy spike .... *P. capitata* *
          8. Galea lacking subapical teeth; flowers 15-25 mm long in dense, hairy spike .... *P. oederi* *
        7. Flowers pink to purple
          9. Galea with subapical teeth
            10. Stem leaves few and small, or lacking; flowers spirally arranged; galea twisted .... *P. sudetica*
            10. Stems leafy; galea straight .... *P. langsdorfii*
          9. Galea lacking subapical teeth; flowering spike thick, dense, white woolly .... *P. kanei* *

          * Not described in detail in the guide, but see the conspectus of *Pedicularis*.

BRACTED LOUSEWORT	*Pedicularis bracteosa*

General Erect perennials **up to 1 m tall**, coarsely fibrous-rooted, or often some of the roots tuberous-thickened; plant glabrous below the inflorescence; stems leafy, unbranched.

Leaves **Finely divided or fernlike**, doubly toothed with short or no stalk, **mostly borne on flowering stems**.

Flowers **Yellowish to sometimes tinged red or purple; upper lip hooded, beakless or with short beak at tip; in dense, elongate terminal cluster** above several hairy, leafy bracts.

Fruits Glabrous, flattened, curved capsules.

Ecology Moist open forest, thickets, meadows, and clearings in the mountains. Fairly common, locally abundant at subalpine to alpine elevations (occasionally lower) south of 55°.

Notes: Pedicularis capitata (few-flowered lousewort) also has yellowish-cream flowers that may be tinged with red or purple. It differs from *P. bracteosa* in that the plant as a whole is much smaller, the leaves are mostly basal, and the flower cluster is shorter, more compact, and has fewer (2-4) flowers. Also the upper lip is strongly arched and hooded, with two small teeth near the tip. • Thompson women incorporated the leaf pattern in basket designs. • The common name *lousewort*, applied to most species of *Pedicularis*, dates back to the 17th century. It was formerly thought that cattle grazing in fields where *P. sylvatica* grew in abundance became infested with lice. It is more likely that these pastures were poor and supported weak, unhealthy, and lice-ridden stock. Another common name, "wood betony," is also applied to *P. bracteosa*; *betony* comes from an old Gallic word meaning medicinal plant. Also called "fernleaf."

FIGWORT FAMILY

LABRADOR LOUSEWORT — *Pedicularis labradorica*

General Biennial or short-lived perennial from taproot, 10-30 cm tall; stems single or several, **simple or (usually) branched**, leafy, **becoming increasingly hairy towards top** of plant.

Leaves Basal leaves small; lower **stem leaves deeply cut and coarsely toothed**; leaves gradually becoming smaller towards top of stem.

Flowers **Yellow with red spots**; upper lip hooded, **lacking beak but with pair of long teeth near tip;** lower lip three lobed and fringed with very small hairs; **few (5-10) flowers** in small, loose, terminal clusters or in axils of stem leaves.

Fruits Glabrous, flattened, curved capsules.

Ecology Dry to wet forest, swamps, shrub-carrs, thickets, clearings. Common at low-medium to subalpine elevations in the North, and in the southwestern part of the region (usually on cold soils).

Notes: Pedicularis racemosa (sickletop lousewort) is about the same size but has clustered, unbranched stems, coarsely toothed but undivided leaves, and creamy white flowers with strongly arched upper lips that have sickle-shaped, downwardly curved beaks. It is a species of subalpine coniferous forests, openings, and dry meadows, and occurs only in the southeastern-most part of our region.

ELEPHANT'S HEAD — *Pedicularis groenlandica*

General Perennial; stems **unbranched, often clustered**, 20-50 cm tall, **glabrous**, sometimes reddish-purple.

Leaves Basal leaves **finely divided, fernlike**, the divisions sharply toothed; stem leaves several, progressively smaller towards top of stem.

Flowers **Pink-purple to reddish**; upper lip strongly hooded and beaked, **resembling the head and trunk of an elephant**; flowers many in dense, terminal spike.

Fruits Glabrous, flattened, curved capsules.

Ecology Fens, shrub-carrs, swamps, seepage areas, edges of mountain streams. Uncommon, scattered from low to subalpine elevations in the North and in the southwestern part of our region (i.e., Chilcotin and adjacent Tweedsmuir Park).

Notes: Pedicularis ornithorhyncha (bird's-beak lousewort) also has deeply divided, toothed leaves and reddish-purple flowers, but its upper lip is extended into a straight beak, 2-4 mm long, which resembles the beak of a bird. It is primarily a coastal high-elevation species, but is fairly common in subalpine and alpine heath and meadows along the western boundary of our region. • Many lousewort species are edible. Young stems and roots can be eaten raw or boiled until tender, but should only be eaten in an emergency. • The common names "elephant's head" and "birds-beak" both describe the appearance of the flowers.

LANGSDORF'S LOUSEWORT — *Pedicularis langsdorfii*

General Perennial from thick woody stem base, often with a **stout taproot** as well; stems 5-30 cm tall, **unbranched but clustered**, glabrous to woolly-hairy, especially above.

Leaves Basal and along stem, **finely but shallowly divided (comblike)**, divisions round toothed.

Flowers Purple with **hooded upper lip**, lacking beak, but with **pair of slender teeth** near tip; several to many in dense, elongate, terminal clusters.

Fruits Glabrous, flattened, curved capsules.

Ecology Dry to moist, grassy, alpine tundra and heath, and gravelly alpine ridges; common at high elevations throughout the region.

Notes: The similar *P. kanei* (woolly lousewort; = *P. lanata*) has a dense spike covered in thick, white-woolly hairs. The upper lip lacks the two teeth. The leaves are less deeply divided, even more comblike. • The shoots and thick yellow taproots of *P. kanei* were eaten by Inuit people in Alaska. Shoots were mixed with other greens (e.g., *Sedum integrifolium*). Frozen, fermented greens can be cut up in winter and served with seal oil and sugar as an Inuit-style ice cream. Roots were and still are dug and eaten as a vegetable. Children like to suck the nectar from the flowers. In parts of the U.S.S.R. the leaves are used to make tea. • The tops are browsed by caribou and reindeer.

SUDETEN LOUSEWORT — *Pedicularis sudetica*

General Perennial, 5-50 cm tall; stems stout, **unbranched, mostly single**; densely hairy upwards (in flowering spike).

Leaves Mostly basal, **finely divided (fernlike)**, divisions doubly toothed; a few leafy bracts below the flowers.

Flowers Reddish purple, pink or bicoloured; **upper lip hooded and twisted, lacking beak but with pair of teeth near tip**; many in spirally arranged, dense, hairy, terminal cluster (compact at first, later becoming elongate).

Fruits Glabrous, flattened curved capsules.

Ecology Moist alpine tundra, heath, open subalpine forest, shrub-carrs, and seepage areas. Common at subalpine to alpine elevations, mostly north of 54°, extending south to the Chilcotin.

Notes: A very variable species. As with *P. kanei*, roots and shoots were or still are eaten by Inuit people.

YELLOW MONKEY-FLOWER — *Mimulus guttatus*

General Annual from fibrous roots or perennial from creeping stolons or rooting from stem nodes; stems erect or trailing, simple or branched, to 50 cm tall, sometimes small and dwarfed, *glabrous (usually)* to sparsely hairy.

Leaves In pairs, oval, coarsely toothed, lower ones stalked, upper ones clasping stem, smooth or covered with fine hairs.

Flowers *Yellow*, lower lip with one large or several small crimson to brownish-red spots, throat of flower hairy; flowers large, trumpet shaped (strongly 2–lipped), several to many in loose terminal clusters.

Fruits After flowers drop, the fused sepals become inflated and surround a many-seeded capsule.

Ecology Wet ledges, crevices, weeping rock faces, seepage areas, along streams, near springs, wet ditches and clearings; from low to high elevations in the mountains; common throughout the region.

Notes: *Mimulus tilingii* (mountain monkey-flower) is a dwarf, somewhat creeping, alpine species with a few terminal yellow flowers that are very like (and just as large as) those of *M. guttatus*. The flowers look almost too big for the stems. *M. tilingii* grows in mossy alpine seepage and along stream banks, in our region only in the southwest (south of 54°) and along the east side of the Coast Mountains. • The name "monkey-flower" comes from the grinning facelike flower. The Latin *mimulus* means little actor – the diminutive of *mimus* meaning an actor in a farce or mime.

PINK MONKEY-FLOWER — *Mimulus lewisii*

General Perennial from stout, branching rhizomes; stems thick, clustered, mostly simple, 30-70 cm tall, *sticky and softly hairy*.

Leaves Large, clasping stem in pairs, oval shaped with sharply pointed tip, conspicuously veined, widely spaced teeth on margin.

Flowers *Rose-red to pale pink*, lower lip marked with yellow and a few hairs; few, large, showy, trumpet shaped, strongly 2-lipped.

Fruits Oblong capsules.

Ecology In and along streams (especially ice-cold ones) and in other wet seepy openings, also in the forest along slide tracks, at moderate to high elevations in the mountains. Scattered, locally abundant in areas of wet climates south of 55°, most common in the southeastern part of the region, occasional in the Skeena-Nass transitional area.

Notes: Sometimes called "Lewis' monkey-flower," after Merriweather Lewis of the Lewis and Clark Expedition of 1806. • The monkey-flowers have very sensitive 2-lobed stigmas (female parts) that will close if touched with a pin, straw, piece of grass, or an insect's tongue.

193

GORMAN'S BEARDTONGUE *Penstemon gormanii*

General Perennial from woody rootstock; stems several, clustered, erect, 15-50 cm tall, smooth below to hairy among flowers.

Leaves *Basal leaves spoon shaped*, lacking teeth; stem leaves linear to oblong, lacking stalks.

Flowers Violet to purplish, sometimes white, hairy in throat, *large (to 20 cm long)*, tube shaped, with 5 rounded lobes, twice as long as broad, in terminal cluster.

Fruits Elliptical capsules.

Ecology Dry mountain slopes, old dunes, sandy clearings, and gravelly areas (road cuts); scattered at low to medium elevations, *only in the North from around Cassiar to the Yukon border*.

Notes: The name "beardtongue" ("beard's tongue") comes from the fact that the flower throat and especially the lower lip of many *Penstemon* species are very hairy (hence a bearded tongue). • *Penstemon* comes from *pente* (five) and *stemon* (thread) because the flower has five stamens (male parts) − four fertile and one sterile.

SMALL-FLOWERED PENSTEMON *Penstemon procerus*

General Perennial from woody stem base; stems tufted, erect, to 40 cm tall, smooth.

Leaves *Oval to lance shaped*, lacking teeth, basal ones with short stalks, stem leaves lacking stalks and arranged in opposite pairs.

Flowers Blue-purple sometimes tinged pink (occasionally white), fused to form tube, not strongly 2 lipped, *small (8-12 mm long),* 1 to several in dense clusters arranged in whorls around the stem and at its tip.

Fruits Capsules.

Ecology Dry sandy banks, gravelly ridges, grassy hillsides, dry meadows, and open woods. Common throughout at low to subalpine and occasionally alpine elevations, except lacking from Quesnel Highland.

Notes: Penstemon procerus is sometimes called "tall beardtongue."

FIGWORT FAMILY

AMERICAN BROOKLIME — *Veronica americana*

General Perennial from shallow creeping rhizomes, or rooting from trailing stems; stems somewhat succulent, simple, erect or ascending, 10-70 cm tall, **glabrous**.

Leaves Usually 3-5 opposite pairs on flowering stem, oval to lance shaped, **short stalked**, sharply pointed and toothed.

Flowers Blue (violet to lilac), saucer shaped, not strongly lipped, with 2 large, spreading stamens, **in long, loose clusters along stem**.

Fruits **Round** capsules.

Ecology Wet ground or shallow water, marshes, seepage areas, along springs and streams, wet clearings and ditches, and skidder tracks. Scattered at low to medium elevations throughout the region.

Notes: Leaves are edible and used widely as a salad vegetable and pot herb. Care should be taken to avoid plants growing in polluted water. • Brooklimes have been used for centuries to treat urinary and kidney complaints and as a blood purifier. • The name "brooklime" comes from Europe where *V. beccabunga* grows along streams or brooks in wet mud where birds may become trapped or "limed" (an expression for ensnaring birds in sticky materials). • The name "veronica" is also used. It may be derived from an Arabic word meaning beautiful memory, in reference to the pretty flowers. An alternative derivation is that some flowers bear markings resembling those on the handkerchief of St. Veronica after she used it to wipe the face of Jesus as he carried the cross (the *vera iconica*, meaning true likeness)

ALPINE SPEEDWELL — *Veronica wormskjoldii*

General Perennial from shallow rhizomes; stems simple, erect, 7-30 cm tall, sparsely to densely **hairy, sticky or glandular among flowers.**

Leaves All on stem in opposite pairs, elliptic to oval or lance shaped, rounded to pointed at tip, slightly toothed, smooth to hairy.

Flowers Blue-violet with cream-coloured centre, saucer shaped, with prominent style and 2 stamens, few to several in **cluster at top of stem;** flower stalks sticky-glandular.

Fruits **Heart-shaped, hairy** capsules.

Ecology Meadows, streambanks, seepage areas, and moist open slopes, at moderate to high elevations in the mountains throughout the region.

Notes: The name "speedwell" was applied originally to *V. officinalis,* which was used medicinally as a strengthening and wound-healing plant and against coughs. Alternative meanings are get well, prosper well, or go on well. Another meaning comes from the fact that the petals fall off as soon as the flowers are picked; hence, farewell, good-bye, or God speed, being equivalent to speedwell.

COW-WHEAT · *Melampyrum lineare*

General Slender **annual** with simple or few-branched stems, 10-30 cm tall.

Leaves Leaves **opposite**, with short stalks, linear or lance shaped.

Flowers White or pinkish, **tubular** with yellow patch in throat, 2 lipped, **surrounded by green leafy bracts**.

Fruits Curved, asymmetrical capsules, few seeded.

Ecology Dry well-drained sites, usually in partial shade; dry pine stands, especially on coarse outwash, terraces, or old beach ridges; rocky slopes and ridges. Sporadic, locally common at low to medium elevations south of 55°.

Notes: The name "cow-wheat" was originally applied to the European *M. arvense* which was "freely cropped by passing cattle, to which it was fed in times of scarcity." Linnaeus claimed cows produced the most yellow butter after eating it. Another source says it is because its seed resembled wheat, but was useless to man. Despite all this, the Canadian *M. lineare* is much too small and scattered to be a forage plant.

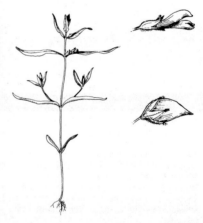

DWARF MISTLETOE — *Arceuthobium americanum*

General Small, glabrous, yellowish or greenish brown, **leafless, fleshy** plants **parasitic on the branches of pines. Stems emerging from the host, segmented**, 2-6 cm long, usually tufted, the segments mostly 1-2 mm thick; accessory branches often several per node in whorls.

Leaves Reduced to tiny opposite scales.

Flowers Greenish yellow, small, inconspicuous; male flowers on short lateral stems, 2 to several per node; female flowers on short stalks, 2 to several and whorled at each node.

Fruits Greenish or bluish, sticky, egg-shaped berries that explosively eject single, sticky seeds.

Ecology *Parasitic almost exclusively on pines*, and usually on lodgepole pine, but also reported on whitebark pine; throughout the southern part of our region except at high elevations, apparently lacking from the North.

Notes: Causes witch's broom — a disorganized growth of the tree. Mistletoe infections can cause significant reductions in the growth of lodgepole pine. • The common name appears to be derived from the Old English word *mistletan. Tan* means twig; some sources say *mistl* means different, hence different-twig. Others say *mistl* comes from Old German *mist* meaning dung, in that birds eat the berries and the seeds are deposited on trees in sticky bird droppings.

BASTARD TOAD-FLAX — *Geocaulon lividum*

General Perennial; stems single or clumped, 10-25 cm tall, from creeping, threadlike, reddish rhizomes; **parasitic on the roots of other plants**.

Leaves **Alternate**, thin, **oval, blunt tipped**, bright green or frequently yellow-variegated, a condition caused by lodgepole pine's comandra blister rust, of which *Geocaulon* is the alternate host.

Flowers Greenish purple, small, inconspicuous, in slender-stalked, 2-4 flowered, axillary clusters; usually only centre flower fertile.

Fruits Succulent, **scarlet to fluorescent orange berrylike drupes**; edibility questionable, not recommended.

Ecology Dry to moist, open woods and bog forests, throughout the region from the lowlands to middle elevations.

Notes: The species is also known as *Comandra livida*. • Turner (1978) reports that Okanagan children sucked the nectar from the flowers and the Lillooet sometimes ate the berries and "removed the tough outer rind by placing them in their moccasins and walking down a hill on them." Called the "dog berry" by the Yukon River Indians, it is considered edible but not palatable. It could, however, be eaten in an emergency. • The name toad-flax refers in part to the European species *Linaria vulgaris*, which has flax-like leaves. The "toad" part may be an error in translation from an old herbal in which *L. vulgaris* was described as a plant used to treat "buboes" (boils). The Latin word for buboe is *bubonio*, whereas the word for toad is *bufo. Geocaulon lividum* is a bastard toad-flax because it is not the real one.

STINGING NETTLE — *Urtica dioica*

General Perennial *1-3 m tall*, with strong, spreading rhizomes and armed with *stinging hairs* (otherwise glabrous to hairy).

Leaves *Opposite*, narrow lance shaped to oval or heart shaped, *coarsely saw toothed*.

Flowers Greenish, inconspicuous, without petals, *clustered in drooping bunches* at the stem nodes.

Fruits Flattened, lens-shaped achenes.

Ecology Moist, shaded lowlands to mountain slopes; in deep rich soil. Meadows, thickets, open woods, streambanks, often growing *en masse* in disturbed habitats such as avalanche tracks, middens, slash piles, barnyards, roadsides.

Notes: Stinging hairs are hollow, arising from a gland containing formic acid. As the brittle hair tips are broken, acid is secreted causing an irritating rash on contact with skin. Nevertheless, the leaves can be cooked and eaten as greens when young. • Called "Indian Spinach," the young leaves and stems were eaten by both coastal and interior tribes, but it is questionable as to whether this was a traditional use or was introduced by Europeans. The plants were, however, an important source of fibre for making fishnets, snares, tumplines, etc. Fishnets were often dyed with alder to make them invisible. • Both the Gitksan and Carrier report that it was used medicinally either as a counter-irritant or decoctions of roots and leaves were taken internally for a wide variety of ailments (kidney, liver, gallbladder, lung, bladder, and diabetes).

ALPINE BISTORT — *Bistorta vivipara*

General Erect perennial from a short, thick rhizome, with 1-several flowering stems mostly 10-30 cm tall.

Leaves *Mostly basal, with long stalks*; leaf blades narrowly oblong to lance shaped, glabrous, shiny above, grayish below; stem leaves 2-4, becoming much smaller and more sessile higher up the stem.

Flowers *White* (to pink) with greenish bases, small, 5-lobed; several to many in a terminal *spike-like cluster with lower flowers replaced by bulblets* (which sometimes sprout while still on the mother plant).

Fruits Brown, shiny, three-angled achenes (nutlets).

Ecology Shaded woods, moist meadows and streambanks, to alpine tundra and heath; throughout the region, but common primarily at high elevations.

Notes: Both the leaves and rhizomes are eaten by the Inuit of Alaska and Siberia. The leaves are mixed with other greens and eaten cooked. The starchy rhizomes are boiled and mixed with seal oil, added to stews, or eaten raw. They are said to taste like almonds. • Care should be taken when eating them as various members of the family this plant belongs to (Polygonaceae) contain hydrocyanic acid. • Clustered in the axils of stem leaves one can often find small pink bulblets. These are dislodged by the wind and roll away to form new plants, hence the species name *vivipara*, meaning to produce live young. The common name is from the Latin words *bis* which means twice and *torta* meaning twisted, refering to the contorted rhizome.

LAMB'S-QUARTERS — *Chenopodium album*

General *Annual*, 2-100 cm tall, usually with several to numerous short branches, greenish to grayish-mealy (*covered with flaky scales*); stems often purple striped with age.

Leaves *Egg or diamond shaped*, alternate, somewhat firm and succulent, coarsely but irregularly toothed or lobed; *lower surface grayish green and covered with mealy particles*.

Flowers Greenish, tiny, *in dense clusters or spikes* in the leaf axils and at the stem tips.

Fruits Black, shiny, flattened, circular nutlets, often covered with a thin, white, papery envelope.

Ecology Disturbed sites, especially cultivated land, gardens, roadsides. Common at low to medium elevations throughout the settled parts of the region.

Notes: Chenopodium capitatum (strawberry-blite) is a native species scattered at low to medium elevations throughout the region, on roadsides, gravel bars, and in cultivated areas. It is a glabrous (not mealy), yellow-green plant with flowers in globose heads that form interrupted spikes and become red and berrylike in fruit. • *C. album* is a very characteristic and often abundant weed of agricultural areas, originally from Eurasia but now naturalized in much of North America. Its leaves can be eaten raw or boiled; formerly an important potherb but was ousted by the related spinach. • "Lamb's-Quarters," or more correctly *lammas quarter* was originally given to *Atriplex patula*, because it bloomed about the first of August, which was the time of a traditional harvest festival.

CURLY DOCK — *Rumex crispus*

General Robust *taprooted perennial*; stems unbranched below flower clusters, 50-100 cm tall.

Leaves *Oblong to lance shaped*, rounded at base, to 5 cm wide by 40 cm long, with crisp, curly edges; basal leaves with long stalks; stem leaves sessile, reduced in size upwards; above each leaf base a membranous sheath surrounds the stem.

Flowers Greenish to dull rusty brown, inconspicuous, small and numerous, *whorled in dense clusters* (to 40 cm in length) along upper part of stem and its branches; petals with a grainlike enlargement centred towards the base.

Fruits Smooth, *winged achenes, reddish brown*, shiny, triangular in cross-section.

Ecology Waste places, roadsides, meadows, cultivated fields and pastures. Scattered at mostly low elevations throughout the settled parts of the southern half of the region; uncommon in the North.

Notes: Rumex acetosella (sour weed) is another widespread, introduced weedy species, but is smaller (20-30 cm tall) with basal leaves that are shaped like an arrowhead, but with the basal lobes flaring outward. *R. acetosa* ssp. *alpestris* (garden sorrel) has egg shaped to triangular leaves that are shaped like an arrowhead, but with basal lobes downwardly curved. It is a native species of lowland to subalpine meadows and thickets, scattered throughout the region but most common in the North. • In rocky places at high elevations, look for the mountain sorrel (*Oxyria digyna*), which has distinctive kidney- to heart-shaped, long-stalked basal leaves from which arise several 10-30 cm tall stems carrying long, crowded clusters of greenish flowers or reddish, winged fruits. • Curly dock is a European weed now widely established. Rubbing irritated skin with dock leaves is an effective folk remedy for stinging nettle.

199

WESTERN SPRINGBEAUTY   *Claytonia lanceolata*

General Glabrous perennial from a ***globose***, easily detached corm; flowering stems 5-15 cm tall.

Leaves Basal leaves lance shaped, 1-few, with largely underground stalks, seldom seen at flowering time; stems with a pair of opposite, sessile leaves below the flowers; leaves somewhat fleshy.

Flowers ***Usually white***, sometimes pink or pinkish-lined, few to several (3-20) in loose, often nodding clusters; petals 4, joined together for 1-2 mm at base.

Fruits One-celled, three-valved, egg-shaped capsules, each with 3-6 black shiny seeds.

Ecology Open grassy slopes at middle elevations to subalpine and alpine meadows, usually where moist at least early in the spring, often particularly abundant at timberline in moist meadows and near snowbanks, where it flowers early and wilts as soon as the capsules mature. ***Only in the southernmost parts of our region*** (south of 53°).

Notes: The plant varies greatly in size, depending both upon the relative size of the corm and local growing conditions. In general, alpine plants are smaller, have fewer and smaller flowers, and have smaller but relatively broader leaves. • The corms are palatable when cooked and taste rather like potatoes. Often referred to as "Indian Potato," they were an important source of carbohydrate for the Shuswap, Carrier, and Chilcotin Indians. They were dug just after flowering and boiled, steamed, or dried for later use. The Shuswap stored them in deep earthen pits just like potatoes. Because they are so small, a single meal would require the destruction of a large number of plants, and this charming little flower could easily be wiped out of an area by repeated harvesting.

ALASKA SPRINGBEAUTY   *Claytonia sarmentosa*

General Glabrous perennial from long, ***slender rhizomes***, as well as from runners; flowering stems 5-15 cm tall.

Leaves Basal leaves elliptic to egg shaped, 1-few, with sheathing stalks; stems with a pair of opposite leaves below the flower cluster; leaves somewhat fleshy.

Flowers ***Pink*** (fading whitish), in 2 to 8-flowered, loose, nodding clusters; petals 4, basally united.

Fruits Egg-shaped capsules, each with 2-6 black, shiny seeds.

Ecology Moist mossy places in subalpine scrub and alpine tundra especially in seepage areas, near snowbeds, and on streambanks. Common in the ***northwestern part of the region*** (Cassiar Mountains, Boundary Ranges, Alsek Ranges).

Notes: Although this species is not reported as edible, the leaves and underground portions of several species of *Claytonia* and the closely related *Montia* are edible.

FIELD CHICKWEED — *Cerastium arvense*

General Tufted or clumped perennial, with trailing stems, glandular-hairy on upper part of stems and among the flowers, 10-25 cm tall.

Leaves Opposite, 1-2.5 cm long, **narrow, greyish green, fine-hairy, pointed at tip; most stem leaves with secondary leafy tufts in their axils.**

Flowers White, **fairly showy**, commonly 3-6 in an open, flat-topped cluster, on glandular-hairy stalks; petals 5, deeply notched at the tip, **8-12 mm long**, two to three times longer than the sepals.

Fruits Cylindrical, many-seeded capsules opening by 10 teeth.

Ecology Dry ground on rock outcrops, screes, grassy slopes, and meadows; also dry open forest and clearings. Sporadic throughout the region except in areas of wetter climates, at low to high elevations but usually below timberline.

Notes: Cerastium beeringianum (Bering chickweed) is a matted to sprawling, arctic-alpine species that could be confused with *C. arvense*, but has broader, generally apically rounded leaves that lack sterile shoots in their axils, and fewer flowers. • The name chickweed derives from the fact that this species and *Stellaria media* (the common chickweed that infests your garden) were considered wholesome food and were fed to chickens, goslings, and cage birds, especially if they were ill.

BLUNT-LEAVED SANDWORT — *Moehringia lateriflora*

General Perennial from rhizomes or stolons; stems thin, ascending to erect, single or in small clumps, minutely hairy, 5-20 cm tall.

Leaves Opposite; basal leaves smaller than the 3-7 stem leaves, which are **egg shaped to oblong or lance shaped, rounded at the tip**, and minutely hairy.

Flowers White, small, erect, solitary or 2-5 in terminal clusters; petals 5, **4-8 mm long**, two to three times longer than the sepals.

Fruits Capsules opening by 6 teeth.

Ecology Meadows and grassy slopes, thickets, open, relatively dry deciduous and mixed forest – often with trembling aspen; fairly common throughout at lower elevations except in dense coniferous forest and in muskeg, rarely to subalpine elevations.

Notes: This species is also known as *Arenaria lateriflora* • For comment on the meaning or derivation of *wort,* see *Stellaria calycantha.*

NORTHERN STARWORT — *Stellaria calycantha*

General Low, often matted perennials from long rhizomes; stems slender, prostrate to ascending or erect, 5-50 cm long, glabrous to sparsely hairy.

Leaves Opposite, sessile, elliptic to narrowly lance-shaped, 0.8-4 cm long, the **margins minutely saw-toothed**; thin, glabrous except for a few long basal hairs.

Flowers White or greenish, small, solitary and axillary or more commonly in open, terminal groups; petals shorter than sepals, or lacking.

Fruits Straw-coloured to purplish capsules, much longer than flowers, opening by 6 teeth.

Ecology Wet meadows, thickets, streambanks, glades, open moist forests, clearings, and roadsides. Throughout the region, but mostly at lower to middle elevations.

Notes: A variable species in terms of size of leaves, flower size, degree of branching of the inflorescence, and hairiness of the stem. • The name *wort* is found frequently in compound plant names. It is derived from the old English *wyrt* that generally means plant or vegetable and was often applied to plants having some medicinal values.

CRISP STARWORT — *Stellaria crispa*

General Low, spreading, often clumped or matted perennials from slender rhizomes, glabrous throughout; the stems weak, prostrate to ascending, mostly simple, 5-30 cm long.

Leaves In numerous pairs, lance to egg shaped, sessile, or lower ones short stalked, sharp pointed at tip; **thin margin translucent** and minutely crisped like potato chips.

Flowers White, very small, single in axils and at stem tips; sepals 5; petals lacking (usually) or shorter than sepals.

Fruits Straw coloured or brownish capsules, nearly twice as long as the sepals, opening by 6 teeth.

Ecology Moist sites, mostly in the lowlands or at mid-elevations; shady wet forests, clearings, thickets, streambanks, seepage areas. Mostly in the wetter portions of the southern half of the region.

Notes: Occasional specimens are similar to *S. calycantha*. • *Stellaria media* (chickweed) is a widespread introduced weed of cultivated fields, gardens, lawns, and pastures. It is an annual with prostrate, branching stems. Unlike the other Stellarias of our region, chickweed has stalked, not sessile, and broadly oval leaves.

LONG-STALKED STARWORT · *Stellaria longipes*

General Low perennials from slender rhizomes, forming small to large tufts or mats; stems slender, essentially glabrous, 5-20 cm tall, 4-angled.

Leaves Opposite, sessile, *stiff, shiny*, linear to narrowly lance shaped, sharp pointed, sometimes hairy at the base, otherwise glabrous, the margins smooth.

Flowers White, rather small (petals 3-8 mm long), single, or few to several in loose clusters, on *slender, erect stalks*.

Fruits Purplish to black, shiny capsules, opening by 6 teeth.

Ecology Moist soil on streambanks, lake shores, rocky slopes, alpine scree, mountain meadowland, and open forest; also weedy in disturbed areas (e.g., along mining roads). At moderate to high elevations throughout the region, descending to lowlands in the North.

Notes: This species represents a complex of entities (many of which have been called separate species by some taxonomists) variable in colour, pubescence, bracts in the inflorescence, and number of flowers. One of these forms, known as *S. longipes* ssp. *altocaulis* or as *S. monantha*, is likely to be noticed because its glaucous leaves give the plant a distinctly blue-green colour, in contrast to the fresh green of other subspecies. • In our region, *S. longipes* is probably the most common and widespread species of a group of dwarf, tufted, alpine perennials in the pink family (*Caryophyllaceae*). Most have small narrow leaves and all have fairly small white flowers, but *Stellaria* and *Cerastium* have deeply notched or 2-cleft petals whereas *Minuartia* (*Arenaria*) (sandworts) and *Sagina* (pearlworts) have entire or shallowly notched petals. They are all plants of rocky alpine slopes, scree, ledges, and tundra.

S. longipes ssp. *altocaulis* (inset)

MOSS CAMPION · *Silene acaulis*

General Glabrous, tufted perennial from woody roots and branched, thickened stem base, forming *compact, hemispherical or flat cushions* up to 50 cm broad; stems 3-4 cm tall, with densely crowded branches.

Leaves Mostly basal, *withering and persistent* for many years, linear to narrowly lance shaped, *stiff*, glabrous, sharp pointed, sessile.

Flowers Showy, *pink*, lilac, or pale purple (rarely white), single, sessile or short stalked.

Fruits Three-chambered capsules.

Ecology Moist but well-drained areas in high mountains, in rock crevices or on cliffs and ledges, on gravelly, exposed ridges and turfy tundra barrens. Common alpine species in suitable habitats throughout the region.

Notes: This is one of our most beautiful alpine cushion plants and is an excellent plant for rock gardens. • Craighead *et al.* (1963) describe, with stirring patriotism, the occurrence of this species with alpine forget-me-not and white phlox in the Teton-Yellowstone area: "Growing thus together, they appear to be a single cushion of varicoloured flowers — the red, white and blue symbolizing the complete freedom that comes to all outdoor lovers in the vastness of the mountains." • The name campion (or champion) comes from Europe, where flowers of red campion (*Silene dioica*) were used to adorn chaplets (wreaths) placed on heads of champions at public games.

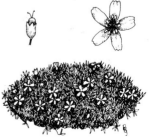

203

HOLBOELL'S ROCKCRESS · *Arabis holboellii*

General Biennial from taproot; stems solitary or few, 20-50 cm tall, hairy near the base.

Leaves Basal leaves entire or somewhat toothed, lance shaped, *finely hairy*, tapering at the base to slender stalks; stem leaves sessile, usually closely hairy, getting smaller towards top of stem, often *with tiny earlike flanges (auricles) at the base*.

Flowers *Pink or pinkish-purple to white*, small, with four petals that are 5-10 mm long, several to many in terminal clusters that elongate with age.

Fruits *Long, narrow*, flattened *podlike* "siliques" on short stalks that are abruptly bent near the base, so that the siliques point back down the stem.

Ecology Dry, gravelly, rocky, or sandy slopes, river terraces, or roadsides; in grassland, scrub, or open woods. Scattered throughout the region in suitable habitats at low to medium elevations.

Notes: There are five or six relatively common species of *Arabis* or rockcress in our region. *Arabis drummondii* (Drummond's rockcress) is similar in general appearance and habitat to *A. holboellii* but is shorter, has white or pinkish petals, and bears its siliques stiffly erect or slightly spreading. *Arabis glabra* (tower mustard) is a tall (up to 1.5 m), stout, introduced weed with bluish-green, unbranched stems that are hairy only at the base, creamy-white flowers, and stiffly erect siliques. It occurs in disturbed habitats at low elevations throughout, but most commonly in drier parts of the southern half of the region. • The name "cress" derives from an old Indo-European word meaning to nibble or eat. The leaves of cresses were (and are) widely used for salads. *Arabis* species are closely related to the cresses, but grow in dry, rocky places − hence rockcress.

ALPINE DRABA · *Draba alpina*

General *Dwarf tufted* perennial, closely branched from the base, forming small cushions usually less than 5 cm high; *branches densely clothed with old, persistent leaves*; flowering stems 1-few, hairy, 3-13 cm tall.

Leaves All *basal* (rarely 1 on stem), broadly lance shaped to oblong or elliptic, *hairy on both surfaces*; midribs often conspicuous in age and persistent.

Flowers Bright *yellow*, small, with four petals that are 4-5 mm long; flowers 2-7 in loose terminal clusters.

Fruits Short, flattened, *oval to elliptic* "silicles," hairy or glabrous.

Ecology Alpine tundra, snowbeds, scree, and crevices in cliffs or boulder fields; strictly a high elevation species, primarily in the northern mountains of our region.

Notes: Draba is a taxonomically difficult genus of 15 or so species in our region. Generally, the species are annual, biennial, or perennial; from taproots; often with simple or variously branched hairs; with a basal rosette of leaves or sometimes with stem leaves; with small, yellow or white flowers; and with relatively short, oval to lance-shaped, flattened fruits. Some species grow in lowland habitats (usually disturbed or open grassy areas), but most are small, tufted, or cushion-forming alpine species. Positive identification usually requires material with both flowers and fruits, and reference to technical floras and keys. • Regardless of their technical difficulty, Drabas are charming plants, especially in the alpine tundra, where they produce little explosions of colour under extremely trying circumstances.

SHEPHERD'S PURSE — *Capsella bursa-pastoris*

General Finely hairy annual; stems 10-50 cm tall, simple to (usually) branched.

Leaves Basal leaves in a rosette, with petioles 3-6 cm long, broadly lance shaped, more or less entire to toothed or pinnately divided; stem leaves alternate, sessile and **clasping** (pair of ear-like lobes at base of leaf), lance shaped to oblong, irregularly toothed.

Flowers **White**, small (petals 2-3 mm long, sepals smaller), usually numerous; at first clustered densely along the stem, later spreading out as they mature and fruits develop.

Fruits Strongly **flattened, triangular to heart-shaped silicles**; seeds numerous, sticky when wet. Typically buds, flowers, and fruits are present all at the same time on a single plant.

Ecology Waste places, roadsides, fields, paths, gardens, barnyards. From low to medium to sometimes subalpine elevations throughout the region, common in most places where there is human-caused disturbance.

Notes: Originally from Europe, shepherd's purse has become a very widespread weed throughout the region and most of North America and can be troublesome in cultivated fields and gardens. Shepherd's purse often harbors fungi that can be transmitted to cabbage, turnips, and other members of the mustard family. • Shepherd's purse, western tansymustard, Holboell's rockcress, and alpine draba are members of the large mustard family (Brassicaceae). Many, including shepherd's purse and western tansymustard, are weedy species of disturbed sites, but the family also includes important agricultural plants such as broccoli, cauliflower, rapeseed (canola), and, of course, mustard. Mustard family species have 4 petals, 4 sepals, and silicles or siliques for fruits. • The distinctive fruits are responsible for both the scientific and common names. *Capsella* is Latin for little box, *bursa* for purse, *pastor* for shepherd.

WESTERN TANSYMUSTARD — *Descurainia pinnata*

General Taprooted, greenish annual; stems 10-50 cm tall, simple to freely branched, **with fine, starlike hairs** and sometimes also glands, especially on the flowering branches.

Leaves Mainly on the stem, alternate, broadly lance shaped in outline, 3-10 cm long, **2-3 times pinnately divided** into narrow segments; upper leaves smaller and less divided.

Flowers Pale to bright **yellow** (occasionally white), small (1.5-3.5 mm long), on slender stalks in an open cluster

Fruits Relatively **long and narrow pods** (siliques), 4-20 mm long, about 1.5 mm wide, somewhat club-shaped or elliptic and rounded at tip; 10-20 seeds mostly in two rows; fruiting stalks spreading horizontally, about as long as pods (averaging 12 mm).

Ecology Disturbed soil on relatively dry sites, roadsides, gravel bars, overgrazed grassland. Scattered, locally abundant at low to medium elevations throughout the region, most common in the southern half.

Notes: A widespread, native but weedy, and very variable species (it has been described scientifically in at least 4 different genera, besides *Descurainia*, and at least 30 different species!). Two other weedy species of *Descurainia* also occur in similar habitats in the region, and all three are difficult to distinguish. *Descurainia richardsonii* (Richardson's tansymustard) is gray-hairy generally, has narrower siliques pointed at the tip and shorter ascending fruiting stalks; the siliques are about 10 mm long on stalks about 5 mm long. *D. sophia* (flixweed) is a European species that is also gray-hairy, has leaves that are more intricately divided (2-3 times), and narrow linear siliques with 10-20 seeds in a single row (siliques about 8 mm long on spreading stalks about 6 mm long).

205

PINK CORYDALIS — *Corydalis sempervirens*

General Annual or biennial, glabrous throughout, *pale green and glaucous*, from taproots; stems 1-few, usually erect, 0.2-1.0 m tall, occasionally much branched, *rather soft and with watery juice.*

Leaves Alternate, much divided.

Flowers Showy, *pink with yellow tips*, spurred, three to ten or more in loose terminal cluster(s).

Fruits *Long thin podlike* capsules that are constricted between the seeds and usually curved; seeds black and shiny.

Ecology Open woods or scrub, rocky hillsides, burnt clearings, roadsides; mostly in disturbed soils. At low to medium elevations throughout the region.

Notes: Corydalis aurea (golden corydalis) has yellow flowers and spreading or straggling stems that are usually much branched. Both of these species are most common in disturbed areas and behave as weeds. In the northern forests they occur right across the continent, and are most abundant for a few years immediately after disturbances such as wildfire. They apparently bank their seeds in the forest floor for decades or even centuries, until germination is triggered by disturbance, exposure, and warming of the soil. *Geranium bicknellii* behaves similarly. • *Corydalis* is Greek for crested lark. Presumably, the rather ornate flowers were thought to resemble this bird.

BLUE CORYDALIS — *Corydalis pauciflora*

General Perennial, *dark green*, glaucous and glabrous, from deep, tuberous roots; stems usually 1, erect, 5-15 cm tall.

Leaves Few (2-5), clustered near the base of the stem, *once-divided in threes*, the leaflets lobed.

Flowers Showy, *sky blue to blue-purple* (sometimes lilac), prominently spurred, two to six on short stalks in small terminal cluster.

Fruits *Short thin podlike* capsules that are straight and not constricted between the seeds.

Ecology Seepage sites in alpine tundra; often with species such as *Claytonia sarmentosa* and *Arnica lessingii*. Scattered but locally common in the mountains of the North, sporadically south to 55° or so, on cool moist north slopes of the higher peaks.

Notes: This lovely small plant is easy to overlook. The small blue-purple flowers are unusual in both shape and hue.

LANCE-LEAVED STONECROP · *Sedum lanceolatum*

General Glabrous, succulent perennial; stems 5-20 cm high, tufted.

Leaves Alternate, ***narrowly lance shaped***, but ***rounded in cross-section and fleshy***; mostly near the base (the stem leaves tend to drop off before the plant flowers) and crowded on sterile shoots.

Flowers Bright ***yellow***, in dense clusters; parts in five; petals narrowly lance shaped, 6-9 mm long.

Fruits ***Erect*** follicles.

Ecology Dry, open, grassy slopes, sandy benches, ridges, and outcrops; usually on rocks or gravel. Scattered throughout, mainly on south slopes at low to medium elevations, and more common in the southern half of the region.

Notes: Sedum divergens (spreading stonecrop) could perhaps be confused with *S. lanceolatum*, but is a mat-forming succulent with prostrate stems and ascending flowering branches; opposite, berry-like, egg-to spoon-shaped leaves; and strongly divergent follicles. *S. divergens* also generally grows at higher, subalpine-alpine elevations (often in temporarily moist, gravelly habitats) than does *S. lanceolatum*. *S. stenopetalum* (worm-leaved stonecrop) could be encountered in the driest, southernmost parts of the region. It is similar to *S. lanceolatum* but has strongly keeled, persistent leaves; widely divergent follicles at maturity; and upper leaves that often have sterile, bulbil-like flowers in their axils. • The rounded leaves of *S. divergens* were considered to be more of a berry than a green by interior natives. They were harvested in the spring before the flowers appeared. The Niska, Gitksan and Haida ate them raw as a dessert after a meal — to sweeten and freshen breath. • The leaves of all stonecrops are edible, but eaten only in moderation as some have emetic and cathartic properties and can cause headaches.

ROSEROOT · *Sedum integrifolium*

General Glabrous, ***succulent*** perennial with branched rootstocks that produce annual stems, 5-20 cm tall and ***clothed with many persistent leaves; rhizomes thick***, fleshy, scaly, and ***fragrant when cut***.

Leaves ***Oval to oblong, flattened***, irregularly toothed to smooth edged, much smaller and scalelike below, ***larger further up the stem***.

Flowers Usually ***dark purple, sometimes yellow***; densely clustered at tips of leafy stems; parts often in fours; petals oblong, 2-4 mm long.

Fruits ***Red or purplish*** follicles, more or less erect with divergent tips.

Ecology Alpine scree, talus, cliffs, and ridges (usually where moist in spring), sometimes also in grassy tundra or even moist turfy sites; at high elevations throughout, but more abundant on richer, less acidic bedrock types.

Notes: This species is also known as *S. rosea*. • Native people in Alaska ate the succulent leaves and young shoots raw or boiled them as greens. The Inuit would eat the boiled rootstocks with walrus blubber or other fats. The plants are best collected before the flowers appear as they tend to become bitter and fibrous in late summer. • Decoctions of roseroot were also used by Alaskan Athapaskan groups for sore throats, colds, and as an eye-wash. • The common name roseroot derives from the fact that the rhizome when cut or bruised emits the fragrance of roses. • Another common name, "king's crown," may refer to the flowers, which are arranged in a dense, crownlike cluster at the top of the stem.

ROUND-LEAVED SUNDEW — *Drosera rotundifolia*

General Small, insectivorous perennial, 5-25 cm tall.

Leaves Sticky glandular, **spreading**, in basal rosette, 3-7 cm long; **blades round to broadly egg shaped or wedge shaped**, at least as broad as long, fringed **with long, reddish, glandular hairs (tentacles)** that exude drops of sticky fluid; leaf stalks glabrous.

Flowers **Small, white**, fully open only in strong sunlight; few (3-10) in a coiled cluster, all on one side of the stem.

Fruits Many-seeded, partitioned capsules.

Ecology Sphagnum bogs, fens, and wet meadows; fairly common throughout the region, but mostly at low to medium elevations. *D. rotundifolia* grows especially on higher and drier parts of the bog surface, mostly associated with Sphagnum moss.

Notes: Sundews are commonly pollinated by the same insects they use for food — mosquitoes, midges, and gnats! • The sap is acrid and has the reputation for curdling milk. Fresh leaves were used in Europe in the preparation of cheeses and junkets and for removal of warts. The sap also contains an antibiotic effective against several bacteria and was used to treat tuberculosis, asthma, bronchitis, and coughs.

LONG-LEAVED SUNDEW — *Drosera anglica*

General Same as for *D. rotundifolia*, except leaves.

Leaves Sticky glandular, often reddish, **ascending to erect**, in basal rosette, 3-10 cm long; blades **spoon shaped to oblong or linear**, at least twice as long as broad, **fringed with "tentacles."**

Ecology Fens, swamps, wet meadows; less commonly in acid *Sphagnum* bogs; scattered throughout the region at low elevations and more frequent in the North – less common overall than *D. rotundifolia*. *D. anglica* tends to grow in lower and wetter, mucky parts of the wetland surface.

Notes: Drosera anglica entraps insects in a similar manner to *D. rotundifolia*. • A Mediterranean drink, called "Rossolis," is made from a mixture of sundew blended with raisins and brandy. • The common name is thought to come from a mis-spelling of the Saxon word "sin-dew," which means always dewy – for indeed it is! The name *Drosera* comes from a Greek word also meaning dew. • Another common name for *D. anglica* is "great sundew."

BUTTERWORT — *Pinguicula vulgaris*

General *Insectivorous* perennial with fibrous roots; stems 3-16 cm tall.

Leaves All basal, *greenish yellow*, forming rosette, succulent, broadly lance shaped to elliptic, smooth edged *with inrolled margins; greasy-slimy on upper surface*.

Flowers *Lavender purple*, rarely white, 15 mm or more long; petals in funnel-like tube *with spur* and white hairs in throat; nodding flowers *borne singly* on leafless, sticky stem.

Fruits Round capsules.

Ecology Moist sites generally; fens, tamarack swamps, bogs and mossy seeps, rocky drip-faces; low elevations to subalpine meadows, scattered in the North, uncommon to the south.

Notes: Pinguicula villosa (hairy butterwort) is a less common, smaller species with densely glandular flowering stems and smaller (up to 8 mm long) flowers. It typically grows in wetlands at low to medium elevations, in the northwestern part of the region. • Butterworts (and sundews) usually grow on sites low in available nutrients and supplement their diet by entrapping insects. Insects stick to upper slimy surface of the leaves. The margins tend to roll inwards to prevent insects escaping. The plant secretes juices that digest the soft tissues of the insect. • The plant supposedly encouraged or protected the milk-producing capacity of cows, so ensuring a supply of butter. Yorkshire farm women annointed the chapped udders of cows with butterwort juice. It was also thought to protect cows from elf arrows, and human beings from witches and fairies. • The name "butterwort" comes from the greasy feel of the leaves, as if melted butter had been poured over them. *Pinguis* means fat.

WILD GINGER — *Asarum caudatum*

General *Evergreen* perennial, with extensive rhizomes; *stems trailing, rooting freely, sometimes forming large mats*.

Leaves *Heart to kidney shaped, dark green, two arising from each node*, leaf stalks and veins finely hairy.

Flowers *Purplish brown, solitary, bell-like* flowers with 3 widespreading sepals, each tapering to long point.

Fruits Fleshy capsules.

Ecology Rich bottomlands, moist shaded woods, frequently in thick leaf-mould that often hides the flowers. In our region, virtually restricted to the "big bend" area of the Fraser River and the middle Skeena and Nass valleys.

Notes: The whole plant when crushed has a *strong smell of lemon-ginger*. This scent was valued by the Thompson and Okanagan natives, who mixed it with sphagnum moss to make a soft, sweet-smelling bedding for infants. The roots can be eaten fresh, or dried and ground as a ginger substitute. • The word "ginger" dates back to the thirteenth century and means horn-root or root with a horn shape and has generally been applied to plants with this particular flavour or smell.

209

BICKNELL'S GERANIUM   *Geranium bicknellii*

General *Annual or biennial, much branched*; stems 20-60 cm high, with spreading hairs, from slender taproot.

Leaves Small, 2-7 cm broad, deeply 5 parted, the lobes further divided into pointed, narrow lobes, hairy and glandular on veins.

Flowers *Pale pink-purple, small,* usually two per stalk.

Fruits Five-parted capsules that *open explosively, splitting lengthways from the bottom, and flinging the 5 seeds away* from the parent plant.

Ecology Common along roadsides in recent clearcuts and on disturbed soil, where it behaves like a weed. Widespread at low to middle elevations throughout.

Notes: This species, together with *Corydalis sempervirens* and *C. aurea*, is very abundant for a few years after disturbances such as wildfire or clearcutting followed by slashburning. Apparently, its seeds remain on the forest floor for decades or even centuries, and germination is triggered by disturbance, exposure, and warming of the soil.

NORTHERN GERANIUM   *Geranium erianthum*

General *Perennial* from thick, long, scaly, rhizomes and woody stem-base; stems hairy, 60-80 cm tall.

Leaves Deeply divided into 3-5 irregularly lobed, narrow segments, blades broader than long; basal leaves long stalked, stem leaves stalkless.

Flowers *Blue to pink-purple,* in loose, 3- to 5-flowered clusters; petals twice as long as sepals; *flower clusters usually not higher than the surrounding leaves.*

Fruits Five-parted capsules, the styles fused to form a central pointed column. When dry, the central column splits into 5, each part suddenly recoiling and carrying with it part of the capsule, and at the same time flinging out the seed (somewhat like a sling-shot).

Ecology Moist open forests, meadows, roadsides, and clearings to above timberline; abundant in the western part of the region (essentially in Pacific drainages — Skeena, Nass, Alsek, Stikine), occasionally further east.

Notes: The name "geranium" when translated means crane's-bill or stork's-bill and refers to the fruit with its central pointed column of fused styles that resemble the long bills of cranes or storks.

WHITE GERANIUM — *Geranium richardsonii*

General *Perennial*; stems with glandular hairs, 40-80 cm tall, erect, from short woody stem-base.

Leaves Basal leaves long stalked, stem leaves stalkless, opposite; leaf blades deeply divided into 5-7 irregularly lobed main segments, sparsely hairy.

Flowers *White or sometimes pinkish, with purple veins*; petals with long hairs at base; *flower clusters higher than surrounding leaves*.

Fruits Five-parted capsules splitting open as described for *G. erianthum*.

Ecology Moist meadows, glades, thickets, open forest (usually deciduous); seems to be most at home in the light shade of aspen groves. Low to middle elevations, frequent in the southern half of the region, scattered in the North.

Notes: Occasional light lavender-flowered specimens are found. They could be the result of hybridisation with *G. viscosissimum* or perhaps *G. erianthum*.
• *G. viscosissimum* (sticky geranium) is glandular-hairy all over especially on leaf and flower stems, and has large red-purple flowers, strongly veined with purple. • The type and quantity of hairs on the petals and the colour of the flowers help to distinguish *G. erianthum* and *G. richardsonii*. Where flowers are lacking, the lower side of the leaves of *G. erianthum* are uniformly hairy, whereas those of *G. richardsonii* are only hairy along the veins. Neither are as sticky-hairy as those of *G. viscosissimum*.

ENCHANTER'S NIGHTSHADE — *Circaea alpina*

General *Tender juicy* perennial, *from tuberous slender rootstock*, 10-25 cm tall, simple or branched.

Leaves *Opposite, heart shaped to egg shaped, with pointed tips, toothed*, short-hairy especially on lower surface, *leafstalks with narrow wings*.

Flowers *White to pink, small* in terminal clusters of 8-12; *petals 2, each deeply two-lobed*.

Fruits Oblong, *pear-shaped capsules, covered with hooked or straight hairs*.

Ecology In cool, damp woods and other moist, rich sites, often along streams, from valley bottoms to subalpine elevations on mountain slopes. Throughout our region, except in the Chilcotin.

Notes: The name "enchanter's nightshade" results, in part, from some confusion. *Circaea* was named after the Greek goddess Circe — the enchantress — who supposedly used this plant "as a tempting powder in some amorous concerns" (Hitchcock *et al.* 1955-69). • The application of "nightshade" to this plant is, however, a mystery. It was originally applied to the plants *Atropa belladonna* (deadly nightshade) and *Solanum dulcamara* (woody nightshade). Somehow, it was subsequently transferred to *Circaea*. • The origin of the word "nightshade" in relation to these two other species is in itself a mistake. An old herbal describes *A. belladonna* as a *solatrum* or soothing anodyne. In translation this was mistaken for the words *solem atrum*, which mean black sun or eclipse.

211

ALPINE WILLOWHERB — *Epilobium anagallidifolium*

General *Low, usually matted perennial*, spreading by *rhizomes and stolons*; stem *5-20 cm tall*, simple to branched, often reddish purple; *roots slender and loose*.

Leaves Generally opposite, about equally spaced, in 2-3 pairs, sometimes without but usually with short stems, *oblong to egg shaped, with smooth to wavy margins*.

Flowers *Pink to rose-purple (occasionally white); single to few, small, nodding to erect*; petals notched.

Fruits Linear to club-shaped capsules; seeds about 1 mm long, smooth.

Ecology Moist banks and rocks, scree slopes, and alpine meadows, near seepage sites and springs, and along streams, often above timberline. Throughout the region at high elevations, although the species occasionally descends to lower elevations on floodplains.

Notes: The white-flowered *Epilobium lactiflorum* (white-flowered willowherb) of medium to high elevations and the pink to purplish flowered *E. hornemannii* (Hornemann's willowherb) at low to medium elevations are both larger (10-40 cm tall) species that have leaves with toothed margins.

PURPLE-LEAVED WILLOWHERB — *Epilobium ciliatum*

General Perennial, *rhizomes short or lacking, bulb-like buds (offsets) present or absent*; erect stems from basal leafy rosettes, *0.5-1.5 m tall*, simple or branched above, hairy and/or glandular in the upper part of plant.

Leaves *Opposite*, lance shaped to oval or elliptic, pointed, toothed, short stalked or sessile.

Flowers White, pink, or rose-purple, *small (2-8 mm long)*; few to numerous in erect, terminal cluster.

Fruits Hairy capsules, 3-10 cm long; seeds somewhat rough and hairy.

Ecology Moist habitats generally; streamsides, lakeshores, moist woods and thickets, glades, meadows, disturbed sites such as roadsides and clearcuts. From low to subalpine elevations throughout the region.

Notes: Part of a large complex, including what some taxonomists distinguish as *E. adenocaulon*, *E. glandulosum*, and *E. watsonii*. Highly variable, with a great range in several morphological features. *E. ciliatum* ssp. *ciliatum* (the widespread, weedy subspecies) is usually branched above, has relatively narrow and uncrowded stem leaves, and smaller, usually paler flowers than the typically unbranched ssp. *glandulosum*, which has broader stem leaves that are often crowded around the flowers, larger darker-purple flowers, and also has the bulblike offsets from rhizomelike roots. • *E. palustre* (swamp willowherb) differs in that it produces long, threadlike, above-ground runners that end in buds that can produce more plants. Also, the leaves of *E. palustre* are linear to lance shaped and the petals are white to pink. The plant is generally gray-hairy, and grows in bogs, swamps, and other wetland types.

FIREWEED · *Epilobium angustifolium*

General *Perennial from rhizomelike roots; stems usually unbranched, 0.5-3 m tall*, often purplish in the upper part.

Leaves *Alternate, narrowly lance-shaped*, veins visible on undersurface.

Flowers *Rose to purple, large*, several, in elongated terminal cluster.

Fruits Narrow, green to red, dehiscent seed pods (capsules), which split open and disgorge hundreds of fluffy, white seeds.

Ecology Common and abundant throughout our region in disturbed areas, *especially on recently burned sites*; also in open coniferous, deciduous, and mixed forests, meadows, and along riverbars; from low to subalpine elevations.

Notes: Especially evident along roads and railways and on old burns, hence the common name. It is sometimes grown as an ornamental, but is apt to become a bothersome weed. • The young stems were peeled and the succulent "marrow" (pith) was eaten raw by Shuswap, Carrier, Niska, Gitksan and probably other northern interior natives. Sometimes the whole stems were cooked by boiling or steaming. The Siberian Inuit ate the roots raw. • After eating the marrow, the Haida and Gitksan dried the stem peelings and twisted them into a type of twine used for fishing nets. Coastal groups mixed the seed "fluff" with hair from mountain goats or dogs and used it for weaving or padding. • Both the Gitksan and Alaskan native people reputedly used the roots and leaves as poultices for sores or rheumatism. • The flowers have a lot of nectar which makes an excellent honey.

BROAD-LEAVED WILLOWHERB · *Epilobium latifolium*

General Low-growing, matted perennial with a stout woody base, *non-rhizomatous; stems usually reclining to erect, 5-30 cm tall*.

Leaves Usually *alternate, lance shaped to elliptic or oval*, sessile or nearly so, *somewhat fleshy, often with white-grey bloom*, veins not distinct on under surface.

Flowers *Pink to rose-purple*, sometimes white, *large and showy*, 3-12 in loose, short, terminal, leafy cluster.

Fruits Hairy capsules, 3-10 cm long.

Ecology Sandy and gravelly soils on riverbars, streambanks, roadsides, and ditch banks, and on drier subalpine to alpine slopes, often on talus or scree. Occasional in the valley bottoms of the southern half of the region, more abundant at higher elevations and in the North.

Notes: Within the species there is considerable variation in the size and shape of the leaves. The albino-flowered form is fairly frequently encountered. • *Epilobium luteum* (yellow willowherb) has opposite, oblong-lance-shaped to egg-shaped leaves, and large, yellow flowers, and is scattered (locally common) on streambanks and in wet forest openings from medium to high elevations mostly along the Coast Mountains in the western part of the region. • The young plants of *E. latifolium* were picked, before flowering, and mixed with other greens by Alaskan Inuit. The inner stems (marrow) were eaten by the Bella Coola people. • This species is also called "river-beauty."

213

BUNCHBERRY — *Cornus canadensis*

General *Trailing, low, somewhat woody at base,* widely rhizomatous, 5-20 cm tall.

Leaves *Evergreen, 4-7 in terminal whorl, oval-elliptic,* 2-8 cm long, green above, whitish beneath, veins parallel.

Flowers Consist of *4 white to purplish tinged, petal-like bracts surrounding a central cluster of small greenish-white to purplish flowers.*

Fruits Bright *red, fleshy, berrylike drupes*; although pulpy, they are sweet.

Ecology In dry to moist, coniferous and mixed woods and forest openings from valley bottoms to subalpine elevations. Widespread throughout the region.

Notes: Reported to have an explosive pollination mechanism, whereby the petals of the mature, but unopened, flower buds suddenly reflex and the anthers spring out simultaneously, catapulting their pollen loads into the air. The trigger for this explosion appears to be a tiny "antenna" just over 1 mm long that projects from near the tip of one of the four petals in bud. • The Gitksan ate them mixed with other berries. Two or three handfuls of bunchberries were added during cooking to berries that were being prepared for drying, especially saskatoons. The bunchberries act like a kind of glue or thickening agent, holding the berry cake together and preventing it from cracking on drying. Bunchberries were sometimes steamed and preserved for winter use, but often they were considered only good for bears and birds. • The Sechelt name for bunchberries means *the one that pretends to be salal* because they taste a little like salal berries. The name "bunchberry" comes from the fact that the berries are all bunched together in a terminal cluster. Also called dwarf dogwood (see *C. stolonifera*).

WILD SARSAPARILLA — *Aralia nudicaulis*

General *Widely rhizomatous* perennial with short, stout, erect, woody stems (barely reaching soil surface) from which the leaves arise. The *above-ground shoot consists of a single compound leaf that, when reproductive, arches over a short stalk that bears the flowers.* Often forms large clones in undisturbed forests.

Leaves Generally *single and compound,* 30-50 cm long, with three *major divisions that each have 3-5 leaflets with finely toothed margins.*

Flowers *Small, greenish white, in 3-7 umbrella-shaped clusters or balls that are hidden from sight beneath the leaves on naked flowering stems.* Flowers with both sexes or unisexual, male and female flowers on separate plants.

Fruits *At first greenish-white, then dark purple, plump berries.* Edible, but not very palatable. This species seems to produce fruit sporadically.

Ecology Moist shaded forests, often in mixed-wood stands, on medium to rich sites. Scattered (locally abundant) throughout the southern half of our region at low elevations, but absent from Fraser Plateau and uncommon northwards.

Notes: The Bella Coola Indians formerly made a beverage by boiling the rhizomes of this plant in water. Decoctions were also taken as medicine for stomach pains and may have been used medicinally by the Carrier and Gitksan. • *Aralia nudicaulis* gets its common name "wild sarsaparilla" because it has medicinal properties similar to those of the tropical prickly vine sarsaparilla (*Smilax officinalis*). The name comes from the Spanish *zarza parilla* meaning little prickly vine, though our wild sarsaparilla has no thorns or prickles.

NORTHERN STARFLOWER — *Trientalis europaea* ssp. *arctica*

General Perennial from **short, *horizontal rhizomes that are slightly thickened*** at the top, but not tuberous; stems erect, 5-15 cm tall.

Leaves *Main leaves oval-elliptical to broadly lance shaped, with rounded tips, in a whorl of 5-6* at the top of simple stems; lower leaves few to several, very much smaller.

Flowers *Single, white (with pink tinge), starlike flowers borne on each of 1-3 thin stalks* that arise from centre of leaf whorl; petals sharply pointed.

Fruits Spherical capsules, splitting into 5 parts when dry.

Ecology Muskeg; wet spots in coniferous forest, often on sphagnum moss; open seepage areas, boggy soils, wet thickets and meadows, up to alpine tundra. In suitable habitats from low to high elevations throughout the region.

Notes: Also known as *T. arctica*. • *Trientalis latifolia* (broad-leaved starflower) is a more southerly species that overlaps in range with *T. europaea*. It differs in that the stem leaves, below the terminal whorl of main leaves, are reduced to inconspicuous scales, and it has tuberous rhizomes. In general, the leaves of *T. latifolia* are larger and broader, and the flowers more pinkish than those of *T. europaea*. *T. latifolia* is scattered in forests and openings at low elevations, mostly in the southern half of our region.

SPREADING DOGBANE — *Apocynum androsaemifolium*

General Perennial, from rhizomes; *erect, branched stems, 20-50 cm tall; with milky sap*.

Leaves *Opposite, simple, oval to oblong lance shaped, spreading and drooping*.

Flowers *Small, pink, bell shaped*, showy in terminal and lateral clusters, sweet scented.

Fruits Very long (5-12 cm), narrow, cylindric pods; *numerous seeds, each with long tuft of cottony hairs*.

Ecology On well-drained soils, usually in warm, dry places, along roadsides, on open hillsides and ridges, and in dry forest. Widely scattered at low elevations throughout the region, but merely locally abundant, generally in areas of warmer, drier climate.

Notes: Used widely by northern interior native groups as a source of fibre for making twine for a great variety of uses, e.g., fish-nets, animal traps, sewing, weaving baskets, and generally holding things together. The native people preferred to get the fibre from the related *A. cannabinum* (hemp dogbane) because the bush is larger and the fibres are longer and tougher. But where hemp dogbane was not available, they would use spreading dogbane as a poor substitute. Some *A. cannabinum* was traded to Carrier and other northern Athapaskan groups. An excellent account of fibre preparation is given in Turner (1979). • A close look at the pink flowers will reveal deeper pink lines ("honey guides") to lead insects into them. • The plant is toxic to livestock, and sickness and death have been reported from its use for medicinal purposes by humans. • The name "dogbane" may, in part, come from the fact that the milky sap is very bitter and the plant is avoided by browsing animals.

INKY GENTIAN — *Gentiana glauca*

General Perennial, low growing, *glabrous, yellowish green, stems and leaf rosettes from creeping rhizomes*; stem 4-15 cm tall, erect.

Leaves *Basal rosette leaves oval to spoon shaped, somewhat succulent*; stem leaves smaller, oval-elliptical, in 2-4 pairs.

Flowers *Deep blue, or greenish inky blue, rarely yellowish or white; erect, tubular, bell shaped*; petals shiny (glaucous) with accordion-like folds joining them.

Fruits Oval capsules.

Ecology Alpine tundra, alpine and subalpine heathlands, and meadows. Common at high elevations throughout the region.

Notes: The unusual inky greenish-blue colour of the flowers is very attractive. • The European *G. lutea* was supposedly named after an Illyrian king called Gentius who discovered its medicinal properties. The root was a source of "medicinal bitters" (tonic) and a flavoring for liqueurs. • This species is also called "glaucous gentian."

NORTHERN GENTIAN — *Gentianella amarella*

General *Annual or biennial from taproot*; stems erect, simple to branched, 10-30 cm tall.

Leaves Basal leaves elliptic or lance to spoon shaped; *stem leaves 5-8 pairs, more lance shaped.*

Flowers *Pink-purple, violet, or lilac, rarely white, with fringe of hairs in tubelike throat*; several to many in terminal and lateral clusters.

Fruits Cylindrical capsules.

Ecology Open woods, thickets, and meadows, clearings, and moist areas in general, up to subalpine meadows. From low to subalpine elevations throughout the region, but sometimes overlooked because it is relatively inconspicuous and flowers late in the growing season.

Notes: Gentianella propinqua (four-parted gentian) is a very similar plant. The main difference between these two little annual gentians is that the flowers of *G. propinqua* do not have a fringe of hairs in their throats, and the tips of their petals have a much sharper point than those of *G. amarella.* • The genus *Gentianella* can be distinguished from *Gentiana* by the lack of folds between the flower petals.

TALL JACOB'S-LADDER   *Polemonium caeruleum*

General Perennial, from horizontal rhizome, **stems *solitary, erect, 40 cm to 1 m tall, glandular-hairy above*.**

Leaves ***Mainly basal, tufted, divided into 19-27 leaflets*** that are opposite or not quite opposite (offset), ***lance shaped to elliptic***, and sharply pointed.

Flowers ***Pale blue or purplish, bell shaped in loose terminal clusters; petal lobes pointed and with tiny fine hairs along their margins.***

Fruits Round capsules.

Ecology Moist to wet meadows, seepage areas, streambanks, heathlands, thickets, shrub-carrs, and open forest. Middle to high elevations; common in the North, less frequent south of 56°.

Notes: The common name refers to the ladderlike arrangement of the leaflets, surmounted by blue flowers, and alludes to Jacob, who, according to Genesis, climbed the ladder and at the top reached heaven. • The scientific name comes from the Greek *polemos* (war) because two kings apparently took to the battlefield over who first discovered the (alleged) medicinal properties of this plant.

SHOWY JACOB'S-LADDER   *Polemonium pulcherrimum*

General Perennial from taproot, with ***several loosely erect, clustered stems from branched, thickened stem base, 5-35 cm tall; plants glandular or glandular-hairy***.

Leaves ***Mainly basal, tufted***, stem leaves reduced; ***leaflets 11-25***, opposite or offset, ***egg shaped to circular, with strong skunky odour***.

Flowers ***Blue, with yellow centre***, showy, bell shaped; in crowded clusters; ***petals rounded***.

Fruits Capsules.

Ecology Dry, rocky or sandy places; roadsides, exposed slopes, or alpine ridges, often on gravelly soil. Valley bottoms to alpine throughout the region (alpine specimens dwarfed), but less common in areas of wet climates.

Notes: If you look closely at their beautiful flowers, you can see a bright orange ring at their base. • The skunklike smell of the bruised leaves earns this plant another common name, "skunk-weed." But in spite of the smell it lives up to its scientific name *pulcherrimum*, which means very handsome.

OTHER FAMILIES

TALL BLUEBELL — *Mertensia paniculata*

General Perennial; stems solitary to several from a somewhat woody base, *20 cm - 1.5 m tall*, hairy to smooth.

Leaves *Oval to lance shaped with prominent veins*, coarsely hairy on both sides; basal leaves long stemmed, lance shaped, blunt tipped; stem leaves narrower, sharp pointed, almost sessile.

Flowers *Blue*, sometimes pink or white, *bell shaped, drooping* with protruding styles; few to many in branched, open clusters.

Fruits Four small nutlets.

Ecology Moist forest, streambanks, gravel bars, moist meadows and thickets, woodlands into the subalpine. Typically a boreal species and common in the North, less frequent and scattered in the southern part of the region (south to 53°).

Notes: Sometimes called "lungwort" because of its similarity to the European lungwort, *Pulmonaria officinalis*, a plant believed to be good for lung diseases.

MOUNTAIN FORGET-ME-NOT — *Myosotis alpestris*

General Low perennial, stems *densely tufted*, more or less erect, hairy, 10-30 cm tall, with withered leaves at base.

Leaves Basal leaves *spoon to lance shaped*, hairy; upper leaves more lance shaped and stalkless.

Flowers *Bright blue (rarely white) with yellow centre*; in clusters of several all coming from one side of stem.

Fruits Nutlets; black, blunt, and shiny.

Ecology Moist subalpine and alpine meadows, and alpine tundra. Common at high elevations throughout the region.

Notes: Also known as *M. asiatica.* • One source says the common name "forget-me-not" dates back to 1561 when it was applied to the genus *Myosotis*. Traditionally a blue flower was worn to retain a lover's affection. • Another source says the name was originally applied to another plant (*Ajuga chamaepitys*, the ground pine) because of the nauseous taste it left in one's mouth. There seems to be a great deal of confusion as to exactly how the name came to be transferred to *Myosotis*. • See *Silene acaulis* for some inspirational words about this species. • *Myosotis* comes from the Greek *mus* (mouse) and *ous* (ear), hence, mouse ear, in reference to the soft long hairs on the leaves.

NORTHERN BEDSTRAW *Galium boreale*

General Perennial; mostly 20-60 cm tall with numerous, clustered, simple or few-branched stems, erect, square, smooth stems from creeping rhizomes.

Leaves *In whorls of 4* on stems, narrowly lance shaped, pointed but *blunt tipped, strongly three nerved*.

Flowers White to slightly creamy, very fragrant when in full flower, small but *numerous in showy terminal cluster*.

Fruits Dry nutlets covered *with straight or curly (not hooked) hairs*.

Ecology Open fairly dry forests (especially deciduous and mixed), dry open ground, grassy meadows, clearings, and roadsides. Common from lowlands to timberline throughout the region.

Notes: Northern bedstraw is a member of the coffee family, and its fruits can be roasted and used as a coffee substitute. The roots are a source of dyes. The Blackfoot of Alberta used them to make a red dye for their arrow tips. If the roots are boiled too long, the dye turns yellow. • The plant was used by Alaskan native people in hot packs and poultices. A liquid decoction was applied to external sores and infections. • "Bedstraw" derives from "Our Lady's Bedstraw," the common name of *G. verum*. Legend has it that the Virgin lay on a bed which was a mixture of bracken and *G. verum*. The bracken did not acknowledge the child's birth and lost its flowers, but the bedstraw welcomed the child and blossomed.

OTHER FAMILIES

SMALL BEDSTRAW — *Galium trifidum*

General Perennial; stems square, numerous, from very slender, creeping rhizomes, 5-50 cm tall, often much branched, *slender, weak, and lax, tending to scramble on other vegetation*.

Leaves Leaves mostly *in whorls of 4*, lacking stalks, linear to narrowly elliptic, rounded and *blunt tipped, 1 nerved*.

Flowers Whitish, small, *solitary or in 3's* on long narrow stalks at branch tips.

Fruits Two round, *smooth* nutlets.

Ecology Marshes, fens, swamps, banks of sluggish streams, wet ditches and clearings. Scattered at low to medium elevations throughout the region.

Notes: Small bedstraw is somewhat similar to northern bedstraw, but is generally smaller, crawls along the ground rather than growing upright, has 1-nerved leaves, and is a plant of wet habitats.

SWEET-SCENTED BEDSTRAW — *Galium triflorum*

General Perennial; stems square, 20-80 cm tall, *prostrate or sometimes ascending and scrambling on other vegetation; branched, strongly bristly*.

Leaves *Vanilla scented*, mostly (5) 6 in a whorl, sometimes 4 on small branches, narrowly elliptic, *1 nerved, with hooked hairs on underside midrib, and rounded but sharp-pointed tip*.

Flowers Greenish white, small; *3 flowers per stalk in loose, open clusters from axils* of leaves along stem.

Fruits Nutlets covered with *hooked bristles*.

Ecology Moist open forest, thickets, and streambanks, usually in partial shade. Common at low to moderate elevations throughout the region.

Notes: The plant smells strongly of vanilla, especially when dry, hence the name "sweet-scented bedstraw." The Blackfoot of Alberta used the dried flowers as a perfume.
• *G. triflorum* is in the coffee family; dried and roasted fruits may be used as a coffee substitute.

220

MARSH VALERIAN — *Valeriana dioica*

General Perennial with fibrous roots from a stout branched rhizome or woody stem-base; stems mostly 10-40 cm tall, smooth or nearly so.

Leaves *Basal leaves simple*, oblong to narrowly oval, stem leaves opposite, divided into 3 or more pairs of oval to lance-shaped lobes.

Flowers White, small, numerous, tubular, packed into a tight hemispherical to flat-topped head; styles and stamens protrude giving head a fluffy appearance.

Fruits Numerous achenes, each with feathery plumes that aid wind dispersal.

Ecology Moist meadows, grassy openings, and shrub-carrs; scattered throughout the region at low to moderate elevations.

Notes: The rhizomes have a strong odour that is sweeter than that of *V. sitchensis*. The Shuswap, Gitksan and Carrier used preparations of valerian roots, sometimes mixed with grease, as perfume for the face and hair and as a disinfectant. Some Thompson (southern interior) natives mixed powdered roots and leaves with tobacco for flavouring. •The rhizomes are reported to be edible and might have been eaten by native people in B.C. • An extract of the rhizome of the European species *V. officinalis* has long been used as a sedative, and it is possible that *V. dioica* was also used medicinally by native groups here. • *V. officinalis* is said to be very attractive to cats and rats, and the Pied Piper is reputed to have carried roots in his pocket to lure the rats out of Hamelin. • One source says that the name "valerian" is derived from Valeria, a part of Hungary where *V. officinalis* grew. Another proposes that the name comes from the Latin *valere* which means to be healthy and refers to its medicinal properties. It is also possible that the plant was named to honour Valerius, a Roman doctor reputed to have first used the plant as medicine.

SITKA VALERIAN — *Valeriana sitchensis*

General Fibrous-rooted perennial from a stout, branched rhizome or woody stem-base; stems square, somewhat succulent, 30-120 cm tall, smooth or occasionally short-hairy.

Leaves Large, opposite, in 2-5 pairs on stem, *stalked, all divided into 3-7 coarsely toothed leaflets*, the terminal one being largest and broadest.

Flowers Pale pink fading to white, small, numerous, tubular, arranged in dense terminal, hemispherical to flat-topped cluster; flowers sweet scented; stamens protrude giving head a fluffy appearance.

Fruits Numerous achenes, each topped by feathery plumes that aid wind dispersal.

Ecology Moist meadows, thickets, streambanks, and open subalpine forest. Widespread and often abundant at medium to (more commonly) high elevations throughout the region.

Notes: The rhizomes have a strong odour that some find unpleasant. The Alaskan Tlingit name for this plant means medicine that stinks, and crushed roots were applied to a mother's nipples when weaning a child or to sore muscles, or were blown onto animal traps for luck. Used by the Gitksan, Carrier and Shuswap as a perfume and disinfectant. The Gitksan mixed it with bear grease and wiped it on their faces and hair. The Shuswap bathed their race horses with it. Some Thompson men mixed the dried, powdered root with tobacco for flavouring. • There are reports that some North American native peoples ate the roots and used the plant medicinally. • Sitka valerian is responsible for the strong, sour odour detected in subalpine meadows after the first frost.

221

MOUNTAIN HAREBELL   *Campanula lasiocarpa*

General Perennial from thin branching rhizome; stems 1 to several, 2-15 cm (*usually less than 10 cm*) tall, smooth or slightly hairy.

Leaves Basal leaves small, more or less egg shaped, sharply toothed; *stem leaves narrow, sharply toothed*, lacking stalks, becoming progressively smaller up the stem.

Flowers Deep lilac-blue, usually single, large (23-30 mm long), broadly bell shaped; *sepal lobes very narrow, toothed and hairy*.

Fruits Papery capsules covered with hairs.

Ecology Common and widespread on stony slopes and scree, alpine tundra and heath; generally high above timberline in mountains throughout the region.

> *Notes:* A similar, but generally more dwarf alpine species is the much less common *C. uniflora* (arctic harebell). This species has a smaller flower (l5 mm long) which is much narrower and more funnel shaped. The lobes of the calyx are smooth, and the leaves are not toothed but merely wavy around the margin.

COMMON HAREBELL   *Campanula rotundifolia*

General Perennial with a slenderly branched woody base or system of rhizomes arising from an eventual taproot; *stems 10-50 cm tall*, ascending or erect, more or less glabrous.

Leaves Basal leaves stalked, oval to heart shaped, coarsely toothed, usually withering before flowers appear; *stem leaves thin, lance or linear shaped*.

Flowers Purplish blue, rarely white, single or 2-8, large, bell shaped, on thin wiry stems in loose cluster, nodding; the *sepals glabrous*.

Fruits Nodding oblong capsules.

Ecology In a wide variety of habitats – grassy slopes, gullies, canyons, rocky open ground, and near waterfalls. Scattered at low to medium (sometimes subalpine) elevations throughout the southern half of the region and also north along both the Coast and Rocky mountains.

> *Notes:* This is a very variable species: to 50 cm high at lower elevations, to l0 cm high in the alpine; the leaves long and sparsely hairy on wetter sites, much shorter and hairier on dry ones. • The origin of the name "harebell" is obscure. It may have come from the fact that the plant grew in grassy places frequented by hares. Another suggestion is that it should be "hairbell" in reference to a hairy flower stalk, but since the flower stalks are mostly glabrous, this is unlikely.

BUCKBEAN — *Menyanthes trifoliata*

General **Aquatic to semiaquatic** perennial from thick, submerged rhizomes, covered with old leaf bases; flowering stems erect, glabrous.

Leaves Leaves alternate, crowded near base of flowering stem, each **divided into 3 elliptic, long-stalked leaflets.**

Flowers **White**, usually purplish-pink tinged; petals **covered with long white hairs on inner surface**; very attractive, few to several on long, leafless stout stems.

Fruits Round to oval capsules.

Ecology Bogs, fens, marshes, and lake and pond margins; at low to medium elevations in suitable habitats throughout the region.

Notes: The rhizomes were used by Alaska tribes as emergency food (Finns and Lapps called the bread made from this "missen" bread or "famine" bread). They were dried, ground and washed in several waters to remove the bitterness and then dried again. • The bitter leaves have been used to make a bitter tonic which, taken in large doses, had a cathartic and emetic effect. Buckbean tea was also used to relieve fever and migraine headaches, for indigestion, to promote appetite and to eliminate intestinal worms. It was used externally to promote the healing of ulcerous wounds. • Dry leaves have been used as a substitute for hops in brewing. • The foliage is similar to that of broad beans, which may have given rise to "buckbean" (or "bogbean," another common name). The original name may have been "goat's bean," derived from the French *bouc* for goat. It was used to treat scurvy, and the name "buck" may have derived from *sharbock*, the German word for scurvy. • The name *Menyanthes* derives from the Greek *men* (month) and *anthos* (flower), either because it was said to last one month or because it was once used medicinally to bring on menstruation.

YELLOW WATERLILY — *Nuphar lutea* ssp. *polysepala*

General **Aquatic** perennial from thick, submerged rhizomes; flower stems thick, fleshy, long, arising from rhizomes.

Leaves **Floating** (sometimes partially or wholly submerged), **round or heart shaped with long stalks** (to 2 m long), leathery, 10-40 cm long.

Flowers **Yellow** (tinged with green or red), **single, large, waxy, cup shaped, floating**; petals yellow or greenish, small, lance shaped, hidden by numerous reddish or purplish stamens; centre of flower dominated by large knoblike stigma.

Fruits Many-seeded, oval capsules.

Ecology Ponds, shallow lakes, sluggish streams, throughout the region at low to moderate elevations.

Notes: The rhizomes were and still are used medicinally by the Gitksan and Wet'suwet'en (Carrier). Rhizomes were peeled, sliced, air-dried, and stored sliced or powdered. Rehydrated slices were applied as a poultice to aching joints, broken bones, and skin ulcers. Powder was sprinkled on food and eaten. A weak decoction of fresh rhizome was drunk as an appetite stimulant or tonic. Mixed with devil's-club, yellow waterlily was an important medicine for tuberculosis victims. • Alaskan tribes ate the rhizomes boiled or roasted, and they are said to be sweet and rich in starch. The seeds were a highly sought-after food source for coastal U.S. natives. Turner (1978) reports no evidence of B.C. natives eating either seeds or rhizomes and comments that the latter are extremely bitter even after several boilings. • This species is also called "yellow pond-lily" and "spatterdock," a name for which no explanation has been found so far, although the broad leaves often spatter the surface of water near docks.

SKUNK CABBAGE — *Lysichiton americanum*

General Perennial herb 30-150 cm tall, from fleshy, upright underground stems. *Entire plant has skunky odour.*

Leaves Simple, often huge, lance shaped to broadly elliptic, *30-120 cm long*, 10-70 cm wide, on stout stalks.

Flowers *Greenish yellow*, arranged on a spadix (a spike of flowers on a thick, fleshy axis) surrounded by a *bright yellow spathe* (the large bract which surrounds a spadix).

Fruits Greenish to reddish, *berrylike* and pulpy, 1 or 2 seeded.

Ecology *Very wet, swampy* sites in forests and openings where it's too wet for trees. Scattered and locally common in suitable habitats, at low to medium elevations in areas of wetter climates in the southern half of our region.

Notes: Calla palustris (water arum) is another member of the arum family that occurs sporadically in the region. It has a long thick rhizome, heart-shaped leaves, a white spathe, red berries, and grows in swamps, bog pools, and often floating along the margins of ponds and sloughs. • Some native people refer to skunk cabbage as "Indian wax paper" because all groups with access to the large shiny leaves traditionally used them in many of the same ways as waxed paper, such as lining food-steaming pits, and wrapping or covering food. Turner (1978) notes that only the Lower Lillooet ate the rootstocks and that their name for the plant means hot, like pepper. • Crystals of calcium oxalate in skunk cabbage leave a burning sensation in the mouth, but roasting the rootstocks destroys the crystals, in skunk cabbage and its Polynesian relative taro (both are in the arum family and are an important source of starch for the local native peoples). • The genus name *Lysichiton* (spelled *Lysichitum* in some works) is from the Greek *lysis* (loosening) and *chiton* (tunic), in reference to the spathe. • Also known colloquially as "swamp lantern."

CATTAIL — *Typha latifolia*

General Perennial herb, *with pithy, cylindrical stems*, to 2 m high or more; from coarse rhizomes.

Leaves Alternate, *flat, long and narrow* (grasslike), somewhat spongy, 1-2 cm broad, grayish green; base sheathing the stem.

Flowers Tiny, numerous, borne in a *terminal cylindrical spike*: lower portion (with female flowers) 15-20 cm long, 1-3 cm thick, dark brown, persistent; upper portion (with male flowers) cone shaped, disintegrating and leaving the stem apex bare above the persistent female inflorescence.

Fruits Dry, ellipsoid, about 1 mm long; designed to float, with *numerous long slender hairs* at the base.

Ecology In marshy areas, ponds, and wet ditches in slow-flowing or standing water. Scattered and locally abundant in suitable habitats, at low elevations throughout our region.

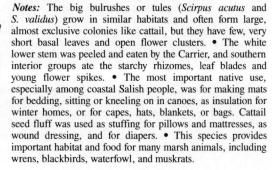

Notes: The big bulrushes or tules (*Scirpus acutus* and *S. validus*) grow in similar habitats and often form large, almost exclusive colonies like cattail, but they have few, very short basal leaves and open flower clusters. • The white lower stem was peeled and eaten by the Carrier, and southern interior groups ate the starchy rhizomes, leaf blades and young flower spikes. • The most important native use, especially among coastal Salish people, was for making mats for bedding, sitting or kneeling on in canoes, as insulation for winter homes, or for capes, hats, blankets, or bags. Cattail seed fluff was used as stuffing for pillows and mattresses, as wound dressing, and for diapers. • This species provides important habitat and food for many marsh animals, including wrens, blackbirds, waterfowl, and muskrats.

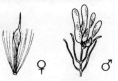

♀ ♂

Grasses

Of all the world's flowering plants, the grass family (Poaceae) are undoubtedly the most useful to humankind. They supply sugar from sugar cane and cereal grains such as wheat, barley, oats, corn and rice; are used for forage and turf; and are available as materials for weaving, adobe, or bamboo structures. Furthermore, grains such as barley can be brewed into beers and whiskys. Many species of wildlife, from large grazing mammals to waterfowl, depend on grass and grassland or wetland habitats for food, shelter, and completion of their life cycles.

Grass flowers are small and are borne in the axils of a small inner bract, the **palea**, and a larger outer bract, the **lemma**; the flower, lemma and palea together are called a **floret**. Below the florets are two bracts, the **glumes**; florets and glumes together are called a **spikelet**. Leaves of most grasses sheath the stem before diverging as a narrow blade, and where the sheathing part joins the blade are two distinctive organs useful for identification: the **ligule** and the **auricle**. Grass stems are hollow and round in cross-section. If your "grass" specimen has either a solid stem or is triangular in cross-section, refer to the section on "Sedges and Rushes" (p. 254).

The grass family is very large and complex. In British Columbia there are over 300 grass species, most of which are indigenous. Only the most common species encountered in the northern part of the province are presented here.

Grasses in general were used widely by Indian peoples for lining steam-cooking pits, wiping fish, covering berries, stringing food for drying, spreading on floors, or as bedding.

To assist in identification, the grasses are picture-keyed into first tribes and then into genera. Detailed drawings of the flowering parts are provided to illustrate characteristics of individual species. For more information on B.C.'s grasses, see Hubbard (1969).

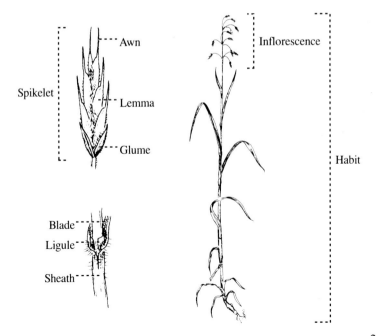

Picture-Key to Common Grass Tribes

1. Inflorescence a spike (spikelets without stalks) .... *Hordeae*
(Barley tribe)

1. Inflorescence a panicle (spikelets with stalks) ....

   2. Each spikelet with 1 flower; glumes small .... *Agrostideae*
                                         (Timothy tribe)

   2. Each spikelet with 2 to many flowers (florets) ....

      3. Glumes shorter than first floret (lowest enclosed lemma); lemmas awnless, or awned from near the tip .... *Festuceae*
                                        (Fescue tribe)

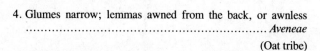

      3. Glumes equal to, or longer than first floret (lowest enclosed lemma)...

         4. Glumes narrow; lemmas awned from the back, or awnless .... *Aveneae*
                                        (Oat tribe)

         4. Glumes broad, boat-shaped; lemmas awned from a notched apex, or awnless...................................... *Phalarideae*
                                    (Canarygrass tribe)

Picture-Key to Grass Genera
Hordeae (Barley tribe)
Inflorescence a spike

spikelets solitary at each node	spikelets two at each node, alike	spikelets three at each node, lateral pair reduced to awns

 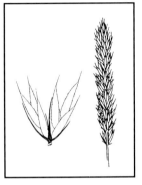 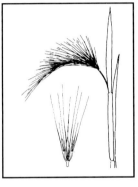

Agropyron
(wheatgrass)
page 231

Elymus
(wildrye)
page 232

Hordeum
(barley)
page 233

Phalarideae (Canarygrass tribe)
Spikelets 3-flowered;
glumes broad, boat-shaped

panicle open or tufted	panicle compact; spikelets crowded, all turned in same direction

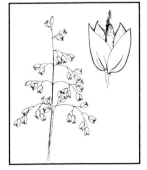 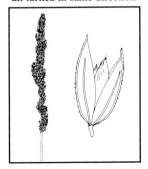

Hierochloe
(sweetgrass)
page 236

Phalaris
(canarygrass)
page 253

Picture-Key to Genera

Aveneae (Oat tribe)

Spikelets 2 to many-flowered; glumes equal to or longer than first floret

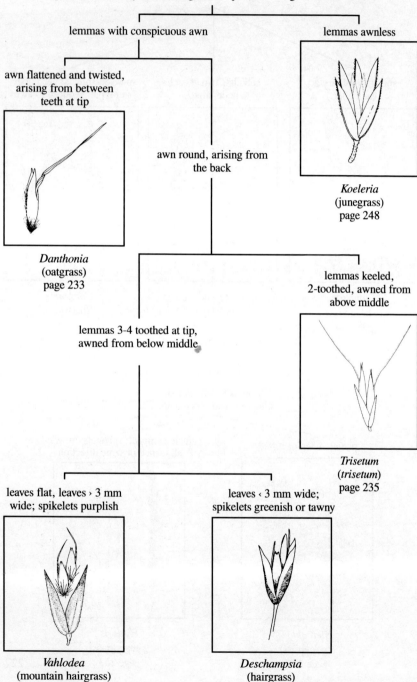

lemmas with conspicuous awn

lemmas awnless

awn flattened and twisted, arising from between teeth at tip

awn round, arising from the back

Koeleria
(junegrass)
page 248

Danthonia
(oatgrass)
page 233

lemmas keeled, 2-toothed, awned from above middle

lemmas 3-4 toothed at tip, awned from below middle

Trisetum
(*trisetum*)
page 235

leaves flat, leaves > 3 mm wide; spikelets purplish

leaves < 3 mm wide; spikelets greenish or tawny

Vahlodea
(mountain hairgrass)
page 234

Deschampsia
(hairgrass)
page 234

Picture-Key to Genera
Agrostideae (Timothy tribe)
Spikelets 1-flowered

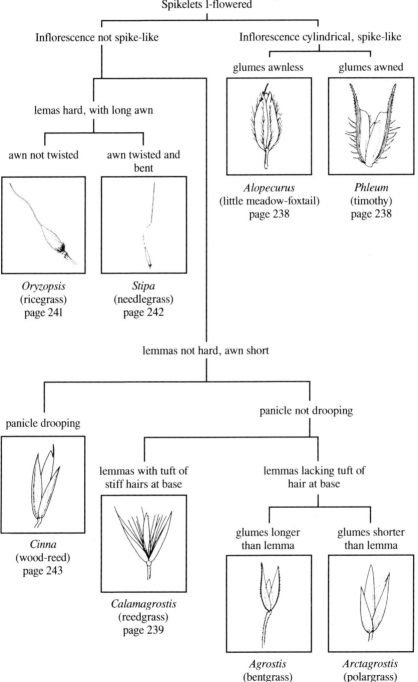

Inflorescence not spike-like

Inflorescence cylindrical, spike-like

glumes awnless

glumes awned

lemas hard, with long awn

awn not twisted

awn twisted and bent

Alopecurus
(little meadow-foxtail)
page 238

Phleum
(timothy)
page 238

Oryzopsis
(ricegrass)
page 241

Stipa
(needlegrass)
page 242

lemmas not hard, awn short

panicle drooping

panicle not drooping

lemmas with tuft of
stiff hairs at base

lemmas lacking tuft of
hair at base

Cinna
(wood-reed)
page 243

glumes longer
than lemma

glumes shorter
than lemma

Calamagrostis
(reedgrass)
page 239

Agrostis
(bentgrass)
page 237

Arctagrostis
(polargrass)
page 237

Picture-Key to Genera

Festuceae (Fescue tribe)

Spikelets 2 to many-flowered

Lemmas with awns

spikelets small; leaves narrow	spikelets large; leaves flat, broad	spikelets long, slender; glumes purplish	spikelet short and broad; lemmas bristly

Festuca (fescue) page 247	*Bromus* (brome) page 244	*Schizachne* (false melic) page 243	*Dactylis* (orchardgrass) page 252

Lemmas without awns

spikelets small; leaf tip boat shaped	spikelets long; lemmas striated	spikelets long; lemmas not striated	low plants; male and female heads separate

Poa (bluegrass) page 249	*Glyceria* (mannagrass) page 246	*Puccinellia* (alkaligrass) page 245	*Distichlis* (saltgrass) page 245

BLUEBUNCH WHEATGRASS — *Agropyron spicatum*

General A *bunchgrass* with numerous erect stems 60-100 cm tall, often forming large clumps.

Leaves Flat or loosely inrolled, *blue-green*, hairy on the upper surface, *previous year's leaves persistent* and curled at base of plant; auricles short and claw-like; ligules short (1 mm long) and collar-like.

Inflorescence Spike slender; *spikelets usually shorter than internodes*; lemmas without awns in var. *inerme*; lemmas with awns 1-2 cm long in var. *spicatum*.

Ecology Common, often abundant in grassland and open forests on dry southerly slopes. At low to medium elevations, only in the southernmost portions of our region (*generally south of Quesnel*).

Notes: This species was used by the Okanagan as tinder and for stuffing moccasins in winter. The straws were placed in newly pierced ears to keep the holes open. Lillooet people dried their berries on it. • This native grass is excellent forage for both domestic stock and wildlife, but is susceptible to damage from overgrazing.

SLENDER WHEATGRASS — *Agropyron trachycaulum*

General Slender, *loosely tufted* perennial, 50-90 cm tall.

Leaves Scabrous, usually flat; several along a stem; auricles absent or short; ligules very short (to 0.5 mm).

Inflorescence Spike slender, 8-20 cm long; *spikelets overlapping*, about 2 to 2.5 times as long as the internode; lemmas awnless or with awns 1-3 cm long.

Ecology Grassland, meadows, rocky slopes, shrub-carrs, and open forest on dry to moist sites. Widespread at low to medium elevations *throughout the region*.

Notes: *Agropyron repens* (quackgrass) is a rhizomatous European species that has become well established in the settled portions of our region as a vigorous, persistent weed. • Slender wheatgrass has been divided into several distinct varieties. It provides good forage for livestock; tolerance to grazing is low.

231

BLUE WILDRYE — *Elymus glaucus*

General Tufted perennial usually forming small clumps, 0.5-1.5 m tall.

Leaves Usually *lax, scabrous, flat or slightly inrolled*; auricles usually well developed, claw-like and clasping; ligules short (about 1 mm long).

Inflorescence Spike erect, stiff, 5-15 cm long; spikelets mostly 2 flowered and overlapping; *lemmas with long (10-20 mm) conspicuous awns.*

Ecology Open forest (coniferous and deciduous), dry to moist openings and clearings. Common at low to medium elevations throughout the region.

Notes: This grass may have been used by southern interior natives in basketry. The split, flattened stems were superimposed over the weave. • This is one of our tallest grasses, and provides forage for both domestic stock and wildlife.

FUZZY-SPIKED WILDRYE — *Elymus innovatus*

General Tall, erect, perennial sod-forming grass; noted for its deep-spreading root system, 0.5-1 m tall.

Leaves *Thin, stiff, and inrolled*; auricles well developed, claw-like; ligules very short (to 0.5 mm long).

Inflorescence Dense, erect, *very fuzzy* spike 5 to 12 cm long; spikelets 3 to 5 flowered and hairy; *lemmas short awned (to 3 mm long).*

Ecology Open forest, south-facing grassy slopes, clearings. Fairly common, locally abundant at low to high elevations throughout the northern part of the region except for Haines Triangle, also in the Blackwater River area (on coarse soils).

Notes: Considered of low palatability, but does provide forage for domestic stock in boreal regions and is an important native forage plant. Important winter forage for mountain sheep in the northern Rockies.

FOXTAIL BARLEY · *Hordeum jubatum*

General Tufted, 30-60 cm tall, stem erect or curved at base.

Leaves Greyish green, rough and hairy, less than 5 mm wide; auricles lacking; ligules short (to 1 mm long).

Inflorescence *Spike* usually nodding; glumes awnlike, 2-6 cm long; lemmas with equally long awns.

Ecology Moist open ground, meadows, roadsides, disturbed sites in general. Very common weedy species at low elevations throughout our region.

Notes: This species is easily recognized by the *"foxtail" of long purplish awns.* A similar species, *H. brachyantherum* (meadow barley), has a narrower spike, with awns less than 2 cm long, and can sometimes be found on the margins of wetlands and ponds on the southern Fraser Plateau. *Sitanion hystrix* (squirreltail) also resembles foxtail barley, but usually has two spikelets at each node, whereas *Hordeum* has three. •The barbed awns of foxtail barley can cause great distress to grazing animals, leading to irritation of their mouths, ears and eyes. A disease called "necrotic stomatitis" can affect populations of various ungulates, both wild and domestic, where damaged mouth tissues are prone to infection, sometimes leading to death. Range managers state that feeding on this species gives stock "bad breath," probably resulting from mouth infections.

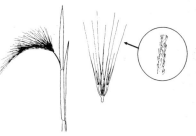

TIMBER OATGRASS · *Danthonia intermedia*

General Densely tufted, 5-40 cm tall.

Leaves Mainly basal, to 3 mm wide, long-hairy on the lower surface, old leaves remaining; *long hairs where leaf blade joins the stem*; auricles absent; ligules a fringe of hairs, to 1 mm long; sheaths very hairy.

Inflorescence Spikelets few, borne in a dense, tuftlike panicle; lemmas hairy at base and margins only; *awn twisted, up to 1 cm long.*

Ecology Grassland, meadows, shrub-carrs, open forest, grassy alpine tundra. Common but not abundant, from valley bottoms to above timberline in the southwestern part of the region; also occasional on grassy, southerly slopes in the North.

Notes: One of the first grasses to have growth in the spring. This is a distinctive grass with *large, oatlike spikelets* which often turn purplish.

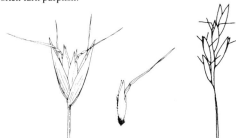

233

TUFTED HAIRGRASS   *Deschampsia caespitosa*

General Densely tufted with numerous stems 20-120 cm tall; roots fibrous.

Leaves *Rather stiff, narrow*, flat to folded, to 3 mm wide; auricles lacking; ligules prominent, pointed, up to 10 mm long.

Inflorescence An open, loose *panicle 10-25 cm long*, often nodding; spikelets *bronze and glistening*, usually darkening at maturity; lemmas thin, awned from near base.

Ecology Meadows (sometimes in pure stands), shrub-carrs, gravelly river bars, lakeshores, and (occasionally) alpine tundra. Widespread but scattered, from low to high elevations throughout the region.

Notes: One of several grasses used by the Tlingit of Alaska to imbricate fine spruce-root baskets. • This is a variable species with a broad ecological amplitude (coastal salt marshes to alpine tundra) and a range from the Arctic to high altitudes in the tropics.

MOUNTAIN HAIRGRASS   *Vahlodea atropurpurea*

General Loosely tufted, 40-80 cm tall.

Leaves *Flat, soft, deep green*, tips more or less prow-like; auricles absent; ligules 1.5-3.5 mm long, hairy.

Inflorescence An open, loose *panicle, 5-10 cm long*, often nodding; *spikelets relatively large and often purplish* in colour at maturity; lemmas awned from the middle.

Ecology High elevation mountain meadows, alpine heath, snowbeds, streambanks, and open subalpine forests. Scattered, locally abundant at high elevations in areas of heavy snowfall.

Notes: Mountain hairgrass is referred to in some texts as *Deschampsia atropurpurea*. • Though this species is sometimes found in the upper subalpine where forest stands thin to "parkland," its true home is above treeline.

NODDING TRISETUM — *Trisetum cernuum*

General Tufted, 60-120 cm tall.

Leaves *Flat, lax*, 5-10 mm broad, with thin prominent tips, glabrous; auricles absent; ligules 1.5-3 mm long.

Inflorescence An *open, loose panicle* 15-30 cm long, often nodding; *lemmas with long bent awn* from near middle; *second glume wider than first, with a sharp tip.*

Ecology Moist forest, clearings, streambanks. Common at low to subalpine elevations in wetter parts of the southern half of the region.

Notes: Nodding trisetum could be confused with false melic (p. 243), which lacks a sharp tip on the larger glume, has longer lemmas, narrower leaves, and longer callus hairs.

SPIKE TRISETUM — *Trisetum spicatum*

General Erect, densely tufted bunchgrass 10-50 cm tall.

Leaves Stiff, to 5 mm wide, relatively short, folded to flat, finely hairy; auricles absent; ligules 0.5-2 mm long.

Inflorescence *Dense, spikelike* (often turning dark purple) *panicle*, 5-15 cm long; *lemmas with long bent awn* from near middle; glumes nearly equal in size.

Ecology Generally on dry soils, rock outcrops or rocky slopes, but occasionally in moist areas, dry open forest, and alpine tundra. Widespread at low to high elevations throughout our region, but rarely abundant.

Notes: Important forage plant when abundant in the alpine and subalpine.

235

COMMON SWEETGRASS — *Hierochloe odorata*

General Erect, often solitary, usually **purplish-based stems 30-60 cm tall**; spreading from long rhizomes; sweet smelling.

Leaves Stem leaves short and broad (to 8 mm wide); non-flowering shoots often have long blades; auricles absent; ligules 3-5 mm long.

Inflorescence **Panicle open**, pyramidal in shape; spikelets lustrous golden yellow, tulip shaped; glumes broad; lemmas hairy, **awnless**.

Ecology Moist meadows, lakeshores, streambanks, riparian areas; widely scattered from **low to medium elevations** throughout the region.

Notes: This grass was widely used by native people across North America to make fragrant baskets. In B.C. it was definitely used by southern interior groups and possibly also by some northern groups as a personal and household fragrance and air freshener. The fragrance is due to the presence of coumarin.

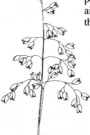 

ALPINE SWEETGRASS — *Hierochloe alpina*

General Erect, short, **reddish-based stems**, about **20 cm tall**; spreading from short rhizomes.

Leaves Stem leaves few and short; basal leaves longer; ligules short (to 0.6 mm long), with fringe of hairs at tip.

Inflorescence **Panicle tuftlike**; spikelets tawny, 3-flowered: first lemma with short awn, second lemma with a **longer bent awn**, third lemma awnless.

Ecology Alpine tundra. Common, but rarely abundant, throughout the region.

Notes: Another name for the genus is "holy grass," as the species are burned as an incense in religious rituals by some native groups. This small mountain grass is distinctive with its few, bronze-coloured spikelets.

HAIR BENTGRASS — *Agrostis scabra*

General Densely tufted perennial with scabrous stems 20-50 cm tall; roots fibrous.

Leaves *Numerous, fine,* short, scabrous, mainly *basal*; auricles absent; ligules 2-3 mm long.

Inflorescence *Panicle large, diffuse, flexuous,* often purplish; spikelets borne near the branch tips; glumes equal, small; single lemma delicate, with or without a fine awn; glumes and panicle branches also scabrous.

Ecology Dry to wet disturbed areas generally; also on dry rocky slopes and gravelly river bars. Common at low to moderate elevations throughout our region.

Notes: An introduced species, *Agrostis stolonifera* (redtop), has a stiff panicle with spikelets forming at the base of branches. Selections of redtop are among several species of bentgrass extensively used as lawn grasses and turf grasses. It is also locally abundant following disturbance, especially in the northeast. • Species of *Agrostis* are also called "ticklegrass"; play with the panicle to find out why! The panicle breaks away with age, rolling along the ground like a tumbleweed in the wind.

POLARGRASS — *Arctagrostis latifolia*

General Perennial, 0.6-1.5 m tall; slowly expanding growth by rhizomes produces a dense bunchlike appearance.

Leaves *Wide, flat, and erect* with an acute tip, mostly along stem (i.e., *not basal*); ligules long, up to 5 mm long.

Inflorescence Open panicle with long, usually ascending branches; spikelets often purplish at maturity; *glumes unequal,* nearly as long as spikelet; *lemmas awnless.*

Ecology Wet meadows, fens, gravel bars along rivers. Scattered at low to subalpine elevations north of 57°.

Notes: Extremely variable species; provides forage for wildlife. It is tolerant of being submerged during spring runoff, and is currently being investigated for its agricultural potential.

237

TIMOTHY — *Phleum pratense*

General A short-lived perennial that forms large clumps; stems smooth, stiffly erect, up to 1 m tall; **base bulbous** with fibrous roots.

Leaves Wide and flat, tapering; auricles absent; ligules 2-3 mm long.

Inflorescence *Panicle very dense, spikelike, cylindrical*, many times longer than broad, up to 10 cm long, *about 10 mm thick*; spikelets crowded, flattened; glumes strongly ciliate on keels and with short, stout, curved awns.

Ecology Roadsides, pastures, clearings; introduced (from Eurasia) and partly naturalized near settled areas. Common from low to medium elevations, throughout the region wherever it has been introduced.

Notes: This palatable, leafy grass is one of the more important domestic hay grasses in North America, and one of our more common causes of hay fever. *Phleum alpinum* (alpine timothy), a common native grass in the subalpine and alpine, is similar but smaller (to 50 cm tall) and has a shorter (less than 5 cm long), wider panicle. • Timothy is named for Timothy Harris, the 19th century U.S. agrologist who championed its use in domestic pastures.

LITTLE MEADOW-FOXTAIL — *Alopecurus aequalis*

General Erect or spreading, stems 15-60 cm tall, often with a curved base underwater.

Leaves Flat, 1-4 mm wide, lax when submerged; auricles absent; ligules 4-8 mm long, pointed.

Inflorescence *Slender, spikelike panicle*, 2-7 cm long, *about 4 mm thick*, pale green; lemma with short awn attached near middle.

Ecology Muskeg, riverbanks, roadside ditches and shallow ponds, streamsides, and wet clearings. Common at low elevations throughout the region.

Notes: This grass looks somewhat like a small timothy plant.

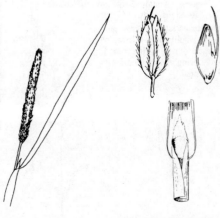

BLUEJOINT   *Calamagrostis canadensis*

General Tufted, coarse perennial up to 2 m tall; has creeping rhizomes and forms tussocks.

Leaves Numerous, elongate, **rather lax; collars usually lacking hairs**; auricles absent; ligules 3-8 mm long.

Inflorescence Nodding panicle **10-25 cm long**, from narrow and rather dense to loose and relatively open; lemma with usually straight awn, and numerous **callus hairs nearly as long as lemma**.

Ecology Moist to wet forests, meadows, wetlands and clearings. Common and often abundant, from low to high elevations throughout our region.

Notes: One of the grasses used by the Tlingit of Alaska for imbrication of fine spruce-root baskets. • Very aggressive colonizers after disturbance; moderate forage value for livestock and also an important food of bison in the North. Particularly abundant in the northeast portion of our region, where it is often the dominant species on disturbed sites.

PURPLE REEDGRASS   *Calamagrostis purpurascens*

General Tufted, 30-70 cm tall.

Leaves Flat or slightly inrolled, **rather thick; collars indistinctly pubescent**; ligules 2-4 mm long.

Inflorescence Dense panicle, usually pinkish or purplish, 5-12 cm long; lemma with **bent awn that sticks out** from the glumes, numerous **callus hairs about 1/3 length of lemma**.

Ecology Grassy ridges, rocky slopes, dry open forests, shrub-carrs, alpine tundra, clearings, **often on calcareous or alkaline sites**. Scattered at low to high elevations throughout the region except for areas of wetter climates.

Notes: Plants are usually well spaced. The large, straw coloured heads are conspicuous late in the season.

GRASSES

PINEGRASS — *Calamagrostis rubescens*

General Erect, 60-100 cm tall, with long rhizomes, usually forming extensive cover; *base of plants reddish*.

Leaves *Long*, 2-4 mm wide; *collars hairy*; auricles absent; ligules to 5 mm long.

Inflorescence Dense panicle, yellowish green to purple, 7-15 cm long; bent awn on lemma often sticks out from glumes; *callus hairs less than 1/2 the length of lemma*.

Ecology Dry woods and clearings. Common, often abundant, at low to medium elevations south of the Nechako River on the Fraser Plateau.

Notes: One of a group of plants, including species of the grass *Poa* and the sedge, *Carex concinnoides*, which have all been identified by modern day native informants as timbergrass. Timbergrass was

used by interior native people to make soapberry beaters, in the preparation of dried soapberry cakes, or for covering food. The Okanagan and Thompson wove socks and insoles from it for their moccasins. • This common yellow-green grass carpets the dry coniferous forests of the southernmost part of the region, rarely forming heads except in open sunny areas. Pinegrass is not very palatable to grazing animals except for new spring growth.

SLIMSTEM REEDGRASS — *Calamagrostis stricta*

General Rhizomatous perennial 40-100 cm tall.

Leaves Long, *tough and wiry,* 2-4 mm wide, usually involute; auricles absent; ligules 2-4 mm long.

Inflorescence Panicle narrow, congested, 5-15 cm long, generally pale green but sometimes purple tinged, turning brown late in the season; straight awn slightly exceeding the lemma, *callus hairs two-thirds as long as lemma*.

Ecology Fens, marshes, streambanks, lake margins. Plants are usually widely spaced, but occasionally form dense stands. Scattered throughout the region at low to moderate elevations.

Notes: The *long, narrow, spikelike panicle* makes this wetland grass distinctive. Previously known as *C. neglecta*. This species is similar to *C. inexpansa* (narrow-spiked reedgrass) which has longer ligules (to 6 mm) and generally broader leaves.

ROUGH-LEAVED RICEGRASS — *Oryzopsis asperifolia*

General Tufted, with erect, spreading stems 20-40 cm long; plant usually solitary.

Leaves **Wide, firm, flat**, rough in texture, tapered at both ends; some basal leaves usually lax and laying on ground; auricles absent; ligules short, about 0.5 mm long, ciliate at tip.

Inflorescence Simple, few flowered, spikelike panicle, 5-8 cm long; **glumes 6-8 mm long**; hard, cylindrical lemmas yellowish, with awns 5-10 mm.

Ecology Dry to moist open forests and clearings. Scattered at low to moderate elevations in the southern half of our region.

Notes: The ricegrasses can dominate dry forested sites in southern parts of our region, their clusters of decumbent basal leaves forming characteristic circles on the herb-poor forest floor.

SHORT-AWNED RICEGRASS — *Oryzopsis pungens*

General Tufted perennial 15-30 cm tall, usually loosely clumped.

Leaves **Long, slender, and rather stiff.**

Inflorescence Narrow panicle 3-6 cm long; **glumes 3-4 mm long**; hard, cylindrical lemmas with short awns (1-2 mm).

Ecology Very dry forests and openings, usually on sandy or rocky soils. Scattered at low to moderate elevations throughout all but the wettest parts of the region.

Notes: This is a small grass which increases in abundance in disturbed areas. The inflorescence of ricegrasses is somewhat similar to that of the true rices (*Oryza* spp.).

241

STIFF NEEDLEGRASS — *Stipa occidentalis*

General Strongly tufted, robust, 40-80 cm tall, *flowering stalks erect*.

Leaves Thin, stiff, usually inrolled, white hairs present on upper surface; auricles absent; ligules about 0.5 mm long.

Inflorescence Relatively *narrow, lax panicle* 10-20 cm long; lemmas with bent *corkscrew-twisted awns* 3-4 cm long.

Ecology Dry grassy ridges, open rocky slopes. Scattered at low elevations of Fraser and Nechako plateaus, also on dry warm grassy south slopes along major rivers (e.g., Stikine, Peace) in the North.

Notes: This species is also known as *Stipa columbiana*.

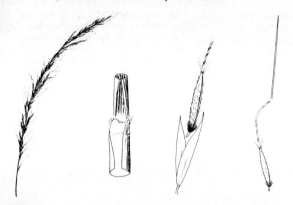

SPREADING NEEDLEGRASS — *Stipa richardsonii*

General A tufted perennial 40-100 cm tall, *flowering stalks arched near top*.

Leaves Mostly basal, inrolled, usually 15-25 cm long; auricles absent; ligules to 0.5 mm long.

Inflorescence A *loose open panicle*, the spikelets slender and drooping; lemmas with bent *corkscrew-twisted awns* about 3 cm long.

Ecology Grassy ridges, open rocky slopes, and dry open forests. Scattered at low elevations of Fraser and Nechako plateaus, also on dry warm grassy south slopes along major rivers in the North.

Notes: Corkscrew-twisted awns will work their way into the ears of domestic pets. This grass often forms solid stands at the edge of dry forests.

NODDING WOOD-REED — *Cinna latifolia*

General Rhizomatous, 60-120 cm high, sometimes bulbous at base.

Leaves Thin, soft, and **wide (7-15 mm) in the middle, rapidly narrowing quickly to a sharp tip**, rough to the touch, **borne at right angles to the stem**; auricles absent; **ligules hairy, 4-8 mm long**.

Inflorescence **Open drooping panicle** 15-30 cm long, whole spikelets detach at maturity leaving a bare stem; lemmas with a short straight awn or awnless.

Ecology Moist woods, meadows, wet areas along streams, and moist disturbed areas. Widespread and abundant in wetter climates, locally common on wetter sites in drier climates, at low to medium elevations south of 55°, extending northward along the Coast and Rocky Mountains.

Notes: Increases tremendously on disturbed sites. One of the grasses used by the Tlingit of Alaska for imbrication on fine spruce-root baskets.

FALSE MELIC — *Schizachne purpurascens*

General Loosely tufted from a decumbent base, glabrous, 50-100 cm tall.

Leaves Flat, 2-3 mm broad, lax, narrowed at base; auricles absent; ligules to 1 mm long.

Inflorescence **A few-branched drooping panicle, often purplish**; lemma 10 mm long, **long bent awn from just below the teeth at the tip**, with callus hairs at the base somewhat like a *Calamagrostis*.

Ecology Open grassy or wooded, moist to dry and rocky areas, often at forest edges. Scattered, locally abundant in the southern half of the region at low to subalpine elevations, most common in dry to moist climates; uncommon further north.

Notes: Appears similar to nodding trisetum (p. 235), which has a shorter lemma (5-6 mm) and wider leaves, and to some bromes, but with smaller seeds.

PUMPELLY BROME *Bromus inermis* ssp. *pumpellianus*

General Rhizomatous, generally sod forming, 50-80 cm tall; ***stems with hairy nodes.***

Leaves Flat with prominent veins, up to 12 mm wide; auricles usually present on some leaves; ligules 0.5-2.5 mm long.

Inflorescence ***Ascending to erect, narrow panicle,*** 7-20 cm long; spikelets large, relatively narrow, often purplish tinged; ***lemmas fuzzy-hairy and short awned (2-3 mm long).***

Ecology Meadows, dry grassy slopes, margins of dry forest, disturbed areas. Scattered at low to high elevations throughout our region.

Notes: This native species can be distinguished from the introduced smooth brome (*B. inermis* ssp. *inermis*) by the presence of hairs on the lemmas and at the stem nodes. Smooth brome is well established in disturbed areas, old fields and meadows, and is an important component of hayfields and pastures.

COLUMBIA BROME *Bromus vulgaris*

General Tall (60-100 cm), slender, loosely tufted; ***stems often with hairy nodes.***

Leaves Lax, flat, and usually hairy on at least one surface; auricles lacking; ligules 3-5 mm long.

Inflorescence ***Open, drooping panicle*** with slender branches; spikelets few flowered; ***lemmas hairy only on margins; awn more than 5 mm long.***

Ecology Shaded to open forest, openings, thickets, moist to dry banks, to subalpine meadows and dry rocky slopes. Common at low to subalpine elevations in the southern half of our region.

Notes: Very similar to fringed brome (*Bromus ciliatus*) which has shorter awns (2-4 mm) and shorter ligules. Fringed brome grows in similar habitats at low to medium elevations throughout our region.

ALKALI SALTGRASS — *Distichlis stricta*

General A sod-forming shortgrass (10-30 cm tall) with vigorous, **scaly rhizomes**.

Leaves Yellowish green, **short, stiff and erect, closely two ranked; old leaves persistent**; auricles absent; ligules short, to 0.5 mm long, fringed with hairs.

Inflorescence **Panicle small with large, compressed spikelets**; male and female flowers form on separate plants; **lemmas hardened, unawned**.

Ecology Saline or alkaline meadows, occasionally on dry slopes. Scattered, locally common; **only in the Chilcotin in our region**.

Notes: This coarse grass often forms a uniform cover over large areas in the parkland/pond country of the Chilcotin.

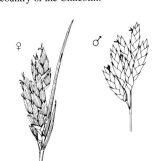

NUTTALL'S ALKALIGRASS — *Puccinellia nuttalliana*

General Tufted, 40-80 cm tall, with fibrous roots.

Leaves Smooth, short, becoming folded.

Inflorescence **Panicle spreading**, 6-20 cm long; spikelets tiny (like droplets), 4 to 7 flowered; glumes small; lemmas narrowed to an obtuse tip but **without awns**; auricles absent; ligules 1-3 mm long.

Ecology Wetland meadows, seepage areas in gullies and on cutbanks, usually where alkaline. Sporadic at low to medium elevations throughout the region, common only in the Chilcotin, but also here and there along the Peace and Liard rivers.

Notes: Continuous stands of this grass provide considerable forage in wetlands; often found growing with akali saltgrass in the Chilcotin. This species also grows in salt marshes along the coast.

TALL MANNAGRASS — *Glyceria elata*

General Loosely tufted, somewhat succulent perennial with creeping rhizomes, 1-1.5 m tall.

Leaves Flat, lax blades, 6-12 mm wide; auricles absent; **ligules 3-6 mm long, short-hairy**.

Inflorescence Oblong panicle, **with spreading branches** 15-30 cm long; spikelets 6 to 8 flowered; glumes small; **lemmas firm, prominently 7 veined**.

Ecology Streamsides, wet meadows, lake margins and shady moist woods. Scattered throughout the southern half of the region at low to medium elevations.

Notes: The similar fowl mannagrass (*G. striata*), a wetland species scattered throughout the region, has narrower leaves (2-6 mm). Reed mannagrass (*G. grandis*) has 6-15 mm wide leaves, large open panicles, and glabrous ligules. • Good forage for domestic stock and wildlife.

NORTHERN MANNAGRASS — *Glyceria borealis*

General Aquatic (usually) perennial, up to 1 m high, loosely tufted from creeping rhizomes.

Leaves Flat or folded, sometimes floating, usually **2-5 mm wide**; auricles absent; **ligules 5-10 mm long**.

Inflorescence Panicle long and narrow, up to 20 cm long, **with ascending branches**; long, cylindrical, many-flowered spikelets; **firm lemmas with 7 prominent veins**.

Ecology Wetlands (except bogs), streambanks, lake margins; **often found in standing water**. Scattered, locally abundant in suitable habitats at low to medium elevations south of 55°, uncommon in the North.

Notes: Sometimes forms solid stands in fens and marshes. One of the grasses used by the Tlingit of Alaska to imbricate fine spruce-root baskets.

ALTAI FESCUE · *Festuca altaica*

General Densely tufted, coarse, 50-100 cm tall; **old sheaths and leaf bases persist for many years, forming large firm tussocks.**

Leaves Basal leaves numerous, **stiff**, long, narrow, with a rough surface; auricles absent; ligules short (to 1 mm long), fringed at tip.

Inflorescence Panicle open, drooping in age; **spikelets large, lustrous, green or purplish bronze**; lemmas 7-12 mm, tapering to a point, but **not awned.**

Ecology Open forest, meadows, and grassland at middle elevations in the Chilcotin; grassland, thickets, meadows and open forest from low to high elevations in the North. Common and abundant, often dominant, at all elevations north of 57°, south mainly at high elevations to about 51°.

Notes: Large tufts of this tall grass stand out in alpine areas. Sometimes it grows in long lines down windswept gravelly ridges. This is the dominant bunchgrass of subalpine grasslands in the broad upper valleys of the North.

WESTERN FESCUE · *Festuca occidentalis*

General Tufted, with a few slender stems 25-70 cm tall.

Leaves Narrow, **lax, soft**, mostly basal, **in large tufts**; auricles absent; ligules to 0.5 mm long, fringed at tip.

Inflorescence Panicle open, usually drooping at the top; spikelets 3 to 5 flowered; lemmas about 5 mm long, tapering to a slender awn **4-10 mm long**.

Ecology Widespread in dry to moist forest, frequently on rocky slopes and clearings. Common at low to medium (occasionally subalpine) elevations in the southern half of our region.

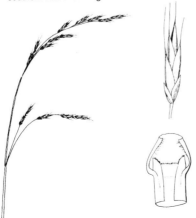

247

ROCKY MOUNTAIN FESCUE — *Festuca saximontana*

General A small, **densely tufted** grass 25-50 cm tall.

Leaves Very slender, tightly rolled, **erect**, in a distinct basal cluster; auricles absent; ligules short (to 0.4 mm), finely fringed at tip.

Inflorescence Panicle **narrow**; spikelets 3 to 5 flowered; lemmas tapering to an awn **1-2 mm long**.

Ecology Dry open forest, ridges and grassland; also found on steep rocky slopes up into the alpine. Scattered and locally common at all elevations, throughout the region except in areas of wetter climate.

Notes: This variable species has been divided by some taxonomists into several varieties, growing to different heights with different leaf lengths. One of these, *Festuca brachyphylla*, is a dwarf (5-15 cm tall) alpine species, common throughout at high elevations.

JUNEGRASS — *Koeleria macrantha*

General **Densely tufted** with smooth, erect stems 20-50 cm tall; lower sheaths often pubescent.

Leaves Slightly inrolled, bluish-green, and usually covered in short hairs; auricles absent; ligules 0.5-2 mm long, hairy, fringed at tip.

Inflorescence **Dense, spikelike panicle**; spikelets 2 to 4 flowered; lemmas **awnless or with a very short awn**.

Ecology Grassland, rocky ridges and open forests, on well-drained soils. Scattered, locally abundant, from low to high elevations primarily in the southern half of the region, occasionally in low elevation grasslands in the North.

Notes: A good forage grass, but the plants are usually widely spaced.

ALPINE BLUEGRASS — *Poa alpina*

General Tufted, with mats of basal leaves, short, from 5 to 30 cm tall.

Leaves *Short, flat*, wide (2-5 mm), crowded at base of stem; *persistent light-coloured sheaths* present at base; auricles absent; ligules 1-3 mm long.

Inflorescence Panicle open, about as long (*2-6 cm*) as broad; spikelets large, 3 to 6 flowered; lemmas hairy on lower half but with *no cobwebby hairs* at base.

Ecology High elevation meadows and tundra, rocky slopes, often abundant where the ground has been compacted (e.g., along game trails). Common throughout the region, sometimes descending to lower elevations in the North on gravel bars and avalanche tracks.

Notes: Poa is a difficult genus taxonomically, and some of the 15 or so species that occur in our region are difficult to tell apart. • The bluegrasses rank high both as forage plants for wild and domestic animals, and as cultivated pasture and turf grasses. This species increases in abundance on disturbed sites.

ARCTIC BLUEGRASS — *Poa arctica*

General Loosely tufted, *with creeping rhizomes*; stems 10-40 cm tall, often purplish and curved at base.

Leaves Mostly basal, *flat or folded*, 2-3 mm wide, tips boat-shaped; auricles absent; ligules 1-3 mm long.

Inflorescence Open pyramidal panicle, *5-10 cm long*; spikelets large, often purplish; lemmas usually with *tuft of cobwebby hairs at base.*

Ecology Common above timberline in meadows, tundra, shrub-carrs and along stream edges, descending to subalpine elevations in the North. Widespread throughout the region.

Notes: A variable species that has been divided into several varieties. It is also called *P. grayana* by some taxonomists.

GLAUCOUS BLUEGRASS — *Poa glauca*

General *Densely tufted*, 10-30 cm tall, with stiff, *glaucous* stems.

Leaves Mostly basal, narrow; a few leaves part way up the stem; auricles absent; ligules 0.5-2 mm long, hairy.

Inflorescence Panicle *compact, narrow*, with ascending branches; spikelets few, green to purplish; lemmas with short hairs and *no basal tuft of cobwebby hairs*.

Ecology Grassy slopes, dry gravelly ridges and rock outcrops. Widespread throughout the region except in areas of wetter climates, from low to subalpine elevations.

Notes: A wide-ranging and variable species. Includes what some taxonomists have distinguished (mostly to the south of our region) as *Poa rupicola*.

INLAND BLUEGRASS — *Poa interior*

General *Densely tufted*; erect greenish stems about 30 cm tall.

Leaves Short, *rather lax*, 1-2 mm wide; auricles absent; ligules mostly 0.3-1 mm long.

Inflorescence Panicle a slender pyramid, 5-10 cm long; spikelets broad, 2 to 4 flowered; lemmas somewhat hairy and *with cobwebby hairs at base*.

Ecology Dry open forest, meadows, and openings; sometimes near rock outcrops. Scattered in areas of drier climates at low to medium elevations in the southern half of the region, occasionally northwards to 58°.

FOWL BLUEGRASS — *Poa palustris*

General *Tall* (40-100 cm), *loosely tufted*, with fibrous roots; stems usually curved and purplish at base.

Leaves Soft, flat or folded, slender (1.5-3 mm wide) and boat shaped at tips; auricles absent; *ligules 2-5 mm long*.

Inflorescence Panicle *open, loose*, 10-30 cm long, *with fine spreading branches*; lower branches in whorls of 4 or 5; lemmas usually bronze at tip, *cobwebby at base, about 2.5 mm long*.

Ecology Widespread in wetlands, moist forest, wet ditches and clearings. Throughout the region at low to medium elevations.

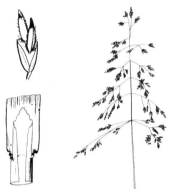

KENTUCKY BLUEGRASS — *Poa pratensis*

General Erect, 30-80 cm tall, with long creeping rhizomes, forming a dense sod.

Leaves Flat to folded, 2-4 mm wide, numerous, with distinct boat shaped tips; auricles lacking; *ligules 1-3 mm long*.

Inflorescence Panicle open, *pyramid shaped*, tending to be curved one-sided when mature, usually with 3-5 branches at each joint; *lemmas about 3.5 mm long, with basal cobwebby hairs.*

Ecology Widely adventive in open forest, thickets, meadows, clearings, roadsides, from low to medium elevations through most of the region, at least near settlements and other human "developments."

Notes: Kentucky bluegrass is the state flower of Kentucky, "the bluegrass state." Mandolin player Bill Monroe, a Kentucky native, named his band the "Bluegrass Boys," and the fast and furious country-tinged music they played came to be called "bluegrass" music. It is appropriate that this species has become widely naturalized in central and northern B.C., home to so many good bluegrass players and festivals. • This extensively used lawn and pasture grass is highly tolerant of close grazing and mowing.

251

ALKALI BLUEGRASS — *Poa juncifolia*

General Tall (40-100 cm), **strongly tufted**, often forming large clumps.

Leaves Numerous, 10-30 cm long, narrow and folded to flat and up to 3 mm wide; auricles absent; **ligules thickened, hairy**, 0.5-2 mm long.

Inflorescence Panicle narrow, 6-20 cm long; branches erect; spikelets 3 to 6 flowered, **lemmas without basal cobwebby hairs.**

Ecology Grassland to open dry forest, often where alkaline. Scattered mostly in areas of drier climates in the southern half of the region.

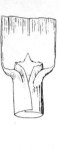

ORCHARDGRASS — *Dactylis glomerata*

General Strongly tufted perennial; hollow stems to 1 m tall, from short rhizomes.

Leaves Sheaths split open partway; blades flat, glabrous, roughened, **3-10 mm wide**, early growth light bluish-green; ligules 3-7 mm long, somewhat hairy; auricles absent.

Inflorescence **One-sided** panicle 3-10 cm long, the branches ascending to erect; **3- to 5-flowered** spikelets flattened and borne at the end of branches in **congested asymmetric heads**; lemmas **5-8 mm long, stiffly hairy on the keel**, with an awn-tip to 1 mm long; glumes 4-6 mm long, with a soft awn-tip, **outer glume stiffly hairy on the keel**.

Ecology Disturbed sites (especially roadsides) and pastures; widespread and often locally abundant at low to medium elevations; throughout but most common in the southern half of the region, near areas of human habitation or disturbance.

Notes: This weedy species is introduced from Eurasia. Orchardgrass is cultivated for hay, and is also used in grass-seeding mixtures on clearings and for erosion control along road cuts. • The genus name is from the Greek *dactylos* (finger), perhaps in reference to the stiff branches of the panicle.

REED CANARYGRASS — *Phalaris arundinacea*

General Perennial, **with long scaly pinkish rhizomes**, to 1.7 m tall; stems hollow.

Leaves Flat, **to 15 mm broad**, roughened; sheaths open, margins overlapping; ligules 4-9 mm long, usually tattered and turned backward, slightly hairy; auricles lacking.

Inflorescence Panicle compact (at least initially), to 25 cm long; spikelets **3 flowered, crowded on side branches** of the inflorescence; **fertile lemma to 4 mm long, shiny, flax-like**; sterile lemmas to 2 mm long, brownish, hairy; glumes about the same size, 4-5 mm long, minutely hairy.

Ecology Wet places in disturbed sites, including clearings, ditches (especially along roads), marshy spots and depressions, streambanks, and along edges of wetlands. Scattered and often locally abundant, more common in the southern half of the region; at low to medium elevations around areas of human habitation or agricultural activity.

Notes: With this grass, the Okanagan made mats for eating on and drying food, and peaked hats for native doctors. A type of rope was also made for binding fish weirs. The Upper Stalo of the Fraser River used the smooth, stout stems for imbrication of baskets. • It's not clear whether reed canarygrass is entirely introduced or is indigenous in parts of the north and has extended its range through human influence. • It may be called "canarygrass" either because the related *Phalaris canariensis* is the source of canary seed or because it was described from the Canary Islands.

Sedges and Rushes

Sedges (family Cyperaceae) and rushes (family Juncaceae) somewhat resemble grasses in their long, narrow parallel-veined leaves and inconspicuous flowers. They are most easily distinguished through examination of their stems: those of sedges are generally triangular in cross-section and solid, with the leaves in 3 rows (vs. 2 rows for grasses); those of rushes are round and also solid ("pithy"). Remember: "sedges have edges and rushes are round". Both provide important forage and habitat for a variety of wildlife species.

It is possible that several sedges may have been used by interior natives in the same manner as grasses were used; i.e., for food preparation, bedding, and on floors.

More information about sedges in our region is provided in Roberts (1983) and Taylor (1983).

> "Oh, what can ail thee, Knight at arms
> Alone and palely loitering;
> The sedge is wither'd from the lake,
> And no birds sing." (Keats, La Belle Dame Sans Merci)

Features of the *Cyperaceae* (Sedge Family)

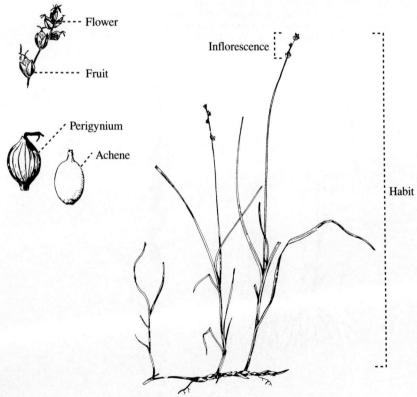

254

Features of the *Juncaceae* (Rush family)

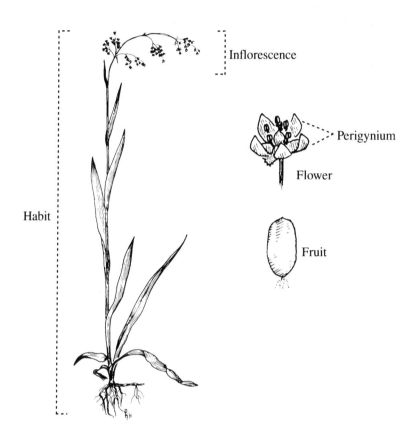

Inflorescence

Perigynium

Flower

Fruit

Habit

Key to Common Sedges (*Carex* spp.)

1. Long inflorescence (longer than 5 cm); cylindrical spikes
  2. Spikes nodding on long stalks
    3. Male flowers at base of female spikes .... *C. mertensii*
    3. Separate male spike at tip of stem
      4. Spikes small (less than 3 mm wide) .... *C. capillaris*
      4. Spikes large (more than 3 mm wide)
        5. Scales black
          6. Bract longer than inflorescence .... *C. saxatilis*
          6. Bract shorter than inflorescence .... *C. podocarpa*
        5. Scales brown
          7. Male spike longer than 13 mm .... *C. limosa*
          7. Male spike shorter than 13 mm .... *C. paupercula*
  2. Spikes without stalks or with short stalks
      8. Perigynia with hairs .... *C. lasiocarpa*
      8. Perigynia without hairs
        9. Leaves and sheaths with hairs .... *C. atherodes*
        9. Leaves without hairs
          10. Perigynia with prominent beak .... *C. rostrata*
          10. Perigynia without beak .... *C. aquatilis*
1. Short inflorescence (shorter than 5 cm); spikes varied
    11. Multiple spikes
      12. Many−flowered spikes; each spike with more than 15 perigynia
        13. Spikes clustered towards end of stem
          14. Scales brown
            15. Each spike with male flowers above female.... *C. diandra*
            15. Each spike with male flowers below female
              16. Soft, wide leaves, greater than 2 mm wide .... *C. macloviana*
              16. Narrow, stiff leaves, less than 2 mm wide .... *C. phaeocephala*
        14. Scales black
            17. Perigynia green or bronze .... *C. media*
            17. Perigynia blackish−purple .... *C. albonigra*
        13. Spikes not clustered; lower spikes separated from others
            18. Perigynia without winged margins .... *C. canescens*
            18. Perigynia with winged margins
              19. Perigynia wide (2 to 2.5 times as long as wide) .... *C. aenea*
              19. Perigynia narrower (2.5 to 4 times as long as wide) .... *C. praticola*
      12. Few-flowered spikes; each spike with less than 15 perigynia
        20. Perigynia with hairs
          21. Some spikes near the base of plant, widely separated from terminal spikes ....*C. rossii*
          21. All spikes on the upper part of a long stem, above the leaves
            22. Male spike small (3 to 6 mm long) ....*C. concinna*
            22. Male spike large (8 to 20 mm long) .... *C. concinnoides*

20. Perigynia without hairs
    23. Perigynia with a prominent beak
        24. Perigynia spreading; spikes have a star-like appearance .... *C. interior*
        24. Perigynia not spreading .... *C. siccata*
    23. Perigynia without a beak
        25. Spikes with stalks; bract long and leaf-like .... *C. aurea*
        25. Spikes without stalks
            26. Three spikes close together at end of stem .... *C. tenuiflora*
            26. Small, well-separated spikes .... *C. disperma*
11.   Single spike
            27. Perigynia beakless, pale green .... *C. leptalea*
            27. Perigynia with beak
                28. Very long, slender perigynia (more than 5 mm long) *C. pauciflora*
                28. Perigynia less than 5 mm long
                    29. Narrow leaves (less than 1 mm wide) *C. dioica* ssp. *gynocrates*
                    29. Wide leaves (about 2 mm wide) .... *C. nigricans*

LOW NORTHERN SEDGE — *Carex concinna*

General Small, loosely tufted, from slender, scaly rhizomes; stems slender, *smooth*, arching, up to 20 cm high; brownish and somewhat shreddy at the base.

Leaves Clustered near the base, narrow (*about 2 mm wide*), much shorter than stem.

Inflorescence Small terminal male spike, *3-6 mm long*, surrounded by 2 or 3 few-flowered female spikes.

Perigynia *Hairy*, plump, three angled, twice as long as the broad, dark reddish-brown scales; *3 short, dark stigmas*.

Ecology Open coniferous forests (often where rocky or sandy and relatively dry), but also in muskeg, shrub-carrs, and clearings. Widespread and common throughout the region, at low to moderate elevations.

Notes: C. concinnoides closely resembles this species, but is larger with a longer male spike (8 mm or more). • The species name of both of these sedges is from *concinnus* which means well proportioned, neat, or elegant, perhaps in reference to the tidy inflorescence.

NORTHWESTERN SEDGE — *Carex concinnoides*

General Loosely tufted from long, slender, scaly rhizomes; stems slender, *smooth*, erect to curved, 15-23 cm high, dark purplish brown at the base.

Leaves Clustered near the base, *2-5 mm wide*, usually shorter than the stem.

Inflorescence Terminal male spike, *without a stalk, 8-22 mm long*; female spikes 1 or 2, few flowered.

Perigynia *Hairy*, plump, obscurely three angled, wider and longer than the dark, purplish-red scales; *4 or 3 long brownish stigmas*.

Ecology Dry open coniferous forests, forest edges, rocky slopes and ridges, clearings. Common at low to moderate elevations in the southern half of our region (to about 57°), especially in areas of drier climate.

Notes: C. richardsonii is similar to this species in appearance and habitat, but has rough stems and longer leaves, and the male spike is stalked. • This sedge was commonly used by the Okanagan for laying under and over food in steam pits, lining moccasins and covering and lining berry baskets. Turner (1979) reports that this plant was referred to by one informant as "timbergrass" — the name also given to pinegrass (*Calamagrostis rubescens*).

ROSS' SEDGE — *Carex rossii*

General Low, dense *tufts*; stems slender, 10-30 cm high.

Leaves Narrow (1-2.5 mm wide) and thin but firm, somewhat spreading, at least some longer than the stem, **with purplish sheaths at the base**.

Inflorescence Terminal spike male, 2 or 3 few-flowered female spikes clustered below; bracts well developed, leaflike, usually longer than the inflorescence; *additional spikes on long stalks near the base of stem*, widely separated from the terminal spikes.

Perigynia Few per spike; longer than the scales, three angled, *covered with short hairs*, with a stalk-like base; 3 stigmas.

Ecology Well-drained, open forests, gravelly or rocky slopes and flats, cutbanks, roadsides, clearings. Widespread and common throughout the region, usually at low to medium elevations but also on dry sites in subalpine zones.

Notes: There are in this region at least four other species of similar appearance and habitat to *C. rossii*. *Carex peckii* (Peck's sedge) and *C. pensylvanica* (long-stoloned sedge) both have hairy perigynia and purplish leaf sheaths like *C. rossii*, but lack the lower female spikes on basal stalks, and are sporadic mostly in the eastern part of the region. *C. obtusata* (blunt sedge) and *C. supina* (spreading arctic sedge) also have brown or purplish leaf sheaths, but have glabrous, leathery, shiny perigynia, and typically occur in dry grasslands and on open, rocky or sandy slopes.

HAY SEDGE — *Carex siccata*

General Stems *usually arising singly* (occasionally 2 or 3 together) from a slender, long-creeping, brown-scaly rhizome; fertile stems slender, 20-60 cm tall; *sterile stems prominent with long, soft leaves*.

Leaves Narrow (1-2 mm wide), flat or somewhat channeled; dried leaves often clothing base of stem.

Inflorescence Spikes 2-8, forming *a cylindrical head*, lower spike slightly separated from others.

Perigynia About 5 mm long (including the **long, prominent beak**), conspicuously longer than the brownish scales, two angled, *wing margined*; 2 stigmas.

Ecology Dry, usually sandy soil in open forests. Scattered, locally common, in suitable locations at low to medium elevations throughout the region.

Notes: The long, soft leaves are similar to those of pinegrass (*Calamagrostis rubescens*). • Also known as *C. foenea*.

SOFT-LEAVED SEDGE — *Carex disperma*

General *Loosely tufted* from long slender rhizomes; *stems very slender, weak, usually nodding*, clothed with old leaves at the base.

Leaves Narrow (*about 1-2 mm wide*), thin, soft, mostly shorter than stem, *light green*.

Inflorescence Very small greenish spikes, *few-flowered, well separated from each other; male flowers at top of spikes*.

Perigynia Plump, greenish to brownish and shining at maturity, small (but longer and wider than the whitish-green scales), with faint lines, 2 angled; 2 stigmas.

Ecology Moist to wet forests, seepy openings, wetlands, streambanks. Very common and widespread at low to moderate elevations throughout.

Notes: Can be confused with *C. loliacea* (ryegrass sedge), which also has few-flowered, well-separated spikes, but its spikes have male flowers at the base and strongly lined perigynia spread at right angles to the stem. *C. loliacea* occupies similar habitats but is less common.

GREY SEDGE — *Carex canescens*

General *Densely tufted*, from short, black rhizomes, often forming large clumps; stems erect to spreading, 10-50 cm high, brownish at base, clothed with old leaves.

Leaves Clustered near the base, long (but not longer than the stems), soft, flat, *2-4 mm wide, bluish-green*.

Inflorescence *4-7 small spikes along stem*, lower ones separated; *male flowers at the base of each spike*.

Perigynia Small (but longer than the straw-coloured scales), yellowish green to whitish brown, *with a very short beak*, 2 angled, 15-30 per spike; 2 stigmas.

Ecology Swamps, fens, bogs, streambanks, lake margins, wet meadows. Common at low to subalpine elevations throughout the region.

Notes: Also known as *C. curta.* • *C. brunnescens* (brownish sedge) closely resembles this species, but has smaller spikes with fewer, more strongly beaked perigynia.

SPARSE-LEAVED SEDGE — *Carex tenuiflora*

General ***Loosely tufted*** from long, slender, yellowish-brown rhizomes; stems fine but firm, arching, 20-30 cm tall, roughened beneath the head, brownish and clothed with old leaves at the base.

Leaves ***Narrow (0.5-2 mm wide)***, soft, some almost as long as stem, ***greyish-green***.

Inflorescence ***Three small, whitish-green spikes closely bunched at tip of stem***; male flowers at the base of each spike.

Perigynia Oval, beakless, shorter than the yellowish-white scales, ***pale green with distinctive lines***, 2 angled; 2 stigmas.

Ecology Sphagnum bogs, fens, swamps, occasionally in seepage areas in forests. Fairly common at low to medium elevations throughout the region.

Notes: This sedge can be recognized by the 3 small spikes bunched at the tip of the slender stem.

GOLDEN SEDGE — *Carex aurea*

General ***Loosely tufted*** from long slender rhizomes with short runners; stems slender, from very short to greatly exceeding the leaves (5-40 cm tall), light brown at the base.

Leaves From near the base, 2-4 mm wide, more or less flat.

Inflorescence Male spike narrow, terminal; 3 to 5 oblong female spikes with 4-20 flowers each, upper ones on short stalks, lower ones on long stalks; long, leaflike bracts.

Perigynia Rounded-egg-shaped, beakless, ***coarsely ribbed***; ***golden to orange when mature***, 2 angled; scales reddish brown, shorter and narrower than perigynia, widely spreading at maturity; 2 stigmas.

Ecology Wet gravelly sites (gravel bars, lakeshores, streambanks), muskegs, fens, seepage meadows. Common and widespread but usually only locally abundant, from low to subalpine elevations throughout the region.

Notes: The round, golden perigynia make this sedge distinctive. ***The spikes often lie on the ground when ripe***. • Some taxonomists recognize two other species in this group: *Carex bicolor* (two-coloured scale sedge), in which the sheath of the lowest bract has black, earlike flanges at its mouth and the perigynia are bluish white; and *Carex garberi* ssp. *bifaria* (= *C. hassei*), in which the terminal spike has female flowers above, male flowers below. Both of these species are sporadic mostly north of 58°.

261

BRISTLE-STALKED SEDGE — *Carex leptalea*

General *Tufted from a threadlike creeping rhizome*; stems very slender, erect but weak, 10-40 cm tall.

Leaves *Narrow (about 1 mm wide)*, thin, *soft, lax*, shorter than stems, *deep green.*

Inflorescence Solitary, few-flowered, narrowly oblong spike, less than 15 mm long; male flowers at tip.

Perigynia Broadly lance shaped *with a distinctive, beakless, rounded tip*; *green with fine lines*, longer and wider than the yellowish-green scales, somewhat two edged; 3 stigmas.

Ecology Bogs, fens, wet meadows, lakeshores, streambanks, mossy seepage areas in forests. Common and widespread (but often overlooked) from low to middle elevations throughout our region.

Notes: Carex chordorrhiza (cordroot sedge) has 3-5 small spikes that are tightly clustered and appear as a single head or spike, but its stems arise singly from a long branching rhizome or stolon. It too is a species of bogs, fens, and lakeshores (often on floating mats infilling ponds) but is sporadic throughout the region except for a centre of abundance in the Fraser Basin (Nechako, Parsnip, and middle Fraser drainages).

YELLOW BOG SEDGE — *Carex dioica* ssp. *gynocrates*

General Stems arising *singly or a few together from a long, slender rhizome*, stiff, smooth, sometimes curved, 5-20 cm tall, clothed with old leaves at the base.

Leaves Clustered near the base, narrow (about 0.5 mm wide), channeled, *stiff*, shorter than stems.

Inflorescence Solitary spike with male flowers at the top, or male and female spikes on separate plants.

Perigynia Egg shaped, *plump*, brown, *glossy with fine lines*, short beaked, becoming widely spreading at maturity, 2 edged; *2 stigmas.*

Ecology Open mossy forests, bogs and fens; found throughout the region at low to moderate elevations.

Notes: Also known as *C. gynocrates.* •*Carex scirpoidea* (single-spiked sedge) also has solitary spikes that are either all male or all female, but it has stout scaly rhizomes, leaves to 3 mm wide, and a hairy perigynia with 3 stigmas, and it grows in tundra, heath, and on rocky slopes and ridges mostly at high elevations throughout the region.

INLAND SEDGE — *Carex interior*

General ***Densely tufted*** from short, dark rhizome; stems slender, wiry, up to 40 cm high.

Leaves Slender, 1-3 mm wide, thin, flat or channeled, shorter than stems.

Inflorescence 3 or 4 small, sessile, few-flowered spikes; male flowers at the base of terminal spike.

Perigynia ***More or less pear shaped***, plump, firm, longer than the yellowish brown scales, widely spreading at maturity, 2 angled, thick margined; ***beak less than one-third the length of perigynium***; 2 stigmas.

Ecology Fens, wet meadows, limey seepage areas, occasionally in bogs. Fairly common at low to moderate elevations north of 57° and in the eastern part of the southern half of the region.

Notes: The spreading perigynia give the inflorescence of this species *a distinctive star-like appearance*. *C. angustior* (narrow-leaved sedge; = *C. stellulata*, *C. echinata*) is similar in appearance and habitat, but has a beak more than half the length of the perigynium, and *C. laeviculmis* (smooth-stemmed sedge) has perigynia that are broadest near the middle, rather than near the base.

FEW-FLOWERED SEDGE — *Carex pauciflora*

General Stems up to 30 cm tall, single or a few together from a very slender rhizome, stiff, brownish and curved at the base.

Leaves ***Narrow (0.5-1.5 mm wide)***, usually channeled, shorter than to as long as the stems.

Inflorescence ***Spike solitary***, ***very small***, without a bract, male flowers at the top of spike.

Perigynia ***Few (usually less than 7), 6-8 mm long***, narrowly lance shaped, longer than the light brown scales, greenish brown, ***bent back downwards at maturity***, 3 angled; 3 stigmas; both scales and perigynia falling off at maturity.

Ecology Scattered in fens and bogs, at low to moderate elevations throughout the region.

Notes: The long, reflexed perigynia distinguish this species. • *Carex microglochin* (few-seeded bog sedge), an uncommon species of peaty, often calcium-rich wetlands and shores, is similar but tends to be smaller (usually about 10 cm high) and has perigynia that are 3-5 mm long.

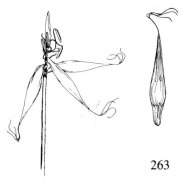

263

SEDGES AND RUSHES

RUSSET SEDGE — *Carex saxatilis*

General Stems **up to 80 cm tall**, single or a few together from a long, tough rhizome, **reddish at the base, basal sheaths shredding**; dried leaves of previous year conspicuous.

Leaves Almost as long as stems, yellowish green, stiff, 2-3 (5) mm wide, flat or somewhat channeled, occasionally partitioned by whitish, knotlike crosswalls.

Inflorescence Male terminal spike; 1 to 3 dark, widely separated, **slender stalked and slightly nodding**, female spikes.

Perigynia Smooth, shiny, reddish brown, oval, with a short beak; scales dark brown, smaller than perigynia; **usually 2 stigmas**.

Ecology A plant of open rocky lake margins, fens, wet meadows, and stream edges. Scattered at low to subalpine elevations throughout the region.

Notes: Also known as *Carex physocarpa.* • *Carex membranacea* (fragile sedge) is much like *C. saxatilis* but has sessile, erect female spikes, and grows in wet tundra and shallow ponds at high elevations north of 58°.

SLENDER SEDGE — *Carex lasiocarpa*

General Tall stems, **up to 120 cm high**, in loose tufts from long-creeping, tough, scaly rhizomes, **reddish at the base, lower sheaths shredding**.

Leaves As long as and often exceeding the stems, **narrow (2 mm or less in width)**, margins rolled inwards, partitioned by whitish, knotlike crosswalls.

Inflorescence Two male spikes above; lower spikes female, **without stalks**; lowest bract long and leaflike.

Perigynia **Inflated**, leathery, dull brown, **densely hairy** with beak divided into **two short, upright points**, wider than the reddish-brown scales; **3 stigmas**.

Ecology Common in fens, and at the edges of streams and lakes; often occurs in extensive pure stands in standing water. Found throughout, at low to medium elevations, but more common in the southern half of the region.

Notes: C. lanuginosa (woolly sedge) is similar to this species in appearance and habitat, but has wider, flatter leaves, and perigynia with two long, somewhat spreading points. It apparently does not occur north of about 55°.

SHORE SEDGE — *Carex limosa*

General One or a few stems from a long slender scaly rhizome; ***roots covered with yellowish felt***; stems slender, 20-60 cm tall, reddish at the base.

Leaves Few per stem, much shorter than stem, ***glaucous***, deeply channeled, 1-3 mm wide.

Inflorescence Male terminal spike, ***15-25 mm long***; 1-3 ***nodding, slender-stalked,*** female spikes below.

Perigynia Bluish green to straw coloured, broadly egg shaped, leathery, 3 angled but flattened; ***scales about as long as and wider than perigynia, with broad tip;*** 3 stigmas.

Ecology Common in fens and bogs throughout the region, from the lowlands to lower subalpine elevations.

Notes: C. paupercula closely resembles this species in appearance and habitat, but has shorter male spikes (less than 12 mm) and long narrow scales that taper to a point. *C. livida* (pale sedge) grows in similar habitats and also has bluish green leaves, but has roots without yellowish felt and erect, loosely flowered female spikes.

POOR SEDGE — *Carex paupercula*

General Plants clustered in tufts, sometimes with many stems, from long slender rhizome; stems slender, up to 80 cm tall, reddish brown and clothed with old leaves at the base; ***roots covered with yellowish felt.***

Leaves Shorter than stem, 2-4 mm wide, flat with slightly inrolled margins.

Inflorescence Short male terminal spike, ***4-12 mm long***; 3-4 female spikes below, ***nodding*** on slender stalks.

Perigynia Bluish green to brown, broadly egg shaped to elliptic, leathery, 3 angled but flattened; ***scales narrower but longer than perigynia, pointy tipped***; 3 stigmas.

Ecology Widespread in peaty wetlands at low to subalpine elevations throughout the region. Often found growing with *C. limosa, C. chordorrhiza* or *C. tenuiflora.*

Notes: Also called *C. magellanica* by some taxonomists. • *Carex paupercula* and *C. limosa* are our two wetland sedges with characteristic yellow-felted roots. *C. macrochaeta* (large-awned sedge) has similar roots and inflorescence but has scales with long-pointed tips and typically grows in higher elevation meadows, avalanche tracks, and seepage areas.

265

SEDGES AND RUSHES

Conspectus of Large Water Sedges

	Carex rostrata	*Carex atherodes*
Plant	in clumps from stout, long, scaly rhizomes	clumps from stout, long, scaly rhizomes
Leaves	glabrous; sheaths brown	pubescent, the short hairs visible to the unaided eye; sheaths shredding, becoming weblike
Spikes		
Perigynia	inflated, abruptly contracted to a beak with short teeth, strongly spreading at maturity	inflated, narrowing very gradually to a beak with long teeth
Comments	A very widespread and common sedge, found in mixed and pure stands.	Widespread but merely locally common, often forming pure stands, particularly in wetlands that normally dry up in summer.

Carex aquatilis	Carex sitchensis	Carex exsiccata (also known as C. vesicaria)
clumps from stout, long, scaly rhizomes	densely clustered, with short rhizomes or none	short rhizomes or none
glabrous, glaucous-green; sheaths reddish	glabrous, sheaths reddish	glabrous; sheaths shredding, becoming weblike
erect, all nearly sessile	lower spikes nodding on stalks greater than 3 cm long	
flattened, egg shaped, with very short beak	similar to those of C. aquatilis; scales narrow, pointed, white-tipped	many ribbed, gradually tapering to a long beak; reddish tinged and not spreading at maturity
A very widespread and common sedge, found in pure and mixed stands, often with C. rostrata. Early in the season, the glaucous-green of C. aquatilis and the yellow-green of C. rostrata help to distinguish these species in vegetative form.	occasionally found scattered among C. aquatilis; often in pure stands at moderate elevations, mostly in the southern half of the region.	

BEAKED SEDGE — *Carex rostrata*

General Thick stems, up to 120 cm tall, in large clumps from short stout rhizomes and long creeping stolons, sometimes forming a dense sod; base light brown, thick, spongy, conspicuously clothed with old leaves, and with **sheaths not shredding and becoming weblike**.

Leaves Upper leaves long, **exceeding stems, yellowish green, rather thick**, more or less flat, up to 12 mm wide, conspicuously partitioned by whitish, knotlike crosswalls between the veins.

Inflorescence Long, with cylindrical spikes; 2 to 4 overlapping male spikes at the top; densely flowered, short-stalked or sessile, erect female spikes below; lowest bract leaflike, longer than spikes.

Perigynia **Inflated**, membranous but firm, **shining, yellowish green to straw coloured**, egg shaped, **several ribbed**, abruptly tapering to a beak with **two short points**, spreading at maturity; scales reddish brown and narrower than, but about as long as, the perigynia; 3 stigmas.

Ecology A very common, large water sedge that prefers perennially wet areas, at low to moderate elevations throughout.

Notes: There are five common species of large water sedges in this region that have the same general appearance. All have stout stems, wide leaves that are partitioned by whitish, knotlike crosswalls between the veins, and a long inflorescence with cylindrical spikes. The leafy bract below the lowest spike is equal to or longer than the inflorescence. They often grow in solid stands in shallow water or very wet soil, forming a dense sod. These sedges are a common component of wetland hay in ranching country, and are valued as food for waterfowl.
• Characteristics which can be used to distinguish between these five species of large water sedges are described in the conspectus (pp. 266-267).

AWNED SEDGE — *Carex atherodes*

General Thick stems, up to 120 cm tall, in large clumps from long slender rhizomes; stems stout, reddish tinged and with **sheaths shredding and becoming weblike** at the base.

Leaves Few to several, not clustered at the base, **generally not as long as stems, dull green, thin**, flat, up to 12 mm wide, conspicuously partitioned by whitish, knotlike crosswalls between the veins; **leaves and sheaths hairy**.

Inflorescence Long, with cylindrical spikes; 2 to 6 erect male spikes above; widely separated, short-stalked or sessile, erect female spikes below; lowest bract leaflike, longer than the spikes.

Perigynia **Inflated**, somewhat leathery, **yellowish green to light brown**, broadly lance shaped, **many ribbed**, gradually tapering to a beak with **two long, spreading points**, ascending to spreading at maturity; scales reddish brown and narrower than, but more or less as long as, the perigynia; 3 stigmas.

Ecology A widespread, but merely locally common, large water sedge of marshes and fens; often forms solid stands, particularly in wetlands that normally dry up in summer. Scattered throughout the region at low to moderate elevations.

Notes: C. rostrata and *C. exsiccata* (inflated sedge; = *C. vesicaria*) are similar to this species in appearance and habitat, but lack the hairy leaves and stem.

WATER SEDGE   *Carex aquatilis*

General ***Rather slender*** stems in ***dense clumps*** from ***thick, scaly, cordlike rhizomes***, up to 100 cm tall; base reddish tinged, thick, surrounded by long brown scales and clothed with old leaves.

Leaves Numerous, as long as or shorter than stems, ***glaucous-green***, flat or somewhat channeled at the base, up to 8 mm wide.

Inflorescence Long cylindrical spikes; 1-3 male terminal spikes; ***short-stalked or sessile, erect*** female spikes below; lowest bract long and leaflike.

Perigynia ***Small (2-3 mm long)***, ***light green***, egg shaped, ***strongly flattened***, abruptly ***very short beaked***; scales blackish, narrower and shorter than perigynia; 2 stigmas.

Ecology Bog, fens, marshes, wet meadows, streambanks, shallow ponds. A very common wetland species from low to high elevations throughout the region; often mixed with *C. rostrata*.

Notes: C. rostrata and *C. atherodes* are similar, but both lack the small, flat perigynia, and *C. aquatilis* has glaucous-green leaves. *C. sitchensis* (Sitka sedge), even more similar to *C. aquatilis*, has short or no rhizomes, lower spikes tending to nod on longer stalks, and scales with distinctive white tips. It occupies similar wet habitats in the southern half of the region and north along the Coast Mountains.

HAIRLIKE SEDGE   *Carex capillaris*

General ***Tufted*** from short rhizomes; stems very slender, 10-50 cm tall, dark and somewhat shreddy at the base.

Leaves ***Mostly from near the base***, shorter than stems, flat, thin, 1-3 mm wide.

Inflorescence Male terminal spike; 2 or 3 female lateral spikes, ***nodding*** at the end of ***long slender stalks***; lowest bract leaflike, ***with a long tubular sheath***.

Perigynia ***Small (2-3 mm long)***, greenish brown to shiny bronze when mature, lance-egg-shaped, 3 angled, tapering to a short beak, longer but narrower than the light brown scales; 3 stigmas.

Ecology Moist, open forests, bogs, shrubby wetlands, stream and pond margins, peaty seepage areas. Fairly common at medium to high elevations throughout the region.

Notes: C. vaginata (sheathed sedge) resembles this species in appearance and habitat and has a similar distribution, but has more erect spikes and larger perigynia (more than 3 mm long).

269

THICK-HEADED SEDGE — *Carex macloviana*

General ***Densely tufted*** from short, blackish rhizomes; ***numerous stems usually 25-50 cm tall*** (sometimes up to 75 cm) with lots of old dry leaves at the base.

Leaves Several per stem, 2-4 mm wide, flat, much shorter than stem.

Inflorescence Several sessile spikes crowded into a ***dense head***; male flowers hidden at the base of each spike.

Perigynia Copper coloured to dark olive-green at maturity; egg shaped, flattened, wing-margined and tapering to a well-defined beak; scales brownish, about as wide and long as perigynia; 2 stigmas.

Ecology Dry to moist open forest, thickets, meadows, grassy slopes, gravelly shores, clearings, shrub-carrs, sometimes in peatlands. Common, widespread, and in a variety of habitats, from low to subalpine elevations throughout the region.

Notes: C. pachystachya and *C. microptera* closely resemble this species, but differ in microscopic details of the perigynia. Some taxonomists maintain that there should be just one, variable species: *C. macloviana*.

BRONZE SEDGE — *Carex aenea*

General ***Densely tufted***; slender, wiry stems ***up to 100 cm tall***, bent over at the tip

Leaves Shorter than stem, soft, flat, 2-4 mm wide.

Inflorescence 4-8 sessile spikes in ***a loose, curved cluster***; lower spikes well separated; male flowers at the base of each spike.

Perigynia Dull green ***becoming bronze, egg shaped***, flattened, wing-margined, and tapering to a long beak; scales brownish, as large as, and concealing, the perigynia; 2 stigmas.

Ecology Open, dry to moist forest, meadows, clearings; often grows in profusion in disturbed areas. Common at low to moderate elevations throughout the region.

Notes: C. praticola (meadow sedge) closely resembles this species but has shorter stems, narrower perigynia, and silvery-green spikes.

MEADOW SEDGE — *Carex praticola*

General ***Densely tufted***; stems slender, ***20-80 cm tall***, somewhat nodding towards the tip.

Leaves Shorter than stem, flat, 1-3 mm wide.

Inflorescence 4-7 sessile spikes, forming ***a loose, slightly nodding spike***; the two lowest spaces between nodes 3 to 10 mm long; male flowers at the base of each spike.

Perigynia ***Pale green or whitish, glossy, narrowly egg shaped***, flattened, wing-margined, ***up to 6 mm long***, tapering to a long slender beak; scales reddish brown with silvery-white margins, as large as and concealing the perigynia; 2 stigmas.

Ecology Dry to moist meadows, grassland, clearings, thickets, and occasionally in open forests. Scattered at low to medium and sometimes subalpine elevations throughout the region.

Notes: *C. petasata* (pasture sedge) closely resembles this species, but has larger perigynia (5-8 mm long), overlapping spikes, and occurs only in dry grassland.

DUNHEAD SEDGE — *Carex phaeocephala*

General ***Densely tufted***, often forming large clumps; stems slender but stiff, ***10-30 cm tall***, clothed in old leaves at the base.

Leaves Shorter than stem, stiff, usually channeled, about 2 mm wide.

Inflorescence ***2-6 sessile spikes*** aggregated into a stiff, straw-coloured head; male flowers at the base of each spike.

Perigynia Straw coloured to dark brown, oval egg-shaped, flattened, up to 6 mm long, abruptly tapering into a short beak; ***margins green winged***; scales reddish brown, as large as and concealing the perigynia; 2 stigmas.

Ecology A fairly common alpine species; often found in rocky, grassy tundra and on open scree slopes; occurs in the mountains throughout the region.

Notes: *Carex bipartita* (two-parted sedge; = *C. lachenalii*) is an alpine species of wet tundra and snowbeds, has 1-4 spikes, and perigynia with sharp-edged (not winged) margins.

GRACEFUL MOUNTAIN SEDGE — *Carex podocarpa*

General *Loosely tufted from slender rhizomes*; stems slender, erect, *10-60 cm tall*, dark reddish brown and somewhat shreddy at the base.

Leaves Shorter than the stem, flat, *2-5 mm wide*, abruptly pointed; *basal leaves reduced to scales*.

Inflorescence Male terminal spike; lateral female spikes, usually drooping on long slender stalks.

Perigynia *Green to straw coloured and blackish tinged*, egg shaped to elliptic, flattened, about 4 mm long, abruptly short beaked; scales purplish black, pointed, *with inconspicuous midrib, about as long as the perigynia*; 3 stigmas.

Ecology Widely distributed in subalpine and lower alpine meadows, seepage areas, streambanks, and wet heath; throughout the region.

Notes: C. microchaeta (small-awned sedge) and *C. spectabilis* (showy sedge) are similar to this species in appearance and habitat, but *C. microchaeta* has coarser leaves concentrated at the base of the stem (and tends to grow in drier, more exposed tundra habitats and at slightly higher elevations), and *C. spectabilis* has scales in which the midrib extends to a point, and is a sedge more commonly found in the southern half of the region, extending north along the Coast Mountains.

MERTENS' SEDGE — *Carex mertensii*

General *Densely tufted*, often forming large clumps; stems *up to 120 cm tall*, sharply triangular and *narrowly winged*, very rough on the angles.

Leaves Shorter than the stem, flat, *4-7 mm wide*, from the lower half of stem; basal leaves reduced to scales.

Inflorescence 6-10 large, cylindrical spikes crowded together and *drooping* on slender stalks; male flowers at the base of most spikes.

Perigynia *Whitish, oval, papery and flattened*, with very small, red-tipped beak; scales dark reddish brown with lighter midrib, *much smaller than perigynia*; 3 stigmas.

Ecology Moist to wet forest openings, open rocky slopes, often in disturbed areas such as roadsides and clearings. Common from moderate to subalpine (not alpine) elevations in the southern half of the region, extending north along the Coast Mountains but infrequent in the interior of the northern half.

Notes: This large sedge is distinctive with its broad, colourful spikes. Probably the only species it could be confused with in this region (especially if specimens were immature) is *Carex atrata* (black-scaled sedge), which has scarcely flattened perigynia, more or less erect spikes, and is scattered in high elevation meadows throughout the region.

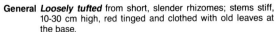

TWO-TONED SEDGE — *Carex albonigra*

General *Loosely tufted* from short, slender rhizomes; stems stiff, 10-30 cm high, red tinged and clothed with old leaves at the base.

Leaves Much shorter than the stem, clustered near the base, flat, firm, 2-5 mm wide.

Inflorescence *2-4 closely clustered, short-stalked, black* spikes; *male flowers at the base of terminal spike*; lateral spikes female.

Perigynia Dark reddish brown to purplish black, egg shaped, *flattened*, about 3 mm long, abruptly short beaked; *scales reddish black with conspicuous pale margins and tips*, about the same size as the perigynia; 3 stigmas.

Ecology Occurs on coarse, well-drained soils of exposed wind-swept areas; widely distributed in the alpine down to the upper subalpine zone throughout the region.

Notes: The erect black spikes and two-toned scales make this mountain sedge distinctive. • *C. microchaeta* looks similar and occupies the same kinds of exposed tundra habitats, but its terminal spike has only male flowers, and the lateral spikes have fairly long stalks. *C. atrata* lacks the strongly flattened perigynia of *C. albonigra*.

SCANDINAVIAN SEDGE — *Carex media*

General *Loosely tufted* from short, slender rhizomes; stems slender, 10-70 cm tall, purplish red and with old leaves at the base.

Leaves Much shorter than the stem, clustered towards the base, flat, 2-3 mm wide.

Inflorescence 3-4 sessile to short-stalked, erect spikes *3-8 mm long and closely packed at tip of stem*; male flowers at base of terminal spike; lateral spikes female.

Perigynia Bluish green when young, bronze later, oblong egg-shaped, *2-3 mm long*, 3 angled, abruptly short beaked; scales purplish black, shorter than perigynia; 3 stigmas.

Ecology Moist, partially open habitats (seepage areas, streambanks, thickets, gravelly shores, shrub-carrs). Widespread from medium to subalpine elevations throughout the region.

Notes: This species is similar to *C. atrata*, which has longer spikes (greater than 10 mm) and larger perigynia (greater than 3 mm). *Carex enanderi* (goose-grass sedge; = *C. eleusinoides*) is also similar but has distinctly ribbed perigynia and is scattered (locally abundant) on peaty, gravelly margins of high elevation ponds in the western part of the region, especially along the flanks of the Coast Mountains.

BLACK ALPINE SEDGE — *Carex nigricans*

General *Tufted from stout creeping rhizome, often forming hummocky mats*; stems stiff, 5-30 cm tall, light brown and clothed with old leaves at the base.

Leaves *Numerous, densely packed near base of stem*, usually shorter than stem, flat or channeled, stiff, 1-2.5 mm wide.

Inflorescence *Spike solitary* with male flowers at top; no bract at base.

Perigynia Brownish, lance to narrowly *egg shaped, stalked at the base*, tapering into a short beak at the tip, *spreading at maturity and soon falling off*; scales dark brown, much shorter than perigynia; *3 stigmas*.

Ecology *Snowbeds, wet meadows, and tundra*, margins of rivulets and ponds. Widespread throughout at high elevations; common especially in high-snowfall areas, less so in drier climates of the northern half of the region.

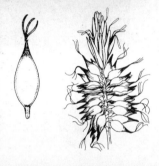

Notes: This species could be confused with *C. pyrenaica* (Pyrenean sedge), which lacks a rhizome, has less widely spreading perigynia with 2 stigmas, and often grows in grassy tundra and in snowbeds on rocky ridges and boulder fields. • Also watch for three other small tufted alpine species with single spikes, all of which occur in rocky windswept tundra and on high exposed ridges. *Carex nardina* (spikenard sedge) has wiry curved stems, an oblong spike, and lance-shaped perigynia narrowed to a stubby base. *C. capitata* (capitate sedge) has wiry straight stems, a globose spike, and egg-shaped perigynia rounded at the base; it also occurs in subalpine meadows and wetlands. *Kobresia myosuroides* (which is not a true sedge) has wiry stems, a narrow linear spike, and loose, unsealed perigynia.

LESSER PANICLED SEDGE — *Carex diandra*

General *Tufted, forming large loose clumps*; stems erect, *30-70 cm tall*.

Leaves Shorter than stem, grayish green, flat or channeled, narrow, *1-3 mm wide; sheaths dotted red at the top*.

Inflorescence Several spikes *closely aggregated into a dense, dark-brown head; male flowers at the top of each spike*.

Perigynia Dark brown, glossy, *egg shaped, tapering to a long flattened beak, stubby stalked at base*; scales light brown, wider but shorter than perigynia; 2 stigmas.

Ecology Common in wetlands, particularly fens, throughout the region at low to moderate elevations.

Notes: *C. prairea* (prairie sedge) and *C. cusickii* (Cusick's sedge) are similar to this species, but both have sheaths that are copper tinged at the top. *C. stipata* (awl-fruited sedge) is bigger all over, up to 100 cm tall with yellowish-green, 4- to 10-mm wide leaves, and often grows in wet clearings and ditches. Compare also with *C. arcta* (northern clustered sedge), which superficially resembles *C. diandra* and can occur in similar habitats but has spikes with male flowers at the base.

NARROW-LEAVED COTTON-GRASS — *Eriophorum angustifolium*

General Stems arising **singly or a few together from widely spreading rhizomes**, rounded, up to 70 cm tall, clothed at the base with dark brown sheaths.

Leaves **Both at the base and along the stem**; stem leaves flat below the middle, triangular and channeled toward the tip, **2-6 mm wide**.

Inflorescence 2-8 spikelets; 2 or more **long leafy bracts**; spikelets drooping.

Fruits Dark brown to black, 3-angled, seedlike achenes, each surrounded by numerous, long (2-3.5 cm) **white bristles**; scales brownish or greyish, **the slender midrib not reaching the tip**.

Ecology Fens, bogs, and margins of streams. Widespread and common from low to high elevations throughout the region.

Notes: Also known as *E. polystachion.* • *E. viridi-carinatum* (green-keeled cotton-grass) closely resembles this species in appearance and habitat but has bracts shorter than the inflorescence, and the midrib of the scale extends to the tip.

CHAMISSO'S COTTON-GRASS — *Eriophorum chamissonis*

General **Extensive beds growing from spreading rhizomes**; stems rounded, up to 50 cm tall, clothed at the base with dark brown sheaths.

Leaves **Mostly near the base, very narrow (0.5-1.5 mm wide)**, channeled throughout.

Inflorescence Solitary spikelet at tip of stem; no leafy bracts.

Fruits Brown, 3-angled, seedlike achenes, each surrounded by numerous long, normally **cinnamon-coloured bristles; scales blackish**, the slender midrib not reaching the tip.

Ecology Fens, bogs, wet ditches; scattered throughout the region at low to medium elevations.

Notes: Also called *E. russeolum* ssp. *rufescens*, this species is distinguished from others having a single head by the rust-coloured bristles and spreading rhizome. *Eriophorum scheuchzeri* (Scheuchzer's cotton-grass) is similar but has silky white bristles. • Two other single-headed species are fairly common in this region. Both are densely tufted (sometimes tussock forming), but *E. vaginatum* (sheathed cotton-grass) has translucent grey scales with broad whitish margins, whereas *E. brachyantherum* (short-anthered cotton-grass) has more or less opaque, greyish to greenish black scales without conspicuous whitish margins. Both are peatland species, but *E. brachyantherum* is more common and widespread.

275

TUFTED CLUBRUSH — *Trichophorum caespitosum*

General *Densely tufted, often forming tussocks*; stems slender, circular in cross-section, 10-40 cm tall, clothed with leaf sheaths at the base.

Leaves Several light brown, scale-like leaves at base of stem; *single stem leaf about 1 cm long.*

Inflorescence *Single, 2-4-flowered terminal spike*; midvein of lowest bract prolonged into a blunt awn (about as long as spike).

Fruits Brown, narrowly egg-shaped, 3-angled, *seedlike achenes, each surrounded by 6 delicate white bristles about twice as long as the achene.*

Ecology Bogs, fens, wet tundra, from lowland to alpine; throughout the region in suitable habitats.

Notes: Also called *Scirpus caespitosus.* • *T. alpinum* (Hudson Bay clubrush; = *Scirpus hudsonianus*) is similar but its stems arise in a row from a short rhizome, and the perigynium is surrounded by 6 much longer white bristles (up to 2.5 cm).

SMALL-FLOWERED BULRUSH — *Scirpus microcarpus*

General Stems *usually clustered*, from a *sturdy rhizome*, stout, *triangular, up to 1.5 mm tall.*

Leaves Several, *both from the base and the stem, flat, 10-15 mm wide*; leaf sheaths often purplish tinged and with whitish, knotlike crosswalls.

Inflorescence Numerous short spiklets in *small clusters at the end of spreading stalks*; bracts several, leaflike.

Fruits Pale, lens-shaped, seedlike achenes, each surrounded by *4-6 slightly longer bristles.*

Ecology Swamps, sloughs, streambanks, wet ditches and clearings. Fairly common at low to moderate elevations throughout the southern half of the region, less so in the North.

Notes: Also known as *S. sylvaticus* and *S. rubrotinctus.* • The related *Scirpus acutus* and *Scirpus validus* (bulrushes) were called "tule" and were widely used by coastal and southern interior Salish, and to a lesser extent by the Carrier, for weaving into mats. The natives did not distinguish between the species used. Both of these big bulrushes are uncommon in low-elevation marshes and shallow water sporadically through the region.

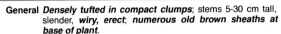

BELLARD'S KOBRESIA — *Kobresia myosuroides*

General ***Densely tufted in compact clumps***; stems 5-30 cm tall, slender, ***wiry, erect***; ***numerous old brown sheaths at base of plant.***

Leaves Several, equalling or somewhat shorter than stems, ***very narrow (about 0.5 mm wide), wiry.***

Inflorescence Spikes solitary, ***narrow***, 1-3 cm long, seldom more than 2 mm thick.

Fruits ***Seedlike, shiny brown achenes loosely wrapped*** by ***light brown scales***; 3 stigmas.

Ecology Dry alpine slopes and rocky ridges in the mountains, typically the most exposed sites with the least snow; also occurs in shrub-carrs, meadows, and gravelly shores at lower elevations; sporadic throughout the region.

Notes: Also known as *Kobresia bellardii*. • This plant is easily mistaken for a sedge, but can be distinguished by the exposed "seeds" and conspicuous brown sheaths. *Kobresia simpliciuscula* (simple kobresia) has several spikes tightly clustered in an oblong head, and occasionally occurs in peaty or gravelly wet areas north of 58°.

SMALL-FLOWERED WOODRUSH — *Luzula parviflora*

General Stems solitary or in small tufts from rhizomes, ***20-80 cm high***.

Leaves Both basal and along stem, ***large (5-10 mm wide)***, flat, with a few long white hairs on margins; ***stem leaves 4 or more.***

Inflorescence Single or paired flowers in a nodding, open panicle.

Fruits Brown, egg-shaped capsules with numerous small seeds, surrounded by brownish bracts that are equal to, or shorter than, the capsule.

Ecology Moist sites in open forests, thickets, meadows, and heath. Widespread and common, from low to high elevations throughout the region.

Notes: This species can be distinguished from other open-flowered woodrushes by its height (usually more than 30 cm), and the presence of 4 or more broad stem leaves. • *Luzula wahlenbergii* (Wahlenberg's woodrush) is very similar but has only 2-3 stem leaves that are 1-5 mm wide, and in our region is less common and grows mostly at high elevations. *L. arcuata* (curved alpine woodrush) is another small (5-25 cm high) alpine species but has narrower leaves and several clusters (of 3-5 flowers each) at the tips of slender, drooping or arching branches. *Luzula spicata* (spiked woodrush) has a single, nodding spike and is widespread in alpine tundra throughout the region.

277

ARCTIC RUSH · *Juncus arcticus*

General *Stems in rows from a thick, horizontal rhizome*, rounded, 10-80 cm tall.

Leaves *All basal*, mostly reduced to pointy-tipped sheaths.

Inflorescence Flowers several to many, clustered on one side of the stem, with a *long rounded bract above appearing like a continuation of the stem*.

Fruits Egg-shaped capsules with numerous small seeds.

Ecology Common in wetlands, wet meadows, and gravelly shores. Scattered, locally abundant, from low to subalpine elevations throughout the region.

Notes: The long bract, plus the many flowers per stem, help to distinguish this species from other rushes. *Juncus filiformis* (thread rush) grows in similar habitats but the bract of its inflorescence is longer, about as long as the stem itself.

DRUMMOND'S RUSH · *Juncus drummondii*

General *Small mats of tufted stems from short rhizomes*; stems round in cross-section, 5-40 cm tall.

Leaves *All basal*, reduced to mere sheaths or sheaths with short bristle-tips.

Inflorescence 1 to 3 flowers at the end of each stem; *lowermost bract even with the top of inflorescence*.

Fruits Oblong-elliptic capsules with *rounded, notched tip* and numerous small seeds tailed at each end.

Ecology Moist gravelly slopes, heaths, snowbeds, and meadows. Common at high elevations throughout the region.

Notes: The short bract, and the few flowers per stem, help to distinguish this species from other low rushes. • *Juncus mertensianus* (Mertens' rush) occurs commonly in similar subalpine/alpine habitats, but has leafy stems and solitary, blackish-brown rounded heads of several to many flowers.

Ferns and Allies

This section contains descriptions of a fairly heterogeneous group of plants referred to as the ferns and their "allies". These are vascular plants: that is, they have internal tubes for transporting fluids (in common with all other plants in this guide except bryophytes and lichens). However, they reproduce not by seeds but by spores (in common with the bryophytes and lichens). This places them in a position morphologically intermediate between the so-called "lower plants" (such as the bryophytes) and the "higher plants" (such as the flowering plants). It also imposes some limits on the biology of the ferns and their allies: because they reproduce by spores, rather than seeds, they must have abundant moisture available for reproduction. Most (but not all!) of these plants are characteristically absent from drier sites. As well, most of the larger ferns are much less common in the boreal forests.

The ferns and allies were used for a number of purposes by native groups in northern B.C., from food and medicine to scouring pads, decoration in baskets, and diaper lining.

Northern B.C. is home to 8 species of horsetails, 7 species of clubmosses, 3 species of selaginellas, 6 species of grape-ferns and rattlesnake-ferns, and approximately 25 species of ferns. This section begins with an illustrated key to the different groups included: horsetails, clubmosses and selaginellas, and ferns (including grape and rattlesnake ferns). Keys are then provided for the species within each group. More information on ferns and allies is provided in Vitt *et al.* (1988) and in Taylor (1973a).

Key to Ferns and Allies

1. Leaves pinnatifid (divided or cut into numerous branches or lobes on two sides of a common axis) and feather like or fan shaped.................FERNS

1. Leaves simple or branch like.

   2. Leaves whorled; stems ribbed .... HORSETAILS

   2. Leaves alternate or opposite; stem not ribbed .... CLUB MOSSES

Horsetails

The horsetails are rhizomatous herbs with aerial, usually hollow, grooved, jointed stems impregnated with silica, making them harsh to the touch. Branches and leaves are borne in whorls at the conspicuous nodes; the leaves are reduced to a series of teeth united by a sheath, and usually lack chlorophyll (the stems and branches are photosynthetic). The spores are produced in terminal cones. The Equisetaceae has a single genus, *Equisetum*, with about 20 species worldwide.

Key to the Common *Equisetum* Species

1. Stems evergreen, usually unbranched (the scouring-rushes).

  2. Stems low and flexible, rather curly and twisted, lacking a central cavity; sheaths with three teeth (a) .... *Equisetum scirpoides*

  2. Stems erect and stiff, with a central cavity; sheaths of the main stem with more than three teeth.

    3. Stems slender, 5-12-ridged, the ridges each bearing 2 rows of tubercles (warty outgrowths or bumps of silica) (b) .... *Equisetum variegatum*

    3. Stems stout, 14-40 ridged, the ridges each bearing 1 or 2 rows of less prominent tubercles, these often forming crossbands (c) *Equisetum hyemale*

1. Stems annual, usually with regularly whorled branches (the horsetails).

    4. Fertile and sterile stems similar; central cavity 1/2 to 4/5 the diameter of main stem; usually in shallow water (d) .... *Equisetum fluviatile*

    4. Fertile and sterile stems dissimilar; central cavity +/- 1/2 the diameter of main stem; usually not in aquatic habitats.

      5. Branches branched; sterile stems with 2 rows of spines on each of the ridges; stem sheaths brownish, the teeth cohering in several broad lobes (e) .... *Equisetum sylvaticum*

      5. Branches usually not again branched; sterile stems with blunt tubercles or cross-ridges on the ridges; stem sheaths greenish, teeth free or nearly so.

        6. Fertile stems permanently whitish or brownish, unbranched, soon withering; sterile stems with smooth or inconspicuous low tubercles and first internodes of the primary branches much longer than the stem sheath (f) .... *Equisetum arvense*

        6. Fertile stems becoming green, branched, persistent; sterile stems with conspicuous tubercles and first internodes of the primary branches shorter than or equalling the length of the stem sheath (g) .... *Equisetum pratense*

SWAMP HORSETAIL — *Equisetum fluviatile*

General ***Stems similar***, solitary or clustered, annual, erect, ***with a large central cavity***, up to 100 cm tall, 9-25-ridged, the ridges smooth or with inconspicuous cross-wrinkles; sheaths green, the teeth dark brown to blackish, persistent, free; ***branches none (usually) to numerous***, whorled; rhizomes creeping, shiny, often reddish.

Cones Short-stalked, blunt-tipped, deciduous.

Ecology Lake edges, marshes, fens, bogs, and other wet sites at low to moderate elevations, throughout our region. Often forms large, conspicuous colonies in ***shallow water***.

Notes: The somewhat similar *E. palustre* (marsh horsetail) is less common in the region and is distinguished by its small central stem cavity (less than 1/3 the diameter of the stem) and its fewer (5-10) stem ridges.
• The black, underground rhizomes of *E. palustre*, and possibly other species of *Equisetum*, were used by the Tlingit of Alaska for decorative imbrication of their spruce-root baskets. • *Equisetum* is from the Latin *equus* ("horse") and *setum* (bristle or horsetail); *fluviatile* means growing in a stream (not a bad description of its habitat).

WOOD HORSETAIL — *Equisetum sylvaticum*

General ***Stems dissimilar***, annual, erect, with a fairly large central cavity. Fertile stems unbranched at first, later with mostly compound branches green to flesh coloured, up to 50 cm tall; sheaths longer than sterile stems, green below, brown upwards, the 3-5 teeth brown, persistent, cohering into several broad lobes. ***Sterile stems*** mostly solitary, green, up to 50 cm tall, ***much branched***, 10-18 ridged, the ridges each with 2 rows of spines; ***sheaths green below, brown upwards***, the 3-5 teeth brown, cohering into several broad lobes; ***branches numerous, whorled, again branched***. Rhizomes creeping, deep in ground.

Cones Long-stalked, blunt-tipped, ***soon deciduous***.

Ecology Moist to wet meadows, shady forests, swamps, bog edges, recent burns and clearings. Throughout the region at low to medium elevations. Usually in more acid, lower-nutrient conditions than the common and meadow horsetails.

Notes: Equisetum arvense and *E. pratense* are of similar size, but have simple branching. Wood horsetail is our only species with branches that branch again several times. • The species name *sylvaticum* means of the forests, emphasizing that this species is most commonly found in forested habitats.

MEADOW HORSETAIL — *Equisetum pratense*

General *Stems dissimilar*, annual, erect, with central cavity. Fertile stems unbranched at first, later becoming branched like the sterile stems, up to 50 cm tall; sheaths pale, the 8-10 teeth brown, white-margined. *Sterile stems* mostly solitary, whitish-green, up to 50 cm tall, *much branched, branches fine, 10-18 ridged, the ridges with conspicuous tubercles*; sheaths pale green, inflated, the 8-10 teeth slender, brown, *white-margined*; branches numerous, whorled, *first internode of primary branches equal to or shorter than the stem sheath*. Rhizomes creeping, black.

Cones Long-stalked, blunt-tipped, *soon deciduous*.

Ecology Moist forests, meadows, streambanks, and clearings at low to moderate elevations throughout the region.

> *Notes:* Meadow horsetail may have been used by natives as a type of sandpaper. Branched species of *Equisetum* are called "horsetail" because the stems and branches resemble a horse's tail. • *Equisetum* species have an affinity for gold in solution, concentrate it more than most plants, and have been used as indicators for the metal.

COMMON HORSETAIL — *Equisetum arvense*

General *Stems dissimilar*, annual, erect, with central cavity. Fertile stems unbranched, usually thick and succulent, brownish to whitish, soon withering, up to 50 cm tall; sheath with 8-12 teeth, large, brown, pointed. *Sterile stems* solitary or clustered, slender, green, up to 70 cm tall, *much branched, 10-12 ridged, the ridges with inconspicuous low tubercles*; sheaths green, appressed to stem, the 10-12 teeth brownish or blackish, persistent, free; branches numerous, whorled, *first internode of primary branches longer than the stem sheath*. Rhizomes creeping, branched, dark-felted, tuber bearing.

Cones Long-stalked, blunt-tipped, *persistent*.

Ecology Moist to wet forests, meadows, swamps, fens, and alpine seepage areas, often weedy (as in roadsides and cutbanks), throughout the region from lowlands to alpine.

Notes: The sterile stems are easily confused with meadow horsetail — the latter, however, has more conspicuous tubercles on the stem ridges, stem sheaths that are equal to or longer than the first internodes of the primary branches, and white-tipped teeth. • The cell walls are impregnated with silicon dioxide, making them rough to the touch and perfect for polishing objects. The stems were used by Interior and Coastal native people like sandpaper for smoothing and polishing surfaces, especially wooden objects such as canoes, dishes, arrow shafts, and gambling sticks. • Ancient Romans ate *E. arvense* shoots like asparagus, and also used them for tea and a thickening powder. • One of the most widespread plants in the world, often a bad garden weed (sometimes called devil guts).

SCOURING-RUSH *Equisetum hyemale*

General ***Stems similar***, solitary or clustered, unbranched, **rough to touch, whitish green, evergreen**, with central cavities, **up to 1.5 m tall, 18-40-ridged**, the ridges with 2 rows of tubercles or these appearing as cross-bars; **sheaths green to ashy gray**, the teeth dark brown to blackish, irregularly persistent, free, and usually also with **two black bands**, one at the tip and a second medial or basal band. Rhizomes creeping, slender, blackish.

Cones Short-stalked, **pointed, persistent**.

Ecology Common on moist to wet sites along major streams and rivers, on open sandbars as well as in shaded alluvial forests, at low to moderate elevations throughout the region.

Notes: This species was used by interior natives as sandpaper. The Gitksan report that the sweet liquid that oozes out from cut stems was an important source of clean water for hunters out on the trail. The Carrier boiled the stems and drank the water for kidney problems and as a diuretic. • The name "scouring-rush" was given to this species because it was used in Europe for scouring utensils made of wood or pewter.

NORTHERN SCOURING-RUSH *Equisetum variegatum*

General ***Stems similar***, clustered, unbranched, **evergreen**, erect, with central cavity, up to 40 cm tall, **5-12-ridged**, the ridges with 2 rows of tubercles; **sheaths green**, the 10-12 teeth black, **white hyaline-margined**, persistent, free, with hair-like, deciduous tip. Rhizomes creeping, shiny, black.

Cones Small, short-stalked, **pointed, persistent**.

Ecology Wet meadows, marshy shores, sandy stream and riverbanks, clearings and roadsides, at low to subalpine elevations throughout our region.

Notes: The peeled stems, base of the plant, roots and rhizomes were eaten by some native groups, either cooked or raw. Northern scouring rush was used by the Gitksan people for bladder problems. • This species can usually be distinguished from dwarf scouring-rush by size alone, but northern scouring-rush has a central cavity and dwarf scouring-rush has none.

DWARF SCOURING-RUSH — *Equisetum scirpoides*

General *Stems similar*, kinked, numerous, clustered, unbranched, green, **evergreen, without a central cavity, up to 20 cm tall, 6-ridged**, the ridges each with a single row of conspicuous blunt tubercles; sheaths enlarged upwards, with a black band above green base, the *3 teeth* thin, usually with transparent margins. Rhizomes creeping, slender, brown, shallow, branched.

Cones Small, very short-stalked, *pointed, persistent*.

Ecology Grows among mosses and in humus on wet to moist sites, cold mossy forest, hummocks in swamps, streambanks, from lowland fen or bog edges to alpine tundra. Throughout the region, particularly common in coniferous boreal forests.

Notes: The *thin, flexible, zigzag stems* and *small size* are characteristic. • The species name *scirpoides* means rush-like, echoing the common name "scouring-rush". This species is also called "goosegrass" in some areas.

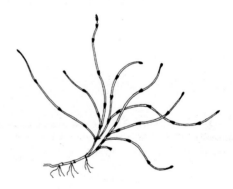

Key to the Common Clubmosses

The clubmosses and spikemosses all have small, narrow, evergreen leaves that are more or less spirally arranged, or sometimes in opposite pairs, and have sporangia in cones or in leaf axils.

1. Spore sacs in leaf axils, not forming terminal cones .... *Lycopodium selago*
1. Spore sacs in distinct terminal cones.
    2. Cones four-angled, sessile; stems short-creeping, sometimes mat-forming; leaves abruptly awn-tipped. .... *Selaginella densa*
    2. Cones round in cross-section, sessile or stalked; stems extensively creeping with erect branches or tufted and dichotomously branched.
        3. Ascending sterile branches simple or forked.
            4. Cones solitary, stalkless at the ends of densely leafy branches ...... *Lycopodium annotinum*
            4. Cones 1-6, stalked on leafy-bracted stalks .... *Lycopodium clavatum*
        3. Ascending branches freely forked (treelike, bushlike or fanlike).
            5. Ascending branches treelike; leaves numerous in 6-8 rows ...... *Lycopodium obscurum*
            5. Ascending branches bushlike or fanlike; leaves flattened in 4 to 5 rows.
                6. Cones stalkless, usually less than 2 cm long; sporophylls toothed marginally above the middle .... *Lycopodium alpinum*
                6. Cones stalked, more than 2 cm long; sporophylls toothed marginally throughout or entire at the base. .... *Lycopodium complanatum*

General Horizontal stems in the form of creeping rhizomes well below the surface of the ground, rooting throughout. Erect stems, up to 30 cm tall, irregularly branched, **bushy-forked, appearing treelike**.

Leaves Numerous, 6-9 ranked, long-pointed.

Cones *Stalkless, solitary at the branch tips*, sporophylls broadly ovate.

Ecology Moist forests, thickets, openings, and bog margins, scattered at low to medium elevations mostly south of 57° in this region.

Notes: Lycopodium spore powder (vegetable sulphur) is highly inflammable and was once used for flash photography. • The genus name *Lycopodium* is from the Greek *lycos* (wolf) and *podus* (foot) after a fancied resemblance of club-moss leaves to a wolf's paw. • This and some other species of *Lycopodium* (ground cedar and running clubmoss) have been observed to form "fairy rings" when growing in openings or old fields. • *L. complanatum* is called "ground-pine" because the plant resembles a miniature coniferous tree. This species is called *L. dendroideum* in some guides.

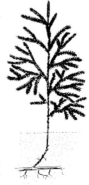

285

ALPINE CLUBMOSS — *Lycopodium alpinum*

General Horizontal stems creeping on surface of ground, up to 50 cm long, rooting throughout, sparsely leafy. ***Erect stems*** up to 10 cm tall, whitish, ***tufted, forked several times, branches somewhat flattened.***

Leaves *4 ranked, partially fused to stem*; in three forms: the dorsal ones lance shaped, the ventral shorter and trowel shaped, the marginal leaves lance shaped, concave.

Cones *Stalkless, solitary at the branch tips*; sporophylls broadly triangular, toothed above.

Ecology Medium dry to moist sites in open, higher elevation forests and subalpine and alpine heath and tundra, throughout our region in suitable habitats.

Notes: L. sitchense (Alaska clubmoss), a species with 5-ranked, essentially similar leaves, is sometimes difficult to separate from the above; it occurs mostly in the western parts of our region, but also in snowy mountains in the southeast. • The Gitksan may have used this plant (or *L. sitchense*) in medicinal preparations. • The species name *alpinum* and common name "alpine clubmoss" emphasize the higher elevation distribution of this species.

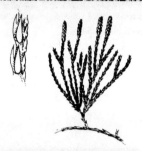

GROUND-CEDAR — *Lycopodium complanatum*

General Horizontal stems creeping on or near surface of ground, up to 1 m long, rooting throughout. ***Erect stems*** whitish green, ***much branched, up to 35 cm tall, flattened*** (cedarlike).

Leaves *4 ranked, partially fused to stem*; in three forms: the dorsal ones with an elevated base, the ventral ones smaller and awl shaped, the marginal ones lance to awl shaped.

Cones *Usually two to three on a forked, long stalk*, sporophylls triangular, toothed except for the base.

Ecology Moist to dry forests and rocky slopes, sandy openings, throughout the region at low to medium elevations.

Notes: The foliage of this species somewhat resembles that of western redcedar. • Ground-cedar is somewhat similar and apparently related to *L. alpinum*, from which it can be distinguished by larger size, loose elongated branches, much-reduced ventral leaves, stalked cones and (to some extent) habitat.

RUNNING CLUBMOSS   *Lycopodium clavatum*

General   Horizontal stems creeping on surface of ground, sometimes arching, to 1 m or more long, rooting throughout, leafy. ***Erect stems irregularly branched, up to 25 cm tall.***

Leaves   Bright green, ***crowded, ascending to spreading***, about 10-ranked, ***lance shaped, tipped with soft white bristles.***

Cones   ***Several (2-4) on a forked, long stalk***; sporophylls rounded, irregularly toothed throughout.

Ecology   Moist to dry open forests or edges of swamps and bogs; openings, clearings, and roadcuts (often on sandy soil); sometimes in high elevation heath and tundra. Scattered at low to high elevations throughout the region, much more common to the west along the Coast Mountains, uncommon in the Chilcotin.

Notes: Used in modern times by the Bella Coola and Nootka for making Christmas wreaths. The Gitksan recognize this plant and call it "otter belt." It may have been used in medicinal preparations. • The spore powder is very flammable, and was used formerly in fireworks, stage lighting, and early flash photography.

STIFF CLUBMOSS   *Lycopodium annotinum*

General   Horizontal stems creeping on or near surface of ground, sometimes arching, up to 1 m long, rooting throughout, leafy. ***Erect stems shiny, simple or once to twice forked, up to 25 cm tall.***

Leaves   8 ranked, whorl-like, ***usually spreading, firm, pointed.***

Cones   ***Stalkless, solitary at the branch tips***; sporophylls rounded, toothed throughout.

Ecology   Moist forest, thickets, bog margins, and subalpine heath, common and widespread from low to subalpine elevations throughout the region.

Notes: In recent times the plant has been used to make Christmas decorations. • While there are no reports of the spores of *Lycopodium* species being used by B.C. native groups, the spore powder (known as vegetable sulphur) was supposedly used by other North American natives as a drying agent for wounds, nose bleeds and diaper rash. The spores may also be used today as a dusting powder for condoms and a body powder for bedridden patients.

FIR CLUBMOSS — *Lycopodium selago*

General *Horizontal stems short*, withering but persistent. **Erect stems simple or several times dichotomously branched**, usually clustered, *often forming tight, more or less flat-topped tufts*, up to 20 cm tall.

Leaves 8 ranked, **usually ascending, crowded, lance shaped, firm, pointed**.

Cones Not obvious; s**porangia borne in the axils of ordinary foliage leaves at the branch tips.**

Ecology Moist, open, usually subalpine forests, parkland, heath; bogs; shaded, acid cliffs and boulders; alpine heath and tundra. Scattered, rarely abundant, at low to high elevations throughout the region.

Notes: Fir clubmoss is reported to contain a chemical that may be effective against Alzheimer's disease. • This species is called *Huperzia selago* in some guides.

COMPACT SELAGINELLA — *Selaginella densa*

General *Greyish green, densely tufted,* low growing; main stems **forming cushion mats** up to 10 cm wide; numerous, erect to ascending, short branches.

Leaves Spirally arranged, **closely crowded and appressed**, grooved down the middle of the back, lance shaped, often ciliate margined, long pointed, up to 2.5 cm long. **Hair-points yellowish**, forming tufts at ends of branches.

Cones *4-angled*, stiffly erect at the branch tips; sporophylls broadly egg shaped, long pointed, ciliate margined.

Ecology Dry, exposed ridges and rock outcrops, occasionally in dry forest, valley bottoms to alpine tundra; scattered in suitable habitats, mostly in the southern half of our region.

Notes: Selaginella sibirica (northern selaginella) is a closely related species with more intricate branching and white hair-points on its leaves. It occupies similar habitats in the North. • *Selaginella selaginoides* (low selaginella) also occurs sporadically throughout the region. It is easily distinguished by its more open habit, its shorter, more prominently spined leaves that lack hair-tips, and its more lance-shaped sporophylls. In contrast to the other two species, it prefers wet, turfy seepage, streambanks, fens, and bogs. • This species is also known as "common selaginella" and "dense spike-moss."

Ferns

The grape or rattlesnake ferns (*Botrychium* spp.) are relatively small ferns with fleshy roots and short, vertical, subterranean stems (rhizomes) that bear a single leaf divided into a sterile expanded blade and a fertile, spikelike or panicle-like portion. The spore sacs are free (not aggregated in sori) and are short stalked, sessile, or sunken in the leaf tissue.

The "true ferns," have creeping or erect rhizomes (often very scaly) and often large, stalked, erect or spreading fronds. The frond blades are curled in bud (fiddleheads) and usually lobed or divided or variously compound. Fertile and sterile fronds are most often alike, but dissimilar in some genera. The spore sacs are grouped together in sori, which are sometimes enclosed or covered by a membranous indusium.

Key to the Common Ferns

1. Plants with sterile leaves only; sporangia (spore sacs) borne in clusters on a leafless stalk
    2. Sterile blade once pinnate, with 2 to 5 pairs of fan-shaped "leaflets" .... *Botrychium lunaria*
    2. Sterile blade 2-3 times pinnate, cut in a lacy, fern-like manner .... *Botrychium virginianum*
1. Plants with sterile and/or fertile leaves; sporangia (spore sacs) borne on the leaves
    3. Rhizome and leaves with hairs only, lacking scales; stipes (leaf stalks) tall, stout and erect
    .... *Pteridium aquilinum*
    3. Rhizome (and often the leaves) scaly and hairy; stipes shorter, relatively slender and usually reflexed.
        4. Sterile and fertile fronds dissimilar, the ultimate segments of the fertile fronds narrow and elongate with margins strongly inrolled toward the lower surface.
            5. Sterile and fertile fronds 2 - 3 times pinnate; plants up to 30 cm tall; occurring on rocky, dry sites .... *Cryptogramma crispa*
            5. Sterile and fertile fronds once pinnate; plants 1 - 2 m tall; occurring on rich alluvial sites .... *Matteucia struthiopteris*
        4. Sterile and fertile fronds similar, the ultimate segments of the fertile fronds broader with margins flat.
            6. Indusium (protective covering for the spore sacs) lacking (in *Woodsia* sometimes inconspicuous).
                7. Leaves glabrous or occasionally glandular, not ciliate margined ....
                .... *Gymnocarpium dryopteris*
                7. Leaves with hairs and ciliate margins .... *Thelypteris phegopteris*
            6. Indusium present.
                8. Indusium elongate, fronds large, tapering toward narrow base ....
                .... *Athyrium filix-femina*
                8. Indusium not elongate, fronds small or large.
                    9. Indusium radiating in hairlike or deeply lacerated segments, veins not reaching margin of frond .... *Woodsia* spp.
                    9. Indusium hoodlike or horseshoe shaped.
                        10.Indusium cup shaped, hoodlike .... *Cystopteris fragilis*
                      10.Indusium horseshoe shaped, veins not reaching margin, stipes scaly ...
                      .... *Dryopteris assimilis*

MOONWORT   *Botrychium lunaria*

General   Erect **yellowish green** herb, **10-25 cm tall**.

Leaves   More or less sessile, glabrous, **pinnate, with 2-5 pairs of roundish to fan-shaped pinnae**. Stipe equalling or exceeding the length of sterile blade.

Reproductive   Fertile stalk 0.5-8 cm long, equalling or exceeding the length of the fertile spike. Fertile spike 1-7 cm long, 2-3 pinnately compound, the numerous sporangia mostly sessile and free.

Ecology   Grassy slopes, meadows, turfy ledges, open deciduous forest, hayfields; scattered at low to high elevations throughout the region, but often overlooked.

Notes: Botrychium spp. are not "true ferns," as their sporangia (spore sacs) are born in grapelike clusters on a naked stalk, rather than on leaves as in "true ferns." They are commonly referred to as "grape ferns" or "rattlesnake ferns." • *Botrychium* is from the Greek word *botryos* (a bunch of grapes) in reference to the sporangia; *lunaria* and "moonwort" both refer (presumably) to the lunate shape of the pinnae.

RATTLESNAKE FERN   *Botrychium virginianum*

General   Erect herb, **15-80 cm tall**.

Leaves   **Sterile blade** continuous with stipe, soon glabrate, thin, triangular in outline, **2-4 times compound, much-divided**. Stipe equalling, or more often exceeding, the length of sterile blade.

Reproductive   Fertile stalk 3-20 cm long, equalling or exceeding the length of the fertile spike. Fertile spike 2-15 cm long, 2-3 pinnately compound, the numerous sporangia mostly sessile and free.

Ecology   Moist, often deciduous forests, thickets, and meadows from low to moderate elevations throughout, but less common in the northern half of the region.

Notes: The species name *virginianum* means that this species also grows in Virginia (many species are named after Virginia, because that's where a lot of North American botanists began collecting.) • This plant is presumably named "rattlesnake" fern because the fertile spike emerging from between the sterile leaf somewhat resembles the tail of a rattlesnake (for a similar reason the related *Ophioglossum vulgatum* is called "adder's tongue").

OSTRICH FERN — *Matteucia struthiopteris*

General ***Sterile fronds*** numerous, ***clustered, erect and spreading, up to 2 m tall***; fertile fronds numerous, clustered, rigid, erect, shorter than the sterile ones, up to 75 cm tall, ***turning dark brown***; stipes short, dark green to black at base on sterile fronds; stipes short, dark brown, equalling or slightly shorter than the blade on fertile fronds; rhizomes creeping, branched below ground surface, beset with numerous brown scales.

Leaves Sterile blades ***lance shaped, tapering at both ends*** (with a diamond-shaped profile), ***pinnate-pinnatifid***, pinnae 20 or more pairs, offset, lower ones progressively reduced, pinnules oblong, blunt; ***fertile blades oblong, once-pinnate***, pinnae 20 or more pairs, offset, crowded, spreading-ascending, margins recurved, segments undulated.

Sori Elongated, covered by curved-under margins of pinnae; indusium not evident.

Ecology Moist to wet forests along major streams and rivers, edges of swamps. Locally common and abundant at low elevations along some of our larger river systems (e.g., Skeena-Kispiox, Fraser north of Quesnel, Peace, Liard). Indicator of ***rich alluvial*** sites and bottomlands.

Notes: Of all our ferns, the fiddleheads of this species are the largest, tastiest, and safest to eat. It is locally abundant in Gitksan territory and around Prince George, and was probably eaten.
• The name "ostrich" fern refers to the featherlike arrangement of the leaf segments. • *Matteucia* is named for Italian physicist Carlo Matteuci (1800-1868).

LADY FERN — *Athyrium filix-femina*

General ***Fronds all fertile, clustered, erect and spreading, up to 1.5 m tall***; stipes short, fragile, scaly at the base, much shorter than the blades; rhizomes stout, ascending to erect, beset with scales and old petiole bases.

Leaves Blades narrowly to broadly ***lance shaped, tapering at both ends (with a diamond-shaped profile), 2-3 times pinnate***; pinnae 20-40 pairs, offset, lower ones progressively reduced, basal pinnae lance shaped; pinnules 15-30 pairs, offset, toothed to pinnatifid.

Sori ***Elongate and curved***, with elongate and curved indusium.

Ecology Moist to wet forests, thickets, openings, slidetracks, streambanks, gullies, meadows, and clearings at low to subalpine elevations; widespread, locally abundant in the southern half of our region, except for the Chilcotin (where it occurs sporadically on fluvial sites); rare in the North.

Notes: At first glance this fern could be confused with *Dryopteris assimilis*. The latter, however, is broadly triangular (not diamond shaped) in outline, with the blade not tapering towards the base.
• The fronds of this fern were used by native people for laying out or covering food, especially berries for drying. The fiddleheads were eaten in the early spring when they were 7-15 cm tall. They were boiled, baked, or eaten raw with grease. • *Athyrium* is Greek for "without a shield" — this is perhaps because the indusium is ultimately forced open; *filix-femina* means lady fern (at one time believed to sneak around at night to mate with *Dryopteris filix-mas*, the male fern).

291

SPINY WOOD FERN — *Dryopteris expansa*

General *Fronds clustered, erect and spreading, up to 1 m tall*; stipes scaly at the base, usually shorter than the blades; rhizomes stout, ascending to erect, beset with chaffy brown scales.

Leaves Blades *broadly triangular to egg shaped to broadly oblong, 3 times pinnate*; pinnae 5-20 pairs, slightly offset, *the lowest pair broadly triangular and asymmetrical;* pinnules up to about 12 pairs, slightly offset, the two most basal pinnules much larger than the others, ultimate segments toothed.

Sori *Rounded*, partially covered by the rounded indusium.

Ecology Moist forests and openings, at low to moderate elevations throughout the region, sporadic in the Chilcotin, and less common in the North.

Notes: This species is also know as *D. assimilis*, *D. austriaca*, and *D. dilatata*. • Rhizomes of this fern were an extremely important source of starch for many central and northern interior native groups, especially the Gitksan, Niska and Carrier. The rhizomes, dug in the fall or even from under the snow, were baked in pits overnight and then peeled like bananas and eaten. They taste a little like squash. •*Dryopteris fragrans* (fragrant fern) has evergreen, leathery, narrow, pinnate-pinnatifid fronds that are glandular, scaly, and have a sickly sweet smell. It is a species of cliffs, boulders, and talus slopes north of 57°. • *D. filix-mas* (male fern) is a large fern with non-glandular fronds that have the broadly lance-shaped outline of lady fern, but are 1-2 rather than 2-3 times pinnate. Male fern occupies wooded slopes, avalanche track thickets, and shaded talus, and occurs sporadically at low to medium elevations in the Skeena-Nass transitional area and also along the big bend of the Fraser River. • *Dryopteris* is the classical Greek name for this fern, from *drys* (oak) and *pteris* (a fern).

BRACKEN — *Pteridium aquilinum*

General *Fronds large, solitary, erect*, deciduous, *up to 1.5 m tall; stipes stout*, straw colored to greenish, longer than the blades; rhizomes spreading, much-branched below ground surface, beset with numerous hairs.

Leaves *Blades triangular, 2-3 times pinnate, hairy*; pinnae 10 or more pairs, mostly opposite, the lowest pair narrowly to broadly triangular, upper ones progressively reduced and lanceolate; pinnules 10 or more pairs, offset, ultimate segments round-toothed, *margins recurved*.

Sori *Marginal, continuous*; indusium not evident.

Ecology Open sites, roadsides, clearings, often weedy at low to moderate elevations. Sporadic, very uncommon in the Chilcotin, otherwise locally abundant south of 55°, and in extreme northwestern B.C.

Notes: Both the Gitksan and Carrier Indians ate the long, black rhizomes. These were peeled and eaten raw, baked in pits overnight and eaten with meat or fish, or roasted and pounded into

a kind of flour. Although the fiddleheads may have been eaten by some groups and are popular with Japanese people, they have been implicated in livestock poisoning and in stomach cancer, and should probably not be eaten. Furthermore, a South American study found a three-fold higher incidence of gastric cancer in humans who drank untreated milk from cattle that habitually ingested bracken from heavily-infected pastures. • A cosmopolitan species.

OAK FERN — *Gymnocarpium dryopteris*

General **Fronds usually solitary (but often in masses), erect**, deciduous, **up to 35 cm tall**; stipe shiny, straw colored, scaly at the base, equalling or more commonly longer than the blades; rhizome elongate, slender, creeping, beset with a few brown fibrous scales.

Leaves **Blades broadly triangular, 2-3 times pinnate, glabrous**; pinnae up to 20 pairs, mostly opposite, the lowest pair triangular and asymmetrical; pinnules up to about 12 pairs, usually offset, the two most basal pinnules larger than the others, ultimate segments round-toothed.

Sori **Small, circular, lacking an indusium.**

Ecology Moist forests and openings, rocky slopes; common and often abundant at low to subalpine elevations throughout our region, except essentially absent in the Chilcotin.

Notes: Oak fern is a characteristic "indicator species" of moist sites. As moisture levels increase other indicator species become more abundant: devil's club (*Oplopanax horridus*) on wet sites, horsetails (*Equisetum* spp.) on very wet sites. •*Gymnocarpium* means naked fruit, because there's no indusium. • The close relationship of *Gymnocarpium dryopteris* to *Dryopteris* is reflected by its inclusion in the latter genus by some taxonomists as *D. disjuncta*.

BEECH FERN — *Thelypteris phegopteris*

General **Fronds usually solitary, erect**, deciduous, **up to 40 cm tall**; stipes slender, brown basally, straw coloured upwards, sparsely scaly, equal to or more usually longer than the blades; rhizomes slender, creeping, sparsely scaly.

Leaves **Blades triangular to egg shaped, pinnate-pinnatifid, beset with hairs and scales**, the latter mainly on the midribs; pinnae hairy, 10-25 pairs, opposite to offset, sessile, the **lowest pair usually reflexed downward**, the others attached nearly at right angles to the stipe, upper ones progressively reduced; pinnules 10 or more pairs, usually offset.

Sori **Small, more or less circular; indusium lacking.**

Ecology Moist, rich forests, streambanks, wet cliffs, and rocky seepage slopes at low to subalpine elevations. Scattered, locally common, through the southern half of our region, except for the Chilcotin, north along the Coast Mountains to Alaska-Yukon. Most abundant on basic or calcium-rich rock.

Notes: Thelypteris is Greek for female (*thelus*) fern (*pteris*); see notes under *Athyrium* regarding the nocturnal behaviour of these ferns. This species is also called "cowboy fern" because the lowest pair of pinnae points downwards like spurs, or spread out like bowed legs.

ROCKY MOUNTAIN WOODSIA   *Woodsia scopulina*

General   ***Fronds clustered, erect and spreading, 10 to 20 cm tall, brittle***; stipes short, stiff, brown basally, straw coloured upwards, shorter than the blades; ***rhizomes*** creeping, ascending, ***beset with numerous scales and old stipe bases.***

Leaves   Blades oblong, lance shaped, tapering at both ends, pinnate-pinnatifid to 2-times pinnate; pinnae 6-20 pairs, opposite or offset, lower ones reduced, ***densely to sparsely white-hairy and stalked-glandular, especially below;*** pinnules 2-8 pairs, opposite or offset, toothed.

Sori   ***Rounded; indusium deeply lacerated*** (divided into linear lobes).

Ecology   Dry cliffs, crevices, rock slides and talus slopes at low to high elevations. Scattered, locally common throughout southern half of the region, uncommon in the North.

Notes: The genus *Woodsia* is named in honour of English botanist Joseph Woods (1776-1864); *scopulina* describes its habitat (of the rocks or cliffs).

OREGON WOODSIA   *Woodsia oregana*

General   ***Fronds clustered, erect and spreading, up to 30 cm tall***; stipes short, stiff, brown basally, straw coloured upwards, shorter than the blades; ***rhizomes*** creeping, ascending, ***beset with numerous scales and old stipe bases.***

Leaves   Blades lance shaped, tapering at both ends, pinnate-pinnatifid to 2 times pinnate; pinnae 6-18 pairs, opposite or off-set, lower ones reduced, ***glabrous or somewhat glandular below***; pinnules 2-6 pairs, offset, round-toothed.

Sori   ***Rounded; indusium with radiating, hairlike segments.***

Ecology   Dry cliffs, crevices, rock slides, and talus slopes, at low to high elevations. Throughout the southern half of our region.

Notes: This species grows in similar habitats to *Woodsia scopulina*; the Rocky Mountain woodsia, however, has numerous hairs and stalked glands on the lower sides of the blade.

FRAGILE FERN — *Cystopteris fragilis*

General *Fronds usually clustered, erect, up to 30 cm tall*; stipes straw coloured, short, glabrous, equalling or shorter than the blades; *rhizomes* short, creeping, *densely scaly.*

Leaves *Blades lance shaped, tapering at both ends, 2-3 times pinnate*, axis glabrous except for a few hairs towards the base of the pinnae; pinnae 8-18 pairs, often offset, lower ones reduced; pinnules 3-8 pairs, often offset, irregularly toothed.

Sori *Small, roundish, partially covered with a hoodlike, somewhat toothed or lobed indusium.*

Ecology Moist to dry, rocky forests and openings, rock cliffs, crevices, and ledges, talus slopes, common and widespread from low to high elevations throughout the region.

Notes: This species is sometimes confused with *Woodsia oregana*, a fern with numerous old stipe bases and an indusium with radiating, hairlike segments. •*Cystopteris montana* (mountain bladder fern) is a sporadic but often overlooked species of shady, moist to wet forest, glades, rocky slopes, and streambanks. It occurs at medium to subalpine elevations, probably in most of the region except the Chilcotin and the Fort Nelson Lowland, typically on nutrient-rich or calcareous sites. *C. montana* looks more like a *Gymnocarpium* or *Dryopteris*, with triangular-ovate, twice-pinnate leaves, but has a hoodlike indusium. • *Cystopteris* is from the Greek for bladder (*kystos*) and fern (*pteris*), referring to the hoodlike indusium; *fragilis* means brittle (the stems).

PARSLEY FERN — *Cryptogramma crispa*

General *Sterile fronds numerous, clustered, erect and spreading, up to 20 cm tall*; stipes straw coloured to greenish, equalling or longer than blades; *fertile fronds numerous, erect, taller than the sterile ones, up to 30 cm tall*; stipes straw coloured to greenish, longer than the blades; rhizomes short, ascending, branched, *beset with scales and old stipe bases.*

Leaves *Sterile blades egg shaped, thick*, crisply firm, *glabrous, usually 3 times pinnate*; pinnae mostly 3-10 pairs, offset, largest at the base; pinnules 3-5 pairs, offset, finely toothed; *fertile blades broadly lance shaped, 2-3 times pinnate*; pinnae mostly 3-10 pairs, opposite to somewhat offset; pinnules (ultimate ones) with inrolled margins.

Sori *Along the length of fertile pinnules, covered by inrolled margins*; indusium not evident.

Ecology Fairly dry rocky, open sites (cliffs, ledges, crevices, talus slopes) at moderate to high elevations. Sporadic in suitable habitats throughout the region, except not east of the Rocky Mountains.

Notes: Cryptogramma is Greek for hidden (*krypto*) line (*gramma*), referring to the way the leaf margin hides the sori; *crispa* refers to the crisped fronds. • Called "parsley fern" because the fronds look somewhat like parsley.

Bryophytes

"Bryophytes" is a term used to described three large groups of small plants – the mosses, liverworts and hornworts. Hornworts are the smallest group, and are neither common nor widespread in northern B.C., so they are not treated here.

All of the plants described previously in this guide contain internal tubes for transporting food and water within them; they are vascular plants. Bryophytes lack these tubes; they are non-vascular plants. As well, most of the plants described previously reproduce themselves with seeds. Bryophytes (along with ferns, clubmosses and horsetails) lack seeds, reproducing instead with spores. Because they cannot effectively transport food and water internally, and because they require water for reproduction, bryophytes are small plants, and are often more abundant in wetter places. Almost all of the mosses and liverworts in this region are common throughout the northern hemisphere, from boreal Canada to Scandinavia, the Soviet Union, China and Japan.

Bryophytes consist of two generations: the gametophyte, the mosses and liverworts we see carpeting the ground throughout central and northern B.C.; and the sporophyte, a capsule raised above the gametophyte by a stalk (seta). Sporophytes are only present when conditions are right, and in liverworts usually last only for a day or less.

Apart from the sphagnum mosses, most native people did not distinguish among the many mosses and liverworts that they used. Mosses, in particular, were used throughout the province for many household tasks including lining pits and as a source of moisture for both cooking and molding wood, wiping the slime off fish, stuffing mattresses and pillows, lining babies cradles and bags, and covering floors. Mixed with pitch, mosses were used to caulk canoes and in more modern times they were mixed with mud to chink log cabins. Most groups preferred sphagnum moss, but would use other species if it was not available.

As with other sections of the guide, this section describes only the most common bryophytes in central and northern B.C. More information can be obtained from Vitt *et al.* (1988), Schofield (1968), or Conard and Redfern(1979).

"If it were not for the mosses, it is difficult to say how barren the woods would be or how much beauty would be lost to nature."

E.M. Dunham, How to Know the Mosses, 1916.

Mosses

Liverworts

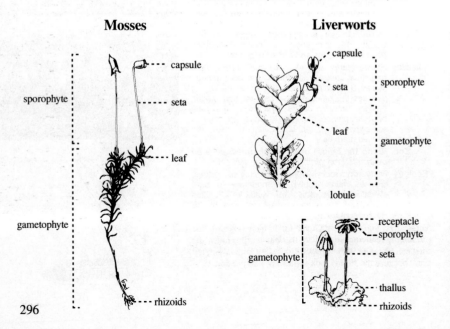

RED-STEMMED FEATHERMOSS — *Pleurozium schreberi*

General **Stems orange to reddish**, irregularly **pinnately branched**, ascending, 5-12 cm tall, forming light green to yellow-green **mats**.

Leaves Oblong to oval, rounded at the tips, inrolled at the sides.

Sporophyte Almost never seen (see Notes); seta red to yellowish, 2-4 cm tall; capsules cylindric, 2-3 mm long, horizontal.

Ecology In most forested habitats, particularly abundant in dry open forests, uncommon in the open (e.g. bogs, shrub-steppe); common and abundant from low to subalpine elevations throughout the region.

Notes: The most common and widespread moss in central and northern interior British Columbia. The red stem visible through fairly transparent leaves is characteristic, hence the common name. This species usually occurs in combination with our other "feathermosses" (step moss and knight's plume), and they often form a continuous mat in mature coniferous forest. • Evidence of sexual reproduction (i.e., capsules) is rare in *P. schreberi*, and there is no known mechanism of asexual reproduction. This is somewhat unusual in a moss distributed fairly widely around the globe. Crum (1976) suggests that a lack of male plants may underlie the sexual difficulties in *Pleurozium*. • The word *Pleurozium* comes from the Latin *pleuro* meaning ribs and presumably refers to the arrangement of the branches on either side of the stem which resembles a rib cage. • Also known as "big red stem" by some forest ecologists.

STEP MOSS — *Hylocomium splendens*

General Olive green, yellowish or reddish green, stems creeping, 2-20 cm long, stems and branches reddish, often with branches on branches; current year's growth arising from near the middle of the previous year's branch, producing **feathery "fronds" in step form**; forming springy **mats**.

Leaves 2-3 mm long, oval, entire, wide base abruptly narrowed to the tip.

Sporophyte Uncommon; seta red-brown, 1-3 cm tall; capsules brown, inclined, 1.5-3 mm long, with a long beak on the lid.

Ecology Soil, humus, decaying wood; wide range of forest habitats; also moist thickets and tundra; common and widespread, from the lowlands to the alpine tundra throughout the region.

Notes: This moss is indeed "splendens". Specimens of lesser vigour may resemble red-stemmed feathermoss. Since a new "step" is produced each year (+/-), the age of this moss may be estimated by counting the "steps." Those who learned stepmoss on the coast may be surprised to discover the less robust, once to twice pinnate specimens of the northern interior (vs. 2-3 times pinnate on the coast), described by some as var. *alaskanum*. • *Hylocomium* means living in the forest.

KNIGHT'S PLUME — *Ptilium crista-castrensis*

General Green to golden-green, 3-12 cm long, branches somewhat upright to drooping; **symmetrical, feathery tapered branches, plumes "well groomed"**; in decorative **mats**.

Leaves Branch leaves pleated, ovate, to 2 mm long, all curled in the same direction towards the branch below; stem leaves pleated, curled towards the stem base.

Sporophyte Seta reddish, 2-4.5 cm tall; capsule chestnut brown, nearly horizontal, 2-3 mm long, curved.

Ecology On humus, logs, sometimes on boulders and tree bases, in coniferous and mixed forest; common and often abundant at low to subalpine elevations throughout the region Red-stemmed feathermoss and knight's plume are the characteristic mosses of northern British Columbia.

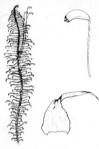

Notes: Knight's plume could be mistaken only for *Drepanocladus uncinatus*, which is not so evenly branched and much less common in our region. • *Ptilium* means plumelike, *crista-castrensis* means crest (*cresta*) of the castle (*castrensis*) all referring to the elegant, regularly pinnate branches similar to the plume of a knight's helmet (hence the common name).

WIRY FERN MOSS — *Thuidium abietinum*

General Yellow or dark green to brown; stems to 12 cm high, stiff; **branches simple** (not divided), **feathery** (somewhat like *Ptilium*), erect or ascending; with **abundant fuzz on stems**.

Leaves Furrowed, oval, 1.2-1.8 mm long.

Sporophyte Seta reddish, 2-5 mm tall, wavy; capsule 2-3 mm long, strongly curved and inclined.

Ecology **Dry, calcium-rich areas**, exposed rocks, soil or sand, talus, or humus in open, dry forests. Scattered (locally abundant) at low to subalpine elevations in areas of drier climates throughout our region.

Notes: T. recognitum is a similar species, but the main stems are branched 2-3 times (vs. unbranched in *T. abietinum*), the plant is smaller (never more than 9 cm tall), and it grows in moist to wet, shady sites. • The name *Thuidium* implies a resemblance to *Thuja* (redcedars) because of the feathery branching; *abietinum* means like *Abies* (the "true firs"), presumably a similar reference. Despite these similarities, it should be relatively simple to separate this moss from the large conifers.

ELECTRIFIED CAT'S-TAIL MOSS — *Rhytidiadelphus triquetrus*

General Bright to dark green or yellow green **mats or clumps**; **stems sprawling to erect** to 20 cm long, orange red, **irregularly to regularly branched**; branches tapered, curved down at tips.

Leaves Gradually narrowed, pleated, **sticking out from stem**; **apical tuft of leaves more ruffled than those below.**

Sporophyte Seta 1-5 cm long; capsule red-brown, inclined, 1.5-3 mm long.

Ecology Humus, soil, logs, stumps, ground cover; in coniferous and deciduous forest; particularly abundant in some floodplain forests. Scattered and often locally abundant from low to medium elevations throughout the region.

Notes: Bent-leaf moss (*Rhytidiadelphus squarrosus*) is similar, but its leaves taper abruptly to a slender, channelled tip. Lanky moss (*Rhytidiadelphus loreus*) is thinner than *R. triquetrus* and has tidier stem tips; typically a coastal species, it is scattered at low to medium elevations in areas of wettest climates in this region. •*Rhytidiadelphus* means brother of *Rhytidium*, implying a fraternal relationship between the genera.

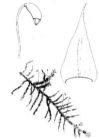

PIPECLEANER MOSS — *Rhytidiopsis robusta*

General Glossy green, yellow to brownish green, stems few-branched, prostate, often mat forming; **branches pudgy**, to 15 cm long, branch ends usually curved; **stem covered in green "fuzz".**

Leaves 3-4.5 mm long, close packed, curved, **longitudinally furrowed, wrinkled**, oval base narrowed to a point, edges rolled under.

Sporophyte Seta reddish brown, 2-3 cm long; capsule to 3 mm long, inclined, curved.

Ecology Litter, humus, decaying wood in coniferous forest, often forming carpets around subalpine fir; scattered at medium to subalpine elevations throughout the region except in the Northeast; most common in areas of high snowfall.

Notes: This species occurs in the same habitat as, and often grows side-by-side with *Brachythecium* spp. •*Rhytidiopsis* means looking like *Rhytidium*. The individual branches look like small pipecleaners − hence the common name.

CRUMPLED-LEAF MOSS   *Rhytidium rugosum*

General *Yellow, greenish yellow or golden brown, erect*, branched on one side or with symmetrical, regular feathery branches with hooked tips, *fuzzless stems*; erect to fairly erect stems 2-8 cm high; forming *loose mats*.

Leaves Crowded, curved one way, *furrowed and rumpled*, narrowed to a long, thin tip, edges rolled under.

Sporophyte Seta red, 2-2.5 cm; capsule brown. The sporophyte of this moss has never been recorded in British Columbia.

Ecology *Dry, well-drained, thin soil, exposed calcareous areas, dry tundra*; uncommon but locally abundant at medium to high elevations in suitable habitats throughout the region.

Notes: Often occurs with *Thuidium abietinum* and *Aulacomnium turgidum*. • *Rhytidium* comes from the Latin *rhytidio* meaning wrinkled and refers to the rumpled leaves.

WAVY-LEAVED MOSS — *Dicranum polysetum*

General **Light to yellow green, large (7 cm or more in height)**, covers large areas of ground, **stem covered with whitish "fuzz"** (matted rhizoids), good for sitting on.

Leaves To 1 cm long, **held well out (more or less at right angles) from stem, wavy edges.**

Sporophyte 1-5 setae per plant, 2-4 cm long; capsules 2-4 mm long, inclined or horizontal, curved.

Ecology Ground, rocks, and decaying wood in open dry to moist forest; common and locally abundant at low to medium elevations throughout the region.

Notes: Male plants in our common *Dicranum* species (including this one) are just tiny buds on the leaves of female plants. This may combine the advantages of having the sexes on separate plants (outbreeding) with the convenience of having both sexes on the same plant (reproduction is more sure), and may explain why species of *Dicranum* are very commonly seen with sporophytes. • Vitt *et al.* (1988) list the common name "electric eels" for this species, as the leaf arrangement makes the plant look like it was "hit with an electric shock!" • *Dicranum* refers to the forked nature of the peristome teeth; *polysetum* means many setae per plant (most Dicranums have only one).

CURLY HERON'S-BILL MOSS — *Dicranum fuscescens*

General **Green to dark green**, unbranched, **1-4 cm tall**, stems reddish brown; small to sizable patches and cushions.

Leaves **Curved to the same side**, long, narrow, pointed end; contorted when dry, keeled in upper part (V-shaped).

Sporophyte Seta yellow to dark, 1-2 cm long; capsule light or dark brown, inclined, to 4mm long, furrowed lengthwise when dry, asymmetrical; can have a small bump just above the base on the lower side.

Ecology **Usually on wood**: rotten wood, base of living trees; common from low to subalpine elevations throughout the region.

Notes: Broom moss (*Dicranum scoparium*) is a similar species, but its leaves are very glossy, and are not "crispy" when dry, whereas leaves of *D. fuscescens* are not glossy, and are quite "crispy" when dry. Broom moss also tends to grow in looser mats than curly heron's bill moss. *D. pallidisetum* is another very similar species of subalpine elevations (see NOTES under *D. pallidisetum*). • The common name curly heron's-bill moss is presumably in reference to the leaves that are curved and long-pointed like a heron's bill.

PALE-STALKED BROOM MOSS — *Dicranum pallidisetum*

General Pale to dark green, 1-6 cm tall.

Leaves As for *D. fuscescens*, but tubular (U-shaped in cross section) instead of keeled (V-shaped in cross-section), contorted when dry.

Sporophyte Seta 1-2.5 cm long, yellow, darker with age; capsule yellow-brown, darker when old, furrowed, normally paler than *D. fuscescens*.

Ecology Humus, soil, rock, decayed wood, *in subalpine forest and parkland, and alpine heath; higher elevations than D. fuscescens*; throughout the region at appropriate altitudes.

Notes: Schofield (1969) notes that this species is difficult to distinguish from *D. fuscescens* without a microscope; try using the leaf cross-section to separate them. • The species name *pallidisetum* means pale stalk, and refers to the seta.

SICKLE MOSS — *Drepanocladus uncinatus*

General Yellow-brown to brown, stems slightly to irregularly *feathery branched*, 2-5 cm long, *tufts and mats*.

Leaves Long, narrow, pleated lengthwise, *all turned in the same direction, almost curled round in a crescent moon*.

Sporophyte Seta red, 15-30 mm long, wobbly; capsule brown, inclined or erect, 2-3 mm long, curved, almost horizontal.

Ecology Soil, humus, rock, decayed wood, tree bases, wet to fairly dry sites, ranging from gravel bars and wetlands (especially fens and swamps) to upland forest, where usually at the base of trees or boulders. Widespread but usually scattered, from low to high elevations throughout the region.

Notes: The name *Drepanocladus* is from the Latin *drepano* (curved) and *clado* (branch), referring to the sickle-shaped leaves characteristic of the genus; *uncinatus* is from the Latin *uncio* meaning hooked. The terminal group of leaves grows together in a hook-shaped unit, so the growing end of each stem is "hooked" (as suggested by the common name).

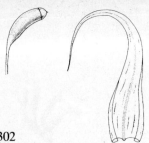

FALSE-POLYTRICHUM — *Timmia austriaca*

General Green, bluish green, red-brown or brown, 3-7 cm high, upright patches.

Leaves Turned up when wet, spreading wider when dry, *orange leaf base wrapped around stem.*

Sporophyte Seta reddish brown, 2-3 cm long, 2-4 per plant; capsule greenish to brown, 3-5 mm long, tilted, cylindric, furrowed when dry.

Ecology On soil and humus in coniferous forest (often in floodplain forests or near streams), soil around rocks, cliffs, rock shelves; scattered from low to medium elevations throughout the region west of the Rocky Mountains.

Notes: This moss *looks like a Polytrichum*. *Timmia* has orange leaf bases. *Polytrichum* has lamellae (green ridges running lengthwise along the leaf "midrib") on leaf surfaces and the leaves appear opaque, whereas *Timmia* has translucent leaves. • *Timmia* is named for Joachim Timm, a German botanist; *austriaca* means from Austria. Mount Timmia on Ellesmere Island was named for this genus, thus making a mountain out of a moss-hill.

STIFF-LEAVED POLYTRICHUM — *Polytrichum alpinum*

General Dull blue-green, brown, or red-brown, 4-16 cm high in vertical tufts, *stem fuzzy at base*; forming loose tufts.

Leaves 8-13 mm long, lean, tapering, concave.

Sporophyte Seta 15-30 mm long, yellow turning brown, 3 angled on top; capsule 3-6 mm long, *rounded in cross-section*, almost straight up to horizontal.

Ecology Rocks, soil, humus on banks, damp shady spots, usually in coniferous forest; fairly common *from low to high elevations* throughout the region.

Notes: This species is described in some other guides as *Pogonatum alpinum*. It differs from other *Polytrichums* in our area by the shape of its capsule (rounded in cross-section). The specific name *alpinum* (of the alpine) describes its habitat further south; in this region it occurs at all elevations.

303

JUNIPER HAIRCAP MOSS — *Polytrichum juniperinum*

General Green, blue-green, to red-brown, 1-13 cm high, **loose tufts of vertical growth, unbranched.**

Leaves 4-8 mm long, straight to slightly curved, pointed up or up and outwards when dry, spreading wider when wet, **toothless clear edges,** folded over forming two narrow shining lines, **leaf tip extended into a reddish point.**

Sporophyte Seta brown, 2-6 cm long; **capsule** reddish brown, 2.5-5 mm long, nearly vertical to horizontal, **square.**

Ecology Soil, humus and rock, stumps, banks, trailsides, dry open woods; frequent after fire; commonest on dry, exposed acidic sites; common and widespread, from low to high elevations throughout the region.

Notes: Species of *Polytrichum* can be recognized by the characteristic *lamellae* on their leaves: dark green ridges running lengthwise along the leaf midrib. • *P. commune* is somewhat similar, but has toothed leaf margins, a reddish brown leaf tip, can grow to 20 cm or more, and typically grows in moist, shady forests. *P. alpinum* resembles the juniper haircup moss, but has different leaves and capsules that are round in cross-section. The juniper haircap moss occurs throughout the world except in some tropical regions. • *Polytrichum* (many hairs) and "haircap moss" both refer to the hairy calyptra (the cap on the capsule); *juniperinum* means like juniper, because the leaves are similar in shape and colour to those of the common juniper (*Juniperus communis*).

AWNED HAIRCAP MOSS — *Polytrichum piliferum*

General Glaucous green to brown, 1-4 cm tall, stem bases leafless, tops crowded with leaves, forming **dense tufts.**

Leaves 4-7 mm long, pointing up when dry, out when wet; entire margin folded in over lamellae; **leaf tip ending in a colourless point** visible from several metres as a whitish coating around each plant.

Sporophyte Seta brown, 3-4 cm tall, thick, wavy; capsules reddish brown, 2-3 mm long, 4- or 5-angled box shape.

Ecology Dry sterile sandy gravelly soil, exposed rocks, roadsides, old fields; scattered from valley bottoms to alpine tundra throughout our region.

Notes: The awned haircap moss is similar to juniper haircup moss; look for the long white "hair point" on the leaves of awned haircap moss. In both of these dry site species, the inflexed leaf margins covering the green lamellae reduce desiccation. *Polytrichum strictum* shares leaf features with these two species, but has whitish fuzzy stems (matted rhizoids) and occupies wetland habitats, typically growing on mounds of *Sphagnum*.

SIDEWALK MOSS — *Tortula ruralis*

General *Overall brick red in colour* (base reddish, top greener) when wet, blackish when dry; 2-3 cm tall, *forming upright tufts with a hoary appearance.*

Leaves *Folded and twisted around stem when dry*, spreading or curved out and down at 90 degrees when moist; *with a blunt end and long hairpoint*, which is sometimes as long as the leaf.

Sporophyte Seta 1-2 cm tall; capsules 2-3 mm long, curved.

Ecology *Sandy soil, rock, dry, sunny, often calcareous sites*; on suitable habitats throughout the region, from lowlands to alpine elevations.

Notes: No other species in our area has similar leaves.
• *Tortula* means twisted, in reference to the leaves and the capsule teeth; *ruralis* means of the countryside.

FIRE MOSS — *Ceratodon purpureus*

General *Green, yellow-brown, or reddish, forming small, dense tufts*, unbranched, to 1 cm tall.

Leaves About 2 mm long, acute, margins curled up or down nearly their entire length.

Sporophyte Seta dark-red to brown, 2-3 cm long; *capsule dark red*, inclined to horizontal with bump at base, 2-4 mm long, cylindric, deeply furrowed.

Ecology Soil, rock, dead wood, or burned, logged-over ground, roadsides, roofs. *A weedy species*, on disturbed sites throughout the region from low to subalpine elevations.

Notes: On burned-over sites, this species often occurs with *Pohlia nutans* and other pioneers such as *Bryum caespitosum*, *Funaria hygrometrica*, and *Marchantia polymorpha*. The deeply furrowed capsules and seta colour *en masse* are good identifying features. • *Ceratodon* is from the Latin *cerato* meaning horn-shaped in reference to the forked capsule teeth; *purpureus* describes the sometimes reddish-purplish colouration of this species.

BRYOPHYTES

YELLOW-GREEN ROCK MOSS — *Rhacomitrium heterostichum*

General Variable colour (green, yellow, brown), **often whitish from the leaf points**, 2-5 cm long, low upright or creeping along the ground; **freely branched mats.**

Leaves 2-2.6 mm long, turned to one side when dry, tip clear (white), brittle when dry.

Sporophyte Seta yellowish to reddish-brown, 3-8 mm tall, twisted when dry; capsule yellowish, erect, 1.2-2.5 mm long, smooth or a bit wrinkled in lines when dry.

Ecology Exposed acidic rocks, gravel, and sand, shaded or sunny; throughout the region, from valley bottom gravel bars to alpine ridges.

Notes: Rhacomitrium canescens is similar. Its leaves end in toothed, minutely bumpy tips, whereas those of *R. heterostichum* end in merely toothed tips.

HOARY ROCK MOSS — *Rhacomitrium lanuginosum*

General Green, yellow, blackish or brown, sometimes whitish from leaf tip colour, 3-15 cm high, erect or spreading over ground, short tufty horizontal branches; **often forms large, whitish gray-green cushions.**

Leaves Erect or curving to one side, 3.5-4 mm long, narrowed to **hoary white leaf tips**.

Sporophyte Seta reddish brown, 4-9 mm long, often in pairs; capsule 1-1.7 mm long, red-brown, erect, a bit tufted.

Ecology Dry, exposed soil, rock and tundra, barren mountain tops; typically at high elevations but descends to valley bottoms on talus slopes, recent lava flows, and (paradoxically) in some peatlands, especially towards the Coast Mountains; widespread throughout the region, except apparently absent in the northeast.

Notes: R. lanuginosum has minutely bumpy (papillose) leaf tips like *R. canescens*, but has a more hoary-white appearance.
• *Lanuginosum* means softly hairy, woolly or cottony and refers to the long, white leaf tips which give the plant a distinctive cottony appearance.

DRUMMOND'S LEAFY MOSS   *Plagiomnium drummondii*

General   ***Clear, light, clean green***, 2-6 cm high, ***stems unbranched and erect with rhizoids on lower stem; forming tufts.***

Leaves   Sterile plants: leaves in more or less two rows, smaller at ends; fertile plants erect, leaves larger at top; small point on tip of each leaf; ***leaves not much changed in drying***, lightly crisped, very clean and crinkly, ***with single-toothed margins.***

Sporophyte   Seta yellow or orangish, 1-3 cm long, ***groups of 2-4 per plant***; capsule yellow, hanging, 2-3 mm long.

Ecology   Soil, humus, bark, tree bases, and rocks in moist forest; scattered throughout at low to subalpine elevations..

Notes: Species of *Plagiomnium* and *Rhizomnium* were formerly all in the genus *Mnium*. Three "segregate genera" are now recognized: *Rhizomnium* for species with entire (untoothed) leaves, *Plagiomnium* for species with singly-toothed leaf margins, and *Mnium* for species with doubly-toothed leaf margins. • Both *P. drummondii* and *P. cuspidatum* (1 seta per plant) are distinguished by leaves that are singly toothed along the upper half of their margins.

COMMON LEAFY MOSS   *Plagiomnium medium*

General   Light yellow-green, ***loose tufts***, 2-7 cm high, ***stems erect to semi-erect and "fuzzy" (with numerous rhizoids).***

Leaves   5-10 mm long, ***when dry contorted and crisped*** (this separates it from *P. drummondii*), largest near end of stem, margins ***singly toothed nearly to base.***

Sporophyte   Setae pale yellow to reddish (when older), 2-5 mm long, 1-3 per plant; capsules brown, hanging, 3-4 mm long.

Ecology   Wet rock, humus, and tree bases in wet forest, streambanks, seeps, springs in clean water; throughout the region in appropriate habitats, from low to subalpine elevations.

Notes: All species of *Plagiomnium* and *Rhizomnium* in this area are commonly referred to as "leafy mosses."

LARGE LEAFY MOSS — *Rhizomnium glabrescens*

General Green to dark green, unbranched upright stems to 3 cm, leafy, *stems reddish-brown, covered with rhizoids at the bottom; in tufts*.

Leaves 3-6 mm long, oval to elliptic with round end, twice as wide as long; *margins entire* (no teeth on margins); widely spreading upper leaves often look like small green flowers; male and female plants separate (the males in a disk-shaped leaf group at the top of the stem).

Sporophyte Seta reddish brown to brown, to 4 cm tall; capsule nodding, 3-6 mm long.

Ecology On the ground, on decaying wood, or on rocks in moist coniferous forests, along streambanks; scattered, locally abundant throughout the southern half of the region in areas of moist climate.

Notes: The similar *Rhizomnium nudum* has leaves as wide as long, and is most abundant in medium to high elevation forests with heavy snowpacks.

COASTAL LEAFY MOSS — *Plagiomnium insigne*

General Green to dark green, unbranched erect plants, leafy, to 6 cm or more tall, *leaves bunched at the top into a "rosette"*, forming tufts or in small colonies; sterile plants along the ground to 12 cm long.

Leaves To 1 cm x 4 mm, concave, leaf bases run down the stem, when torn off the 2 strips (each side of the midrib) come off with the leaf; *margins singly toothed nearly to base*; leaves contorted and crinkled up when dry.

Sporophyte Seta reddish brown to yellow, to 4 cm tall, in clumps from the top of female plants; capsules yellow, nodding, 3-4 mm long.

Ecology Humus, tree bases, and rotting wood in shaded, moist to wet forested areas; scattered in wet climates in the southern half of our region.

Notes: The sexes in this species are on separate plants.

WOODSY RAGGED MOSS — *Brachythecium hylotapetum*

General *Gleaming green, large, relatively few, low, arching branches; often forming large clumps or loose mats,* which can cover large areas.

Leaves Smooth, the middle gently bulging upwards, pointed, with twisted tips; in two rows.

Sporophyte Seta rough with little bumps; capsule brown, curved, horizontal to drooping.

Ecology Humus, needles, decaying wood in moist to wet, coniferous or mixed forest; at low to subalpine elevations throughout all but the northeastern part of our region.

Notes: There are probably 10-15 species of *Brachythecium* in our region, and they can be difficult to tell apart. All species are more or less yellow-green, have lance-shaped, sharply pointed, pleated leaves, and stems that tend to sprawl or creep and branch frequently but irregularly.

SHORT-LEAVED RAGGED MOSS — *Brachythecium oedipum*

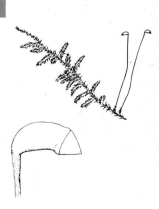

General *Pale yellow green,* stems upreaching to arched, *irregularly branched,* size variable.

Leaves Pointed, 2-2.5 mm long, oblong to lance shaped, twisted at the tip, flattened into two rows; *margins finely toothed.*

Sporophyte Seta orange to red, 1-3 cm tall; capsule brown to very dark brown, horizontal, 1-2 mm long, usually rough.

Ecology Forest floor, humus, rocks, logs, bases of trees; fairly common at low to medium elevations throughout our region.

Notes: This species is also known as *B. curtum.* The name *Brachythecium* means short capsule, in reference to the relatively short, thick capsule on the sporophyte.

GOLDEN RAGGED MOSS	*Brachythecium salebrosum*

General Medium to large moss in *loose, green to yellow-green mats*, stems creeping along the ground or upright, branched irregularly.

Leaves Pleated, long (2-3 mm), lance shaped to slightly broader.

Sporophyte Seta yellow to red, smooth, 1-3 cm tall; capsules inclined or horizontal, 2-3 mm long.

Ecology Shady ground at bases of trees, crawling over logs, leaves; common throughout the region at low to medium elevations.

Notes: B. leibergii is similar, but the leaves are folded into pleats, and the seta surface is rough, not smooth as in *B. salebrosum*. This species might also be confused with *Drepanocladus uncinatus*, which also has leaves all curved in one direction and also sometimes grows on tree trunks.

GIANT WATER MOSS	*Calliergon giganteum*

General *Yellow-green, green, or yellow-brown*, up to 20 cm long or more, in *deep, loose clumps*; *feathery branching*.

Leaves *Standing well out from stem, stem leaves egg shaped and blunt ended*, branch leaves rolled when dry.

Sporophyte Seta cinnamon in colour, 4-7 cm high; capsules curved, 2-3 mm long.

Ecology Marshes, swamps, fens, bog pools, alongside creeks; *often floating or partially submerged*; low to subalpine elevations, scattered (locally abundant) in suitable habitats throughout the region.

Notes: There are several other species of *Calliergon* (e.g., *C. sarmentosum, C. stramineum, C. cordifolium, C. trifarium*) that can be found in similar habitats in our region. • This species is one of a heterogeneous group referred to by some ecologists as the "brown mosses," which includes species of *Calliergon*, *Drepanocladus*, *Tomenthypnum nitens*, *Scorpidium scorpioides*, *Hypnum lindbergii*, and *Campylium stellatum*, and which indicates (in general contrast to *Sphagnum*) "richer" (minerotrophic or calcareous) wetland habitats. • Crum (1973) notes that *Calliergon*, meaning "pretty work, refers to good workmanship or elegance in construction or appearance."

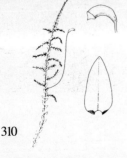

GLOW MOSS — *Aulacomnium palustre*

General Yellow-green, drying brown, 3-9 cm tall, **erect usually unbranched stems with a reddish brown, fuzzy covering.**

Sporophyte Seta red-brown, to 4 cm tall, stalk twisted when dry; **capsule** reddish brown, inclined to almost erect, to 4 mm long, curved, **strongly grooved.**

Leaves Lance shaped to ovate, sharply pointed, 3-5 mm long, twisted when dry.

Ecology **Muskeg, swamps, fens, wet forests, cold, wet disturbed sites**; common throughout the region, at low to alpine elevations.

Notes: Aulacomnium turgidum is a related species, occurring on wet to dry, rocky, often calcareous, alpine tundra, scattered throughout the mountains of our region, except perhaps in the Chilcotin; leaves are blunt rather than pointy, the gametophyte resembles upright scaly cocktail sausages (or large yellow caterpillars [Crum 1973]), and sporophytes are rare. • Mats of glow moss can cover large areas on wet sites. *The yellow-green colour is almost incandescent at times*, hence the common name. It will also grow up the base of bushy plants (e.g., *Spiraea*). Asexual reproduction is common − look for clusters of green, leafy-looking "brood" bodies on the end of short green stalks. • *Aulacomnium* means furrowed *Mnium*, in reference to the grooved capsules.

GOLDEN FUZZY FEN MOSS — *Tomenthypnum nitens*

General **Yellow-green to golden brown**, shiny when dry, 5-15 cm tall, **upright stiff patches**; simple feathery branches often curved down; **stems yellowish green to brown, covered with reddish brown felt.**

Leaves Long, tapered, furrowed, pointed and held upwards along stem.

Sporophyte Seta reddish brown, 2-5 cm long; capsule similar in colour, inclined, 2-3 mm long.

Ecology **Wet, calcium-rich sites, muskeg, swamps, fens, tundra seepage**; widespread in suitable habitats, from low to alpine elevations throughout the region.

Notes: This species commonly forms hummocks on wetland sites. The golden yellow colour and longitudinally folded (plicate) leaves with midribs are good identifying characteristics. • See notes about brown mosses under *Calliergon giganteum*. • *Tomenthypnum* means a fuzzy (or felt-covered) *Hypnum*, another genus similar in appearance; *nitens* means shining; hence, the "golden fuzzy fen moss."

311

COMMON GREEN SPHAGNUM — *Sphagnum girgensohnii*

General *Clean green* or sometimes slightly yellowish (not at all reddish) stems, upright with terminal "bud" of leaves, forming *loose carpets*, branches in bunches of 4-5.

Leaves *Stem leaves large, tongue shaped with a fringed tip*; branch leaves crowded, narrow, ovate.

Sporophyte Seta absent; capsule dark brown to black.

Ecology Cedar and spruce swamps, bog forests, fens, humic drippy banks, *usually in shaded forest habitats* in our region, but in the North can form hummocks in higher elevation shrublands. Common from low to subalpine elevations throughout the region.

Notes: Sphagnum spp. are commonly called "peat mosses" and are widely used in gardening. • When dry, peat moss species can absorb large amounts of fluid. They are also thought to have natural antiseptic properties. For these reasons they have been used throughout the ages for treating wounds, personal hygiene and baby care both by Europeans and by native people throughout B.C. − see *S. capillaceum*.

SHAGGY SPHAGNUM — *Sphagnum squarrosum*

General Bright or pale green, 5-8 cm deep, branches in groups or hanging along stem, prominent terminal "buds," forming *loose carpets*, individual plants well separated.

Leaves *Branch leaves suddenly turned out at a 90 degree angle* (very distinctive character); stem leaves large, long, oblong tongue shaped, somewhat frilly at tips.

Sporophyte "Seta" (pseudopodium) brownish, 6-8 mm; capsule dark brown, to 2 mm long.

Ecology Areas subject to fluctuating water levels, swamps, bog forests, frequently along streams; another typically woodland species at low to medium elevations throughout our region on appropriate sites.

Notes: Some species of *Sphagnum* have antibiotically active properties, along with certain species of *Dicranum, Mnium, Atrichum* and *Polytrichum*. • *Squarrosum* means rough, as when the overlapping leaves have protruding tips that spread in all directions. • Another common name for this species is "shaggy peat moss."

COMMON RED SPHAGNUM *Sphagnum capillaceum*

General ***Red all over to red here and there***, sometimes pink, 5-15 cm long, branches clumped near tip and distributed in bunches of 3-5 along the stem, plant forming ***upright compact cushions with "pompom"-shaped heads.***

Leaves Stem leaves long, concave, pointed; branch leaves slender, pointed.

Sporophyte Seta short (1-2 mm); capsule dark brown, 1-2 mm long.

Ecology On hummocks, in open or shady bogs, black spruce muskeg; often the dominant species in our bogs; locally abundant at low to subalpine elevations throughout the region.

Notes: This species is also known as *S. nemoreum* and *S. rubellum* (= *S. capillaceum* var. *tenellum*). • This species was used especially by northern interior natives (e.g., Tahltan and Gitksan) because it is so abundant in their territories. It was dried and used for bedding, sanitary napkins and baby diapers. Wet *Sphagnum* has healing properties and was placed on wounds. The Carrier believed that red forms caused bad sores. • *Capillaceous* means hairlike or very slender.

POOR-FEN SPHAGNUM *Sphagnum angustifolium*

General ***Green or yellowish (stem often reddish toward tip)***, large, ***loose carpets***, tufted top has 5-way symmetry in branching, young drooping branches in pairs.

Leaves Stem leaves very small, broadly triangular; branch leaves lance shaped, flat and wavy, with tips curved outwards when dry.

Sporophyte Seta short (1-2 mm); capsule dark brown, to 2 mm long.

Ecology Hollows or depressions in open bogs, bog forests, seepage areas in upland coniferous forest; scattered from low to subalpine elevations throughout the region except in areas of drier climates.

Notes: Also known as *S. recurvum.* Many *Sphagnum* species were used for their absorptive and healing properties by native people throughout B.C.

COMMON BROWN SPHAGNUM *Sphagnum fuscum*

General **Brown, brown-green**, stem slender, brown; individually less robust than other peat mosses, **in very compact hummocks; threadlike branches interwoven inside the hummocks.**

Leaves Stem leaves tongue shaped, blunt; branch leaves lance shaped, pointed.

Sporophyte Seta short (1-2 mm); capsule chocolate brown, 1-1.5 mm long.

Ecology **Capping hummocks in older or drier, more acid portions of open bogs, black spruce muskeg, or on isolated hummocks on fens**; common (but only locally abundant) from low to medium elevations throughout our region.

Notes: Look closely at the leaves of the peat mosses (you'll need a microscope) to see why they are so absorptive. Much of the leaf is composed of larger, clear, dead cells – this distinctive characteristic allows leaves of *Sphagnum* to absorb large amounts of fluid and makes them useful in gardening, as surgical dressings, or for personal hygiene.
• *S. fuscum* could be confused with unusually dark red-brown forms of *S. capillaceum* and its var. *tenellum*.
• *Fuscum* means light brown, swarthy or dark coloured; the brown stem separates this species from most other similar species.

STREAMSIDE MOSS · *Scouleria aquatica*

General **Dark to black-green,** to 20 cm long, **floppy;** stems with rhizoids which are also on leaf bases, reddish brown; **forms black mats with streamers of branches just at the high water level of streams and rivers.**

Leaves 3-5 mm long, large teeth, blunt tips.

Sporophyte Seta very short (1.5-2 mm); capsule dark brown to black, 1-2 mm long, upright, nearly spherical with a fringe of exposed red teeth when dry.

Ecology Stream rocks, submerged or emergent, **a characteristic moss of the splash zone of fast-flowing mountain streams and the littoral zone of large rivers.** Low to medium elevations throughout the region except in much of the North, particularly abundant and noticeable along major rivers of the Skeena and Fraser systems.

Notes: As the water level goes down, this species shows up. • This is the only large moss commonly found growing in this habitat.

FAIRY PARASOLS · *Splachnum luteum*

General Intense **translucent green** plants **in little patches on moose dung (usually), with yellow umbrellas or skirts** above them.

Leaves Lightly crisped, pointed, large teeth on the margin.

Sporophyte Seta red, 2-15 cm long; capsule brownish, urn shaped, 1-1.5 mm long, with a broader "parasol," 4.5-11 mm wide, bright yellow.

Ecology **Common on moose dung in soggy spots**, throughout the northern half of the region where moose or caribou live.

Notes: Splachnum rubrum is a similar, but less common, moss with red hypophyses which grows mainly on regurgitated fur and bones from owls and other carnivores. • The hypophysis, or "umbrella," is an interesting organ that has been compared to the leaf of a higher plant (it has stomata and spongy tissue, generally absent from mosses). The species is adapted for spore dispersal by insects; the hypophysis emitting (through its stomata) an odour attractive to many insects, which fly from patch to patch spreading spores onto suitable animal droppings. The seta in this species continues growing even after the spores mature. • The parasol sporophytes closely resemble small mushrooms with long stalks. • The spores of both species are dispersed by flies. Vitt *et al.* (1988), suggest that the parasols might be "airports" for the flies to land on. The flies pick up the spores and then fly to dung where they lay their eggs and at the same time deposit the moss spores.

315

COMMON LEAFY LIVERWORT — *Barbilophozia lycopodioides*

General Pale to yellow green, forming small to large mats; branches 3-8 cm long, **about 1/2 cm wide, unbranched, crawling.**

Leaves **Overlapped like shingles**, attached at a sharp angle across the stem, wavy and crisped, **usually 4 lobed**, wider than long with pointed tips, with 4-7 long cilia at base; underleaves large (to 9 mm long), cleft into 2 lobes.

Sporophyte Rarely seen (even for a liverwort!), reproduction largely asexual.

Ecology Creeping over humus, needles, wood, and rocks, in moist coniferous forests; also in subalpine parkland and shrubby thickets; common at low to subalpine elevations throughout the region except in the Chilcotin.

Notes: Similar to *B. floerkei* (see notes under that species); more similar to *B. hatcheri*; these other two species both have leaves that are more commonly 3 lobed. *B. floerkei* is virtually restricted to high elevations, whereas *B. hatcheri* often grows on rocks, and its leaves are about 1/2 the size of those of the common leafy liverwort.

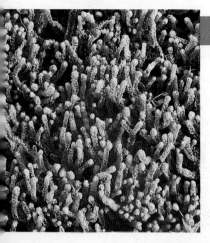

MOUNTAIN LEAFY LIVERWORT — *Barbilophozia floerkei*

General Yellow to dark green, 2-10 cm, **loose to compact tufts, stiff erect stems, few branches.**

Leaves Close together, stiff, spreading, crisped, square-rounded shape, 1-1.5 times as long as wide, **3 lobed**, incurved wavy margins, bottom leaf margin with 1-3 short cilia; underleaves large, cleft into two lobes.

Sporophyte Capsule ovoid.

Ecology In shady subalpine forests of spruce and subalpine fir (also with mountain hemlock, amabilis fir, and whitebark pine), on humus, acid needles, rock slabs, with *Barbilophozia lycopodioides*; fairly common at subalpine elevations throughout the region.

Notes: Similar to *B. lycopodioides*, which has 4, more pointed lobe tips with 4-7 longer, twisted cilia, and is a larger plant generally.

NORTHERN NAUGEHYDE LIVERWORT — *Ptilidium ciliare*

General ***Red brown to copper red***, stems stiff, upright, to 0.5 cm long, ***forming mats, branches single to twice feathery***.

Leaves Unequally divided into 4-5 lobes, (Vitt *et al.* (1988) call them "***hand-shaped***"), partly wrapped around the stem, to 2 cm long by 2.5 cm wide; underleaves to 1 cm long by 1.3 cm wide, bi-lobed, with numerous cilia.

Ecology Dry sites, with lichens (esp. Cladonia), usually on rock or on a thin layer of soil over rock; scattered at subalpine and alpine elevations, throughout the region.

Notes: This species is similar to *P. pulcherrimum*, which also occurs in our region. *P. pulcherrimum* grows on logs (vs. rock or soil for *P. ciliare*), and is more firmly attached to its sustrate than *P. ciliare*.

CEDAR-SHAKE LIVERWORT — *Plagiochila porelloides*

General ***Light green to olive green***, dull shoots unbranched to sparingly branched, to 10 cm long, ***usually in mats or patches***.

Leaves ***Roundish to elliptic***, to 5 mm wide by 10 mm long (quite variable in size), ***margins*** reflexed (bent backwards) and ***usually toothed***; underleaves lacking.

Sporophyte Seta colourless, weak; capsule ellipsoid, to 2 mm long.

Ecology On rocks, soil, streambanks, forest floor and matted around tree bases, also in alpine heath and boulder fields; scattered through the region from low to high elevations.

Notes: Plagiochila is the largest genus of liverworts in the world; *P. porelloides* (often called *P. asplenioides* ssp. *porelloides*), like many northern B.C. bryophytes, occurs in similar habitats at north temperate latitudes around the world.
• The toothed leaves are unusual for a liverwort.

SHINY LIVERWORT — *Pellia neesiana*

General **Thalloid** (i.e., with no differentiation into stems and leaves – in this case, **somewhat straplike and dichotomously branching**), shiny dark green and usually with a red tinge most intense around the midrib, translucent near the edge, no pores visible, less than 1 cm wide, wavy edges.

Sporophyte Spherical capsules on short, transparent stalks.

Ecology Wet banks, seepy ground, wet forest glades, clearings; scattered throughout from low to subalpine elevations, except in drier climates of the southern parts of the region.

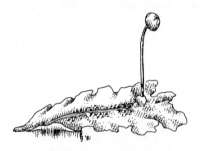

GREEN-TONGUE LIVERWORT — *Marchantia polymorpha*

General **Green to yellow-green, strap-shaped thallus**, 2-10 cm long, 1-2 cm wide, flattened on the surface, **edges of the thallus with wavy lobes**; top surface often with a dark line down the centre, pores visible on the thallus; lower surface brown or purplish brown with numerous yellowish rhizoids.

Sporophyte Produced from under the fingerlike female "umbrella;" plants are unisexual, **male and female receptacles are umbrella-like**, the female receptacle clearly divided into a dozen or more filaments, the male merely lobed.

Ecology Stream sides, wet soil, roadside ditches, rock walls, often on burned ground; scattered in appropriate habitats throughout the region from low to subalpine elevations.

Notes: The umbrella-like male and female structures are distinctive for this charming little plant. You may remember *M. polymorpha* from high school biology class, used as an example of a liverwort.

318

Lichens

British Columbia is home to more than a thousand different kinds of lichens. Of these, however, only a few hundred are widespread and conspicuous. In northern B.C. especially, most of the lichen cover is accounted for by relatively few species – a majority of which are briefly described in the following pages.

A lichen is just a fungus that has discovered agriculture. Instead of invading or scavenging for a living like other fungi – moulds, mildews, mushrooms – the lichen fungus cultivates algae within itself. Algae are photosynthesizers, and so supply the fungus with carbohydrates, vitamins and proteins. In return the fungus provides the alga with protection from the elements.

Lichens come in many different shapes, but they never form leafy stems, as mosses do. The following account recognizes six growth forms: crust, scale, leaf, club, shrub and hair.

Lichens reproduce in several ways. Sometimes the fungal partner produces saucer-like fruiting bodies (**apothecia**). Sometimes the inner "stuffing" (**medulla**) of the lichen may become exposed here and there at the surface as clusters of tiny powdery balls (**soredia**). Or sometimes, again, the upper surface may bear tiny wartlike outgrowths (**isidia**). When soredia and isidia are carried to new localities, as by birds, they may grow into new lichens.

Lichens have traditionally been used as a source of food and dye by the Inuit and, to a lesser extent, by other natives across Canada. Some lichens are thought to possess antibiotic properties, and in medieval times especially, were used in Europe for medicinal purposes. Many species are sensitive to air pollution to differing degrees and have been employed successfully to monitor levels of air pollution, especially sulphur dioxide. Extracts are used as fixatives in perfumes and soaps.

Lichen Life Forms

CRUST: Intimately attached throughout; lacking a lower surface.

SCALE: Tiny shell-like lobes with a cottony lower surface; forming overlapping colonies.

LEAF: Small to large leaflike or straplike lobes, usually with holdfasts and a hard (non-cottony) lower surface.

CLUB: Unbranched or sparsely branched cylindrical stems, usually upright.

SHRUB: Much-branched cylindrical stems, usually tufted.

HAIR: Intricately branched filaments, tufted to pendent.

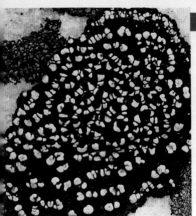

GREEN MAP LICHEN *Rhizocarpon geographicum*

General A ***mosaic crust*** consisting of tiny ***yellowish green "tiles"*** (areoles) set against a ***black background***.

Ecology Forming ***roughly circular colonies over acid rock*** in open sites; more frequent above tree line. Common throughout the region at high elevations.

Notes: In the far north, *R. geographicum* may grow no more than a centimetre in a century; however, individual colonies may persist for thousands of years. It is one of the species commonly used for dating rock surfaces (for example, when studying the movement of glaciers in the Canadian Arctic), a technique known as lichenometry.

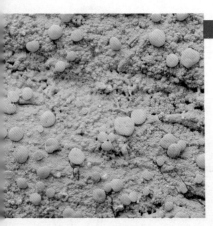

SPRAYPAINT LICHEN *Icmadophila ericetorum*

General A ***continuous crust*** lichen; upper surface ***pale bluish green***, somewhat roughened, typically bearing small ***flesh pink fruiting bodies***.

Ecology Over decaying moss and rotting wood, usually in cool, humid, coniferous forest types, and in bogs. Scattered at low to subalpine elevations throughout our region.

Notes: The spraypaint lichen somewhat resembles a mold. It provides an unusual instance of lichen parasitism, the fungal partner deriving part of its nutritional requirements from the mosses over which this lichen typically grows.

• *Ericetorum* means of the heaths, reflecting the occurrence of this species in heaths and other acidic habitats.

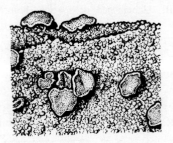

SHINGLE LICHEN — *Hypocenomyce scalaris*

General A ***semi-upright scale*** lichen; lobes **tiny**, to about 0.8-1 mm long, ***shell-like***, loosely overlapping; upper surface pale greyish brown; lower surface and lobe ***margins bearing soredia***.

Ecology Forming loose, shingle-like colonies over trees and charred stumps in open sites in forested zones. Scattered in the southeastern part of the region.

Notes: Shingle lichen is unusually selective in its choice of habitats, *colonizing only soft bark and charred or weather-worn wood.* • *Scalaris* means scale-like or overlapping, in reference to the morphology of the plant.

CLADONIA SCALES — *Cladonia cariosa*

General An ***upright scale*** lichen; lobes **small**, to about 2 or 3 mm long; upper surface pale greyish green to brownish green; lower surface white cottony (hand lens), ***without soredia*** or holdfasts.

Ecology Forming loosely overlapping colonies over humus and sandy mineral soil in open forest and clearings at all elevations. Scattered throughout the region, often best developed on disturbed sites.

Notes: Like other scale lichens of the genus *Cladonia*, *C. cariosa* may give rise to pale white to green, club-like "stems" which, in this case, are vertically "ribbed", and bear dark brown fruiting bodies at their tips. The scales ("squamules") of other *Cladonia* species may be similar, but are usually less consistently upright.

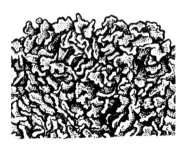

321

BLISTERED ROCKTRIPE   *Umbilicaria hyperborea*

General A *roundish leaf* lichen, 1-4 (5) cm across, attached centrally by a **single holdfast**; upper surface dark brown, *"blistered"*, usually bearing *fruiting bodies*, these concentrically *ridged* (hand lens); lower surface *dark brownish*.

Ecology *On acid boulders in open situations* at all elevations. Common throughout our region, but most abundant above timberline. Probably our most common *Umbilicaria*.

Notes: U. polyphylla is similar in habit and habitat, but is more lobed, has an even upper surface, lacks fruiting bodies, and is sooty black below. The Umbilicarias, or "rocktripes," were used by Sir John Franklin and other early northern explorers as an emergency food. They are also important as a source of scarlet dyes (hard to believe, but true!). The scarlet dyes known in Scotland as *corkir* were used for dying tartan cloth. • Also eaten by the Inuit. Best soaked in soda water first to remove acids which can cause severe intestinal irritation.

LUNGWORT   *Lobaria pulmonaria*

General A *loosely attached* leaf lichen; lobes *broad*, to 2 or 3 cm wide; upper surface *pale brownish green (bright green when moist), broadly indented (pocked)*, bearing *soredia or isidia* along the intervening ridges and along the lobe margins; lower surface pale, mottled white and brown, partly thinly covered in fine hairs (hand lens).

Ecology On trees in humid forest, both coniferous and deciduous. Scattered at lower elevations throughout, most common in areas of moister climates south of about 58°.

Notes: L. linita is similar, but lacks soredia and isidia and typically grows over the ground, especially at higher elevations. • Used by early physicians in the treatment of pneumonia and other lung diseases – owing primarily to its resemblance to that part of the body! • The Gitksan word for this plant means frog's blanket because it resembles the skin of a frog or toad; they may have used it medicinally. • The chapped skin of babies and the feet of adults in Scandinavia were bathed in decoctions of this species. • Research in the U.S. Pacific Northwest has suggested that this nitrogen–fixing lichen may be important in the nutrition of old-growth forests.

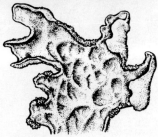

FRECKLED LICHEN — *Peltigera aphthosa*

General A *loosely appressed leaf* lichen; lobes *broad*, 2-5 cm wide, *pale grey-green* (dry) *to bright green* (moist) above, bearing scattered *"warts"*, lower surface without veins or with only broad, *inconspicuous veins*, cottony, blackening abruptly inward of lobe margins.

Ecology On moss, humus, rocks, and decaying logs, typically in or near forest or thickets. Common at all but the highest elevations throughout the region.

Notes: The freckled lichen is easily confused with *P. leucophlebia*, whose lower surface typically bears well-developed veins and darkens gradually inward. The "warts" in these species are actually tiny colonies of blue-green algae, which supply the lichen fungus and its green-algal partner with nitrogen. • The chapped skin of babies and the feet of adults in Scandinavia were bathed in decoctions of this species.

DOG LICHEN — *Peltigera canina*

General A *loosely appressed leaf* lichen; lobes *broad*, to 1.5-2 cm wide; upper surface pale brown or grey, thinly covered in *fine hairs* (especially toward margins: hand lens); lower surface white, *cottony*, bearing narrow, *brownish veins* and dark, *flaring holdfasts* (rhizines).

Ecology On mineral soil and humus, moss, or decaying wood in open places at all elevations. Common throughout.

Notes: Peltigera canina is often difficult to distinguish from other related "dog lichens". However, *P. canina* is unique in combining broad lobes with distinctly flaring holdfasts. • Dog lichen was used in former times in the treatment of rabies — because the fruiting bodies were thought to resemble dogs' teeth.

Peltigera membranacea

TOAD PELT — *Peltigera scabrosa*

General A *loosely appressed leaf* lichen; lobes **broad**, to 2-4 cm wide; upper surface pale greyish brown, *lacking hairs*, but minutely **roughened** (hand lens); lower surface bearing broad **brownish** veins and tufted holdfasts (rhizines), otherwise pale and cottony; fruiting bodies, when present, vertically oriented along lobe margins.

Ecology Over soil and moss in open sites at all elevations. Scattered throughout, more common in the North.

Notes: The *Peltigeras* are among the most conspicuous of ground-dwelling lichens; nowhere are they more varied than in British Columbia, home to at least 27 species. • *Peltigera malacea* is similarly widespread, but grows in coniferous forest and subalpine thickets as well as in openings. *P. malacea* has thick lobes with fine hairs on the upper surface towards the lobe margins; an upper surface which is dull grey when dry, dark blue-green when moist; and a lower surface that is essentially veinless and thickly cottony.

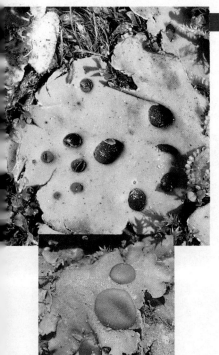

CHOCOLATE CHIP LICHEN — *Solorina crocea*

General A rather *closely appressed* leaf lichen; lobes **broad** relative to length, to 1 - 2 cm wide, upper surface brownish or greenish; *lower surface* veined, **bright orange**, cottony (hand lens); fruiting bodies common, chocolate brown, lying flat on upper surface.

Ecology Over soil in snowbed areas, streambanks, tundra hummocks, especially above tree line. Scattered, locally common throughout our region (except apparently absent in the Peace River district).

Notes: Unlike most lichens, *S. crocea* has two algal partners: one is a green alga, lying in a layer just beneath the upper surface; the other is a blue-green alga, layered just below the green alga. • *Crocea* means saffron or yellow coloured.

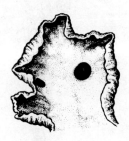

GREEN KIDNEY LICHEN *Nephroma arcticum*

General A *loosely appressed leaf* lichen; lobes very *broad*, to 7 or 8 cm wide; upper surface *yellowish to lime green*, lower surface pale, except blackening toward centre, dull, thinly covered in *fine hairs; fruiting bodies* common, to 2 cm across, positioned *near the lobe margins on the lower surface*.

Ecology Over mossy rock outcrops or on moss and decaying wood in open, usually coniferous, forest and thickets. Scattered at medium to high elevations in the southern half of the region (where it is most frequent in areas of heavy snowfall, particularly subalpine forest), common and abundant in the North, but absent from the extreme northeast.

Notes: Bears the largest fruiting bodies of any lichen, occasionally to 5 cm across.

RAGBAG LICHEN *Platismatia glauca*

General A *loosely attached leaf* lichen; lobes broad, to 1 - 2 cm wide, *pale bluish green to whitish grey* above, often frilly and bearing soredia or isidia, especially along the margins; lower surface white to black, *shiny*, typically *lacking holdfasts* (rhizines); fruiting bodies very rare, positioned along upper margin.

Ecology Mostly on conifer branches and trunks in more humid forest types. Common at low to medium elevations throughout most of the region, uncommon in the far North.

Notes: One of the most variable of lichen species. Some forms have a very tattered appearance.

MOONSHINE CETRARIA   *Cetraria pinastri*

General   A *loosely attached* leaf lichen; lobes small but rather broad relative to length, to 3-4 mm wide, pale *greenish yellow* above, bearing abundant *yellow soredia* along margins.

Ecology   Over the bases and lower branches of conifers in all forested zones and on shrubs such as scrub birch, willows, alders, soopolallie. Common throughout at low to subalpine elevations.

Notes: Most abundant where protected from the winter cold by a layer of snow. • *Cetraria canadensis* could be confused with *C. pinastri*, but lacks soredia and is found most commonly in open lodgepole pine forests in the southern half of the region. • There is some evidence that many of the yellow *Cetraria* species were a source of yellow dyes for B.C. natives.

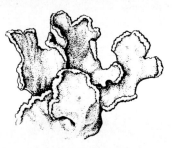

CURLED CETRARIA   *Cetraria cucullata*

General   An *upright leaf* lichen; lobes narrow, to 1-3 mm wide, channelled, to 6 or 7 cm tall, pale *yellowish green* above and below, except often becoming *reddish at base; lobe margins strongly inrolled* and somewhat frilly.

Ecology   Forming colonies over ground in open sites, especially *near or above tree line*. Common at high elevations throughout our region; abundant in windswept, grassy alpine tundra.

Notes: *C. nivalis* is similar, but has broader, more flattened and wrinkled lobes which discolour to yellow-orange, not red, towards the base. The reddish tinge at the base results from the breakdown of protolichesterinic acid – one of nearly 500 chemical substances produced by lichens. These two species have similar habitats and distributions, and can often be found growing together. • *Cetraria tilesii* is a lemon yellow, narrow-lobed species of calcium-rich soil and gravel in alpine tundra, especially in the northern half of the region, and south along the Rockies.

326

General An ***upright leaf*** lichen; lobes narrow to fairly broad, to 7 or 8 cm tall, ***brownish***; lobe margins often somewhat inrolled, bearing tiny ***"spines"***; lower surface ***sparsely flecked*** by tiny white patches (pseudocyphellae; use hand lens to see).

Ecology Over soil or moss in open sites or in open coniferous forest. Common at all elevations, especially in alpine tundra; throughout the region, except in the southeast.

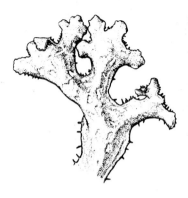

Notes: In *C. ericetorum*, the white patches are restricted to near the lobe margins. • *C. islandica* is among the most highly rated of edible lichens and was widely eaten by the Inuit. It was often dried, powdered and then reconstituted by boiling with water to form a jelly-like gruel. It can also be added to soups and stews. • Traditionally used in Northern Europe in the preparation of bread, porridge, salads and jelly, and sold in Scandinavia as a remedy for coughs and colds. In Switzerland, extracts of *C. islandica* are incorporated into throat pastilles, and herbal sweets and teas. In 17th and 18th century England, it was boiled in milk and drunk for coughs and tuberculosis, and it was a popular laxative in Central Europe.

General An ***unattached leaf*** lichen; lobes narrow, to 2 - 6 mm wide, usually forking at regular intervals, ***upper surface medium brown; lower surface whitish***, except bearing brown patches.

Ecology ***Forming balls over the ground*** (except when caught among shrubbery) at tree line or above. Scattered in windswept alpine tundra in the north.

Notes: Formerly *Cetraria richarsonii*. • Remarkable among plants, *M. richardsonii* grows entirely free of the ground, and disperses by being blown across the alpine tundra by the wind. • *Masonhalea* is named after Mason Hale, renowned lichenologist and author of *How To Know the Lichens*.

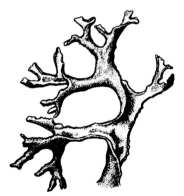

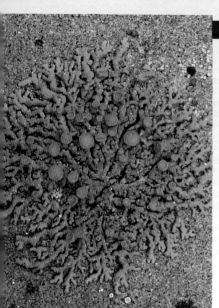

ROCK ORANGE LICHEN   *Xanthoria elegans*

General An *appressed leaf* lichen; lobes very narrow, about 0.5 mm wide; upper surface **bright orange**, generally bearing **many orange fruiting bodies**.

Ecology On limestone and other calcium-rich rocks; also over acid rocks that have been enriched by bird droppings. Scattered throughout at all elevations.

Notes: Another orange species, *X. candelaria*, will often be found over trees: its lobes are upright and bear soredia. • Orange splashes of *Xanthoria* over cliffs have often aided biologists in locating raptor perches and eyries, as well as seabird nesting sites. • Researchers

have determined that patches of this lichen on the graves of members of Sir John Franklin's expedition have only grown to a diameter of 4.4 cm in the century available for growth.

GREEN STARBURST LICHEN   *Parmeliopsis ambigua*

General A *closely appressed leaf* lichen; lobes very narrow, 0.5 - 0.8 mm wide; upper surface pale **yellowish green**, bearing numerous **head-shaped soredia clusters**; lower surface blackening inward of lobe margins, with sparse holdfasts (rhizines; use hand lens to see).

Ecology Forming rosettes over acid-barked trees and shrubs; also over decorticated (barkless) logs. Common throughout the region from low to subalpine elevations.

Notes: P. hyperopta is identical in all respects except in being greyish, not green. *P. ambigua* and *P. hyperopta* are sometimes considered to be chemical forms of the same species, and often grow together. • *Parmeliopsis* means resembling the lichen genus *Parmelia* but *ambigua* means doubtful or uncertain relationship − i.e., a mixed-up lichen! Look for these species especially at the base of conifers.

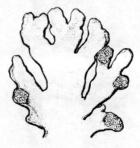

HOARY ROSETTE LICHEN — *Physcia aipolia*

General A ***closely appressed leaf*** lichen; lobes narrow, to 1 - 2 mm wide; upper surface ***pale greyish***, with small white spots, bearing ***numerous fruiting bodies***, these usually with a ***frosted*** appearance; lower surface tan, with numerous pale holdfasts (rhizines).

Ecology Forming rosettes on bark of deciduous trees and shrubs, especially aspen, birch, willow, and alder. Widespread at low to medium elevations throughout our region.

Notes: P. *phaea* is similar, but colonizes acid rock in open sites. • The frosted appearance of the fruiting bodies results from a concentration of calcium oxalate crystals, which in turn derive from the calcium-rich surfaces colonized by this species.

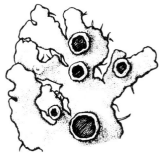
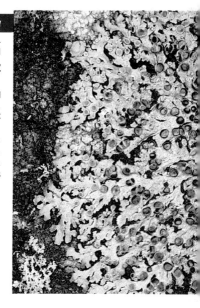

WAXPAPER LICHEN — *Parmelia sulcata*

General An ***appressed leaf*** lichen; lobes narrow, 1 - 3 mm wide; upper surface ***pale greyish***, bearing ***soredia in long narrow cracks***; lower surface black and with numerous black holdfasts.

Ecology On coniferous and deciduous trees and sometimes boulders in forest and openings. Common and widespread from low to subalpine elevations throughout our region.

Notes: P. *saxatilis* is similar, but bears isidia, not soredia, over its upper surface, and usually grows on rock. • Long used by north Europeans and Canadian Inuit as a natural dyestuff, waxpaper lichen yields a variety of hues, from yellowish-brown to dark or even rusty brown. Brown dyes from *Parmelia* were called *crottle* by the Scots. • This species is commonly used by rufous hummingbirds to decorate and camouflage the outside of the nest.

329

LICHENS

HOODED TUBE LICHEN   *Hypogymnia physodes*

General An **appressed leaf** lichen; lobes narrow, 1-2 mm wide, **hollow, bearing soredia on the insides of burst lobe tips**; upper surface pale greyish green; lower surface black, without holdfasts (rhizines).

Ecology On nearly all available surfaces, including trees, moss, boulders and soil. Common and widespread, from low to subalpine elevations.

Notes: H. austerodes is similar, but is usually brownish and bears soredia over the upper surface. • Among the most pollution-tolerant of the macrolichens, *H. physodes* is a familiar species of city parks and boulevards. • *Physodes* means inflated-looking or puffed out.

FORKING TUBE LICHEN   *Hypogymnia imshaugii*

General A **semi-upright leaf** lichen; lobes narrow, 1-2 mm wide, regularly forking, **hollow, without soredia**; upper surface pale greyish; lower surface black, lacking holdfasts.

Ecology On conifers in open forest, most common in areas of moister climate in the southern half of our region.

Notes: One of a small number of lichens restricted to western North America: more than half of B.C.'s lichen species occur in appropriate habitats throughout the northern world.

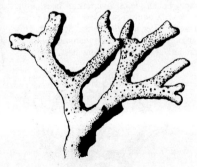

FEW-FINGER LICHEN   *Dactylina arctica*

General An *upright club* lichen, to 1.5-4 cm tall, *pale yellowish green or yellow-brown*, hollow, typically unbranched, *fingerlike*, usually blunt tipped.

Ecology Forming colonies on the ground in alpine tundra, among mosses, dwarf shrubs, or other lichens; often sheltered by rocks or hummocks. Common and widespread in the North (north of 57°), scattered on the highest mountains in the southern half of the region.

Notes: Most so-called arctic or alpine lichens also sometimes occur in the forested zones; *D. arctica*, however, seems to be entirely restricted to the land above the trees. • *Dactylina* is from *dactyl* meaning fingerlike in reference to the appearance of this species.

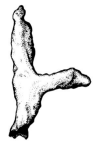

ROCK WORM LICHEN   *Thamnolia vermicularis*

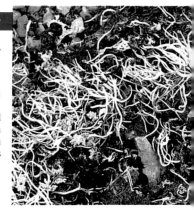

General An upright or *prostrate club* lichen, to 3-6 cm long, *creamy white*, hollow, unbranched or sparsely branched, *wormlike*, pointed tipped.

Ecology Occurring singly or in scattered colonies in wind-blown alpine tundra, on mineral or humus soil, gravel, rock, and among other lichens. Scattered above timberline throughout the region.

Notes: Although *T. vermicularis* lacks fruiting bodies, and has no obvious dispersal mechanisms, it occurs in appropriate habitats from Baffin Island to Antarctica, on every continent except Africa. • *Vermicularis* means wormlike, describing the general appearance of this lichen.

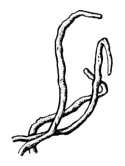

PIONEER CLADONIA — *Cladonia cornuta*

General An ***upright club*** lichen, to ***3-5 cm tall***, pale greyish green, hollow, generally unbranched, tapered and pointed tipped, ***covered in soredia*** (except near the base; use a hand lens).

Ecology Forming colonies over humus and among mosses in conifer forests and forest openings, clearings. Common from valley bottoms to subalpine parkland, throughout the region.

Notes: C. bacillaris is similar, but smaller (1-2 cm tall). • Pioneer cladonia is an early invader after fire, becoming scarce in climax forest types.

ORANGE-FOOT LICHEN — *Cladonia ecmocyna*

General An ***upright club lichen***, to 3-6 cm tall, pale greyish green, except becoming ***orange at base, hollow, sparsely branched, without soredia***, either tapering to points or terminating above in ***narrow cups***, these sometimes ringed with brown fruiting bodies.

Ecology Forming extensive colonies over the ground in forest and openings on humus, decaying wood, and moss. Common and often abundant from low to subalpine elevations throughout, more common in regions of prolonged snows, less so in the drier southern parts of the region.

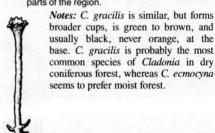

Notes: C. gracilis is similar, but forms broader cups, is green to brown, and usually black, never orange, at the base. *C. gracilis* is probably the most common species of *Cladonia* in dry coniferous forest, whereas *C. ecmocyna* seems to prefer moist forest.

PIXIE CUP LICHEN — *Cladonia pyxidata*

General An ***upright club*** lichen, 1-1.5 cm tall, greyish green, hollow, without soredia, typically unbranched, arising from basal colonies of scale lichens, and terminating in ***flaring cups***, these covered in ***"warts"*** (areoles) and often ringed with ***brown*** fruiting bodies.

Ecology On acid mineral soil and humus, in open forest, scrub, openings, and clearings. Common from low to high elevations throughout the region.

Notes: C. chlorophaea is a soredia-bearing counterpart of *C. pyxidata*. Both are often called "pixie cup lichens," owing to their resemblance to tiny goblets.

Cladonia chlorophaea

RED PIXIE CUP — *Cladonia borealis*

General An ***upright club*** lichen, 1-1.5 cm tall, pale yellowish green, hollow, without soredia, unbranched, arising from basal colonies of scale lichens, and terminating in ***flaring cups***, these covered in ***"warts"*** (areoles) and often ringed with ***red*** fruiting bodies.

Ecology Forming colonies over acid soil and decaying conifer logs. Common from medium to high elevations throughout the region, but most abundant in the North.

Notes: C. borealis is listed in earlier books as *Cladonia coccifera*. *C. pleurota* is the soredia-bearing counterpart of *C. borealis*. • Roughly 70 species of *Cladonia* occur in B.C. Of these, about a dozen produce red fruits; the rest are brown-fruited. • *C. bellidiflora* (shown in the photograph here) also has red fruiting bodies and lacks soredia, but has narrow cups (if at all) and abundant scales on its stalks. It is more common toward the Coast Mountains, and is often called "British soldiers" because of the red fruiting bodies.

Cladonia bellidiflora

333

GREY REINDEER LICHEN   *Cladina rangiferina*

General An ***upright shrub*** lichen, to 5-8 (10) cm tall, **greyish white**, intricately branching from a main stem, the branches hollow and with a dull, **feltlike surface** (use a hand lens); many of the terminal branchlets pointing in one direction (swept to one side).

Ecology Forming extensive carpets over the ground in open coniferous forest (commonly on sandy soils) and in open sites at all elevations, from lowland bogs on *Sphagnum* to alpine tundra. Common and widespread throughout the region.

Notes: In the much more compact *C. stellaris*, the terminal branchlets are divergently branched and a main stem is often lacking; the colour, moreover, tends to pale yellowish green. *C. stellaris* is gathered in some parts of its range for use in wreaths, floral decorations and architects' models; in Fennoscandia it forms the basis of a million−dollar export industry. • Grey reindeer lichen is sometimes prepared and eaten by the Inuit in the same manner as Icelandmoss. Species of *Cladina* and *Cetraria* constitute a large portion of the winter diet of the caribou. The stomach contents of a freshly killed caribou (partly digested reindeer lichens) are considered a great delicacy and are eaten immediately without cooking. They are said to taste like fresh lettuce salad; we have no doubt this is true.

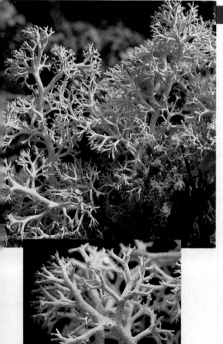

GREEN REINDEER LICHEN   *Cladina mitis*

General An ***upright shrub*** lichen, to 4-7 (10) cm tall, **pale yellowish green**, intricately branching from a main stem, the branches **hollow** and with a dull, **feltlike surface** (hand lens); many of the terminal branchlets pointing in one direction.

Ecology Forming mats over the ground in open coniferous forest and in open sites at all elevations. Common and widespread throughout the region.

Notes: The similar *Cladonia uncialis* differs in having divergent branchlets and a hard outer surface, not at all feltlike. • The *Cladinas* are an important ground cover of northern, boreal and subarctic woodlands throughout the world; as such they are a preferred winter food of reindeer and caribou.

LICHENS

COMMON CORAL LICHEN *Stereocaulon paschale*

General An **upright shrub** lichen, to 3-5 cm tall, pale greyish white, much branched, the **branches solid** and bearing a dense, **coral-like "foliage"** (phyllocladia).

Ecology Forming colonies over open ground at all forested elevations. Common throughout our region; often forming dense colonies on gravelly river terraces and lava flows.

Notes: Easily mistaken for *S. tomentosum*, which has a thick "woollen" covering over its branches (use a hand lens). All *Stereocaulon* species bear secondary algal colonies among the branches: in *S. paschale* these take the form of tiny black tufts, whereas in *S. tomentosum* they are visible as greyish lumps. • The common coral lichen is also grazed by caribou.

SPINY HEATH LICHEN *Coelocaulon aculeatum*

General An **upright shrub** lichen, to 2 - 3 (5) cm tall, dark **brown**, much branched, the branches **solid, shiny**, stiff, and **pointed tipped**.

Ecology Scattered or forming mats on open, generally sandy ground in exposed sites at all elevations but most frequently at high elevations. Common throughout.

Notes: This species is also known as *Cornicularia aculeata*. • *C. aculeatum* is an asexual species, rarely forming fruiting bodies. Throughout most of its range it probably depends for its dispersal on passing animals, to whose fur and feathers its spiny branches would tend to cling; in more exposed sites, however, it is dispersed at least in part by the wind. • *Bryocaulon* (= *Cornicularia*) *divergens* is similar but has longer, reddish brown branches. It grows in windswept gravelly or rocky tundra.

335

SPRUCE-MOSS — *Evernia mesomorpha*

General A semi-erect or pendent **shrub** lichen, to 7 or 8 cm long, pale **yellowish green**, wrinkled, pliable, much branched, the branches somewhat angular and bearing coarse **soredia** (hand lens).

Ecology On conifers in open forest, particularly near bogs in the muskeg of the Fort Nelson Lowland. Scattered from low to medium elevations in the northeastern part of our region.

Notes: E. prunastri is closely related, but has flattened branches with a whitish lower surface. It is common in moist coniferous forests (often on the dead lower branches of spruce and subalpine fir) mainly west of the Rockies. • Spruce-moss has been used since the 16th century in the manufacture of perfumes. Extracts of this lichen act as fixatives so that the perfumes do not evaporate too quickly but last for several hours.

WOLF LICHEN° — *Letharia vulpina*

General An upright or somewhat pendent **shrub** lichen, to 4-6 cm long, bright **sulphur yellow** (chartreuse), much branched, the branches angular, pitted, and bearing abundant **soredia and isidia** (use a hand lens).

Ecology Forming tufts on conifers in exposed sites at all forested elevations. Common but scattered in areas of drier climates in the southern half of our region (south of 57°).

Notes: Wolf lichen contains a poisonous chemical, vulpinic acid. This lichen was formerly mixed with ground glass and sprinkled over wolf bait or mixed with animal fat and nails in northern Europe – apparently to good effect! • An important natural source of brilliant yellow dye for B.C. interior natives, the wolf lichen was used to colour baskets, furs, feathers, porcupine quills and wood, and more recently for dying cloth. This interior species was traded to coastal groups.

BRITTLE HORSEHAIR LICHEN   *Bryoria lanestris*

General A pendent *hair* lichen, to 10 - 15 cm long, **dark brown**, intricately branched, the branches uneven in width (use a hand lens), brittle, and bearing tiny whitish flecks of **soredia**.

Ecology Draping the branches of conifers in forests at all elevations. Common throughout our region.

Notes: Easily confused with *B. fuscescens* and *B. glabra*, which have coarser, more even and less brittle branches, and are more common in drier climates. *B. glabra* has shiny, olive-green to black, even branches with soredia-filled cracks.These widespread lichens disperse entirely by asexual means, including the transport of branch fragments and soredia by birds and other animals. They are not known to produce fruiting bodies. • Closely related species of *Bryoria* (formerly *Alectoria)* were widely used by native groups in B.C. as food, as well as in the making of clothing, footwear, and face masks. Species varied in the amount of vulpinic acid they contained and all had to be cooked before eating. (See Turner, 1978 for methods of preparation.)

VELCRO LICHEN   *Pseudephebe pubescens*

General A small, **prostrate hair** lichen, to 2 cm high, **blackish**, richly branching, and **resembling velcro**.

Ecology Forming patchlike colonies attached to acid boulders, particularly above tree line in exposed tundra and on windy ridges. Common on suitably high mountains throughout the region.

Notes: *P. minuscula* is similar, but has shorter, more flattened branches, the tips of which often become attached to the substrate. • Velcro lichen is mostly restricted to wind-blown sites which hold little snow in winter. Here the dark branches readily absorb the sun's heat − a feature that allows this lichen to be physiologically active even when air temperatures are far below freezing. • The Pseudephebes are among the only hair lichens in which much of the plant, rather than just the base, is attached to the substrate.

COMMON WITCH'S HAIR — *Alectoria sarmentosa*

General A *pendent hair* lichen, to 15-30 cm long, *pale green*, intricately branched, the hollow, shiny branches terminating in unadorned *black tips* (use a hand lens).

Ecology Over conifers in humid forest types at all forested elevations. Common in areas of moister climates in the southern half of our region, and north along the Coast Mountains to Alaska-Yukon.

Notes: In the similar *Ramalina thrausta* the branches terminate in minute, pale green "hooks" (hand lens). Common witch's hair is often used by warblers and vireos in the construction of their nests. • This species is superficially similar to *Usnea* species, but *A. sarmentosa* lacks a central cord. • Along with the black "old-man's beard" lichens (species of *Bryoria*), this plant may have been woven into moccasins or ponchos by southern interior Salish people and used to decorate ceremonial face-masks by the Shuswap people. • *Alectoria* means unmarried, and presumably refers to the relative absence of fruiting bodies in this genus.

POWDERY OLD MAN'S BEARD — *Usnea lapponica*

General An *upright to somewhat pendent hair* lichen, to 4-6 cm long, *pale yellowish green*, much branched, the branches each strengthened by a tough *central cord*, and here and there encircled by rings of *eroding soredia*.

Ecology Forming tufts over conifers and deciduous trees and shrubs, especially at lower elevations but ranging to subalpine forests. Common throughout our region.

Notes: In *U. subfloridana*, another common but more boreal *Usnea*, the branches bear conspicuous "nests" of isidia. • The greenish colour derives from usnic acid — a substance long known to possess antibiotic properties, and now used in the treatment of skin diseases. The chapped skin of babies and the feet of adults in Scandinavia were bathed in decoctions of this species.

Glossary

achenes: small, dry, 1-seeded nutlike fruits

aments: catkins; dry, scaly spikes of a unisexual inflorescence (such as those of willows)

apical: at the apex or tip

apothecia: cup-shaped reproductive structure of ascomycete fungi

appressed: lying close or flat against a surface

areoles: (lichens) small discrete greenish patches on the lichen surface

auricle: a small, projecting ear-shaped lobe or appendage

awn: a bristle-shaped appendage usually at the apex of a structure

awned: with an awn

axil: the angle between the leaf and the stem

axillary: arising from an axil

basally: towards the base

bilobed: divided into two lobes

branchlet: a small branch

bulbil: a small, bulb-like structure often located in a leaf axil, or replacing flowers

calcareous: calcium-rich; soil rich in lime.

cordate: heart shaped

crenate: margin with rounded teeth or scalloped

cultivars: cultivated varieties

decorticated: with the cortex removed

decumbent: reclining or lying flat on the ground, but with ascending tips

dehiscent: (fruit) opening by definite pores or slits to discharge seeds

drupe: fleshy or pulpy, one-seeded fruits, the seed with a stony covering

drupelets: small drupes

eglandular: not glandular

entire: without indentation or division

fens: wetlands of slow-moving, often alkaline water with sedge (not *Sphagnum*) peat underfoot

flexuous: bent in a zig-zag manner

florets: tiny flowers, usually arranged in clusters; used also to describe the specialized flower of grasses

gametophyte: the sexual generation of plants

glabrate: nearly glabrous

glabrescent: becoming glabrate

glabrous: without hairs present

globose: shaped like a sphere

glume: in grasses, one of two empty bracts at the base of the spikelet

hairpoint: a thin, hairlike extension

hyaline: clear, transparent

hybridisation: the process of creating a hybrid by breeding between different species

incurved: curved, upward and inward (referring to leaf margins)

indusium: an outgrowth covering and protecting a spore cluster in ferns

inflexed: incurved

lamellae: flaps on the surface of a moss leaf

lanceolate: lance shaped

lemma: the lower of the two bracts immediately enclosing the individual grass flower

lenticels: slightly raised areas on the bark of stems or roots

ligule:(in grasses) the flat, usually membranous projection from the summit of the sheath; (in composites) the strap-shaped part of the marginal (ray) flower

mericarps: one of the two parts into which the dry fruit of a carrot-family plant splits at maturity

mesic: average in moisture for that climatic region

midrib: the central rib of a leaf

midvein: the central vein of a leaf

minerotrophic: used to describe wetlands nourished by mineral-rich waters

montane: on or of mountains

nectary: a structure, usually of flowers, which produces nectar

oblanceolate: lanceolate with the broadest part above the middle

obovate: egg-shaped, with the narrower end basal

obovoid: obovate

palmately: leaves divided into lobes diverging radially like fingers

GLOSSARY

perigynia: (singular, perigynium) the inflated sacs enclosing the ovary in sedges.

peristome: The apical opening of a moss capsule, often ringed with teeth

petioles: leaf-stalks

photo-synthesizers: plants which photosynthesize; i.e., green plants which produce their food from water, carbon dioxide, and the sun's energy

pinnae: (singular pinna) primary divisions of a pinnate leaf

pinnate: feather formed; of a compound leaf in which the leaflets are placed on each side of the common axis

pinnatified: pinnately cleft half-way to the middle

pinnules: the secondary leaflets of a bipinnate leaf

plicate: folded like a fan

pollinia: (singular pollinium) a cluster of many pollen grains stuck together

pome: a fruit with a core, such as an apple

pruinose: with a fine white waxy, powdery, or granular coating

recurved: curved under (referring to leaf margins)

reflexed: abruptly bent or turned backwards or downwards

reticulate: net veined

rhizoids: filamentous much-branched strands, generally on moss stems, often fixing the moss to its substrate

rhizome: underground, often elongate stem; distinguished from a root by the presence of nodes, buds, or scale-like leaves

seral: of a stage (sere) in ecosystem development

serrate: saw-toothed, having sharp, forward- pointing teeth

serrulate: finely serrate

sessile: without a stalk

setae: (singular seta) bristle-like structures

shrub-carrs: wetlands dominated by shrubs and developed on mainly mineral materials that are periodically saturated but rarely inundated

shrub fens: fens dominated by shrub cover

silicles: like siliques, but shorter, not much longer than wide

siliques: the podlike fruits of certain members of the mustard family, much longer than wide

soredia:(lichens) microscopic clumps of several algal cells surrounded by fungal hyphae and erupting at the thallus surface as a powder.

sori: (singular sorus) a collection of small sporangia on the underside of a fern frond

spikelet: small or secondary spikes; the floral unit, or ultimate cluster, of a grass inflorescence

spinulose: covered by tiny spines

sporangia: (singular sporangium) spore cases

sporophylls: spore-bearing leaves

sporophyte: the spore-producing generation of plants

stamen: the pollen-bearing organ of a flower

stipe: a stalk-like support, such as the stalk supporting the capsule in mosses

stipules: appendages at the base of leaf stalks

stolons: horizontally spreading stems or runners at the ground surface, usually rooting at the nodes or tips

stomata: (singular stomate) specialized pores on leaves allowing for movement of gas and moisture

subapical: almost apical

subcordate: almost cordate

subentire: almost entire

suberect: almost erect

subglobose: almost globose

subsessile: almost sessile

substrate: the surface on which something grows

taproot: a primary descending root

tomentose: densely hairy with matted wool

tomentum: a dense covering of woolly or felty hairs

umbels: an often flat-topped inflorescence in which the flower stalks arise from a common point, much like the stays of an umbrella

umbelliferous: bearing umbels

unawned: not awned

References Cited

Andrusek, B., 1986. Edible wild plants. Canadian Geographic Vol. 105 (4): 65-70.

Argus, G.W. 1973. The genus *Salix* in Alaska and the Yukon. National Museum of Natural Sciences Publications in Botany, No. 2. National Museums of Canada, Ottawa.

_____ 1983. *Salix*. pp 198–214 *in* E.H. Moss. Flora of Alberta. 2nd edition revised by J.G. Packer. University of Toronto Press.

_____ 1992. Salicaceae. in G.W. Douglas, G.B. Straley, and D. Meidinger. The vascular plants of British Columbia. Special Report Series. British Columbia Ministry of Forests. (In press).

Brayshaw, T.C. 1976. Catkin Bearing Plants of British Columbia. Occasional Paper No. 18, Royal B.C. Museum, Victoria, B.C.

_____. 1989. Buttercups, Waterlilies and their Relatives in British Columbia. Memoir No. 1, Royal B.C. Museum, Victoria, B.C.

Carrier Linguistic Committee, 1973. Hanuyeh Ghun Utni-i - Plants of Carrier Country. Summer Institute of Linguistics, Fort St. James, British Columbia.

_____, 1974. Central Carrier Bilingual Dictionary. Summer Institute of Linguistics, Fort St. James, British Columbia.

Clark, L. J., 1973. Wildflowers of British Columbia. Gray's Publishing Ltd., Sidney, B. C.

Conard, H.S. and P.L. Redfern. 1979. How to know the mosses and liverworts. Wm. C. Brown, Dubuque, Iowa.

Coupé., C.A. Ray, A. Comeau, M.V. Ketcheson and R.M. Annas (compilers). 1982. A Guide to Some Common Plants of the Skeena Area, British Columbia. Land Management Handbook No. 4, B.C. Ministry of Forests, Victoria, B.C.

Craighead, J.J., F.C. Craighead and R.J. Davis. 1963. A Field Guide to Rocky Mountain Wildflowers. Houghton Mifflin Company, Boston.

Douglas, G.W. 1982. The Sunflower Family (Asteraceae) of British Columbia. Volume 1 - Senecioneae. Occasional Paper No. 23, Royal B.C. Museum, Victoria, B.C.

_____, G.B. Straley and D. Meidinger. 1989. The Vascular Plants of British Columbia. Part 1 - Gymnosperms and Dicotyledons (Aceraceae through Cucurbitaceae). Special Report Series 1, B.C. Ministry of Forests, Research Branch, Victoria, B.C.

_____. 1990. The Vascular Plants of British Columbia. Part 2 - Dicotyledons (Diapensiaceae through Portulacaceae). Special Report Series 2, B.C. Ministry of Forests, Research Branch, Victoria, B.C.

_____. 1991. The Vascular Plants of British Columbia. Part 3 - Dicotyledons (Primulaceae through Zygophyllaceae) and Pteridophytes. Special Report Series 3, B.C. Ministry of Forests, Research Branch, Victoria, B.C.

Gottesfeld, L.M.J. and B. Anderson, 1988. Gitksan traditional medicine: herbs and healing. J. Ethnobiol. 8(1): 13-33.

Grigson, G., 1974. A Dictionary of English Plant Names. Allen Lane, A Division of Penguin Books, London.

Hale, M.E. 1979. How to Know the Lichens, Second Edition. Wm. C. Brown. Dubuque, Iowa.

Hale, M.E., Jr. and W.L. Culberson. 1970. A second checklist of the lichens of the continental United States and Canada. The Bryologist 63: 137-172.

Hitchcock, C.L., and A. Cronquist. 1973. Flora of the Pacific Northwest. University of Washington Press, Seattle.

_____, A. Cronquist, M. Ownbey and J.W. Thompson. 1955-69. Vascular plants of the Pacific Northwest. Parts 1-5. University of Washington Press, Seattle.

Holland, S. S. 1976. Landforms of British Columbia. A Physiographic Outline. Bulletin No. 48 (2nd edition). British Columbia Department of Mines and Mineral Resources, Victoria, B.C.

Hubbard, W.A. 1969. The Grasses of British Columbia. Handbook No. 9, Royal B.C. Museum, Victoria.

Hultén, E. 1968. Flora of Alaska and Neighbouring Territories. Standford University Press, Standford, California.

Ireland, R.R., G.R. Brassard, W.B. Schofield and D.H. Vitt. 1987. Checklist of the mosses of Canada II. Lindbergia 13: 1-62.

Lauriault, J. 1989. Identification Guide to Trees of Canada. Fitzhenry and Whiteside, Markham, Ont.

Lyons, C.P. 1974 (1st ed. 1952). Trees, Shrubs and Flowers to Know in British Columbia. J.M. Dent and Sons, Toronto and Vancouver.

Meidinger, D. 1987. Recommended vernacular names for common plants of British Columbia. Research Report RR87002-HQ, B.C. Ministry of Forests, Victoria, B.C.

_____ and J. Pojar (compilers and editors). 1991. Ecosystems of British Columbia. Special Report Series 6, B.C. Ministry of Forests, Research Branch, Victoria, B.C.

Moore, R.J. and C. Frankton. 1974. The Thistles of Canada. Monograph No. 10, Canada Dept. of Agriculture, Ottawa, Ont.

Morice, Father A.G., 1892-93. Notes Archaeological, Industrial and Sociological on the Western Denes with an Ethnographical Sketch of the same. Transactions of the Canadian Institute, Session 1892-93.

Moss, E.H. 1983. (Second Edition, revised by J.G. Packer). Flora of Alberta. University of Toronto Press, Toronto, Ont.

Noble, W.J., T. Ahti, G.F. Otto and I.M. Brodo. 1987. A second checklist and bibliography of the lichens and allied fungi of British Columbia. Syllogeus 61, National Museums of Canada, Ottawa, Ontario.

People of 'Ksan, 1980. Gathering What the Great Nature Provided; Food Traditions of the Gitksan. Douglas & McIntyre, Vancouver/University of Washington Press, Seattle.

Pojar, J., R. Love, D. Meidinger and R. Scagel. 1982. Some Common Plants of the Sub-Boreal Spruce Zone. Land Management Handbook No. 6, B.C. Ministry of Forests, Victoria, B.C.

Porsild, A.E. and W.J. Cody. 1980. Vascular Plants of the Continental Northwest Territories. National Museum of Canada, Ottawa, Ont.

Porter, G.L. 1990. Willow Species of Disturbed Sites in theSub-Boreal Spruce Zone in Northcentral British Columbia. FRDA Handbook 004. B.C. Ministry of Forests/Forestry Canada, Victoria, B.C.

Prescott, G.W. 1964. How to Know the Freshwater Algae. W.C. Brown Co., Dubuque, Iowa.

Prior, R.C.A., 1879. On Popular Names of British Plants: being an explanation of the origin and meaning of the names of our indigenous and most commonly cultivated species. Frederic Norgate, London.

Roberts, A. 1983. A Field Guide to the Sedges of the Caribou Forest Region. Land Management Report No. 14, B. C. Ministry of Forests, Victoria, B. C.

_____ 1986. Willows of the Lower Skeena and Bulkley Valleys, and Their Relative Importance as Winter Food for Moose. Unpublished manuscript, B. C. Ministry of Environment, Smithers, B.C.

Schofield, W.H. 1968. Some Mosses of British Columbia. Handbook No. 28, Royal B.C. Museum, Victoria.

Scoggan, H.J. 1978-79. The Flora of Canada. National Museum of Natural Sciences Publications in Botany No. 7 (1-4), National Museums of Canada, Ottawa, Ont.

Smith, H.I., 1920-23. The Uses of Plants by the Carrier Indians of British Columbia (2 volumes). Unpublished Manuscripts prepared for the National Museum of Canada (on file at the Canadian Museum of Civilization, Ottawa).

_____, 1925-27. Ethno-botany of the Gitksan Indians of British Columbia. Unpublished Manuscript prepared for the National Museum of Canada (on file at the Canadian Museum of Civilization, Ottawa, Ont.).

Stotler, R. and B. Crandall-Stotler. 1977. A checklist of the liverworts and hornworts of North America. The Bryologist 80:405-428.

Szczawinski, A.F. 1959. The Orchids (Orchidaceae) of British Columbia. Handbook No. 16, Royal B.C. Museum, Victoria.

_____ 1962. The Heather Family (Ericaceae) of British Columbia. Handbook No. 19, Royal B.C. Museum, Victoria.

_____ and G.A. Hardy, 1975. Guide to Common Edible Plants of B.C. Handbook No. 20, Royal B.C. Museum, Victoria, B.C.

Taylor, T.M.C. 1966. The Lily Family (Liliaceae) of British Columbia. Handbook No. 25, Royal B.C. Museum, Victoria.

_____. 1973a. The Ferns and Fern Allies of British Columbia, Handbook No. 12, Royal B.C. Museum, Victoria.

_____. 1973b. The Rose Family (Rosaceae) of British Columbia. Handbook No. 30, Royal B.C. Museum, Victoria.

_____. 1974a. The Figwort Family (Scrophulariaceae) of British Columbia. Handbook No. 33, Royal B.C. Museum, Victoria.

_____. 1974b. The Pea Family (Leguminosae) of British Columbia. Handbook No. 32, Royal B.C. Museum, Victoria.

_____. 1983. The Sedge Family (Cyperaceae) of British Columbia. Handbook No. 43, Royal B.C. Museum, Victoria, B.C.

Turner, N.J., 1978. Food Plants of British Columbia Indians Part 2: Interior Peoples. Handbook No. 36, British ColumbiaProvincial Museum, Victoria, B.C.

_____, 1979. Plants in British Columbia Indian Technology. Handbook No. 38, British Columbia Provincial Museum, Victoria, B.C.

_____, 1982. Traditional Use of Devil's-Club (Oplopanax horridus: Araliaceae) by Native Peoples in Western North America. Journal of Ethnobiology 2 (1): 1-11.

_____, 1984. Counter-irritant and other medicinal uses of plants in Ranunculaceae by native peoples in British Columbia and neighbouring areas. Journal of Ethnopharmacology 11: 181-201.

_____, L.M.J. Gottesfeld, H.V. Kuhnlein and A. Ceska, In press 1991. Edible wood fern rootstocks of western North America: solving an ethnobotanical puzzle. Journal of Ethnobiololgy

Viereck, L.A. and E.L. Little. 1972. Alaska Trees and Shrubs. U.S.D.A., Forest Service, Agriculture Handbook No. 410.
Vitt, D.H., J.E. Marsh, and R.B. Bovey, 1988. Mosses, Lichens and Ferns of Northwest North America. Lone Pine Publishing, Edmonton, Alberta.
Welsh, S.L. 1974. Anderson's Flora of Alaska and adjacent parts of Canada, Brigham Young University Press. Provo, Utah.

Additional References

Anderson, J.R., 1925. Trees and Shrubs: Food, Medicinal, and Poisonous Plants of British Columbia. Dept. Education, Government of British Columbia, Victoria.
Bailey, L.H., 1963. How Plants Get Their Names. Dover Publications Inc., New York.
British Columbia Forest Service. 1977. Tree Book. Ministry of Forests, Forest Service Information Division. Victoria, B.C.
Cody, W.J., and D.M. Britton. 1989. Ferns and Fern Allies of Canada. Publ. 1829/E, Research Branch, Agriculture Canada, Ottawa, Ont.
Crum, H. 1973. Mosses of the Great Lakes forest. Contr. Univ. Mich. Herb. 10:1-404.
Frankton, C., and G.A. Mulligan. 1987. Weeds of Canada. N.C. Press Limited and Agriculture Canada, Ottawa, Ont.
Garman, E.H. 1973. Guide to the trees and shrubs of British Columbia. British Columbia Provincial Museum Handbook No. 31. Victoria.
Grigson, G., 1974. A Dictionary of English Plant Names. Allen Lane, A Division of Penguin Books, London.
Gledhill, 1989. The Names of Plants. Second Edition, Cambridge University Press, Cambridge.
Gottesfeld, L.M.J., 1991. Plants That We Use: Traditional Plant Uses of the Wet'suwet'en People. Kyah Wiget EducationSociety, Moricetown, British Columbia.
Heller, C.A., 1981. Wild Edible and Poisonous Plants of Alaska. Revised Joint Publication No. 28 — Cooperative Extension Service, University of Alaska and U.S.D.A.
Hosie, R.C. 1969. Native trees of Canada, Queens Printer, Ottawa.
Hulten, E., 1968. Flora of Alaska and Neighbouring Territories. Stanford University Press, Stanford, California.
McGrath, J.W., 1977. Dyes From Lichens and Plants. Van Nostrand Reinhold Ltd., Toronto, Ont.
Mulligan, G.A., and D.B. Munro. 1990. Poisonous Plants of Canada. Publication 1842/E, Agriculture Canada, Ottawa, Ont.
Prior, R.C.A., 1879. On Popular Names of British Plants: being an explanation of the origin and meaning of the names of our indigenous and most commonly cultivated species. Frederic Norgate, London.
Porsild, A.E. 1974. Rocky Mountain Wildflowers. National Museum of Canada, Ottawa, Ont.
Robuck, O.W., 1985. The Common Plants of the Muskegs of Southeast Alaska. U.S.D.A. Forest Service, Pacific Northwest Forest and Range Experiment Station Misc. Publication, Portland, Ore.
Robuck, O.W., 1989. Common Alpine Plants of Southeast Alaska. U.S.D.A. Forest Service, Pacific Northwest Forest and Range Experiment Station Misc. Publication, Portland, Ore.
Richardson, D., 1975. The Vanishing Lichens; Their History, Biology and Importance. David & Charles, London/Vancouver.
Reader's Digest, 1986. The Magic and Medicine of Plants. Reader's Digest Publication.
Schofield, J.J. 1989. Discovering Wild Plants: Alaska, Western Canada, the Northwest. Alaska Northwest Books, Anchorage/Seattle.
Scotter, G.W. and H. Flygare. 1986. Wildflowers of the Canadian Rockies. Hurtig Publishers, Edmonton, Alta.
Stevens, J.E. 1973. Discovering Wild Plant Names. Shire Publications Ltd., Aylesbury, England.
Sweet, M., 1962. Common Edible and Useful Plants of the West. Naturegraph Company, Healdsburg, California.
Taylor, R.J. 1990. Northwest Weeds: The Ugly and Beautiful Villains of Fields, Gardens and Roadsides. Mountain Press Publishing Co., Missoula, Montana.
Taylor, T.M.C. 1970. Pacific Northwest Ferns and Their Allies. University of Toronto Press, Toronto, Ont.
Trelawney, J.G. 1983. Wildflowers of the Yukon and Northwestern Canada Including Adjacent Alaska. Sono Nis Press, Victoria, B.C.
Turner, N.J. and A.F. Szczawinski, 1978. Wild Coffee and Tea Substitutes of Canada. Edible Wild Plants of Canada Series No. 2, National Museum of Canada, Ottawa, Ont.
_____, 1979. Edible Wild Fruits and Nuts of Canada. Edible Wild Plants of Canada Series No. 3, National Museum of Canada, Ottawa, Ont.

Szczawinski, A.F. and N.J. Turner, 1978. Edible Garden Weeds of Canada. Edible Wild Plants of Canada Series No. 1, National Museum of Canada, Ottawa, Ont.
_____, 1980. Wild Green Vegetables of Canada. Edible Wild Plants of Canada Series No. 4, National Museum of Canada, Ottawa.
Viereck, E.G., 1987. Alaska's Wilderness Medicines: Healthful Plants of the Far North. Alaska Northwest Books, Anchorage/Seattle.
Viereck, L.A. and E.L. Little. 1972. Alaska Trees and Shrubs. Agriculture Handbook No. 410. U.S.D.A. Forest Service, Washington, D.C.

Photo Credits

Frank Boas: 27a, 28a,c, 29a, 32a,c, 33a, 34b, 37b, 40a,b, 41b, 42a,b,c, 43a, 44b, 46a, 47c, 48a,b, 49a, 52b, 71a, 75a, 79b, 80a, 82b, 83a,b, 84a,b, 85b,c, 92a,c, 100a, 103b, 126a,b, 127b,c,d, 128a, 129a,c, 130a, 131a,b, 135a,b, 136a,b, 137a, 139b,c, 140a,b,c, 143a, 145a,b, 150a, 151a,b, 152a,b, 155b,c, 156a, 159a, 160a, 165a, 167b, 168a, 169b, 170a, 172a, 177a,c, 178a,b, 179a,b, 180a, 182b, 183a, 184a, 187a,b, 190a, 191b, 192a, 193a, 194b, 195a, 196, 197a, 198b, 201a,b, 203a,c, 205a, 207a,b, 208b, 209b, 210b, 211a,b, 212b,c, 214a,c, 215a, 217b, 221a, 224a, 244b, 262b,d, 276b, 291b, 292b,c, 293a, 297a, 298a,b,299b, 300, 301a,b, 302a,b, 303a,b, 304a,b, 305a,b, 306b, 307, 308a,b, 309a, 311b,c, 312a,b, 313a,c, 314a,b, 316a,b, 317b, 318a, 322b, 323a,b,c, 324b,c, 326a, 332, 333a,b, 334b, 335b

Robin Bovey: 281b, 284a, 287a, 288a,b, 294a, 310a,b, 315a, 317a, 320a,b, 321a,b, 325b, 326b, 328a,b, 329a,b,c, 330a,b, 336a,b,c, 337, 338

Robert Norton: 27d, 34a, 41a, 64b, 72a,b, 88b, 91a, 105b, 138a, 142c, 149a, 181a, 183b, 184b, 195b,c, 197b,c, 218b, 219a, 223b, 236b, 241b, 242b, 243a, 247a, 259a, 260b, 263b, 268b, 271a, 273b, 287b

Jim Pojar: 19a, 22b, 28b,d, 29b, 32b, 33b, 35a,b,c, 36b, 39a, 43b, 45a,b, 47a, 48d, 50a,b, 51a, 52a, 63a,b, 66a, 67a,b, 69a, 74a, 79a, 80b, 81b, 82a, 84c, 85a, 88a,c, 89a,b, 91b, 92b, 97c, 98a,b, 99b, 100b, 101a,b, 107a, 108a, 109a,b, 110a, 111b, 112a, 114a, 115a, 116b, 117b, 119b, 127a, 128b, 129b, 131c, 132a, 142a,b, 143b,c, 144a,b, 146a, 147a,b, 148a,c, 149b, 150b, 153a,b, 154a, 155a, 159b, 160b,c, 164a,b, 165b, 166a,b, 169a, 170b, 171a,b, 172b, 173a, 177b, 180b, 181b, 182a,c, 185b, 190b, 192b, 193b, 194a, 198a, 200b, 202a,b, 204a,b, 206a,b, 208a, 210a, 212a, 213a,b, 214b, 215b, 216a, 217a, 218a, 221b, 222a,b, 223a,c, 224b, 232b, 263c, 281c, 282a,b, 283b, 290a,b, 291a, 292a, 293b, 294b, 295a,b, 297b, 299a, 306a, 311a,d, 313b, 315b, 318b, 322a, 324a, 325a,c, 327, 331a, 334a, 335c

Anna Roberts: 27c, 46c, 49b, 65b, 66b, 69b, 70a, 72c, 73a,b, 74b, 75b,c,d, 76b,c, 104a, 105a, 111a, 116a, 117a, 118a, 119a, 231a,b, 232a, 233a,b, 234a,b, 235a,b, 236a, 237a, 238a,b, 239a,b, 240a,b, 241a,c, 242a,c, 243a,b, 244a,c, 245a,b, 246a,b, 247b, 248a,b, 249a,b, 250a,b, 251a,b, 252a, 253a, 258a,b, 259b, 260a,c, 261a,b, 262a,c, 263a, 264a,b, 265a,b, 268a,c, 269a,b, 270a,b, 271b, 272a,b, 273a,b, 274a,b, 275a,b, 276a, 277a,b, 278a,b, 286a

Other contributing Photographers: Blain Andrusek: 18b, 19c, 21b,c, 23a, 44a, 65a, 99a, 104b, 108b, 113a, 118b, 173b,c, 199a,b, 205b, 281a, 283a, 286b; George Argus: 20b, 68a; B.C.Ministry of Forests: 14a,b,c,d, 15a,b,c,d, 19b, 22c, 24a, 25a,b,d, 156b, 200a, 209a, 220a, 221c, 331b,; Adolf Ceska: 76a, 102a, 125a, 148b, 285a; Ray Coupè: 38a, 48c, 252b; Blake Dickens: 46b, 90a; Katherine Enns: 21a, 120a; Ron Long: 97a,b, 103a, 130b, 191a, 203b, 216b; Robin Love: 36a, 112b; M. Naga: 24b; L. O'Hara: 77a,b; George Otto: 114b, 334c,d, 335a; P.T. Read: 24c; Rick Riewe: 74c, 141b; H. Roewer: 81a, 92d; Joan Rosenberg: 139a; Martin Ross: 39b; Rob Scagel: 64a, 120b, 125b; Nancy and Robert Turner: 141a; E.J. Underhill: 20a, 167a; W. van Dieren: 186a,b; Cliff Wallace: 22a, 47d, 49c; Cleve Wershler: 18a, 25c, 27b, 37a, 47b; Jim Woollett: 38b.

Index to Common and Scientific Names

Primary species described in the guide are in bold-face type; those mentioned in the Notes sections only are not.

INDEX

INDEX

George Argus
Canadian Museum
of Nature, Ottawa,
Ontario

Frank Boas
Bryologist,
Youbou, B.C.

Ray Coupé
B.C. Forest
Service, Research,
William's Lake,
B.C.

Craig DeLong
B.C. Forest
Service, Research,
Prince George,
B.C.

George Douglas
Conservation
Data Centre,
Victoria, B.C.

Trevor Goward
Curator of
Lichens, U.B.C.

Andy MacKinnon
(with his son
James)
B.C. Forest
Service, Research,
Victoria, B.C.

Jim Pojar
B.C. Forest
Service, Research,
Smithers, B.C.

Rosamund Pojar
Naturalist,
Smithers, B.C.

Anna Roberts
Naturalist,
William's Lake,
B.C.